D0946094

KWANI?

Kwani? is published by:
KWANI TRUST
P.O Box 2895, 00100
Nairobi,
KENYA

Tel : +254 (0) 20 4451383

First Published 2007
First Impression
ISBN 996698366-X

Creative Direction / Design Layout: SEVEN PRODUCTIONS
Creative Directors: JUDY KIBINGE & ALFRED MUCHILWA
Mac Designer / Layout: PETER NGUNGUI
Poetry Concept Designs: LENJO MAZA
Cover Illustration / Design: JUDY KIBINGE & ASAPH CHANGE
Cover Poem: RABINDRANATH TAGORE

Kwani Trust is a FORD FOUNDATION grantee.

www.kwani.org

For

David Sadera Munyakei

Table of Contents

KWANI?

Editorial

Let me tell you ...

It never ceases to amaze me how incredible a story-telling space Kenya is. I continue to meet, in bars, in matatus, churches, estate corners and in other public spaces that individual, who is always bound to introduce himself with the magic words that always hold me spellbound: let me tell you ... and I become the receipient of another incredible narrative. This has been going on for a while - ever since I came of drinking age and quickly learnt that a version of the truth on most national or local matters or at least an inkling can be found in the stranger sitting next to me in the pub; that woman in the *mathree*; that cab-driver late at night.

And though the facts matter, it is the inducement of a commonality, the feeling that I share enough with a stranger to care about a shared narrative, to believe the unbelievable, the improbable version; that is what makes me feel more Kenyan than anything else. It is those shared narratives and the will to believe, that truly tell about the nature of the Kenyan condition. And yet, another thing that never ceases to amaze, these narratives never find their way into our official and formal public texts.

Over the last 12 months I have listened to tens of stories and even been lucky to live in some of them. And just like when I started drinking and heard one amazing narrative after the next in pubs all over the city; in *mtaa* corners ... and I thought - Fuck! Fuck! Fuck! Oh shit what an incredible space I live in ... and why doesn't this come out in any of our formal and official mediums that truly tell us about the nature of the Kenyan condition? And yet again, in a time when many are struggling to find a Kenyan identity I realised that it is the common stories that make such a thing recognisable for me ...

Lately, a *Joscom (Jos com bok)* from Tokyo narrated to me, yes, over drinks a tale of woe and laughter, on the crazy shit of living in such a foreign space that he now has trouble believing it. He told me of how he came back with his new Japanese wife a few years ago and immediately lost her to the Kenyan Immigration Authorities after they went through a daily dose of corruption, extortion and threats when trying to clear their belongings. A writer-friend told me, over a period of three days, about her quest into deep Bombay looking for a spiritual healer who had once resided in Kenya but had been deported for political reasons; another writer friend told me about his unbelievable plunge into a Naivasha space full of such unreal colonial eccentricities, oddities, racial tension and murder that the writing of the story has become less about word-count and more of a hand-wringing exercise in self-censorship.

I also met a DJ based in the ethnically 'conscious' downtown of Narok who has decided of all things to become a Kikuyu as he can't amazingly relate to his tribe of birth and now spends different months of the year roaming in between small-town Kenya and elsewhere. I met an 'indigene' and Subaru driving 'forest dweller' who was a small cog in the illegal sale of the Mau forest. I also met a young woman from Banana- that template for Nairobi's peri-urban spaces- who is also a prostitute and specialises in U.N bigwigs. She introduced herself as Mama Jason and through the story of her life explained why the industry is fed by these peri-urban spaces. I was told of life in Wangige - where every other new day is a 40's style Chicago adventure of robbers, cops, guns, blood and hijackers - Nairobi noir at its best! All these reminded me of what it means to be Kenyan.

Then, there are the stories that I lived in ... I spent many hours at Langata Women's prison listening to inmates tell me their story; I pursued Congestina Achieng in the streets of Huruma, and Eastleigh to try and get her narrative of how she became a pugilist and in the process met a young man who gave me an idea of what it means to grow up with boxing as your only hope of staying out of jail. I also met a young female M.C trying to make it in the Kenyan hip-hop scene.

And as different as all these narratives were I could relate to them as they were essentially Kenyan. Though these didn't make it into these pages they remain the reason why we at *Kwani?* do what we do; we recognise that in these stories we share a common identity and, perhaps more importantly, tell others about who we are.

But not all the stories I lived in were about building an identity, the celebration of a commonality or illuminating hidden spaces. One in particular seemed to be the antithesis of all these and continues to baffle in the extreme. I continued over the last year living a story that had been published in *Kwani? 3: The true story of David Munyake*i- the Goldenberg whistleblower. In many ways I had been living the Goldenberg saga before I even met Munyakei and spent many months tracking down his narrative.

I had already started living it when I came of age in the early 90's. The Goldenberg scandal was a defining moment in my life; by almost destroying Kenya's economy it made me, like many others of my age, think it wiser to study, work and seek a future elsewhere. Like many who came of age in the 90's, if Moi was already a looming figure in my consciousness and to all intents my surrogate father, Goldenberg was the divorce that flung many of Kenya's young citizens outside the country. It was a grim time even as a child but a defining moment of what I became. But I now realise it is the stories that I talk about that helped keep it all together.

Goldenberg continued to become part of my life in 2004-2005 when I spent months with David Munyakei- who passed on with little recompense, early on this year. *Kwani?* 3 brought you a story which ended a year before his death. So in August this year I travelled back to the past to visit his family. Once again I re-lived yet another tale of woe through his wife and children- who are still struggling.

As much as I have enjoyed listening to stories over the last 15 years, this is the one story that I for once wished was not Kenyan - but because it is, just like all the others it has to be told. Let us continue sharing our stories. David Sadera Munyakei, from here to eternity- rest in peace.

BILLY KAHORA

Editorial

I hate *githeri.* 4 years of it - six times a week in boarding school, with floating bits of cabbage, cracked teeth and gravel and the dining hall smell of steaming peeling paint and bubbling giant cookers.

After living abroad for ten years, I used to fantasise about boiling *githeri* - about rude *matatu* drivers; about bad speakers screaming near *matatu* ranks, about us Kenyans, who are so bullied by authority figures, we turn on each other, instead of on the authority figure.

We miss old ways. We are terrified about new things - because we have learnt to measure with exactitude what we can expect from a president who is a monarch - and a parliament whose single aim is to make themselves as rich as the wealthiest class of people in the wealthiest nations of the world.

This is why we, not they, are squashing any opportunity for a meaningful new Kenya - run by professional, sane feet-on-the-ground people who did not earn-their stripes as Affirmative Action Vaseline Faced Missionary School Boys (or their children, cousins, uncles and godfathers): people who have lived and thrived in a crumbling Kenya and kept their integrity about them; people who have innovative and bold ideas; people who have had their hands on earth, and their minds in the sky.

One time in South Africa, I was in a cheap country bus, and the driver was drunk. I was terrified, because I was sitting right behind him, and my Kenyan reaction was to pretend it was not happening. I slept. Half an hour later some very rude women - some grandmothers- were screaming. They stood. Picked out the strongest man in the bus, and asked him to stop the driver. Eight or nine people surrounded him. He stopped. The travellers took a vote after some brisk discussions, the driver was dropped off at the nearest police station and a passenger was appointed to take us to Johannesburg. Many of these women were probably illiterate.

Most of this time I was just annoyed. I do not know why I was annoyed. The women were changing a status quo, a way of doing things - good or bad - and maybe this is what annoyed my narrow fearful Kenyan self.

A few weeks after coming home in 2000, I took a *matatu* (express) from Njoro to Nakuru. It was full, and was not supposed to stop along the way - a privilege for which we paid 40 bob. I had been heaving bags of leek since early morning and was dirty and smelly. We got to Technology, and three people were hustled in, elbows in my nose, warm and squirming chicken at my feet; hot breath in my ear - a kiss. A kiss? I had enough. I shouted at the guy to put them down. I started to elbow my way out. Behind me, in Gikuyu, speculation was rife coupled with much nose sniffing as the other passengers made it clear that they were unimpressed with my revolutionary ideas. Who does he think he is? Is he better than us who take this thing? And so on. The conductor was laughing. In annoyance I demanded my money back and then asked them to drop me off. I could hear passengers laughing as I left in a silly, hot-eared huff.

In Kenya, until we are left naked, we will defend the status quo - much has been made of the 500 people who earn 90 percent of the government wage bill; much has been made of the knot of families and connections who have taken ownership of this country - and who are not happy with all the land they own and all the assets, who will still come into our homes and take the very last cent as taxes to fund their referendum campaign, and the elections in 2007. But these days they hardly need to do this work - a whole population of people will defend them, will make velvet carpeting for them and ululate for a loaf of bread. So when I ask a Gikuyu taxi driver in Nakuru. Is business good? He says it was better during Moi. I ask him about the government. He brightens and says, "... but he! Kibaki is a wise one! He is Working!"

For whom? Kenya's rich-poor index has worsened since this government came to power. Cleary the economy is doing well. But for what 5 percent?

"Truly a God. Did you know he was number 1! From Standard 1 until University! And the way he is confusing Raila?" says the taxi guy.

And what has he done for you?

"Oh! We have been telling them *Kaa Mucii. Ka Mucii!* We told them we would help them keep the Luos out of Nakuru." Which brings me to some of the motivations behind this issue:

Over the last two years a kind of insanity has overtaken many Gikuyus. Messiahs have come to "save us" from the "beasts of the west" - and these "beasts of the west" are of course, the problem with Kenya. The same people who had vowed in 2002 to allow a Kenya for Kenyans are now selling Kenya - with their massive vote - to a bunch of people who do not know the price of a pint of milk, or care - except when they own the milk manufacturing plant that stole machinery from a KCC which we built with our money.

Neither do they care about the sisal-producing district, where a whole tribe remains squatters, or the ranch in Laikipia where poor people are herded away by the same army and police forces that are meant to exist to protect them and their sovereignty.

And we are grateful for this love by these people, partly because they do a little work - nowhere enough to be meaningful for Kenya, but sufficient to plant flowers on roundabouts and build one school with CDF.

The real money, our money, ends up, in now legislated ways, into the pockets of the Fortune 500. Parselelo Kantai calls it the Vampire State - and really no state in Africa is as adept as Kenya at misleading its population and channelling all meaningful monies to the few who partner with "international investors" to leave us all bone dry. This is why even poorer countries, countries with less resources and institutions were able to shed their old guard and we can't.

The Kibaki government, like the Moi government and the Kenyatta government and the ODM possible government are all cut from the same original cloth. Although we all see Uhuru and Raila and Kibaki as very different people representing very different ethnicities, they are brothers - of the same class of families who feel they have a royal right to rule. They come from the same eras, the same schools, the same social circuits - they battle things out when we are watching - for we validate their power. But within themselves they have no real problem. This is why former enemies always seem to turn around and become friends when they need to be: because they all need each other - they are in a conspiracy to control the history and future of Kenya - which we are told is all about them, their daddies, their cousins and uncles and in-laws.

Since they are heroes it is their natural right to inherit everything. So every five years we troop off to vote for one of them to inherit our assets - for we are their employees, their citizens and slaves, their children, their feudal chattels. And we are happy when they throw extra shillings on the floor for us. It makes us feel good.

This new era of Gikuyu political power is examined in parts of this issue of *Kwani?* Much of what is discussed here may replicate itself all over Kenya, for these problems are not unique to the Gikuyu. We do not approach it with political essays - more we have some interesting opinions and fiction and blog entries and some heart rending confessions that talk about patriarchy and the family; the fall of the Gikuyu man; the rise of the woman - and all sorts of defenses people have built over the past 40 years, ten years after this community has cut open by a terrible season of attack; and its recovery with the rise of Kenyatta.

What I fear, as a Gikuyu and as a Kenyan, is that the mobile, flexible ambition we had for Kenya is now frozen behind a new dogma chanted by Gikuyus everywhere - that the new *Mtukufus* of Kenya are here to stay, and it is these *Mtukufus* who will save Kenya. Again, a new generation invests our hope not in ourselves; we do not want to challenge a government to be better; we want to be comfortable with the status quo - and that will send us straight back to 1969. To 1988.

Our aim is not to alienate, or to be "comprehensive" - it is simply to provoke conversation. Our newspapers speak in maidenly terms - like old Victorians about "a certain community". We feel we need to name things - and allow conversations to take place - because it is in these secret in-between places that hate and fear build and thrive, when people start to think that at home their close friends and their families are "plotting against them."

We feel obliged to work towards the end of an era of big men, and their families and children. And the way to do this, I believe is to question our own hearts.

The hearts of those in power are not in doubt.

BINYAVANGA WAINAINA

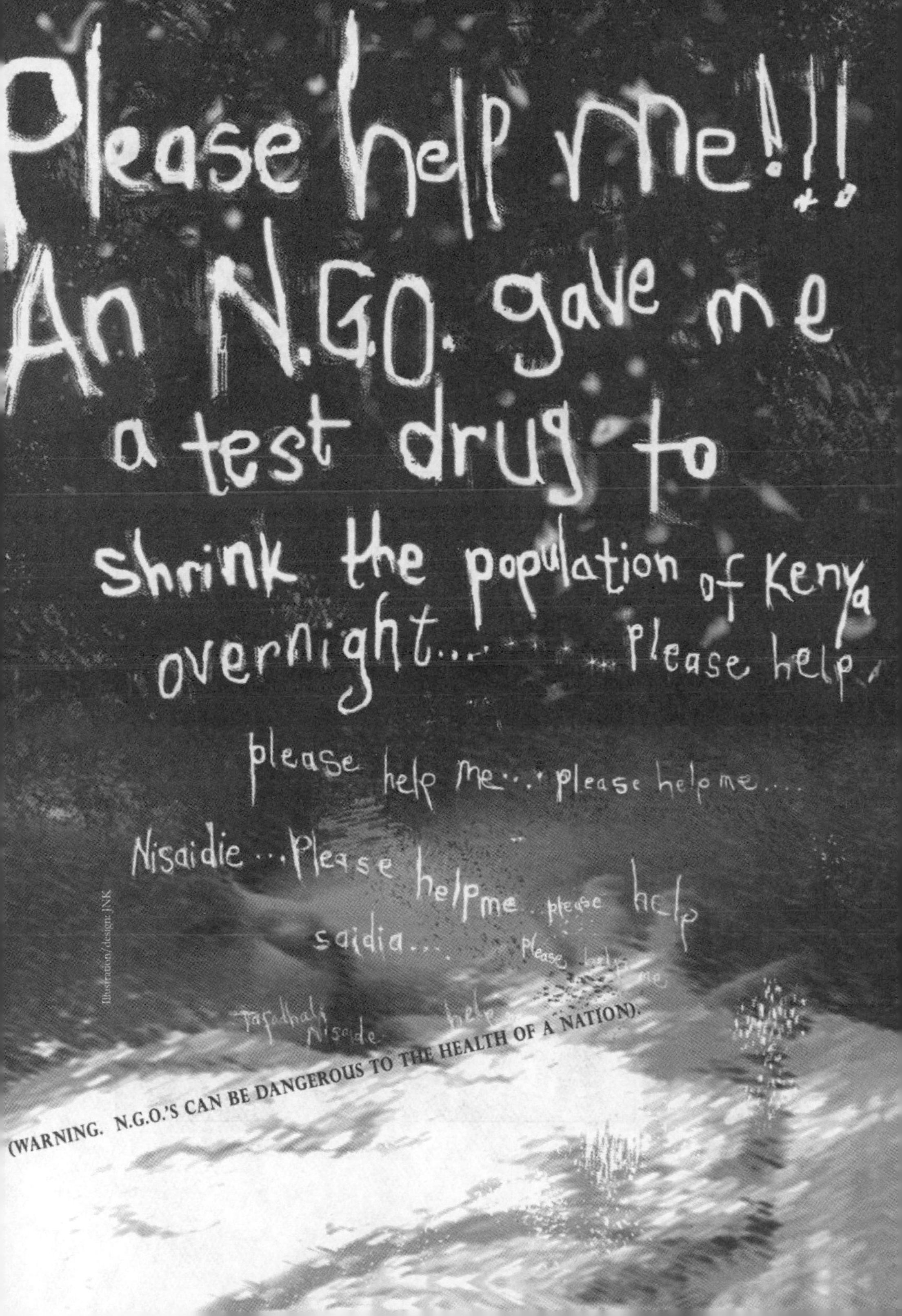

Please help me!!!

An N.G.O. gave me

a test drug to

shrink the population of Kenya

overnight... ... Please help

please help me... please help me...

Nisaidie... Please helpme... please help

saidia... Please help me

Tafadhali Nisaidie help

(WARNING. N.G.O.'S CAN BE DANGEROUS TO THE HEALTH OF A NATION).

Illustration/design: JNK

EDITOR'S NOTE: This strip was first published in FARAFINA

WILL YOUR PEOPLE VOTE FOR ME OR NOT?
WHAT DO YOU SAY?
WE WILL NEVER VOTE FOR YOU.WE DON'T HAVE THE SAME IDEOLOGY!
"IDEOLOGY" HA! HA! HA! HA!
COME MY FRIEND; COME AND SEE "IDEOLOGY"
THIS - IS *IDEOLOGY!*

HOW MUCH DO YOU WANT?

WELL, SINCE YOU WON'T TALK, HERE...

...EACH OF THESE BAGS CONTAINS N5 MILLION. YOU WILL GET FOUR MORE BAGS AFTER THE ELECTION.

BUT REMEMBER, WE HAVE OUR WAY OF KNOWING WHETHER OR NOT YOUR PEOPLE VOTE FOR US...
?!

S-D-P?

P-PR-PROGRESS...

NRC SECRETARIAT, ABUJA...
...THE PROBLEM WITH NIGERIA...
...IS FAILURE OF LEADERSHIP ...
... IN ALL ASPECTS OF OUR SOCIETY...
...FROM THE NUCLEAR FAMILY TO NATIONAL LEVEL AND...
GENTLEMEN, I WANT TO PERFORM...
WHA...?!
?!
HERE IS THE MONEY. N2 MILLION EACH.
NOW WE ARE TALKING.
CORRECT MAN!
EH- EHN!
NA YOU BIKO!
YOU DON WIN!
JJC!
?!

Photograph: Amunga Eshuchi

Kiririkano

'For mami…'

BY WAMBUI WA WANJIRU

Chapter One

The other day, I was talking with Cucu on the phone and she told me a very interesting story. Apparently, Wacu, whom I haven't seen since last year, went home with a white man she intends to marry and caused serious problems.

The guy calls himself 'Njoroge' and has dreadlocks; one of those whites who wear shukas and eat with their fingers when they come to visit you. Wacu and her man alighted from a matatu at noon and walked home from the crowded centre followed by a gang of children who kept singing and calling the man all sorts of names, while running up to touch him and then retreating.

The long and the short of it is that Uncle Maina, when he saw the man, was overcome by a desolation that has had him in bed since then. He hasn't spoken to anyone, just drinks Lucozade and stares at the wall. The doctors say his heart, which used to trouble him, is fine and they cannot find anything physically wrong with him. He won't get out of it, whatever it is; Mama Wacu can't keep up with farm duties, and their workers at the shop in town are having a ball pilfering from the stores.

Cucu was saying that of course, everybody knows it's because Uncle Maina can't stomach the thought of his daughter marrying "that boy," and that everybody is wondering why, of all people, she had to bring that white to the homestead.

"What is wrong with you girls?" Cucu asked me. "Why do you leave these good men here and go bringing the worst from out there, eh?" She sounded very disgusted.

She went on for a long time, telling me how she just might curse us one of these days if we continue like this; how we kids are so directionless, have no manners or sense of self-worth. Then she told me to come home this weekend so that I can shine the living room floor and wash the windows there. I should remember to take some floor polish with me when I go, also rags.

I remember how weird it was spending time with Wacu at her place on Upper Hill where she lives in an expensive flat with a school friend who's dating a German diplomat. Wacu's roommate is Cindy - her best friend from secondary school in Kinangop - and from what Wacu told me, the German pays rent and takes care of all the bills, though he lives with his white wife and three children at their official residence in Muthaiga.

My cousin and I ran into each other at the hyper supermarket on Ngong Road one Saturday morning, around eleven when the heat wasn't bearing down yet, and I am still amazed at the change in Wacu; her new style and affectations. From a simple ruralite, she has metamorphosed into an urban queen, with a way of speaking that mimics television announcers on the glossier new stations. She's thin now, and has some kind of accent that's meant to be foreign, a long weave, and Cleopatra-like eyes whose corners are pencilled across the sides of her face almost to her ears.

I truly was dumbstruck by the change in my cousin, dumb enough not to comment on her transformation though I grew increasingly irritated the more she spoke in her new voice. There was no trace of Wacu as I knew her: no speaking Gikuyu anymore or reflex high-fives. She wasn't slouched to the side with her hand on her hip, the stance in which I everlastingly remembered her. She just stood there in high heels, occasionally brushing back the wisps of weave that fluttered into her new face.

After we'd chatted a while, I invited Wacu home. I had only gone to the supermarket to buy juice and planned on spending the rest of the day lying on the grass by the paw-paw tree. We had closed down our business for the day, Mom had gone to her *kiama* meeting and Cucu was visiting relatives in Elburgon.

"Nituinuke," I told Wacu. "When is the last time you came to our place?" I hoped that familiar surroundings would bring her to reality and shift our relationship back into gear.

"Are you guys still on Riara with those big snakes?" my cousin asked.

"Ya, we're still there," I replied. "But Absalom killed the snakes. In fact the *maperas* are ripe. *Si* you come we eat some?"

Wacu, my other cousins and I had grown up eating the guavas at Cucu's and I knew she would love the ones we have in Riara. They are bigger and juicer than those in Kiambu, and our trees are old and strong.

For the first time that day, my old Wacu bubbled to the surface.

"Ati maperas?" she asked and then laughed in her real voice.

"Kwanza these ones are very deadly," I replied mischievously and opened my eyes wide. Too many guavas give you constipation.

She laughed again and our connection returned.

Wacu declined, but asked me to come along and see her new place, and because neither one of us could handle a bus ride in the coming heat, we hopped into a taxi at the petrol station and headed for Upper Hill where my cousin and her friend Cindy live.

At the flat complex, we found their maid talking with the *askari* at the gate while she waited for Wacu to return and pay her. The maid - Jemimah if I remember correctly - had cleaned the house from top to bottom, washed, ironed and folded, and all she received was a hundred bob.

Just imagine. One hundred shillings for all that work. I was shocked when Wacu pulled the note from her purse and handed it to the woman.

When Jemimah was walking out of the complex, I asked her where she lived and she said she was going to Kawangware 56. Imagine. On foot, and with only one a soc to show for the day's toil. I tried talking to Wacu about it and I'll tell you how that conversation went, in a minute.

The flat is very nice, though Wacu's and Cindy's imaginations could have been more adventuresome with the décor. There's an oversized brown sofa set and a big coffee table (Lamu-style) in the living room, though one can tell the furniture was quickly assembled by those roadside *fundis* on Ngong Road. There were splits in the table, (the wood must have been wet when constructed), and when Wacu went to the bedroom to change into comfortable clothes, I examined it closely and as suspected, found it to be softwood. The *fundis* had stained it with mahogany powder-and-water dye, then held it together with carpenter's glue and thin nails.

By the north wall they have a big display cabinet with odds and ends, a khaki pouf which I liked, small side tables and no books, but some *Cosmopolitans, Msafiris* and a couple of Afro South African fashion magazines I'd never seen before. A small pink rug and plants rounded off the living room and the rest of the flat had standard-procedure furniture. But what I liked most of all in her place was the sun. There are big windows throughout and lots of light. Boy, do I love big windows or what?

Later, while Wacu spoke with someone on the phone, I fried *githeri* and went to the kiosk to buy us a Fanta. It was good to be with my cousin again, though I kept thinking about the maid who was probably walking home in the hot sun, all the way to Kawangware, where the 56 bus cuts a corner and leaves Gitanga Road. All the way from Upper Hill in the heat and dust.

When I was small and lived in Langata, every morning from the bus or car on the way to school, I saw hundreds of people walking to work in town or Industrial Area. And on our way home, those people were walking back again, one behind the other, like a long human snake. I never thought about them - they were just part of the scenery. But now, when I remember Jemimah who made one hundred shillings and then walked to Kawangware in the heat, I wonder how much those people used to make back then and how they survived on it.

"Sasa wewe", I begin, "You're paying this woman only a soc for all the work she has done here today?"

"Ala? Ya," comes the reply, this time in regular-speak. *"Kwanza* she's very lucky that I didn't fire her last week".

I inquire.

"I found that she'd nabbed food. *Haki ya Mungu* these people think with their stomachs," my cousin says.

"What d'you mean?" I ask. "You found she'd carried food on her way out?"

"A-á," says Wacu, "I'd left a certain amount of meat and rice when I left last Saturday and when I came back, she had eaten some of it."

"And on top of that," Wacu adds, "She used to drink tea here like there was no tomorrow, adding sugar as if this is a factory."

She laughs and picks up my plate and puts it on her empty one.

I lean back in my seat and take a sip of Fanta.

"Me the way I see it," I say softly, "You should let her eat and I think you should pay her more. Maybe for her, it's the only square meal she sees in a week. We have to be kind... And what sort of salary is that you're paying her in the first place?"

Then I stop, because the look on Wacu's face makes me realise I should have kept my mouth shut.

Everything changes. Good tidings flutter out of the room.

Wacu stares at the plates, inhales and says,

"First of all you haven't asked me how many people in this building she works for. Eh? Do you know she cleans two other people's places and they each give her a soc?"

She looks at me and adds, "That Jemimah makes over a G every month. And the *junguz* who used to live in number ten gave her clothes and *sufurias* before they went back to Denmark. She's lucky to have a job. What if I had ten kids and made her suffer like other people? Have you asked yourself that? And how much work is there in this house? Just me and Cindy. That's all she has to worry about."

I stare at the plates.

"You know Soni, people like you think that just because you've lived abroad, you understand things better than us. *Kwanza* you're very lucky. If your Mom hadn't managed to go to Europe how do you think you guys would have survived? And where would you yourself have been if you'd never gone to *Stato?* Don't come here and start lecturing me about the way I pay Jemimah."

And with that, Wacu picks up the plates and moves to the kitchen.

The visit ended shortly after that. Wacu got on the phone and stayed on it in her room while I washed up then sat out on the balcony. I couldn't have left immediately because I wanted to set things right with her, so I hung around for a while thumbing through magazines and watching the neighbours get in and out of their cars in the parking area. When Wacu still hadn't come out after an hour, I walked to the bedroom and picked up my bag which lay next to her on the bed.

"Oh, you're going?" she looked at me and asked.

I had actually gone in to get some lip salve but said yes, hoping she would hang up so I could explain myself.

"Okay, see you," this time her accent was back. And just like that, she turned around and went back to her conversation.

I walked out of the flat to the sounds of her phone chatter, down the stairs and once outside stood in the sun for a minute asking myself what had just happened.

At the gate, the askari is waiting.

"Sasa unaenda?" he asks, swinging the big black gate open.

"Ee, sasa 'naenda zangu."

"Haya basi, nenda salama. Na utarudi kututembelea lini?" he adds with a smile.

I smile back. "Sasa... unajua mimi ninaishi mbali sana..."

He starts to laugh.

"Lakini utarudi tu," the man seated on the pavement next to the askari's booth says with finality. He raises his rake for effect.

We all laugh. "Haya basi, m'baki salama," I say, and they raise their hands in response.

Chapter Two

Physically, I'm small - five three and slender - and for many years, sported a head of long straightened hair which is now cut short and natural. After years of lye burns and raw scalps, Mom and I got fed up of the relaxed hair we'd been holding onto (she for decades) and had our heads shorn. We wanted to start afresh, look the way God made us as Africans; how we are meant to be. Afterwards, when she realised how weird we appeared to our customers - two bald women running a hair salon - Mom bought a series of colourful *vitambas* and wrapped her head in them till she had enough growth to plait.

Myself, I've remained bare and like it; because I can wash and go, don't suffer lye burns anymore and have salved my previously guilty conscience by staying away from the lunacy of chemically altered African hair.

Other than that, I suppose I look like your run-of-the-mill Kiambu girl. My skin is very dark and my eyes are humongous. I have long lashes and straight teeth with a gap between the two top incisors, high cheekbones and thin long fingers.

I'm just regular, and for a twenty-six year old girl living in this nineties world, my mood is constant and easy-going, so long as I can laugh, hear a good story and learn new things.

Mom's eyes, unlike mine are brown, and her skin lighter. She's about my height, much thicker and has a long neck. She was born and raised in Kiambu, finished high school there then married Fafa whom she met at a boogie in the city. Mom has only one brother, Uncle Maina (Wacu's dad) and two sisters (they are really Cucu's sister's daughters) Tata Nyambura and Tata Wangui. Tata Nyambura lives in Satellite and Tata Wangui in Banana. But our clan is big, so I have a multitude of aunts, uncles, cousins and cucus and gukas all over the place.

My mother is always calm; nothing overwhelms her, though with her past travails and the episodes she has lived through, she could write two books.

When things went bad for us after Fafa died, Mom moved us all the way to Langata where she opened a chicken kiosk and drove her own private school bus on weekday mornings and afternoons.

When I was in secondary school and things were slightly better, Mom sold car spare parts while I killed and plucked chickens after school and on the weekends. She still kept the bus, helped Cucu at the farm, supplied meat to KQ and rented land in Laikipia where we grew maize. And she put me through university by selling curios all over Europe.

She's kind, has a wry sense of humour, is very strong - both mentally and physically - and is not educated in the *muzungu* sense. Mom taught me how to work hard and not depend on anyone, and she is very humble. Because of her, I can face the flood, which I suppose, is the greatest lesson a child can learn from her parent. My mom is more respectable that some of these people running around here with ten degrees who don't know whether they are coming or going.

People say we look alike which makes me feel good, because my mother is very pretty. I don't know about our resemblance; maybe if we meet someday you will tell me if it's true.

As for home, we've lived in this house since I was 17 and Absalom our gardener comes and goes every day, though he has asked to move into the wooden house at the bottom of the garden. Apparently, his relatives in Kawangware are driving him nuts. Ever since he opened a tailoring business for his wife, her brothers who've never liked him have been trying *"juu chini"* to destroy him. This weekend, he'll hammer a plastic carpet into his new domicile down there. I bought him a mosquito net and a stove to cook on, and we put in a cupboard, table and chairs. He's happy, as we are. His wife will come to live with him and it's good for us because we will have them to talk with.

So that's Soni in a nutshell. I lived abroad for some time, during university, and other than rare trips around here now and then, *mutanipata hapa tuu,* generally minding my own business unless of course, I'm pulled out of my orbit into the chaos of this place.

Chapter Three

Not too long ago, I was down in Grogan buying wimbi for our porridge. It was a January afternoon, hot and dusty, and my ears and throat were itchy from the flour wafting about the room. Kimdas is one of those places where they grind your meal while you wait and a long queue stretched ahead of me that afternoon - a mix of women and men lined up waiting for flour, with me at the end for my four kilos of wimbi.

Outside was shouting and din, and I was irritable. Just getting down to Grogan from the salon had put me on edge and I stood there dreading my walk back, the street throngs, congestion, heat and home time chaos.

So when I heard someone wailing and turned to see a crowd forming outside the entrance to Kimdas, I heaved in distress at the thought of more nuisance.

On the pavement in front of the shop, a short handicapped woman, like the ones you see selling sweets at Kencom, was shaking uncontrollably and wringing her arms, wailing *"Mwana wakwa, mwana wakwa"*.

A crowd was beginning to swell around her and someone asked:

"Wee mama unalia nini?"

Another responded:

"Mtoto wake amepotea,"

"Ati amepotea? Kwani alimuwacha wapi?"

Somebody new walked up and asked:

"Ati ni nini inaendelea hapa?"

The woman was wailing in abandonment,

"Woiii, woiii, woiii, mwana wakwa athire kuu? Woiii, woiii, woiii, Mwathani wakwa."

She threw herself here and there, exhorting the crowd to give her back her child, then pushed her way to the road where she bent down to search under parked cars, all the while crying louder and louder.

By Kirinyaga Road standards, the crowd was small, though a wall of bodies blocked the entrance to Kimdas. People were crossing over to see what was happening and some shopkeepers had walked out of their premises to investigate as well.

Inside the shop, the queue disintegrated and most that had been standing before me made their way outside. A flour-covered Kimdas worker responsible for milling our grain left his post and disappeared into the sea of bodies. I too pushed myself into the mix and turned to a man in a nylon suit who was following the proceedings.

"Boss", I asked him, "Ati ni nini inaendelea hapa?"

Without looking at me, the man in the suit pointed to the handicapped woman and said,

"Huyu mwanamke anauza matunda hapa nje."

I looked at her wares strewn on the pavement in front of us.

"Alienda kupiga simu kwenye hiyo callbox," the man continued, pointing to the booth thirty feet away, "Na alipomaliza kuongea, aligeuka akaona mtoto amepotea."

"Ala!" I exclaimed, and turned to look at the woman.

She was short and had sickly pockmarked skin and looked unhealthy, like someone who hasn't eaten vegetables in a while. In her yellow chiffon dress, head wrap and thick multicoloured sweater, the woman was a carbon copy of three million women in Nairobi, the only difference being that her right leg was encased in a leather and chuma brace. All around her on the ground plastic bags and oranges lay scattered about, some being trampled by the congregation.

People in the crowd were asking all sorts of questions.

"Kwani mtoto alienda wapi?" A stout woman in a green skirt asked the woman in despair.

"Mama," she added to the handicapped woman, "Mtoto wako ameenda wapi? Hakuna mtu hapa unayemjua mwenye pengine amemchukua?"

"Woiiiiii Ngai-e mwana wakwa niathire kuu?!!? Woiii Mwathani Jesu ngwika-atia riu.....?" The handicapped woman was really wringing her arms and appeared ready to collapse any second.

It was a regular Grogan day. Just drama.

Women in the crowd stood cheek in palm, palm in cheek following the unfolding saga, while staring at Mama Kuria with pained expressions. Men asked rapid-fire questions over and over again. Others were giving the rundown to new crowd members who had joined us on the pavement. A number of people were looking under parked cars and between buildings in an attempt to find the missing child, and a fat Power and Lighting employee stopped his motorcycle and offered to ask the police up the hill to come and assist the woman. Even the Kimdas proprietor telephoned his friends around the corner and asked them to look out for the child.

By the time two policemen ambled down the hill and round the corner, we had the following information in hand:

The missing child's name was Kuria, he was three and answered to the name 'Papa'. He and his mother lived in Dandora Kangemi and he was wearing blue trousers, a white sweater and brown shoes. His mother had left him seated on the pavement by the oranges while she went to make a phone call to her sister who worked as a cleaner in Othaya General Hospital. Her sister had asked how Papa was and when his mother turned to look at her son and tell his aunt "he is okay and is eating an orange", she found that he was gone. The woman's name was Ciku or Mama Kuria and she wasn't married. No one she knew on Grogan could have taken her child since everybody around there - the workers, askaris and owners - knew her. She'd been hawking on that pavement for a year.

While crowd members narrated this to the policemen, a man in askari uniform ran up to the handicapped woman. He was panting and sweating profusely.

"Hayuko huko Mama Kuria," The askari panted to the wailing woman, turning her by the forearm to face him. Apparently, he had scoured the road above us to see if Kuria had somehow ended up there.

Mama Kuria trembled and the muscles in her face twitched wildly.

When the policemen began to cross-examine her and the crowd overwhelmed me, I pushed my way to the other side of the road and walked to a soda vendor who seemed to be the only one on the strip not following the afternoon saga. There, I bought a drink, leaned on a parking meter and gulped down the cool Bitter Lemon. The sun drilled into my head. Loud honking, metallic clangs and noise engulfed Grogan and I watched as the crowd across the road began to disperse.

As I was handing the empty soda bottle back to the vendor, a pretty saleswoman walked out of the electronics shop behind us and asked me what was happening across the road.

It was extremely hot, dry and dusty and the two policemen were walking the gesticulating and hobbling woman awaydown the road. Her askari friend was bent over picking oranges into a plastic bag and I stood watching him and the three figures, then turned and began to walk towards the city wondering about Kuria and his mother.

How many times had I read reports in the paper of missing children? "Seven year old John Omwenga, a Standard Two pupil in Happy Tots Primary School disappeared on his way home to Buruburu from school..." Or, "Mary Kivuti, a thirteen year old student at St. Annes Primary in Umoja has been missing from her family home since Monday last week..." I would read the reports, worry about the children and be sad for a few days, then forget about it. What could I possibly do? This place is full of stories like that. So I continued to walk.

Five minutes or so up the hill, I remembered the wimbi and thought of stopping at one of the supermarkets in town. But it was getting late and we had none at home, and by the time I got up to the city centre, supermarket aisles would be packed with after work shoppers. I ran back down the hill to Kimdas and as always, life had moved on. Grogan was ready for the next event.

While standing in a shorter queue, I watched the askari who was now chatting with a passer-by outside, still clutching bags of oranges in his hands. I looked at the pavement. No one could tell that minutes before, two lives had been altered on it. One shattered, and the other?

I paid for my flour and as I was leaving the shop, tapped the askari on the shoulder.

"Chief," I asked, "Wamempeleka huyo Mama wapi?"

The man looked me up and down, stared at me for a few moments before responding,

"Central, kuandika statement."

"Na huyo mtoto atapatikana kweli?" I asked.

He stared at me some more then shook his head.

"Sijui," He replied after a while and turned away.

I said goodbye and went down the road, up the hill and towards the city centre.

At the time, the most important thing on my mind was getting out of town. I could barely walk in a straight line. My head was throbbing, as though two hammers pounded non-stop on my temples. The salon was far away, on the other edge of town the city and I stopped at a call box and phoned my mother.

"Mom," I said when she came to the phone, "I'm not feeling well. I'll see you at home."

"What's wrong?" She shouted. There was a lot of blow-dryer noise in the background.

"My head is paining. This sun is too hot."

"Pole," Mom said. "Buy some medicine at the chemist in Dagoretti and then sleep. But make sure Absalom cuts those branches at the bottom."

"Okay, I will," I replied. "Bye."

"Bye Sweetie, and take care," Mom said and hung up.

I continued to walk slowly towards thethe New Stanley because I wanted to catch a taxi opposite the hotel and get home fast. On Tom Mboya Street, there was commotion outside the Post Office. Two men were arguing loudly and appeared ready to come to blows. I crossed the busy road and on the other side, people were running towards me.

"Kwani ni nini sasa?" I asked a magazine vendor and pointed towards three men who had almost been knocked down by a car when they ran into the street.

"Wanahepa maaskari wa Kanjo," he replied.

The last thing I needed was to get caught in the middle of a hawker and City Council askari melee. When more runners appeared, I turned right and walked all the way to Jeevanjee Gardens, hoping to be as far away as possible from the chaos.

By then, I was fatigued. At Jeevanjee, I sat down on a bench under the canopy of a huge bougainvillea. There were people asleep on the grass and I had to squint when I looked around because a sudden wind kicked dust into the air. The park was clean for a change and the smell of roast chicken wafted from Kenchick behind me, making me hungry. I walked to the shop and bought half a chicken, chips and a soda, then made my way back to the park and sat near Queen Victoria's statue. She was covered in bird droppings and someone had stuck an evangelical crusade poster on her. I wondered what she was still doing here.

Trees spread their branches above, and birds chirped all around and two women on the grass nearby smiled up at me and said hello.

Nairobi is so nice. I ate quickly and wiped my greasy fingers on my jeans, then leaned back on the bench and shut my eyes.

After my father died, every other weekend, Cucu would come to Nairobi. On Sundays, she, Mom and I would go into town, buy chicken and eat either at Uhuru Park, or Jeevanjee Gardens. If we went to Jeevanjee, we would make our way to the ice-cream parlour that still stands where the old Alfa Romeo franchise used to be. That part of the city has been slow to change, though I hear they want to tear down Afro-Unity and the building that houses it, which is a shame. Fafa used to drink there, and when I heard of the end of Afro, memories that anchored me to him were jolted.

I opened my eyes. The two women were gone, as were most in the crowd that had been lying on the grass. At the edge of the park, by the entrance closest to the Salvation Army, I spotted some muscular kauzis making their way towards a tourist couple nearby, got up before the boys saw me sitting alone and headed to find a taxi home.

It was by the shoe shop a few doors from Salgon's on Biashara Street that someone grabbed my arm and made me wince.

"Sisté, ni wewe ulikuwa huko Kirinyaga?" a female voice asked.

I turned around.

A fleshy woman about my height had me in her grip and was staring at me. She asked again in a singsong voice,

"Si umetoka Kirinyaga sasa?"

I pulled away from her and put the bag of wimbi on the ground then rubbed my arm where her fingers had been.

"Tunajuana?" I asked.

"Si umetoka Kirinyaga sasa? Ni wewe ulikuwa umesimana hapo Kimdas, sindio?"

I recognised her as the woman in the green skirt in the Grogan crowd.

"Wacheni kuziba njia," a man said angrily, and then pushed past us into the shoe shop.

The woman in the green skirt moved to the edge of the pavement and I remained where I had been standing. In front of us on the street, there was a cream-coloured taxi and inside, the driver stared lazily at us through half-closed eyes. His passenger side door was open and the driver had his foot on the dashboard and was leaning back in his seat looking very drowsy. He was very handsome.

I looked at the woman who was now smiling, and tried to decide whether to be rude to her because my arm hurt.

"Ee, nimetoka huko sasa," I replied and smiled, indicating my bag of wimbi.

"Oo," she looked at the plastic bag on the ground. "Ni unga ulikuwa umeenda kununua?"

"Ndio," I responded and moved closer to her. "Na hiyo maneno kweli ni ya kusikitiza," I added, referring to what we had witnessed. "Kwani mtoto ameenda wapi?"

"Ai, hiyo maneno ni mzito," the woman shook her head slowly and said. "Lakini huyo mtoto hajapotea."

I stared at her and asked,

"Kwani unasema nini?"

"Wewe hujui maneno inayoendelea hapa Nairobi?" she responded. "Hiyo ni business kubwa sana."

She pronounced it 'mbisines' and I smiled when she said that.

"Haiya! Unacheka?" The woman looked at me in surprise.

"Hapana Auntie," I said, holding back an even bigger grin.

"Eee," she continued. "Na wezi wenyewe wako huko Grogan." She pointed towards that part of town.

I had no time for another Nairobi conspiracy and bent down to pick up the bag of wimbi. I was tired of the city whirl and not about to listen to what was sure to be an outlandish urban legend.

"Mummy wacha nielekee," I said tersely to the woman. "Tutaonana siku ingine."

She looked at me, surprised.

"Unaenda?"

"Lazima nielekee," I replied. What did she think I was going to do? Stand there and listen?

"Okay basi," she said and took a step away from me. "Kwaheri."

I realised from the look on her face that I'd embarrassed her, which made me feel bad. Then I pointed to the taxi.

"Naelekea Dagoretti. Unataka lift?" I asked this with a smile, trying to make things right.

"Oo," she said, surprised. Then she smiled. "Asante lakini bwana wangu anafanya hapa," she pointed to a textile shop three doors down. "Tutaandamana pamoja, asante."

So I said goodbye to the woman in the green skirt, got into the taxi and rode out of the city with my handsome driver, Wanjau Hinga.

Chapter Four

After spending years saving for his car, Wanjau is finally in business for himself and doing well. Before, he drove taxis for a rich uncle who owns a bevy of them in Nairobi, as well as the Ha-Wendo Bar and two hardware shops in Ongata Rongai.

Wanjau grew up in Raini, the second in a brood of eight, and his father died a decade ago. Like mine, his people are Mau Mau, though they weren't at Lari but at Hola and the coast. His great-grandfather was part of the crew that planned Chief Waruhiu's assassination, two of his uncles (also deceased) fought in the forest, and his dad swore the oath shortly before the fighting was over.

His mom Njeri farms in Raini, and most of her children live nearby while the youngest, Kamau, works at Ha-Wendo and shares a home with Wanjau in a walled six house plot behind the bar.

Though he passed his high school exams with flying colours and could have gone on to Nairobi University, Wanjau saw no sense in the endeavour when he could get a head start building his future. So for some years, he worked for his Uncle Ngatia and saved the money to buy a second-hand 504. The car is in good condition and from its proceeds he has managed to buy a plot close to his mother where he is constructing a house slow by slow.

For such a young man, Wanjau is serious. He's thirty-three and when I compare him with my ex-boss who at that age had done nothing except commit every vice imaginable and boast about his father's money, I really wonder.

Wanjau starts work in town early, ferrying customers from backpacker hostels to the airport. Then he goes to Ambassadeur and does the same till one; then off to Biashara Street. He would go to Bombax for the night but because it's slow there, moved to Real Club in Lavington. Wanjau gets home around three in the morning, sleeps, is up and off again.

"When do you rest?" I once asked him.

"Between clients and Sundays."

"And now that you don't come disturbing me in Lavington," he added smiling, "I have more time to sleep."

In the beginning, I was cautious around him because the last thing I needed was romantic tension, which nearly always comes up where these types of friendships are concerned. So I invented a boyfriend and kept it going, till he caught on and told me to stop telling lies. I was embarrassed, but he just laughed.

Wanjau doesn't have a woman; or so he says. The last one vowed to commit suicide if he ever left her and that's when he did. The one before her was the psycho kind who even after he told her things were finished, started hounding the new woman he was seeing. Unluckily, she was beaten up by her rival and the rival's sisters and friends. But when the rival turned out to be an even more unbalanced love, threatening to pour acid on his face if he ever left, Wanjau hit the road.

I can see why they go ballistic over him, because he sure is good looking.

Very dark skin, tall, compact and lean, like those Ngong Gikuyus. Plus he has that detached air that drives many women crazy.

Anyway, from him, I've learnt a lot. When we sat together in the car at Bombax some nights, he'd tell me of the things that have happened to him while driving around this mad city by night.

Like the time two thugs hijacked him and forced him to drive towards Muthaiga while they changed clothes in the back only for the car to run out of petrol outside the GSU compound gate. Or the time a crazy white man pulled a gun on him and inquired whether Wanjau thought he was a rally driver. Wanjau told me that he had just stopped at a house in Onyonka Estate one night past midnight, when a red Pajero screeched to a halt behind and the muzungu burst out wielding a Browning pistol. Both Wanjau and his equally surprised customer stared agape at the wild haired muzungu who yelled obscenities then jumped back in his car and sped away.

When he dropped me home that first time, Wanjau had said that if I ever needed a taxi, I could find him outside Ambassadeur or Salgon's. After that, when I was around Biashara Street and didn't have our pick-up, I rode in his car. Eventually, we became friends. These days I consider him my good pal, though I have given up trying to understand what sort of friendship it is we share.

When I locked the gate behind me, I realised that I had forgotten to ask the taxi man to stop in Dagoretti so that I could buy some re-hydration mix and Panadol. My head was still pounding.

I walked down the hill and behind the house wondering where Ceci was, since any time the gate squeaks, she runs up to bark at 'intruders'. Mom named that dog 'Wangeci'... Absalom was nowhere to be seen but down by the river, there was a pile of Jacaranda branches he must have cut earlier in the day.

"Absalom!!!" I called out in the direction of the store. "Absalom!!!"

There was no answer.

I opened the back door, walked in and stepped on a foolscap sheet of paper. Absalom had left a note:

"Mummy,
Nimempeleka Florence hospitali adungwe shindano. Tutaonana kesho.
Love,
Absalom."

Inside the house, I poured myself a glass of water from the clay filter and sat down to sip it. Then I walked to the corridor and touched the hot water heater. It was warm. In the bathroom, I stripped and stood under the shower, tilting my neck to let the water fall over my temples. After washing, I brushed my teeth, checked my eyebrows in the mirror for stray growth and put on a t-shirt.

I padded barefoot over the cold floors into the kitchen and in the fridge, found some leftover *mukimo* and chicken from the night before. I peeled and cut up a paw-paw and pineapple, then walked into the living room and drew the curtains. The bell rang. The night askari had arrived.

I ran to the bedroom and wrapped a *leso* around myself, and on my way out to unlock the gate, grabbed Mom's sweater that was hanging on the back of a chair in the kitchen, put it on and clutched it around my bra-less chest.

Salim was really ringing that bell.

"Hee, Soni," he said when I walked up the hill and opened the gate, "Nilifikiri mumehama! Habari ya leo?"

"Mzuri sana Salim, na wewe jee?" I replied.

"Salama Baby," he responded and looked over my shoulder towards the river. "Kwani Absalom hayuko?" Every day, when Salim arrives, Absalom is waiting for him. They talk a little before Absalom leaves and Salim settles down for the night.

"Amempeleka bibi hospitali," I replied.

"Ala," he said, "Kwani ni mgonjwa?"

"Hakusema," I replied. "Lakini nafikiri ni ile Malaria inamsumbua."

I told him we weren't expecting visitors that night and after Mom came home, he could do his rounds. Salim has been with us for some years now and knows all our family and friends. During the day, he works as an herbalist in Satellite. Absalom told me that Salim lives near the chief's camp and has a steady flow of clients who go to him seeking remedies where conventional medicine has failed.

Chapter Five

So more about me now.

I was born in a fourth floor government flat in Mariakani, down the road from Mater Misericordiae Hospital in the early seventies, before Marigu-ini slum and rubbish heaps crawled down the riverbank in South B, when life in Nairobi was like a postcard.

Fafa and Mom had stopped to greet Mariakani friends on the way to hospital for her check-up when her waters had burst and I popped out almost immediately after, with a full head of hair, bright focused eyes and a tooth. People who know us still talk about my birth in awe.

Fafa's name was Nugi Werehire - 'Nugi Who Brought Himself', and he died of Leukaemia when I was seven. I still remember him, a short, smooth-skinned balding man with a big stomach who laughed a lot.

My mother's name is Wangari Nugi and I'm their only child Muthoni, though everybody - even non-family - calls me by my Gikuyu pet name, Soni. Both my parents come from Kiambu and have heavy Gumba blood in their lineages. We can name ancestors up to eleven generations back on Mom's side, and nine on Fafa's, and Kiambu is dotted with the homesteads of hundreds of my kin. It seems our people have always lived there, above and below ground, so I consider Mwiruti -

my maternal village - to be my true ancestral home.

If you get off a matatu by the Forestry Department sign on the way to the old Uplands Sausage Factory, there is a murram road to the left. Walk down it for about a kilometre towards the river, cross it and go up the hill to the cow dip. Across the ridge, you'll see a small centre encircled by green farms. That's our village. Mwiruti means 'hard worker', and people there don't joke about work.

At our family farm where Cucu lives, we grow tea primarily, but also herd five cows and *njaus* that graze by the river. We have goats, chickens, ducks, sheep, guard dogs and two cats; and also burn *makaa* to sell. Aside from the tea, Cucu keeps an acre of fast-growing wattle that we burn in pits to make the charcoal. Then we have a vegetable shamba, fruit trees, and also sell milk. Our farm's name is Mutamaiyu because a forest of those trees once covered that section of Kiambu, in the days when our people descended Kirinyaga into the area; before the Gumba went underground or were absorbed into our blood.

It's a nice place.

Guka built a stone house in 1962 after tearing down the one colonialists built here when they stole our land. People thought he had gone mad for demolishing the white people's "perfectly good" house; but after years in the forest with Mau Mau and then more of concentration camp misery in Lari under the British, the last thing my grandfather needed after his release was a reminder of muzungus having been here. And unlike many neighbours who bought back their ancestral land from departing colonialists, Guka had no intention of purchasing what rightfully belongs to us.

When the muzungu occupying our farm (a certain Mr. Clarkson) offered to sell to Guka before Uhuru, my grandfather paid him in cash, got the title deed and the same night, with hooded ex-Lari internee compatriots, waylaid Clarkson and his family in their car and got his borrowed money back - plus whatever else the muzungus were carrying. Clarkson was on his way to the airport or going to Mombasa; to a liner back to the UK or some still colonised part of their empire.

The farmhouse has three bedrooms, a kitchen, toilet and small bathroom. In the kitchen, there's an ancient wood-burning stove, one-tap sink and small pantry. We keep two urns of ghee in there, plus a large cast iron hook on which hangs a fresh side of beef. Our bath water is boiled on the stove and carried into the bathroom, as there's rarely enough water pressure from the tank outside to fill the tub. When I was young, Mom would wash me in a basin in the kitchen by the lit stove.

What else? Well, the sitting room is where our ancestors live. Almost every inch of wall is covered with photographs of my forebears (even Nyerere); one of my great-grandfather in his early KCA days; long ago family-sponsored harambees and gatherings. My great-grandmother Wamucii in Mombasa seeing the Indian Ocean when she was ninety in 1968 (Fafa had taken her there in his Ford Cortina); studio photos chronicling births and weddings; one of my Kaunda-suited dad standing by his new tractor in 1973... There is even one of Guka taken two days before he was detained. In it, he's with my great-great grandfather Muriu, who was well over a hundred years old at the time. Muriu is bent over, swaddled in blankets and has long pierced, drooping earlobes. He smiles widely and is gripping a long walking stick. Behind the two men is a perfectly round cylindrical mud hut. A young child is seated on the ground with a maize cob in his hand. His face is fuzzy and no one can remember who he was.

In that room, Cucu keeps a small Vono bed, because on slow afternoons, when things are quiet at the farm, she naps surrounded by our departed kin. She says she travels into their world in her dreams and becomes strong again.

When Mom again went abroad to sell curios after I returned from the U.S., I lived here alone for a year and a half. Though I missed her tremendously, her letters kept me going. She would write to me, telling me of what she saw around Europe, and ask whether or not I remembered to pay the bills, buy fertilizer and see so-and-so at the Lands office. We also spoke once in a while on the phone, when the lines allowed it, or when I picked it up.

Those were the days.

Looking back, it seems like the sun always shone and because I was without the financial angst that sat like an extra pair of shoulders on many others, life was good. Money was no problem; I picked up the rent from our place in Langata and had a simple budget. Two thousand for electricity and water; groceries varied, depending on whether or not Cucu gave me food I didn't consume quick enough. She was always sending something with my relatives who checked up on me; milk, ghee, eggs and vegetables, enclosing a thousand bob in a note she wrote in flawless Gikuyu cursive. When the food overwhelmed me, I gave it to Absalom. The rest of the money went into the bank.

You'd think that with my mother away, I would be hanging around a hip crowd. Some of the students I'd known abroad were back too, but they are high-class and I'm not, or were trying to be and I wasn't. Despite the fact that we studied at the same university out there, and that I hold the same Economics B.A. they do, the fissures of Kenyan classism ran too deep.

My first months back, I'd spent time with my cousins who harangued me about wasting my mother's money to go abroad "when JKUAT is just here and just look at you now, you're jobless."

In those early days, I had no sight other than the moment, and with boundless time, no job and so much to do in Nairobi, life was excellent.

Every day at one, if in town, I'd aim to be at Kencom where the preacher with the P.A. system breaks it down to idlers and others by the shoe-shine stand at the bus stop. He's the one who tells it like it is, isn't fearful of anything and at one time, was in remand for being 'subversive' (since he spends more time commenting on the political situation than on saving souls).

Once, an old crazy Indian walked past Mister Preacher, shouted and wagged his finger at him. I recognised the Indian because he was usually lying on the ground on Eduardo Mondlane Street muttering or singing songs. The war was almost on, but bystanders restrained the preacher who then berated the Indian and told him that the reason we were all killing time at the stop and mostly jobless was because of his kind and their local allies who had ripped this country apart. The preacher was so angry, I thought he would explode. And after his diatribe and then prayer before which he always requests that you bow your head and then offer something small, I gave him ten bob (though I didn't agree with him blaming other people for our problems). I don't know what that man thought of me. We never spoke when I was there. Maybe he thought I was one of the many Nairobi Born Again; but really, I went to hear him because he inspired something in me, notwithstanding his evangelical zeal; because he struck at the upside-down world with unrelenting fury.

I wasn't out of work for too long, though I never managed to keep a steady job after that. I always quarrelled with my employers and got fired. It seems I could never get along with my bosses who spent their days trying to break me. Also, I couldn't play the game: wouldn't kowtow, bootlick, sleep my way up or undermine my co-workers to move ahead. Where to? I didn't care about office politics or *kichinichiniing* anybody. All I wanted was to work and be left alone. God only knows why, but for whatever reason, life kept thrusting me into the most surreal employment situations, where I found myself surrounded by characters who seemed to have crawled right out of a bad dream.

For eight months after my last position, I stayed indoors and slept, only getting up to shower, walk outside and ask Absalom how things were going, and whether or not he needed anything for the *shamba.* I barely ate, and any forays into town or Langata were quick and took place during hours I wasn't bound to meet anyone I knew.

All those months, I just slept, and thankfully, Mom was gone, because she wouldn't have tolerated any of it if she'd been around. Neither Cucu nor my other relatives knew I was comatose - I had lied to them all about having a job that required me to travel to Lokichogio every week. Absalom covered my tracks whenever relatives dropped in to check on us.

Many a time, I was holed up in the house listening to family members talk with Absalom outside, telling him to say hello to Soni when she returned from the North and that they had just come to make sure I was okay. I didn't pick up the phone for weeks at a time. Absalom would go pay the bills and every odd weekend, I would go to the farm, where I continued to sleep, lying to my grandmother about being tired from work and imaginary travels.

When in Mwiruti, I did the rounds and greeted everybody, then returned to the farm and fell into bottomless slumbers out of which not even a severe beating would have extracted me. I am wholly indebted to my ancestors for not revealing the truth to my relatives, for that whole episode is what saved my life and gave me sanity.

For so long before then I had been weary, feeling confused and out of step, like someone riding in a car backwards. After university abroad, I had no idea what my goals were, other than being an African Success Story - whatever that means. And yet I didn't feel I needed to be rich and 'cultured', or trendy, or very clever and different. Or whatever it is people like me are supposed to aspire to be these days. Unlike so many girls, I wasn't trying to get married – especially to a white man, which most girls around here appear to desire. I didn't want to marry a non-black husband and yet was resistant to many of our men - the bulk of whom fell into the professional/cool/cultured troupe that I've never connected with; while the rest drove me insane with their *siasa* and money obsessions, and maddening superiority complexes when all you have to do is look around here to see that women really run the show.

Minutes after being noisily discharged from my last job, I walked into Muncher's on Kenyatta Avenue and sat by the window and cried. The waiter, who knew me because I was a regular there, kept coming up and asking what the matter was.

I wept hard. Not for the job, which I could have cared less about, nor because of my boss's nastiness. I just cried because I was tired and frustrated and wanted something better, then went home and slept because I didn't know what else to do.

Eight months later I woke up feeling like I had shed three skins. I walked out of the dusty house early one morning, stood on the grass by the kitchen and looked down the garden, with my arms akimbo. A small snake, wet with dew, slithered into a hole behind Ceci's kennel and in the distance, I heard my neighbour harassing her maid.

The gate creaked, shook and swung open. It was Absalom, who saw me and beamed all the way down the hill.

"Umefufuka Soni?" he asked when he came up to me on the grass.

I just smiled and shook his hand. He had gained weight.

"Nyasi imemea vizuri," I said, and pointed to the healthy green lawn.

"Ee, vizuri sana," he replied.

We stood together for a while, looking around our land.

"Asante Absalom," I said after a while. "Umenisaidia sana."

I looked up into his almond shaped eyes.

"Soni," he said and started towards the bottom, "Kila kitu ni mos mos,"

That made me smile wider and I went into the house to call Cucu and say I had been transferred back to Nairobi from Lokichogio.

Mom came back and realised I was never going back to school or settling down in a profession. So we opened a hair salon, and that's what we've been running ever since.

We have serious girls working for us and the place is busy. Mostly university chicks and radio presenters from the stations down the road make up our clientele, though some young men come in now and then (new-money types wanting a manicure), or sugar daddies out to get a girl from our patrons. I go in with Mom in the morning and do the accounts, check on supplies and am in charge of all finances. I also handle the farm and other money. Mom takes care of our workers and patrons. They call her 'Mama Soni' and are happy here. None worry about me since I'm either in the small office at the front of the salon or out on errands. We have a good thing going thank God. The girls trust us as we do them and our customers have been very loyal.

Chapter Six

Soni? Soni-ĩĩ?" Mom's voiced roused me from my deep slumber. "Niwanyua dawa?"

I opened my eyes and lifted my head. Mom was sitting on the edge of the bed shaking me by the shoulder. It was dark, though a bright sliver of light from the corridor slit into the room.

"Did you take some medicine?" she asked again.

"Ca," I replied drowsily, and dropped my head back onto the pillow, "Ndinagura. I forgot."

"And how are you feeling now?" Mom asked.

"It's still paining," I said, touching my forehead. "I'll come out there and drink some water. Just give me a few minutes".

Mom got up and walked out of the room. After some minutes, I heard her running a bath. While she washed, I got up, wrapped my leso around myself and walked out of my the room.

The kitchen's terrazzo floor is always cold and I don't know why I forget to wear slippers every time I go in there. Mom has been talking about remodelling the kitchen but she doesn't want to destroy the terrazzo. It's the old beautiful kind (this house was built in the thirties) and she says that *fundis* these days don't make it like they used to back then.

She bought this house when I was seventeen, from a rich Kiambu family that never used it. I guess they were so wealthy, they could afford to keep an empty house in Nairobi. Mom says that she knew one of their daughters in school and that's how she managed to buy this place from them. It's small, just enough for the two of us, but we're lucky to have so much land with it this close to the city. We have two bedrooms, a kitchen, bathroom, living and dining rooms, and a big sunny veranda at the back. Also a garage and servant's quarters full of junk and boxes, and a pretty wooden cottage down by the river. Apparently, before Independence, two British spinster sisters lived here. They sold the place to the people we bought it from, who then kept it locked up and the grounds unkempt until we took it over.

Sometimes I imagine what this place looked like when the two sisters were here. They probably had submissive 'native' workers and many cats.

I heated up the chicken and *mukimo* and set two plates on the table.

When Mom had changed into her nightdress*nightie*, she walked into the kitchen and asked what we were having for dinner.

"Last night's food," I replied. "And there's a paw-paw and some pineapple there," I said, pointing to the plastic bowl on the table.

"Let me just eat the fruit and I'll drink a glass of milk before I go to bed," Mom said.

She picked up the bowl of fruit, walked into the living room, turned the T.V. on and sat down to watch *'Habari'*. It was nine o'clock.

In the kitchen, I remained standing by the cooker stirring the mukimo so that it wouldn't stick to the sufuria bottom and burn.

"And what has this one done today?" I heard Mom ask sarcastically when the announcer began his account of Moi's activities.

I had just finished my banana during the weather forecast when I remembered the Grogan incident. Mom was lying on the sofa, about to fall asleep.

"Oh, I forgot to tell you what happened today Mom," I said. "You know, when I was buying wimbi, a hawker's son was kidnapped?"

"Mm?"

"Yes," I said. "Well he must have been kidnapped; how do you just disappear? Woii, you should have seen how she looked. I thought she was going to die."

"Mm?"

"One minute he was there, the next he was gone. Can you imagine? She just went to use the phone and he disappeared."

"In Grogan?" Mom asked. She was lying there with her eyes closed.

"Ya," I replied. "At Kimdas. Everyone was looking for him but they couldn't find him. The police had to come and take her away."

"What for?" Mom asked.

"What do you mean?"

"Why did they take her away?"

"To write a statement," I said. "And I wonder what that will do."

Mom was quiet but her eyes were now open. She raised herself from the sofa and sat up.

"Hee," she said after a while. "Losing a child is the worst pain there is. How old was the child?"

"I think she said two or three," I replied.

"A girl?"

"Boy."

"Woii," Mom said. "I hope someone finds him and takes him to Dr. Barnados."

"One woman said it's big business down there," I remembered what the lady in the green skirt had said. "Stealing children."

"That's probably true," Mom said. "That place is full of devils," she added. "You should ask Tata Nyambura about that place. She can tell you some horror stories."

"Horror stories?" I asked. "Like what?"

"Sweetie I'm tired," Mom said wearily. She rose to her feet and walked into the kitchen.

"When you see your tata ask her. Goodnight and God bless," Mom said.

"Good night," I replied. "But aren't you going to drink your milk?"

"I'll drink it tomorrow," she said from the corridor. "And pray for that lady and her baby."

"I will," I said. "God bless."

For an hour after that, I watched a dubbed-over Mexican soap opera; something very dramatic. Then I scraped my leftovers into Ceci's bowl and put it out for her.

In the moonlight, I saw Salim's figure. He was seated in an old wicker armchair, in the wooden askari's hut. His bow, arrows and rungu were on the floor by his side. I raised my hand in a goodnight gesture but he didn't respond. He was fast asleep and the jiko's embers before him cast a warm orange glow over the gate.

I locked the doors, washed the dishes and went to bed, into a restless sleep.

Early the next morning, I woke up and cleaned the house. It was chilly outside, but by eleven, I knew the sun would be shining bright.

Ceci was pawing at the kitchen door and when I opened it, she squeezed in through the burglar-proof bars and ran into the house. She ran around the kitchen sniffing the floor for crumbs, licked my foot, squeezed herself out and ran into the garden.

I looked at the terrazoterrazzo and mopped it again then scooped out a cup of wimbi and cooked some porridge for breakfast. Mom's glass of milk was still on the table. I had forgotten to put it in the fridge but after tasting it, found it was still good. Then I showered and while brushing my teeth, heard the gate open. Through the small bathroom window, I saw Absalom walk in carrying the newspaper and a loaf of bread. I rinsed out my mouth, walked to the burglar-proof door and opened it.

"Sasa Absalom?" I asked.

"Fit Soni," he replied. "Habari ya asubuhi?" He walked down three concrete steps and handed me the newspaper.

" Mzuri asante. Habari ya Florence?" I asked.

"Ai," Absalom replied. "Alidungwa shindano huko clinic jana lakini hakulala vizuri. Usiku mzima alishinda akitetemeka tuu."

"Ni Malaria?" I asked.

"Ee," he replied. "Amemeza tembe mpaka amechoka. Sasa tutaona kama hii shindano itamsaidia."

"Na ni kwanini hukumpelekea hizo matawi?" I asked, pointing to the Neem growing by the fence.

"Hiyo kweli itamsaidia?" Absalom sounded incredulous. "Hata Salim aliniambia nimchemshie anywe."

"Itamsaidia Absalom," I said. "Hata mimi nikisikia Malaria inaingia, ninaichemsha."

Absalom stared at the tree for a while and said he would take some leaves home if the injection didn't work. Then he went off to the bottom of the garden.

Mom was in the kitchen sniffing the glass of milk.

"It's good," I said. "I tasted it."

"Just pour it into the porridge," Mom said, handing me the glass.

While we were having breakfast, the phone rang. It was Cucu, wondering whether we'd be going home that weekend. I told her I would drop Mom off that night, but that I would drive back to Nairobi and then return to Kiambu on Saturday after work. I handed Mom the phone and went to make my bed.

While Mom showered, I read the newspaper. On the political front, it was the usual frenzy. I scanned the front page, looked over my horoscope, which seemed to have been recycled from some weeks before, and then scrutinized the National News section. I don't know why, but I wanted to see if they had reported on the missing Kirinyaga Road child. When I found nothing, I sat back and waited for Mom, all the while thinking about Mama Kuria. Would she be back on the pavement so soon after her child's disappearance? And where was he? Maybe he came back on his own. And what about the lady in the green skirt? Was she right? Had he been stolen?

God only knows why but I decided that after dropping Mom at the salon, I might as well drive to Grogan to see, while running my errands in town.

I had prayed for Kuria and hoped he would be found, and after the conversation I'd had with the taxi driver on the way home - about child abductions, 'Devil Worshippers', paedophiles and money-making wizards, my curiosity had been aroused. Also, for some odd reason, I felt guilty about the whole thing.

Mom walked into the kitchen wearing a wax blue, green and yellow boubou. Her head was wrapped in a billowing scarf and as always, she looked stunning. I glanced down at my faded jeans and takkies, and then tugged at the Dawanol t-shirt that had been a free gift from the Kiambu Show the year before.

"The way you dress Soni," Mom shook her head after looking me up and down, "no wonder you can't find a husband."

We both laughed and walked out of the house.

As I was opening the gate, Absalom ran up to Mom who was surveying the work he had done on the Jacaranda the day before.

"Habari Mummy?" Absalom beamed.

"Mzuri sana Absalom," Mom replied. "Soni ameniambia Florence bado ni mgonjwa? Anaendeleaje?"

While they talked, I walked to the pick-up's passenger side and got in. Mom would drive. I turned on the radio and turned it off again when I heard the DJ's fake American twang. Inside the glove box I found a Papy Tex cassette tape. Lucky me, it was the one that had *'Kanda ya Nini'*.

Mom got into the driver's seat and we were off to the salon.

By nine o'clock that morning, I had planned my day. The girls needed five bottles of Porosity, shampoo and as much super relaxer as I could get. There was a big bridal party coming in and all wanted re-touches and treatment. I hadn't been to the bank that week and needed to go and deposit some money. Also, Mom asked me to go and pick up a crate of Guinness for Cucu from Uncle Kinuthia's hotel on Accra Road. My grandmother, since time immemorial, has drunk a bottle of junior Guinness before she goes to bed at night. She once told me that I should start doing the same now, since I'll soon be getting babies. Apparently, if I drink it, my womb will be strong.

I decided to drive first to Muindi Mbingu and buy the stuff the girls needed from a man I know there. Hez wasn't at the shop yet, but I found his mother who gave me the deal her son would have.

I drove back to the salon and found that the girls needed more conditioner. The place was packed. Mom floated about calm and collected, reassuring a little girl who was getting her hair braided, mothering a pregnant lady in the waiting area, chatting with a young politico who was having his manicure done... I am always amazed by her cool. With that kind of thing, I am hopeless and just don't have the skills.

After my second trip to Muindi Mbingu, I decided to remain in the salon and go to the bank sometime that afternoon. So I helped wash heads, give change, paint nails and make small talk. By two o'clock, the wedding party was gone and Mom was sitting in the office eating a cold lunch. The girls had got take-away from a restaurant nearby and they all looked worn out. Business was good.

I emptied the cash box, left some flow money and asked if anybody needed anything else because I was going out.

They didn't, and I told my mother I'd be heading for the bank and Uncle Kinuthia's after which I had things to do.

"When are you coming back?" Mom asked. She looked very sleepy.

"Before six, I hope," I replied. "What do you want me to tell Nduuru?"

"Mugeithie muno," Mom said.

"See you," I told her. "I won't be late."

After the bank, I drove through town, parked in front of Wakirindi Lodge, my uncle's place and looked around for the hotel's askaris who were nowhere to be seen. The last thing I wanted was to leave a pick-up unattended on that road at that hour. Already, I felt car-jackers' eyes on me.

A young boy was standing by the entrance to the hotel and I rolled down the window and waved.

"Kijana!" I called out. "Utanichungia gari tafadhali?"

He ran up to the car.

"Haiya Soni!" he shouted excitedly. "Kari wee?"

"Haiya-e," I responded after recognising him. "Waweru?"

It was Nduuru's younger step-brother Waweru; Uncle Kinuthia's third wife's second son I think... I can never keep track. I hadn't seen him in a year because he is in high-school somewhere in Western and rarely leaves his Mom's farm during holidays.

Waweru took the keys and sat in the car while I went to look for Nduuru inside, whom I found seated at the back of the hotel's restaurant by his office with two other men, talking heatedly, looking more and more like his dad, Uncle Kinuthia.

The strange thing is that whereas Uncle Kinuthia is plain yellow, Nduuru is dark as night. Yet both could be identical twins: tall, big-framed and strong, with the same chiselled features and horrible temper. But where Uncle is quiet, his son is loud. Nduuru's mother is wife number one, Nyokabi; a beautiful ebony-skinned woman who shunned a big- time sixties politician and married Uncle Kinuthia.

Mom's best friend, other than Cucu and Mrs. Nyamu, is Tata Nyokabi, Nduuru's mother. And other than Mom and Cucu, Nduuru is my best friend. He's seven years older than me and I consider him my big brother. He's always taken care of me.

Nduuru was wearing maroon stonewash jeans with zips all over them and a perfectly ironed black and white striped tucked-in T-shirt. On his head, he wore a green khaki safari hat with the picture of a growling lion stamped on to its front. The other men, Njee Wanjohi and a man I know only as 'Munene' are Nduuru's constant companions.

We chatted a bit while one of the waiters went to put a case of beer into the pick-up. At the time, Nduuru was interested in one of our salon girls Wangeci and was always trying to twist information about her from me. That day, because of the men present, he kept hinting about Wangeci, asking me roundabout questions like how our workers were doing and whether or not they were happy with us or not.

What's odd is that in as much as Nduuru is the stereotypical high-spirited energetic Kiambu man, he is one shy person when it comes to women. He just starts stammering and sweating and goes blank around them at first, and it leaves me in stitches when I see it happen.

I had to go.

"Wee, me I have to go," I said and got up from my seat after finishing the cup of tea Nduuru had offered me. "Nitukuaria hindi ingi." Grogan was waiting.

I shook the men's hands and got up to leave. Nduuru walked out with me, adjusting his big-buckled jeans from side to side as we went along. I noticed his shoes.

"Wiikiriti iratu cia con man nikii?" I asked.

He looked down at his white shoes and then up at me.

"Call me we go Tembo!" I shouted to him. I was already on the pavement walking away.

Nduuru raised his hand and waved, hooked his thumbs in his jeans and walked back inside to his friends.

Outside, I found Waweru blasting a reggae tape in the car. I asked him whether he wanted to come along but he said he had to go to the library but could I pick him up later please?

Chapter Seven

Pandemonium slowly enveloped the white pick-up as I descended into the city's schizophrenic half. Pedestrian crowds grew dense, sounds increasingly piercing and smells more pungent. What on earth was I doing down there again chasing after a child I didn't know? And what would I do once I arrived at my destination? With the way things had gone at the salon that morning, Mom was probably busy with the Friday afternoon crowd and needed my help.

As I drove towards Kimdas, my eyes scanned the pavement in search of the handicapped woman. She was nowhere in sight and the only hawker on the ground was a matronly woman seated on an upside down soda crate in front of mango pyramids. She looked like so many others who ply that trade on the streets: burly, polyester dress with a *leso* around her waist; unkempt *matutas* peeking out from under a faded head wrap.

"Maitu wii mwega?" I walked up and greeted her politely after parking the car.

"Ndi mwega muno," she responded. "How many do you want?" she asked, already picking out mangos from her pyramids.

"Give me four please," I said.

I paid her and turned to look at the spot where Mama Kuria's oranges had lain scattered the day before. The woman was counting change from a roll of twenties unearthed from under her left breast.

"I also wanted to buy some oranges from Mama Kuria," I said when she handed me my change. "Yesterday morning, she told me she would have some good ones today."

"Oo," the woman said. 'She's not here today." She stared up at me, as if seeing me for the first time.

"Do you know her?" she asked.

"I buy from her when I'm around here," I lied, keeping my eyes steady.

"Aaa," I added dejectedly. "I really wanted oranges today."

The woman kept staring at me and didn't respond. I thanked her then walked into Kimdas where I bought another packet of wimbi. Luckily, the queue was short this time - just three people ahead of me. But the flour was everywhere and my ears and throat immediately began to itch. At the front, I pointed to the car and asked the owner if he would please keep an eye on the white pick-up outside.

Back on the sunny narrow pavement, the mango hawker was rearranging her wares. I walked to the car and placed my purchases on the beer crate then locked the door, crossed the road and headed to the electronics shop where the pretty saleswoman called Kezia worked.

They sell every conceivable electronic and non-electronic item in that shop: toasters, microwaves, kettles, radios and calculators, as well as bulbs, car mirrors, music systems and even biros and enamel tea sets. It was packed to the beams with merchandise, but business was slow; just one customer paying for a tyre tube. I walked in as Kezia was writing him a receipt, and she smiled brightly when I came up to her.

"Sasa Mummy?" she said and reached an arm across the counter.

"Fit sana Kezia," I replied, hoping I'd remembered her name correctly. My whole body shook as she pumped my hand up and down.

"Nimekuja kukutembelea," I said.

While we were exchanging greetings, a small middle-aged woman walked out of a back office and ordered a male worker in broken Kiswahili to go and sweep the front entrance.

"Wewe wacha makelele!" Kezia turned away from me and shouted to the woman, with my palm still lost in hers. "Kwani ni ma-customer wangapi wameengia hapa leo? Rudi huko ndani na uwache kutusumbua!"

I was pleasantly surprised at this unexpected reaction and turned to look at the woman who frowned, blinked rapidly and took a step back towards the office.

"Ngoja Rakesh narudi," she said to Kezia in a voice meant to be intimidating. "Mimi tashtaki nyinyi yote."

"Si ndio hii simu hapa," Kezia said aggressively and pointed to the phone behind her with her lips. "Iinue umpigie haraka."

Her male co-worker chuckled softly and continued reading the newspaper he had been looking at when I walked in. After the Indian woman disappeared back into the office, Kezia walked out from behind the counter and slipped her arm under mine.

"Omolo," she said to her co-worker, "Akitoka mwambie nimeenda break."

Elbows locked, we walked out of the shop and headed towards an alley.

"Ulifika salama jana?" Kezia asked me as we manoeuvred through the busy walkway.

I was surprised. We had only spoken for a few minutes the day before when I stood outside the shop drinking a soda.

"Ee," I replied. "Na wewe jee?'

"Ndio, asante," she responded. "Haki huyo mwanamke ananiudhi." She was now frowning.

"Usijali," I said and winked at her.

Kezia clicked her tongue and sighed. She pulled me closer to her stout body.

I liked her completely already.

We came to a café in a corner building on whose veranda sat a cobbler with an array of shoes on the wall behind him. The man moved his can of glue to the side when we walked past and into a room in which a loud-talking crowd moved and ate.

Inside, the stench of sweat and hot cooking oil was as overwhelming, and tight-faced waiters weaved about balancing steaming plates while shouting orders over their shoulders to the open kitchen. We found a table in the centre of the packed café and sat down across from one another.

I looked around the room.

It was six full rows of white Formica tables in a long narrow room, bustling with clientele. Brown dirty walls, a framed photograph of a young Moi and a counter on which a glass food display was filled with sambusas, mandazis and queen cakes. We sat on benches.

To my left, a man in a red suit-hat-and-shoe combo was adjusting the collars of his shirt while staring in rapt attention at the miniature scale before him on which a Mwarabu weighed what appeared to be shiny blue stones. The Mwarabu's cream *kanzu* was dirty at the hem, as though it had dragged on the ground while he walked, and he smelled strongly of *firdaus* and kept dabbing at his temples with a grubby handkerchief.

Next to them, seated at the same table, were a woman and her young son. I watched the boy lift greasy chips into his mouth and shuddered. His mother sat back in her chair, looking around and picking her teeth with the edge of a straw. Her plate was empty and on the floor beside her was a sisal basket full of beans.

A long bubbly wound stretched from her ear across her cheek, and I looked away when she caught me staring at her.

Behind Kezia, with his back to the entrance was a cassette tape hawker who was rapidly counting and recounting a thick wad of bills, while talking animatedly with a friend who sat next to him and had very long fingernails I remember.

Then there was a group of *vibarua sugus* in a corner table laughing at something someone said on Kiswahili Service over the transistor radio before them. They were covered in construction dust and looked tired.

People kept coming in and out of the café. At one point, a man at the counter shouted loudly and bolted towards someone outside, leaving his plate of unfinished ugali on the table. Central Africans conversed loudly in Bantu languages, and I got dizzy from the scene and turned back to Kezia to answer her question as to why I was buying wimbi again so soon.

Before I could respond, she ordered a plate of rice and stew for herself and a glass of tea and mandazi for me when I declined the heavy meal. Seconds later, our food arrived.

"Unajua," I began, "Hiyo maneno jana..."

"Unakumbuka yule mama aliyepoteza mtoto?" Kezia interrupted me.

"Mama Kuria?" I asked. "Nimerudi kumtafuta."

"Kumtafuta?" she asked and then continued. "Imagine mtoto hajapatikana."

"Hm," I said. "Kwani ameenda wapi?"

Kezia shook salt into her stew and drank from the glass of water the waiter had splashed onto our table.

"Hata mama wake hakufika Central jana," she continued and scooped some rice into her mouth. "Wale makarao walimwambia arudi hapa atafute mtoto wake vizuri."

"Hawakumsaidia?" I asked in surprise.

"Imagine," Kezia responded. She put her spoon down on the table, picked up the glass and poured water over both hands in turn, spilling it onto the floor. Then she wiped both palms on her skirt and used her fingers to sort through her plate.

"Na yuko wapi sasa?" I queried, "Mama mtoto?"

"Hajaonekana leo," Kezia said.

She picked up a meaty bone from the plate and bit into it.

"Dunia hii," Kezia smacked her lips and continued. "Maisha zamani haikuwa hivi. Na sio Nairobi tuu. Siku hizi hata huko reserve maisha imebadilika." She was now sucking out the marrow.

I bit into my rubbery mandazi.

"Na kwani hakuna mtu mmoja aliyemwona huyo mtoto?" Kezia continued.

"Mimi nimeshinda nikijiuliza hilo swali," I paused chewing and replied. Then I sipped my tea.

Kezia pointed her bone towards Kirinyaga Crescent with her bone.

"Na unajua hapo chini," she looked around, lowered her head and whispered, "*Flying Squad* wenyewe wameingiana na hawa wezi wa watoto."

I was silent but scrunched my face inquiringly.

"Ndio," she said.

Kezia raised her head and drank from her glass. She swallowed loudly, narrowed her eyes at me and continued,

"Nyinyi wababi hamjui yote yanayoendelea hapa."

It was the first time anybody had ever called me that and I smiled.

We talked about the child, wondering where on earth he could have been, whether he was alive or dead. In Grogan, a place teeming with wananchi twenty four hours, how could a three year old child just disappear into thin air? The police... well the police were the police. But somebody must have seen something.

Kezia finished her meal. She placed the bone on her plate and cleaned her fingers on a serviette I fished out of my pocket and handed her.

Then she looked about the room and when satisfied that no one was interested in our conversation, leaned forward and whispered,

"Mummy, hiyo business ya kuiba watoto... *Mtoto kama huyo analeta ngiri ishirini."*

"Ati nini?" I asked.

"Ishirini," Kezia continued and made a peace sign with two fingers. *"Na kuna mdosi mwengine hapa anayehitaji watoto kwa sababu anataka..."*

"Kuwakula?" I widened my eyes and asked expectantly.

Kezia grinned then seconds later, folded her face.

"Tutajuaje Mummy?" She asked quietly.

We sat for a while in silence. The half eaten mandazi lay on a saucer before me. The woman with the bubbly scar had left. I gulped down the rest of my tea and shouted to a waiter behind Kezia for the bill.

WAMBUI WA WANJIRU was born in Nairobi in 1973 and raised there. She is an Orthodox African Traditional Religionist and works in Management in an Equity Group. She enjoys her family, reading, walking and cooking, and has lived and travelled in Africa, Europe, North and Latin America. Kiririkano is excerpted from a larger work of the same name.

Blogguy™ GET YOUR OWN BLOG FLAG? NEXT BLOG>>

Nairobi back in the days

Reminisces about 1980's Nairobi (and '70's for that matter).
22.3.05

Aggression

Ah boys seemed to be very aggressive back then – lakini pia wasichana. Who was it that tokead with the "ngoto"- that thing where you scrape at someone's kisogo with your knuckles, so someone would just be sitting at their desk and they'd get a ngoto. Then there was the "flare", where guys used to flick at each other with their ties – ties zina seem harmless enough until someone flicks at you with one. What about that thing called Green Mamba where you'd wring someone's arms kama kukamua nguo mpaka they had marks like a nyoka?

Who kumbukas the name of that weapon which involved an empty biro pen, bits of tissue (rolled into small balls with spit!), then you'd blow the ball through the biro and those things were ouch yenyewe. Hata on the ceiling there were bits of tissue stuck from that, aah disgusting kabisa. Then there were paper planes, which were used as weapons also – weeh! They had sharp corners which could cause injury.

Halafu kulikuwa na craze ya kukick someone's butt when they weren't looking ("Kadenge na mpira shooti goal") mpaka people started standing with their backs to the wall just in case. There was also that craze of pushing people into the swimming pool – deep end or no deep end (hakukuwa concerns za Health & Safety). The influence of Kungu Fu/ Karate/ Taekwondo etc was also heavy. Kids would go "haaaiiiyyaaa!" (as in those Karate screams) accompanied by sijui a "chopstick" (that thing where you aim with the side of your hands). Wengine walijaribu kickboxing lakini no one could really ruka like that. When a Ninja film was shown on TV the next day kids would wear a ninja-style mask and say "prepare to exhale for the rast" in a Chinese accent.

When a fight broke out everyone would kimbia from their haos to witness it. If it was in chuo we had to keep our voices down or else a teachay would notice, so like one time a chick and a dude were fighting (zile za she knees his balls, he pinches her matiti) and it was more comedy than action, so we were half-falling over, half-applauding in whispers.

Lakini, na sio bias, chicks could maliza a dude 'cause girls used to mature physically quicker than boys. There was this chick in our Esto who was a Muislamu and all the teenies used to mwaga mate at the sight of her. Heh-heh one teenie let it be known to her that he liked her. Wacha! When the chick heard that she banged on his gate and she was like "weeh! Unanikosea heshima!" then she pigad him many ngumis. Woiye, what a crime to be pigiwad for? Lakini that chick was later married off by her paros before she hit twenty.

When two people ajirianad a fight but one of them could clearly foresee that they would be maliziwad, they would ask their housie to standby for backup. Heh! Some housies were mbaya, yani they would fight for their hao's kiddos bila any restraint whatsoever. One of the provocations for a fight was pointing at someone. Ai hiyo tu? Also if there was haramu in a game a fight would tokea. Another provocation was accusing someone of having a crush on someone. Wehseh! Even if it was true it was still a case for "tutafight."

There used to be a hierarchy in our Esto of who had the most nguvu and who had the least – but, weirdly, some people had the reputation of being formidable fighters lakini hakukuwa na any living memory of them actually fighting (hao walitengeneza public relations).

One day there was a blackout, and it was after dark (yani in Nai the sun would go down at sijui 6pm sharp). A fight broke out between two "quoros" and you could only see silhouettes fighting and punching. Baada ya lights returned each side claimed to have won lakini yote iliremain a mystery.

Lakini nowadays it's not ngotos and flares, it's visu and risasi. Back in the day the only weapons we used were sticks and stones and bare knuckles (Rocky style) lakini nowadays kiddos might go too far 'cause weapons are more kawa. Back then, after two people or two quoros fought, after a few weeks or months you'd see them talking and laughing like no one could kumbuka any prior disagreement. Aggression is a part of growing up lakini kids shouldn't take it to the level of visu and risasi. Hata in fact most fights were verbal – thus arose The Mchongoano.

posted by Memoire @ 11:40 AM | 14 comments»

Tuesday, August 29, 2006

SHIBBOLETH

The Epistle of Potash to the Adept

If a lion could talk we could not understand him- Wittgenstein

Potash is a lion; the lion of *(no translation available)*

Read not my words all ye that are of uncircumcised minds. Stiff- necked fools, who think that only their God can be blasphemed. You know what is Blasphemy? Blasphemy is calling me a pagan... heathen!

Cogito Ergo Sum- Rene Descartes

Yaxakaty(?) My thoughts these then that I send to you. You know it is I for we are one. I am in receipt of your summons. To Nairobi I must return, anon. My presence then anticipate; in time for the Third Caucus. Until then this here my herald, a mere messenger that you should not whip- just cut off his head! He is to me worth nothing but to you he is as hot milk. *Vox clamantis in deserto* is what he claims to be; preparing the way. Preparing the way for me—I. I AM. I think I am. *I think therefore I am!*

In the Beginning was the Word- John Bar Zebedee

Words. They are signposts to thoughts. Words. My words are what I send you. I speak to minds saying it like Jesus of Nazareth: EPHPHATHA! Too many runes to scribble and not enough Rizla, to roll these like the scrolls of The Ancients. So what happens when you find them; when you find these words that are, each, filled with mystic value?

Burn them I say. Let the pillar of smoke be your guide. Where there is smoke there is fire; if the smoke is with you, so will be the fire—The Burning Bush. These words will be passed from one mouth to the next as our lore has always been. Words passed on today as they were passed on in the beginning... In the beginning these words WERE!

God is dead- Nietzsche

I see a return to a city in a shambles. A city we love but one that will not love us back. I will return to murky squalor beyond Mabu *(English equivalent= Dickensian* parallels*)*. Our Nairobi where hope is like a foetus- for others it grows but for us it is aborted. Aborted and cast adrift on the Stygian effluent they call Nairobi River.

Our hope, just like us, is too impecunious to afford the boat ride to Hades. So it (we) stays suspended in emptiness- drifting to nowhere. We are the living dead. Miserable souls caught up in the Purgatory of dreams. We knoweth not where we are coming from ... *Ati* Intelligent Design, *na nini... na nini*; Intelligent Design my *patapakata!* (This word means a prosthetic limb that you have been waiting for for three years: *"...Jaribu next week! Angalia room 4B! ...aiih, hiyo file sijui... ati umesema jina yako ni nani?" Et cetera.)*

It is the return to a city where faith cannot move the mountains of garbage. And yet faith is what we live by—faith in our ability to live and die another day. Any other faith has no value.

For where is God when we need him, flying fighter jets in the Middle East? (And the Cedars of Lebanon wither before him, for he is a vengeful God.) That is his *shauri*, anyway, as for us... us we have done buried him: Ashes to ashes and dust to dust- or whatever his most elemental state is, was or plans to be! All we have left is a word without meaning.

God is a swear word: God, pass me the Buddha!

...Ngai!

The Triumphal Entry- (Rear or otherwise?)

"Ye have heard how I said unto you; I go away and come again unto you." (Jn 14:28)

We remain the de trop- urban detritus.

I and my people are one.

posted by POTASH at 09:43 | 8 comments»

POTASH is a regular mid-twenties Kenyan guy trying to afford his next drop of alcohol. He has been in his mid-twenties for too long. His educational background remaining unknown, he continues to describe himself as a pseudo-intellectual. He detests yuppies, development cowboys and preachers who go bang in the night. On a regular Tuesday morning when you are working, he is sitting on a stone, in the mtaa, drinking, waiting for a half-life and writing about it. He confesses to having a longstanding grudge with Matathia.

Tuesday, August 01, 2006

Smoke And Dreams

Even in the village, I keep to the back paths- The Road not Taken! (Now is that your Frost or what? How would I know; literary pursuits went out with big dreams.) I see the local lads sitting on stones, tree stumps, anything. And they wait—just like in the city—wait and talk. It is ten o'clock in the morning already so there might be no casual jobs coming in today. You know, no chance of turning that loose fifty bob. They are nowhere close to raising their quota of the mythical 'a dollar a day' that their families are meant to live by.

So here they are. Yet another day... another missed dollar. In lieu of work, they wait. None of them knows what he waits for. Everyone waits because everyone else seems to be waiting. The Administration Policemen at the Chief's Camp call it, idling with intent. "Intent to do what...?" I wonder "... intent to idle some more?"

And still they wait- wait for a half-life; wait for a shared can of *Napshizzle*; wait for a joint- wait to escape! There goes the neighbourhood: kids who can't tell their dreams from a khat twig on the ground.

Clenched fists salute all around... *"Gota Kizee...* one love... Jah Bless I 'n' I". .. Et Cetera. I perch on an ancient derrière deifying rock. *Juu ya mawe!* In the city, there would have been a used *Kasuku* can or the potholed macadam as an alternative pew, but in the village it is either the 'Hard Rock' or the rusted *debe*. And the *debe* here has the legend, *Italian Aid Fund.* It must be a relic of a Bob Geldorfish Christmas gift circa 1985. In the village, the vortex of time reels anticlockwise!

Yet they haven't missed anything much in those two decades. What has changed, really, beyond the entrenchment of social stratification contrasted against a dearth of equitable means of attaining social mobility? (Note: Equity and not Equality. For those seeking a pigeonhole to thrust me into, I am with Max Weber and not Karl Marx.)

The Oligarchs have successfully thrown a feudal wall of self-perpetuation around themselves with the emergence of a 'democratically elected Aristocracy'. The Petite Bourgeoisie have sold their souls to the Nobility for two dollar CDF contracts and the roads and school roofs that are due to them by right. They have become Knight Defenders of their leaders' failures and wearing their armour of voter's cards, they guard, often with their lives, the transition of the Baronetcies from fathers to sons... to wives; on and on to cousins of varied remove. But the Proletariats; the Proles are still hungry and fighting with the dogs- and eating the dogs at times—for crumbs at the foot of Dives table.

"Sema..."

"Poa..."

"Mhhh...."

"Bangi...?"

"Nikose nikufe...!"

I always got one and a box of Rhino Kubwa matches! It is a conversation starter, a joint is. But most importantly, it helps sustain my Messianic Complex. I am the WAY...

"Got a LIGHT?"

"In TRUTH I got one..."

Druggie Heaven!

The weed and the alcohol is a portal through which these youths try to step away from the harsh realities of this world. It is a street sanctioned Escape Mechanism. Your world may frown at Escapism, but for these youths, it is their only way of stealing glances at a good life. For one furtive moment, albeit in a one-dimensional fantasy world, one can be every thing they deserve to be. Escapism is a journey to the plane of lucid dreams where you become a doctor, a lawyer, a capitalist... momentarily, your dreams are realised and you are living life in Technicolor.

But the good life, particularly the Escapist's simulacrum of it, is like being with a mistress, sooner rather than later you have to put your stuff back into your jeans and take it back home to your frigid wife... ahem!... life, I mean.

A joint is to these kids like a 'file' and 'wittles' to Dickens' Magwitch; it will cut away at their shackles and act as a Placebo of relief against the pulsating pain of life sans meals, past or present. It is their Holy Grail, perpetually they seek it. It is the blood of the Covenant that they drink, in a veritable Dark Mass, to celebrate their "freemasonry as fellow sufferers".

Tings a Gwan na Babylon fi yout' man! is their mantra and they chant it as the Pillar of Smoke rises above the barren earth of their existence and leads them to the Zion Train of Escapism.

Kama takes a Herculean inhalation and blows long, ponderous whiffs on the joint as he watches it rapidly burn itself out like his ambitions. "So they have put aside a billion or two for the youth..." he muses.

"Great Expectations...!" they chorus, eagerly reaching out for the joint as though those two hits are their fair share of the said kitty.

And they could as well take it, in their vaporous dreams that is, for in real life, they never will. I am cynical, yes. That because I have heard Parliamentarians clamouring to play Mr. Jaggers to these Great Expectations. Cynical because these youths have a self-serving politician for their Magwitch, and their Great Expectations will, in the end, turn out to be the Theatre of Broken Dreams.

posted by POTASH at 13:42 | 18 comments»

Tuesday, August 08, 2006

The Philosophers of the Stone

"Yo, our good friend Ms. Rowling gone caught the Agatha Christie Complex."

"Hey, hey P... what you talking?" That is Kiki talking now.

"Yeah," says Deno, "What you mean man?"

"You know that thing Agatha does killing her character...?"

"Yea, yea... "Timi expectorates. (Dude wants to inhale and speak simultaneous like.) "Yeah, the thing our *whachamacallim...* Mr. Watson? He does it..." He gabbles.

"Kinda like." I agree assuming he means Conan Doyle. (Whoa, it's been years since I read that!) "Anyway, see the deal usually is, you do not want folks hijacking your character... er... ghost writing and things see?" I continue.

"James Bond style, huh!" It is that philistine, who thinks *Da Vinci Code* is a classic, talking now. "... Like what's that new one... the movie... called?" Dude is asking now. Like is he serious? He is talking James Bond Movies here... Puhliiz... Who is his mother?

"The spy who shagged you...!" That is my boy Timi now coming through with a repartee. He is a caustic one, Timi. He is when he serves you a regular Timi on ice, eh. His words tend to hang in the air a bit like with that 'don't-mess' cool of an iceberg waiting for the *Titanic.*

"Wha... What? That's the name of the movie...?" philistine is bubbling and gawking or whatever the word is for that stupid expression he is wearing.

"You know what dude..." Kitau takes a mighty swig of *Napshizzle* in punctuation. "Why don't you go check out if there is a new Beyonce video you can get off to?"

"Me, I think..." Dru waxes Cannabis, "Britney Spears preggers is more up his alley!"

"For real...!" Timi agrees while flicking his fingers at Dru. His mouth has already formed a plug and play O of expectation and if you were of a mind to, you could look closely and see his throat muscles spasm with phantom inhalations. "That's the thing for him..." Timi exhales. "But you were saying sum'n else P, *aaaight?"*

"Aaaight...aaaight!" I respond while slipping off the stone slab everyone else is seated on to sit on the ground.

I sit right on the ground next to the used condoms, *veve* twigs and fossilised cigarette butts. Down there is where the heavy gases at. That there is the 20 % (It is obvious I went to a good school, eh. Okay, Deno will tell you that I went to Kathuthiani Mixed Day and Boarding; Ask for Plumber, but do not mind him. He a hater... man... is what he is!) Down there is where the Oxygen is. Above it is the warm gases; the noxious smoke and the Ozone depleting farts of malnourishment.

But what was I saying?

Aaaight!

"aaaaghhhhhttt... so our Ms. Rowlings will kill a major character in Book Seven!"

"What...?"

"The last one...?"

"Which character....?

"Who, eh....?"

Man you should see their faces, now. Messed up like, you know. It is a Kodak, no, a Sony CyberShot DSC-F717, 5.02 Mega Pixels moment. Say cheese! (Okay, but you know we do not do fancy gadgets down here, yes? Sure, sure so you have to settle for this pen-picture. I mean, I am sorry, I know you cannot crop a pen-picture, rotate it and thingamajig it to put on your www, but it is the best I can do, see? *Carpisce.* Yeah, whatever...

But you know what... I am going to sign it: *With Love from the Potash Book Club.* This is just another one for your Ironies of Africa Collection: Street Intellectuals, Uneducated Philosophers, White Collar Hustlers, et al.) These are my people, book critics sans books; yeah, and without a doubt, the best writers you will never read.

"You *jua*," I am telling them. "Stephen King was pleading with her..." At the mention of Stephen King, the boys guffaw. They think I am having them on. You see there is a King story around here. See, usually when we are discussing writers- I mean people who write and not those who copy paste internet stories or those who think Subject + Verb Agreement= Writing and whose primary school-like compositions can be found in [insert local pullout of choice]- there is always the debate over popular vs. highbrow literature. We are all agreed that John Grisham is junk and Danielle Steel is certified trash; but what about Stephen King? I mean, you have to admit the guy is a master story teller. The guy achieves art, doesn't he? We cannot begrudge him his penmanship just because he is popular, can we?

(... I am not an arty writer and neither am I popular. Hey in truth, I probably cannot write to save my *Napshizzle;* but still, down here they call me King, King Shit of Turd Mountain...!)

"Stephen King was pleading with her not to kill Harry Potter." I whisper, conspiratorially.

"Come on now, Harry Potter...!" Dru exclaims.

"...our leading protagonist..." I underline. "The young Massa hisself...!"

"Ms. Rowlings kills young boys..." Timi mutters through teeth firmly clenched on a freshly rolled joint. He peers into the near distance thoughtfully as he pats his jeans in search of a lighter.

"Who does she think she is?" Timi wonders.

"What?" Everyone starts.

"Killing young boys..." Timi seems to be addressing the plumes of smoke jumping out of him like a downed Black Hawk. "Who does she think she is, an Israeli soldier or something...?"

posted by POTASH@17:17 | 16 comments»

POTASH is a regular mid-twenties Kenyan guy trying to afford his next drop of alcohol. He has been in his mid-twenties for too long. His educational background remaining unknown, he continues to describe himself as a pseudo-intellectual. He detests yuppies, development cowboys and preachers who go bang in the night. On a regular Tuesday morning when you are working, he is sitting on a stone, in the mtaa, drinking, waiting for a half-life and writing about it. He confesses to having a longstanding grudge with Matathia.

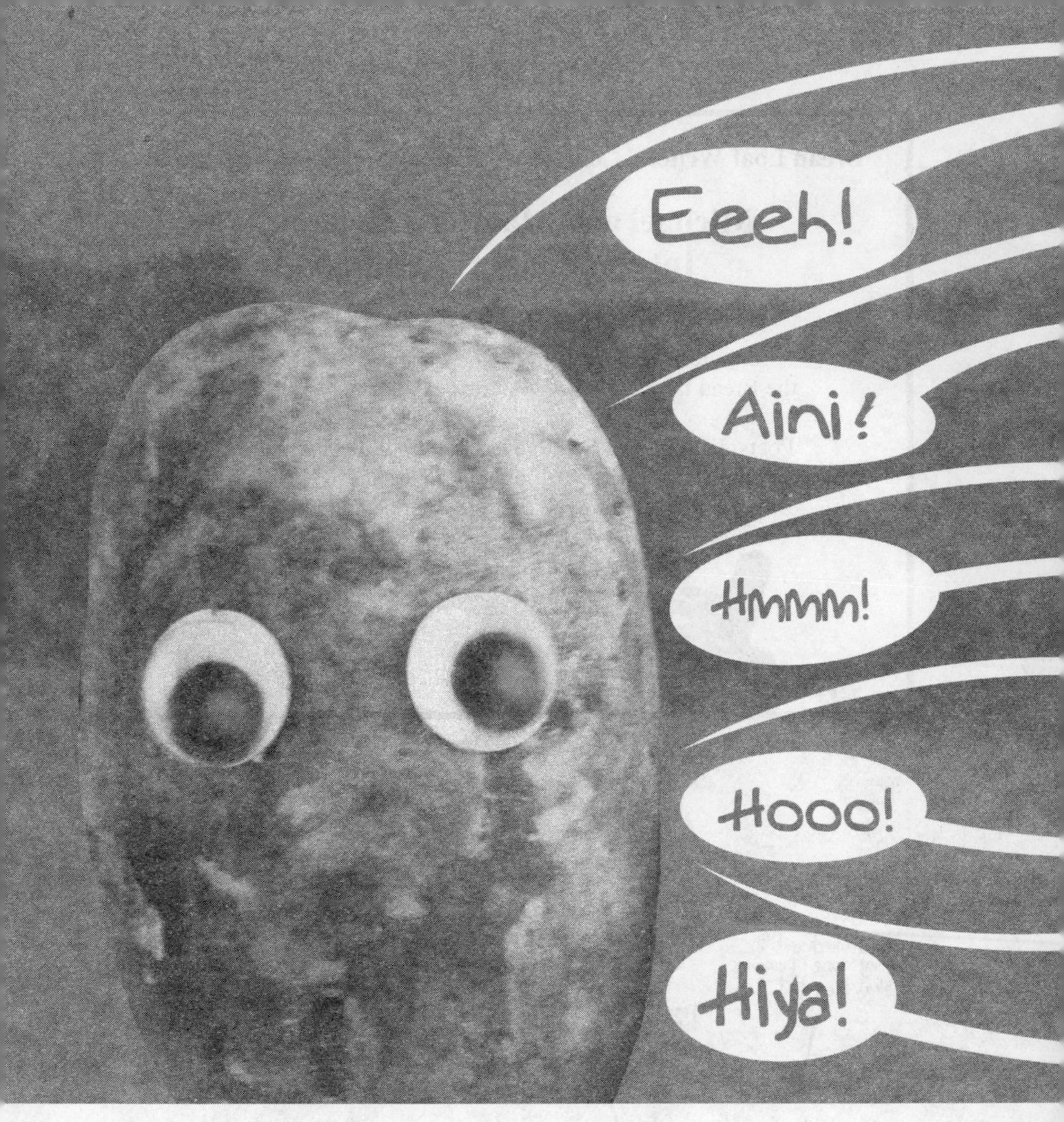

Photography: JNK/ Illustration: The Mindbender
Potato art by: SEVEN

Kikuyu Dialogues

BY CHARLES MATATHIA

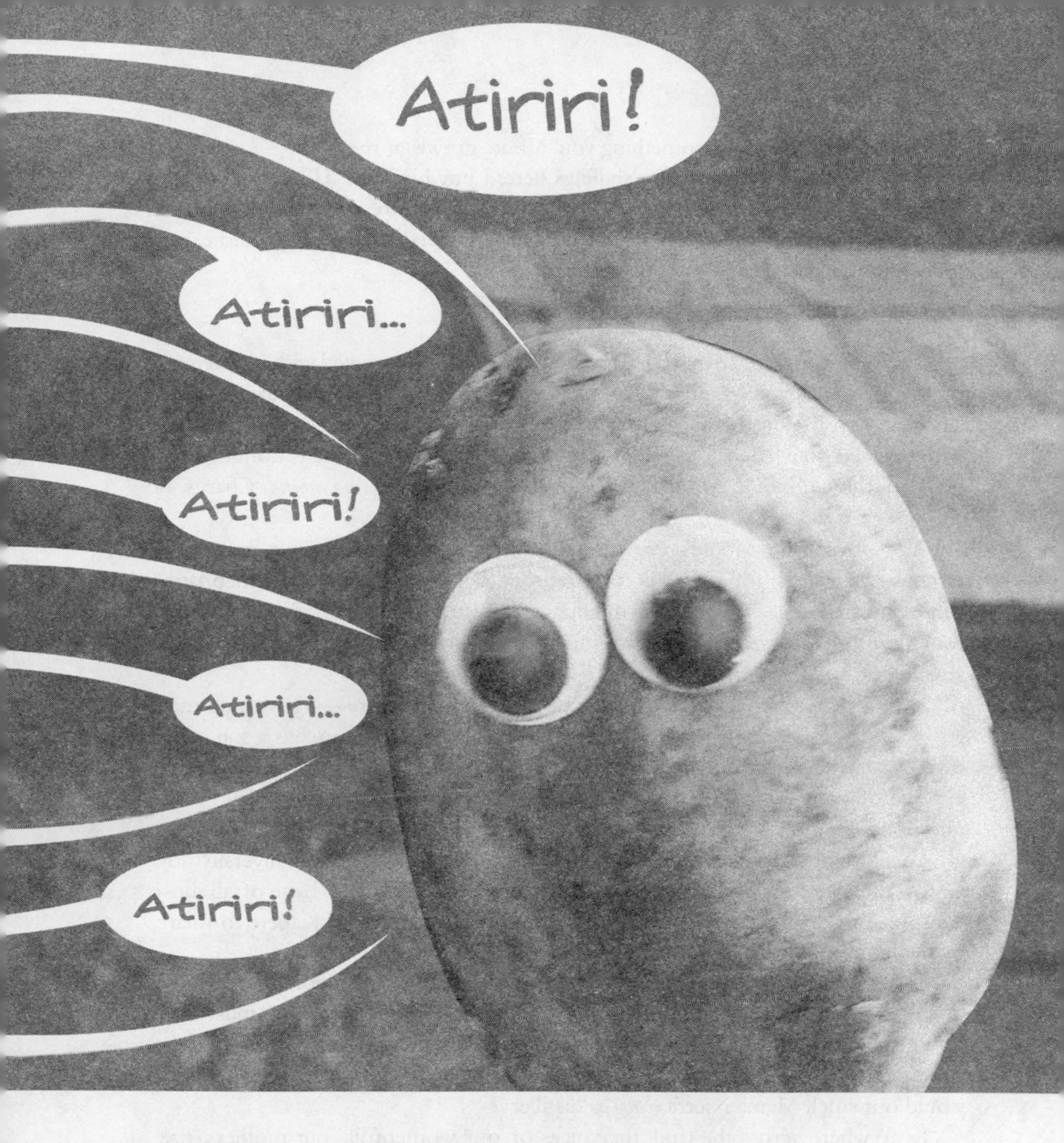

Ndeto ndiikagio ta njuguma! issues are approached with caution is something my grandfather used to say. I need to have some burning questions answered but first I have to set the pace. So I get a couple of old kikuyu men together and buy them a couple of drinks to loosen their tongues.

I am sitting at Mwalimu's place, that is the wines and spirits store, listening to the reminisces of Baba Mbote a.k.a Munio 'John Walker' and Bwana Kamau. 'A man like me...' Baba Mbote is saying, '...you know why they called me John Walker?' At that moment his son walks in. You can feel the pent up tension as Mbote walks towards us.

'gura kiindo...wee!'/ buy something you! Mbote growls at me.

A can of Kane Extra is fifty shillings here, I buy him one. He doesn't bother asking for a chaser. Mbote just swigs, nay, guzzles the entire 205 Mls in the plastic can in one motion. The effect of the alcohol is immediate, what you would expect on an empty belly, and Mbote staggers away.

He spots the outrageously unattractive barmaid.

'K--!'

The expletive he hurls at her is unprintable and yet it is received with indifference by the revellers; even Mbote's own father doesn't winch. His father takes a liberal sip from a bottle of the newly re-launched Citizen Special and surveys the scene with decided nonchalance. Somehow I get the feeling that Mbote is nothing but a chip off the old block. After all as Gikuyu said, wega *umaga na mucii*—Charity, or the lack of it, begins at home.

As it turns out, Mbote's expletive will have to serve as his own version of famous last words, for he is soon passed out, collapsing against the inebriating fumes, warped tables topped with moulting Formica and sweaty bodies attached to foul mouths like a *gunia* of *warus* from the Wangige Market that is across the debris strewn gutter.

Nobody pays him any mind; everyone has grown up here—a grown up man, lest you forget the emphasis. Even Mbote, who is his father's son, has a son of his own. Actually he has four and please do not ask if this is the way to raise sons. It is none of your business, I have been told—'you *imwana* (lads) of today... many questions...'

Yes, Yes, but Mbote whose son was a year ahead of me at the University now lies on the liquor stained concrete as the incontinence that is the bane of all those irresponsible drunks who litter every alley and cattle path from Kabete to Ruare, marks his crotch.

That is all the seed he can sow. A man like Mbote, a once upon a time proud son of Kiambu, do you think he wanted to stop at four? Surely, he must have wanted to try for a daughter, a *Pajero* as Wahome Mutahi was wont to say, to be the apple of his eye. But how could he when the fruit of his loins is this dribble that would out-smell Mama Njeri's *chang'aa* distillery?

Everywhere across the land, the voices of our womenfolk, our mothers, rise; the grumblings can be heard in Muranga, Kangemi and all those other places that didn't make the nine o'clock news, the ferreting out of shebeen queens, the picketing of off-licence bars. But in between times, what do the womenfolk, our mothers do, raise sons?

When I was commissioned to do this report, I wanted to be an objective journalist telling yet another human interest story. Then I met all these Kikuyu men of all ages, watched the interplay between fathers and sons, uncles and nephews and realised that I couldn't isolate myself from the story. As a young man who defines himself as a Kikuyu, ethnically proud but not tribal, mind you, what I saw as I walked through the township alleys, crossed the log bridges and sat in the seedy bars with these men was the son I was and the father I might turn out to be.

At the local bar in the village, I approached a group of old men. They listened to me their faces set somewhere between annoyance, skepticism and disdain as I explained to them the answers that I sought.

'Riu tawe rii, niurutite mburi...?'/ You, have you removed the ceremonial goat? Baba Kim spat at me. Already I was beginning to experience the breakdown in inter-generational dialogue. And to imagine that that was the very thing whose roots I was meant to trace.

Baba Kim's question was taking me to the past. Yet I was interested in the present. This was not about culture and tradition; it was about the realities that I saw in the here and now, the diminishing dialogue between the Kikuyu father and his son. If they were dead set on talking of the tradition they say has been lost, then I would have been interested in knowing what happened to the family unit. And that not only the extensive kinship ties of yore but also the disintegration of the nuclear family. That though, they couldn't answer because as far as they were concerned, they were still the rulers of their roosts. But were they, really?

Everywhere I looked, the women had seen not only a reversal of roles but also, they had taken on non-traditional roles over and above the traditional ones. The Kikuyu womenfolk were, in many homesteads, the nurturers, providers and de facto heads of families. And all the while the men were mere shadows, staggering and blundering behind self- imposed facades of isolation.

When I talked to Mzee Njogu, a retired primary school teacher and an elder at the Anglican Parish, he tut- tutted, *'...maundu maingi.... kimunya amunyire...'*/ 'Many things... the up-rooter (devil) uprooted.' He went on and on about how our people had sinned and fallen short of the glory of God. I nodded with conviction. A sham conviction, though, because I wanted him to move on without rekindling a previous debate we had had on religion a few years back. That was during my first year of Campus and because I had dreadlocks and didn't go to church, he had categorically branded me a *Mungiki* adherent. And all his references to me, to all and sundry, from that day were peppered with, *'...shidwe pepo mbaya....!'* Where is the dialogue?

It was a Sunday evening and as Njogu's wife was about to join us for a cup of tea, three old men came visiting. One was a prominent farmer, the other a retired headmaster of the local high school and the last one, Mr. Githinji had, in his time, been one of those Kikuyus whose operations in the city are unclear; the type that go by the amorphous tag of 'broker'.

As the perfunctory niceties proceeded, I stared at that portrait of Jomo Kenyatta that adorns the sitting room of every Kikuyu man of a certain age. Kenyatta was wearing monkey skin and waving a fly whisk and the caption read: *Mutongoria njamba.*/ Hero and leader. Was that what every Kikuyu man living today was in his household?

Elder Njogu having briefly outlined my quest to his peers, I asked the question that was on my mind. "What kind of silly question is that... by the way, isn't it about time you got yourself a wife?" That was Githinji boiling over.

"The young man is only asking a question..." Elder Njogu's wife interjected. She wore her authority well: Women's Guild Secretary, Retired Deputy Headmistress. Her tone was not of a woman who was used to taking orders; she wasn't your run of the mill submissive wife. Elder Njogu crossed his feet slowly, sipped his *chai* and stared vacantly out of the window. I got the impression that he was trying to make himself invisible.

"Listen," Elder Njogu's wife continued. *"Maundu ni macenjirie..."* Things changed. The way our community lived in the old days is not the way we live today. Men weren't always providers, not in the putting of food on the table kind of way... Their role was mainly security. In the absence of war, Kikuyu men sat and drank beer all day while the women tilled the land, fetched water and firewood and fed the children.

In a way I feel that the men have not been able to adapt into the broader role the new social set up has brought them... Because they were always out there thinking about matters of the tribe with other men, they still try to live that way, sitting in bars with other men. Yet these days the family demands more from the father, his time and his attention. The days of fathers who were distant figures of terror are long gone and yet men still want to be that...

In the old days, children belonged to the community. Everyone could discipline an errant child. There were numerous and time tested rules that ensured that children grew up right. But now, these days, every family unit stands alone. Ideally then, fathers should spend a lot more time moulding their children because the safety net of kinship has been eradicated. Furthermore, what these children learn these days—out there on the school ground and all those other places—is that a family is made up of a father, mother and their children; if they do not see their father, don't you think they will become disillusioned? How can they learn to love and appreciate a man who is never there? There is more than putting food on the table but when you ask some of the children what the role of their father is, they will tell you: daddy *hubuy mkate...*"

Was this woman cool or what? She was giving me good insight, yes, but at what expense? I wanted to hear the men speak for themselves, but they were all silent now. I wasn't quite eager to read this as a microcosm of the role reversal in Kikuyu land. As it were, the previous day a certain old man had told me: *"ungienda wega/* if you know what is good for you....never argue with a woman; either you beat her up if she is bringing *nyokonyoko* or you ignore her." Maybe the men here had chosen to ignore the woman in the room though from the look on Githinji's face, I surmised that if he had his way, he would rather beat her. Githinji is on wife number...uh... I forget!

After several days of scouring for answers, none were forthcoming from the old men that I talked to. They were all adamant that they kept their families together.

But the young men continued to argue that their fathers were mere figure heads, tin gods perched way up there and unwilling to subdivide those measly acres of land and share out resources. Their fathers, on the other hand, said that the young men of today do not listen. They do not value their fathers and are constantly tagging at their mothers' skirts.

But to me that phrase: *'watoto wa siku hizi...mmmh !'*/ 'The children of today! was not mere pontificating and buck passing by the elders but also a regurgitation of a stock phrase by all elders from generation to generation. The old men wanted to lose themselves in nostalgia for their youthful days and conveniently forget that in those days, they too were a vexation to their elders. The young men felt that their old men were blundering, clueless, opinionated idiots who were way past their sell by date.

The burning question then became whether the breakdown in communication that I saw was a recurrent inter-generational struggle, a phenomenon replicated in every age or a chasm that had actually widened this time round?

My answer to that seems to be hinged on the thinking that culture and tradition are dimensions in continuing flux. They are not static entities but are constantly changing, adding new wine to the old wineskins. Therefore then, the frivolity and joie de vivre of youth must be seen as the catalyst for change, essential cogs that keep the wheels of that dynamic we call culture and tradition turning. Then the conservatism of the elders is necessary then, not as an impediment to change but rather as a buffer zone that ensures that change becomes a gradual and manageable process rather than a singular, drastic event.

At this point as I interviewed a couple of men in the 'Third World' section of the city, Riverori, a different angle emerged. It came in the form of an interruption of our conversation by a couple of Mama Vikapus. Now Mama Vikapus occupy an entire demographic of their own. Mama Vikapus, though not of necessity single mothers, tend to be, often times, the bread winners in their households. Most of them see men as an incidental appendage to the family unit and thus dispensable. These women work hard and extremely so for the purpose of keeping their children in school, in food and in clothes.

This in itself brought on greater insight into the story. Suddenly we were exploring the role of the man in this age. The man had been given the role of putting food on the table and as it has turned out that role has been difficult for him to fulfill, what with the rampant unemployment and increased cost of living. The men, in not being able to fulfill this obligation, lose themselves in drink.

The women asked me if I had ever seen a woman hopelessly drunk and lying in the gutter. It was a rhetorical question. Kikuyu women have learned the value of hard work. When the man takes his golden handshake and disappears with a *Gacungwa*/ mistress, will you let yourself starve; what about the children?

Atumia/ women work hard, or so they believe of themselves. They have to, really, when you consider that traditionally the children belong to the woman in kikuyu land. Yes, that is why when the woman runs away or is kicked out by her man, she takes the children with her. So the men, when they feel unable to provide adequately for their families, they cut themselves loose and act like the children are not their responsibility either. But the women, the women always feel obliged to provide for their progeny under all circumstances. When things are hard they gather their children together and, like Mrs. Joe Gargery in *Great Expectations,* 'raise them by hand.'

In a great number of instances, these children do turn out all right. Besides, we Africans do not give too much weight to such things as trauma and all that Freudian pyscho-babble of Penis envy and Oedipal Complexes. But the fact of the matter is that whether these women continue to share a roof with their husbands or not, they are faced by that dilemna of all single mothers, how to raise their children. The single mother seems to have two extremes to choose from: she either smothers her children with affection and the whole kiddie glove treatment or acquires what is known as *'ngoro cia athuri'*/ 'the hearts of men' and their accompanying ironic kind of love. The type of love that is very easy with a switch.

Regardless of whichever extreme she choses, and most sons and daughters from this kind of family set up insist that their mothers maintained the perfect balance, she pushes her weight as the head of the family with the father remaining peripheral and increasingly inconsequential or unknown.

Interestingly, though, it can be argued that the Gikuyu women were, at least nominally, always heads of the family. They were the ones who steered the day-to-day family life but the father's role was clearly defined and enforcable such that the father in being aloof, earned a subtle mysticism and reverence rather than rebuke.

In a great way, things have changed placing emphasis on the nuclear family in such a manner that the parent earns the most respect by not being detached from the nuclear unit.My premise is that some approaches to parenting need have changed with the disintergration of the broader kinship ties. The fact of the matter is that the so called children of today do believe in trauma, it is all there on the Oprah Winfrey show and reality television. Fathers must of necessity come in to bridge the gap that emerged when the mbari and riika support system crumbled.

As for these youths, why, I am young and an apologist for youth; but the truth is that the youth have done some things wrong. As their fathers say "their work is just to drink *bangi...*" That is not necessarily true but I see that bangi, and Mungiki and so called devil worship as metaphors for youthful rebellion, both today and the past. They are mere symbols representing the inevitable breakdown and misunderstanding across generations. The reality of whether or not the young people are actually doing any or all of these things should not be and is not the responsibility of story tellers like me to find out. It is, rather, the duty that every father owes to his son. In an age burdened by 'real-time-push-button' peer pressure and all those negative images in the media, enhancement of dialogue between fathers and their sons is imperative. Fathers need to know what their sons are doing, by asking, and the sons must respond, in a cross-generational language.

Dialogue! Did I find out why it had ceased to exist as I had set out to? Maybe not. The truth is that I got tired of that entire buck passing and apportioning of blame by both sides- the fathers and the sons. At some point I realised that I was constantly getting caught up in a continuous why regress of, 'what came first, the chicken or the egg?' proportions. Fathers were not talking to their sons; sons were not talking to their fathers.

But why weren't they talking to each other? The answer to that seemed to require that I bring along a shoulder shrug dictionary. Or maybe, that I bring in a social scientist with preset jargon clad notions about how people should live with each other. But who needed that? All that was required was that people, fathers and sons, particularly, talk to each other, even if only for a while.

CHARLES A. MATATHIA attended Starehe Boys' Centre and School and is a graduate of the University of Nairobi with a degree in Sociology and Philosophy. He is an essayist, freelance researcher and writer specialising in Development and NGO speak.

GOOGLEPEDIA

Photography: JNK/ Illustration: The Mindbender
Potaot art by: Seven

If you Google, "I hate Kikuyus..."

"But on the other hand other Africans hate Nigerians (no statistics, ... Kikuyus – think they care the god of Kenya. The superiority may be traced back to the ..." ...

"The uprising could be called a failure because the Kikuyus did not win a military ... I hate the guts of them all...I dislike them all with few exceptions."

"If you want to know what keeps Agikuyu out of bed, I mean, Kikuyus ... will not discriminate, I will not hate. I'm unbwogable, and nobody can bwogo me.

Mabeste entertainment...
Quote: plus i'm a kikuyu n' u kno how much kikuyus love money. ...
Dokta are you saying you hate money??
Are you sure you are a kikuyu?

"If YES wins, the Kikuyus should pack their bags and move out of Eldama ...

... The Indians have in fact taken over all the businesses which is why the Kikuyus, who fancy themselves as businessmen and are not bad at it, I hate them. ...

Who cares if you hate the kikuyus? You can go shag a goat for all I care! ...

... councillors and party officials. Speaking to the press later, Mr Nassir denied waging a hate campaign against Kikuyus. Mr Nyenze said, he...
Daily Nation On the Web

"Mashada—OATH TO ENSURE THAT KIKUYUS NEVER, EVER RULE KENYA AGAIN—Online ... I hate turncoats and will always do..."

Confessions of a new Gikuyu generation...
"Thus 'Man Of The House' Status Is Often Established Through Violence And Bluster (Often In Bars)."

Kenyaniyetu - ok any kikuyus in the house
Fact is we kikuyus are God fearing no matter how you put us down we will always rise up and that is because our protector is ... I hate everyone equally..

"grasping, conniving, driven, entrepreneurial and migratory."

"When the wife assumes the role of protector and nurturer, driven by necessity and ability, the man's sole purchase is his physical strength and a hazy memory of the 'good old days."

Concubines provide a shot of potent maleness. With them, he feels powerful and necessary: buying the drinks, paying for the apartment.

> *The rich guy of the 1970s remains much the same: he maintains sole proprietorship, has shrinking assets and few ideas on how to forge ahead. It is arguable whether even in the golden age of the 1970s he was ever really a genuine businessman considering how dependent he was on political patronage to loot assets and establish monopolies.*

From http://www.iupress.indiana.edu/journals/nwsa/nws12-1.html

> Kuhi (a woman) and Huta (a man) were originally married to each other. Later, they decided together that Huta would marry a second woman, Kara, creating a polygamous marriage.Later still, Kuhi entered into a woman-woman marriage with a woman named Wamba. Wamba came to that family as Kuhi's marriage partner, and to assist in raising the children of that household. In this particular case, Wamba could have a sexual relationship with Huta (whom she also informally regarded as a husband), and was not restricted from having sexual relationships with other men outside their household. Later in her life, while still married to Kuhi, Wamba married a woman named Wambui. The result is that this single household contains four marriages: two woman-man marriages and two woman-woman marriages. Such complex relationships do not break any "rules," expectations, or ideals of woman-woman marriages, but are an accepted aspect of such relationships in Gikuyu contexts.

EDITOR'S NOTE:
The full text of this paper is published in this edition of Kwani? as women to women marriage
... NDI MUGIKUYU!
KUOYA KUOYA IS MY BUSINESS
$

Illustration: Celeste Wamiru

From The Blogs...with some changes...

B said...

Last I was home, I had an interesting-perhaps strange-conversation with my sister about Gikuyu women and the men who beat them. It ended up being geographic in nature: In Kiambu, apparently, women castrate men who beat them, or leave them.
I believe in Kirinyaga, beating is seen as routine.

G Said...

This is such a painful conversation. I was forty when I found out my mother was circumcised. I do not know who she is."

C Said...

I do not remember exactly how old I was when my parents separated and later divorced, but I vividly recall the panicky sense of impending change and guilt, suspecting that it was all somehow my fault. While in primary school, the years between six and twelve, I felt like I was the set of the popular American TV show, 'Little House on the Prairie': like the Waltons, my schoolmates all seemed to belong to happy-huggy families whose only dilemmas were how to deal with dad's cute and inconvenient eccentricities. My parents' decision to part ways seemed logical; after all, their own parents were estranged, as were a large number of their siblings. My family seemed to be in a giant Jerry Springer moment that would never end; my father did a disappearing act and my mother took center stage. The men around me became increasingly alienated from their families, their absences became longer, their drinking grimmer and somehow they all seemed to get poorer.

Let me risk the leap from the personal to the political: at its most fundamental, my family's experience arose from a collapsing Gikuyu social contract.

The roots of this crisis stretch as far back as the 1920s. Many Gikuyus are often the first to laugh at the stereotypes other Kenyans foster on them. They regard with rueful pride a reputation for being individualistic, grasping, conniving, driven, entrepreneurial and migratory. To them, the actions that give rise to such a reputation are appropriate responses to the challenge of living and thriving in Kenya. But such conclusions are self-deluding.

With each passing year since primary school (I am now in my early 30s), it has dawned on me that the wholesome image of family harmony and progress that I thought was common outside our home was in fact a hoax. I was on the receiving end of a massive Gikuyu public relations effort: it was OK to be estranged, abused, beaten, stolen from and exploited by your relatives- provided you never let on.

B Said...

...Though fathers were steadily coming home at a later hour and given entirely to conversations relating to the latest epic beer fest, they were still the 'man of the house'. They were invested with the family's *dignitas* and were its public torchbearer. Mothers, I suspect, did not mind this arrangement, provided the men stayed out of their way. These women were engaged in an extraordinary effort to keep up with the Kamaus when it came to educating the children, ensuring a move into the right neighborhoods and acquiring a shamba. Only rarely have I encountered a middle class Gikuyu woman with a single source of income.
The decline of the economy in the 1980s that started as a trickle and accelerated to a full-

fledged recession in the 1990s, was applying the squeeze to 'man of the house' ideas. It was tough to pose as the provider and protector when faced with the sack, as corporations downsized and government largesse was no longer directed to Central Province. The resident Gikuyu in State House during the 1960s and 1970s was no more. To make matters worse, the 1982 coup attempt had prompted President Moi to regard Gikuyu money as a threat he was now committed to neutralizing. For all the heroic bar tales and secret mistresses, the middle class Gikuyu man was caught between the rock of a failing economy and the hard place of declining political backing. It had not always been thus, as I shall explore shortly, but the main rub in the situation was the reaction of women who took it on themselves to maintain the façade of harmony and family progress.

If I were to die even as we speak, that would be the end of it. I would be completely forgotten. No one would ever mention my name. That is simply because there would be no one to carry on my name. Since my husband died he is still remembered by many. But the key reason why he is still remembered is because of me. Someone may pass through here and demand to know "Whose home is that?" Then turn around and ask, "What about the next one?" One would reply, "Did you know so and so? This is his wife's home." Now do you see that the reason he is being remembered is because of me? Because I can be seen. But if I were to die, who will make me be remembered?. . . That is why the idea of marrying another woman came to me. Even now as we speak, if Ngai would bless me with another woman I would appreciate her.

It was in this period that most families splintered and the PR gloss slipped enough for me to hear lurid tales of secret families, alcoholism, depression and disunity.

C Said...

You know this time I was having tea with some mathes; Kikuyu women in Bristol, and one of them said,

"I used to work for People for the Ethnical Treatment of Animals."

F Said...

What is up with the "Gikuyu" social contract, whether falling apart or not? I cannot possibly see how the inclusion of that specificity added

Illustration: Celeste Wamiru

anything at all to your otherwise eloquent and articulate piece. NONE. The point is that we keep reproducing these identities, and then being shocked when people actually suffer as a result. As a political analysis, of course you are correct. I don't have any problems with that part, except to note—again—what a mess these dubious identities create. But to talk about a social contract amongst the Gikuyu disturbs me in ways I cannot even describe—but some of which have to do with the fact that everybody else is falling apart too, everybody else had these sorts of family fantasies, everybody else etc. Apart from the fact that all this talk of 'Gikuyu-ness" reinforces a mythical identity which I find not only bogus but somewhat repulsive: we aren't going to get anywhere at all if we continue even thinking along these lines.

B Said...

The Rwanda comparison: I do not really think there are similarities here. That by invoking tribe we are automatically headed down to the road to mass violence. If anything, the present government's attempt in Rwanda to argue that there is no such thing as ethnicity—so as to forestall future genocides I guess—only reinforces the divide. It reminds me of Nietzsche who said that it is not enough to reach for atheism by simply concluding there is no God, he is present and must be murdered.

Illustration: Celeste Wamiru

You see this kaMuGunda?
One day it wiro mBe aro youahs, But razima tu tunye ka prot kiGine.
...when I Grow up, I wanna Be just like My BaBa....

B Said...

Gikuyu politics are mostly the politics of empty symbolism.

D Said...

Have you ever hard the term some Gikuyus use to describe the other tribes? Nyamu cia Ruguru....beasts from the West....

A dozen promises are issued and a relentless busyness is evident in every corner of government, but none of this should be confused with actual effort which demands too much unselfish commitment. Even as they cynically gut the MOU, the Gikuyu middle classes that once again reign supreme politically, are paranoid about the motivations of other tribes—particularly the Luo. Often in their conversations, I have heard Luo politicians such as Raila being assailed as 'too ambitious'. Never mind that a Luo politician has never held power in Kenya and that Luos since independence have twice united with Gikuyus, to only receive the short end of the stick in the final reckoning. Often, some of my relatives express fear of Luo violence against Gikuyus should Raila or one of his ilk become president. Digging from their inexhaustible store of experience, which they always do with a heavy sigh of regret, they reveal to me that the Luo have a penchant for tribalism in the workplace;

that Kisiis are primitive;
Luhyas are confused;
coastal people lazy;
and Kalenjins stupid.

Hidden from this litany is a Gikuyu sense of personal entitlement to privilege at the expense of everyone.

For the sake of psychologically coping with the alienation from family and community, a sense of victim-hood and moral rectitude is vigorously developed.

Like every paranoid, Gikuyu fears are often a reflection of their own conduct. Being cynical demands you suspect others of similar qualities since it is difficult, in that state, to perceive cooperation and good will as anything more than a cover for sinister designs.

"....He! Do you remember how we felt when Kibaki came into power?"

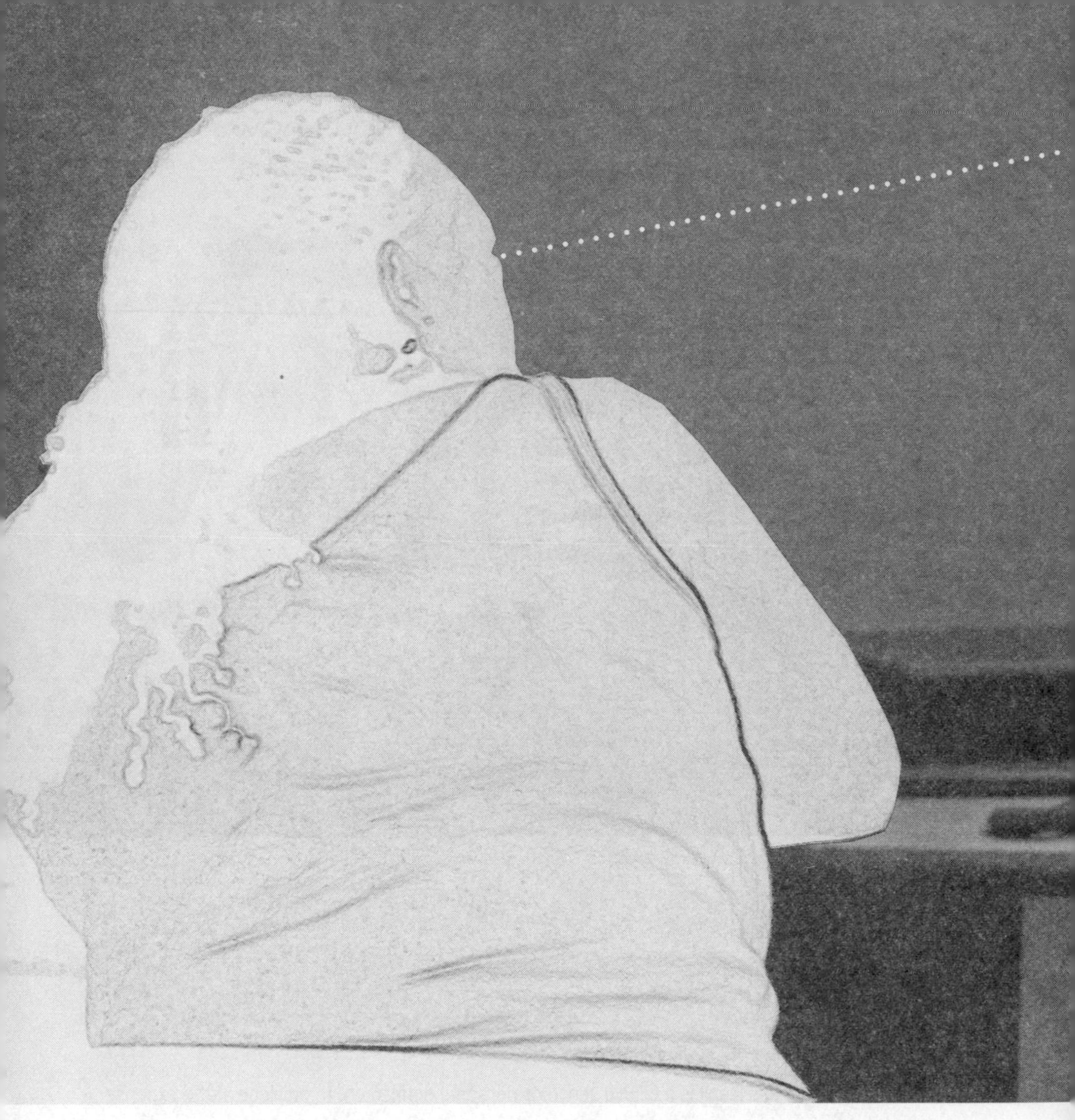

Illustration: Seven

A Kenyan Work Place

BY HAAKASA RENJA

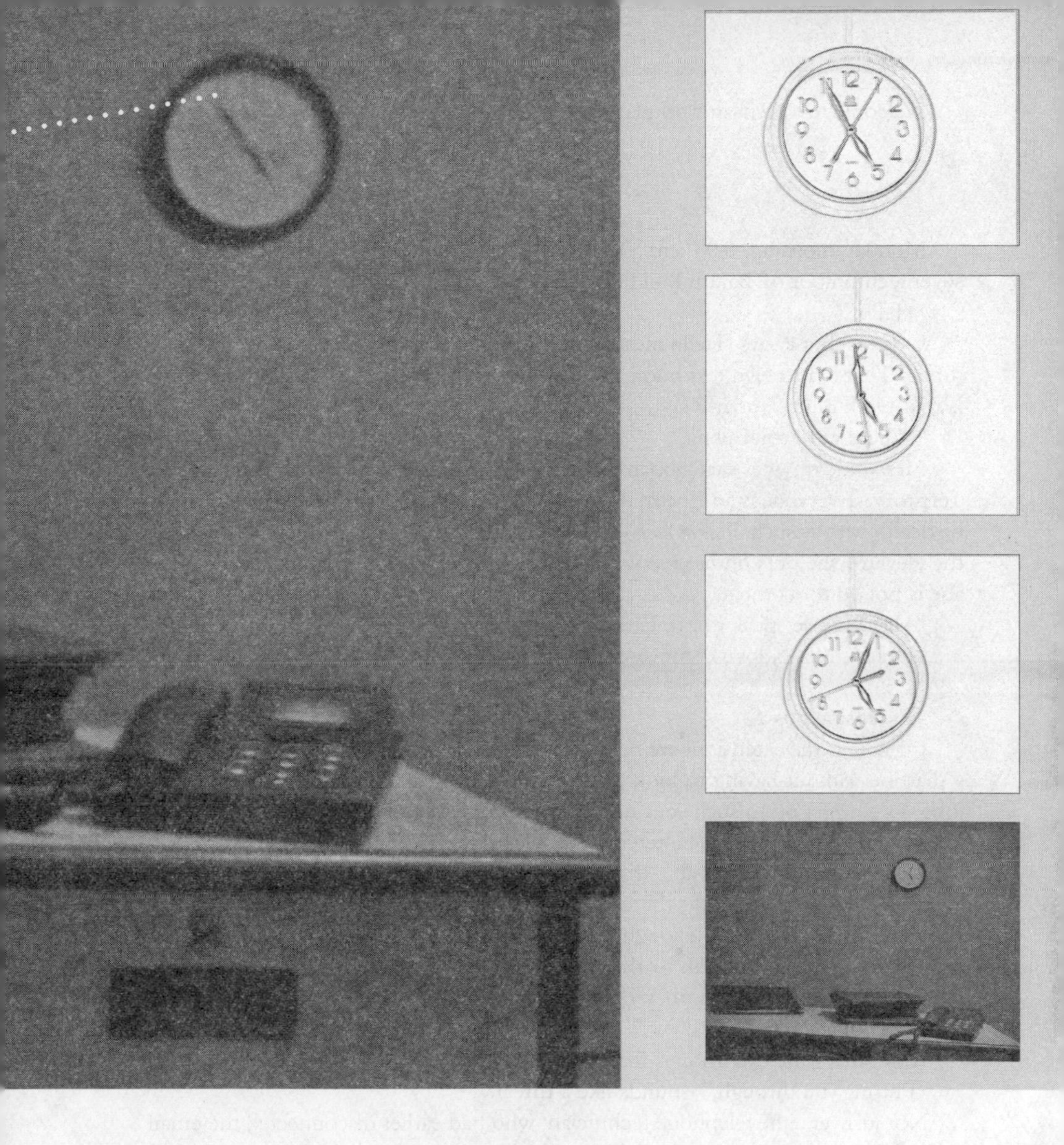

Dark blue ink frozen into ice-cubes. Dark blue ice-cubes piled neatly on top of one another. Arranged in tightly packed columns.

Like rained-on chicken, workers creep into their cold, office cubicles. Avoiding eye contact with anyone they might meet in the corridor—of what use is the intercom if we are to talk face to face?

Open plan office? No way! Your colleagues will see you!

And you might be forced to actually speak with them!

No. We prefer to be shut away. See Nobody, hear Nobody, speak to Nobody. Inside a dull, cold cubicle, like an ice-cube. An ice-cube of dark blue ink.

Welcome to a Kenyan workplace.

Monday morning, 8:00 a.m., Nairobi's Upper Hill area, Baridi Lane, on the seventeenth floor of Barafu Building, the phone rings. A grouchy response,

"Hello."

One text book says, 'Hello means nothing to anyone and is a complete waste of time' That is a foreign text book. This is a Kenyan work place. "Good morning, is that Dark Blue Couriers?"

"Where were you calling."

Mrs. Ndovu, the switchboard operator, believes the workplace is Hostile Territory: Everyone is an Enemy Agent—clients, colleagues, criminals—and must be dealth with as such. *Wakae laini*—they must toe the line. As soon as she steps off the elevator she puts on her mental "military fatigue". When she gets to her desk she is poised for combat.

"May I please speak to Mr. Farasi?" the caller asks.

"Hold," Mrs Ndovu commands.

"... !! ..."

"Extension busy."

Of course the extensions are busy. The intercom is a safe way of launching into a diatribe without having to look anyone in the eye... Besides, ours are sedentary jobs, so why get up to stick your head around someone's door when you can hold lengthy discussions over the intercom. While seated.

The customers must wait. If they are really desperate they can phone again later. If they try frequently, there is a possibility they might eventually speak to someone. If they speak to enough people, they might actually get to speak to the right person. If they speak to the right person, she or he might listen. If they badger him or her enough, they might get a response. If they get a response, it might be satisfactory, if...

Ah! Finally the extension is free.

"Putting you through," sounds like a threat.

Not just yet... the telephone technician, who had earlier disconnected the email line while correcting another problem which nobody remembers, was called in over the weekend to reconnect that line. In the process of reconnecting the e-mail line, he had changed some extension numbers on the switchboard (it is not clear whether this was done inadvertently or maliciously).

However, nobody told the switchboard operator about the extensions. It was kept as a "Monday Morning Surprise!"

Mrs Ndovu, 5' 2" tall and weighing 89 kg, lumbers two metres around the reception desk, six metres down the corridor to the staircase, up a flight of stairs and four and a half metres to Mr. Farasi's office. She stands at the door, panting:

"Your extension is not working. There's a call for you on line two."

"Of course my extension is working. Some extensions were changed on Saturday, when the technician was re-connecting the email line. Try extension 987."

And if you think he's going to make life easy by pressing the flashing light on his telephone set to pick his call on line two, you had better think again.

Mrs. Ndovu turns around heavily, and runs all the way back to the switchboard "Hold on."

Sorry, the caller hung up.

The caller is paying for that call.

The caller will pay for the services you offer (if they are delivered. If...).

The caller's time is being wasted as we talk on the intercom, experiment with our new extensions, plod up and down the corridors...

Yes, the caller is Kenyan.

No, the caller doesn't need this.

Email:

From: Ndovu, M

To: All Dark Blue Staff

Dear All,

Some of your extensions have been changed.

Give me your new extension numbers.

M. Ndovu

Courteous? There's no such word in my mother tongue, does it exist in yours? Civil? Rhymes with evil.

Nobody replied to the email.

"Mrs. Ndovu, one of our new directors is flying in on Wednesday from our JV partners office in Burundi," Mr. Kiboko, the Managing Director, informs the receptionist. Over the intercom, of course. Mr. Kiboko, a man of few words and fewer emotions, is best known for his refusal to evict staff during a bomb scare, demanding that they first complete a leave application form.

"Make sure each person's office is tidy, and let's have these confounded telephones in proper working order before he gets here."

The visitor is going to inspect each person's office? That won't leave much time for anything else. Anyway... does he have a hotel reservation or shall we make one for him? Shall we arrange his transfer from the airport to the hotel? What are his flight details? Will the driver collect him from the hotel and bring him to the office? Are we to prepare an itinerary for his stay in Nairobi? Does anyone care?

Ms. Knowsy Paka is a *"Feelanga"* manager?

A *Feelanga* manager: Feels like a manager. Appears to be one except on the organisation chart. Has the appropriate political clout, which is wielded with abandon.

Knowsy has a BSc– Food Technology, a post-graduate diploma in Graphic Design and one year's work experience as a sound technician in a studio owned by a friend of her father's. She works in the marketing department at Dark Blue Couriers as communications assistant, a position which is somewhat difficult to define. Nevertheless, it comes with a handsome pay-cheque.

At 10:15 a.m. Ms. Paka's scarlet Subaru Impreza swings into the basement parking reserved for senior managers. Dark Blue Couriers pays parking for other staff at the public car park down the road.

"What!" Ms. Paka had exclaimed on hearing about the parking arrangements, "I can't park out there! The paintwork will get damaged! And my remote controlled DVD MP3 player will be stolen! Besides, how am I supposed to get to the office from that parking in the back of beyond? On foot?"

So the VIP parking it was. Along with the key to the VIP elevator, from which all users must be ordered out when Knowsy needs to ride in it. And her elevator ride could last up to 20 minutes, since she has a tendency to keep dashing back to the car for forgotten items—Fendi sun-glasses, iPod, fish-cake, etc.

Knowsy Paka breezes into the office reception. "Good morning, Mrs. Ndovu! Who are you sending that fax to? What emails have you received today?" Knowsy asks, as she reads through all the documents in Mrs Ndovu's 'in' and 'out' trays, walks round the desk and casts her eyes over Mrs. Ndovu's computer screen and on every piece of paper on the desk. "What's this announcement you've photocopied from the newspaper? Make me a copy"—the fact that she's going to read the newspaper herself notwithstanding.

She then strides into the next office and goes through a similar procedure.

If so much as a paper-clip drops from anyone's desk Knowsy is always the first to know. And promptly report it to the relevant manager, even a not so relevant manger, rather like a cat endearing itself to any person with a tuna sandwich.

After reading the newspapers (which must be brought to her desk: it is not her business to go around looking for the newspapers assigned to the department; shouldn't she be getting her own newspapers anyway?), Ms. Paka settles down at her computer and starts her rapid-fire typing. Knowsy has scores of emails to keep up with daily, from her family and friends. Some of them are work related, though, like this one to a cousin's former classmate in Bujumbura:-

Hi, Jean-Yves, there's an Ali ... somebody... visiting our Nairobi office from the JV partners in Bujumbura in a couple of days' time. See what you can dig up on him—does he have a gang of 40 thieves, what's his second name (Baba?), patati patata, and let me have the 411?

The operations manager, Hosea Farasi—Hos—has been phoning Mr. Chui's extension on and off for close to five minutes without any response. Mr. Farasi is always in a hurry and frantically busy. He is involved in a major battle—trying to get things to run the way they ought to. The battle would not be major if only Farasi's team could see clearly on which side they are playing: time and energy is expended tearing one another down. They usually end up handing the trophy to the competition. Farasi tries phoning the next office—Knowsy Paka's—no success. Finally, he hurries to the reception. He can't help noticing a chorus of ringing telephones as he walks down the corridor.

"Mrs. Ndovu, I've been trying to call Chui's extension; why aren't people answering their phones?"

"The extensions were changed"

"Don't we have a policy that any ringing phone must be answered by whoever happens to be near it?"

"The rule I have heard is: 'If you will not solve the client's problem, for heaven's sake do not pick the ringing phone' Nobody wants to speak to a customer who's been driven into a rage by people who don't help... better to have a fresh angry client"

"I'll go to his office"

"You can't. Half of customer service is there, receiving their calls on his direct line."

"I must get the information for my report before tomorrow's meeting"

"That's a communication problem. Knowsy Paka should be able to help"

"She's not answering her phone"

"Oh, I forgot—she's out for lunch"

"Lunch? She only just got here!"

"I'll send Kobe, with a note asking Chui to call you"

Hos Farasi ends up sending a text message to Chui. Even though everyone is fond of Kobe the messenger, a cheerful wiry old man, he is not known for speed. He shuffles along the corridors stopping to have lengthy discussions in flawless Kiswahili, with everyone he meets.

Kobe can never understand why people are so cold, angry, uncommunicative and rude. Someone once told him it was the workload. This explanation puzzles him. Workload? Besides his job as a messenger, Kobe runs a second-hand-clothes stall, and works as a night askari at one of the bosses' homes. And these strong, young people are complaining about their workload?

Ms. Paka phones Mr. Chui's office:

"Why are the telephone costs on the print-out so high?"

"I am quite sure I don't know, I'll find out from Ndovu"

Now you know why the extensions are always engaged—why can't Paka speak directly to Ndovu?

"Why are the telephone costs on the print-out so high?" Chui repeats to Ndovu.

It turns out that since most of the telephone extensions have been changed, Mrs. Ndovu is unable to transfer a number of calls. She is therefore taking messages and staff members are having to call back the clients.

Mrs. Ndovu phones the telephone technician's office:

"Give me Abraham," she demands.

"I'm afraid Abraham is out, can someone else assist you?"

"Give me Isaac."

"I'm sorry he is also out. Would you like to speak to Jacob?"

Jacob is surprised about the switchboard chaos at Dark Blue.

"You people didn't renew your contract with us. So none of our technicians have been to your offices for the past three months."

Ndovu asks Chui (over the intercom) if he knows which company was contracted for the switchboard job last Saturday. Leopold Chui is easy-going so everyone feels comfortable asking him what is going on.

"Well, it wasn't a company as such... Knowsy brought in one of her *relas*—a certain Cunningham Mjanja."

"Do you have his telephone number?"

"He doesn't have a landline...His cell number is 07 something."

"Where is his office?"

"I think he operates from home."

"Where is his home?"

"Er...Knowsy has his contacts."

Cunningham Mjanja has traveled to Madagascar. Knowsy goes to the reception and phones another relative in Uganda to get Mjanja's telephone number in Madagascar. She then phones Madagascar.

The receptionist at the office in Madagascar has difficulty understanding English. Eventually, Knowsy is put through to her relative. Mjanja explains to Ndovu how to check the assigned extension numbers:

"You press the button written 'program.'"

Of all the buttons on the switchboard, "program" is one button you can be sure Mrs. Ndovu has never used.

"Where is it?"

"You see those keys which are..."

Thus Mrs. Ndovu's 45 minute lesson on switchboard programming takes place. Live and exclusive from Madagascar.

Just as they are about to finish, there is a power interruption (no Kenyan workplace is complete without a power interruption) and the switchboard goes off. The programming is lost. Knowsy phones Madagascar again. The lady who answers the phone has difficulty understanding English...

When the telephone print-out from the calls monitoring computer—known to staff as "The Snitch"—arrives, Knowsy will rush to her boss with the computer printout of all outgoing telephone calls.

"Look, boss! Ndovu was on the phone to Madagascar for close to two hours! And here's another call to Uganda! No wonder the telephone bills are so high."

"Send her a strongly worded warning letter at once, Knowsy."

As her *rela*, Mjanja, takes home a handsome fee.

The visitor, Ali Shangaa, after making his own flight bookings, hotel reservations and airport transfers, arrives at the Dark Blue Couriers by taxi, at 9:00 a.m. There is nobody at the reception. Mrs. Ndovu has gone to the PABX room to sort out the switchboard problem. Cunningham, is back in town but is at another client's premises. He takes her through the procedure over the phone.

Ali Shangaa paces back and forth across the reception area. Did he expect someone would come to the reception to meet him? He found his way from his home country to his duty-station, from his duty station to this office, right? And he needs help getting to the meeting room?

Kobe, the messenger, shuffles in and greets him cheerily in his perfect Kiswahili.

"Good morning, sir. Have you been assisted?"

Ali Shangaa lived most of his life in Tanzania; he is quite comfortable with Kiswahili as a working language. He wonders though, who this old man is. Might he be the receptionist? This Kenyan work place is so weird, anything is possible.

"I am here for a nine o'clock meeting"

"Please be seated. I'll fetch the receptionist—she's over there at the back fixing the PABX."

"Your receptionist has some technical qualifications?" Mr. Shangaa asks.

"Not exactly. But she's quite good at this sort of thing. I've seen her at home fixing her sewing machine herself. The technician is directing her over the phone. I'm not so sure about his abilities, though. He's always talking on his cellphone as he works, no wonder he makes such a mess out of everything. This multi-tasking generation—they try to hold down a goat for slaughter with one leg while chasing a chicken with the other... And might I ask please, where you are from, sir?"

Ali Shangaa takes a seat.

"From the Serena Hotel."

"Serena? They must have excellent tennis courts there. And if they don't, it might be a good idea to up-grade them, now that they share a name with a leading tennis player... talking of which, we could use a tennis court over here. These young people are overweight and in terrible shape; they spend all morning sitting in traffic, all day sitting at their desks, all evening sitting in a cybercafe, all weekend sitting in a pub...." Kobe rambles on as he walks to the PABX room.

Ali Shangaa gets up and goes to look for the meeting room. At the end of the corridor an open door reveals a large meeting room. A sign hanging on the door announces "Meeting in Progress."

There's no one inside. Ali looks at his watch: 9:15.

At 9:30, the managers begin to trickle in.

Later, Mrs. Ndovu serves tea and coffee at the side table. Nobody says thank you.

Why should anyone thank you for doing what you are paid to do? We Kenyans will thank you only if you deserve to be thanked- that is, if you've gone out of your way, bent over backwards, gone the extra mile, surrendered your life ... then we might consider thanking you.

Shangaa gets up to serve his coffee.

Where he grew up it is polite to ask if anyone else would like a cup, so he politely asks. But this, sir, is a Kenyan workplace!! Half a dozen managers promptly give the new director their orders:

"Coffee with milk and two spoons of sugar."

Ali Shangaa is... amazed.

"Tea, no milk, one sugar."

Astonished.

"I don't take sugar."

Astounded.

"Put for me two tea bags."

HAAKASA RENJA was born in August 1965 to Ezekiel Ochami Renja of Marama South, Butere and Helen Wanjiru Muthui of Ngecha in Limuru, Haakasa Wambui Renja attended Juja Road Primary School and thereafter proceeded to Ngara Girls High School in Nairobi. She later went to Kianda College and has worked in different capacities in various organisations over the years. She has six older siblings, a teenage son and about a dozen wonderful nephews and nieces aged between one and 32 years, making up the best family on earth.

Photograph: Anonymous

The Return Of The Tribe

BY PAUL GOLDSMITH

THE CONTEMPORARY ROLE OF TRIBES AND CLANS ACROSS THE WORLD

After five hundred years in the cold, the tribe– in concept and practice– is making a comeback. The state is the most important institution in the World, in the evolutionary scheme of things, while the tribe has been ranked for a long time as a lower form of Social Organization. The expanding European nation-state exposed the weakness of tribal societies and fueled the perception of 'tribes' as preserves of superstition and anti-progressive customs.

Tribalism provided a moral pretext for their subjugation; colonialism became the necessary corrective.

The project failed. Tribalism resurfaced as a general explanation for many of post-independence Africa's problems. But radical political economy and the new Afro-consciousness that preceded it across the African Diaspora deemed this tribalism to be a creation of colonialism. The word tribe became pejorative regardless of context, as I discovered when two indignant African American student-colleagues nailed me to the wall for uttering the term during a seminar in 1974: "Tribe is honky, fool!"

Ten days later I was in Africa. I religiously avoided the T word– even though everyone else seemed to use it casually enough. I likewise refrained from uttering the Swahili term *kabila,* conscientiously substituted terms like *umma, ukoo,* or the generic *watu* in its place.

My more perceptive friends noticed my aversion to uttering both 'T' and 'K' words; they laughed and told me that *kabila* is part of Africa's natural order. We are proud of our tribes, they would explain, "It is *ukabila*, tribal politics, that is the problem."

A decade later, I was back in the classroom to teach an introductory course on Africa. The first question I faced was by an African–American student: "Don't all those people over there live in tribes?" I replied, cautiously, "yes, individuals do identify with their ethnic communities, and competition among diverse groups creates special problems, although the ethnic factor camouflages other forces at work..."

I stumbled on in this fashion—while avoiding direct mention of the 'T' word. "Yeah," another hip young student brashly chirped in, "all those Africans belong to different tribes!"

Students, as I discovered, now associated tribe with a positive unambiguous identity, collective pride, and a mutually supportive communal social order. While I was away, young African–Americans had come around to redefine tribe as an alternative to the highly atomized social environment that revolved mainly around sports, soaps, and hip-hop music.

I had no problem understanding this because many of my own generation saw themselves as a tribe apart, a counterculture based on the ideals (and tonsorial fashions) of the founding fathers. This 'rainbow' tribe took its *clue* from the mystical semiotics encoded in the dollar bill: IN GOD WE TRUST and NOVUS

ORDO SECLORUM (the new order of the ages) and the pyramid crowned by an all-seeing eye of providence.

The tribalism of African America appears more associated with the institutional racism pervading the 'new order', and in any event reference to tribe in the negative aspect is no longer an issue. Exasperated administrators responsible for clearing the site of the collapsed World Trade Towers, for example, depicted the unseemly friction between firemen and cops at ground-zero as "the problem of the tribes."

But what is, exactly, a tribe? I don't recall encountering a precise definition during my years of anthropological immersion. Scholars have assembled an array of genetic, historical, and anthropological data to demolish the concept of race, just as the Marxists of the Diaspora dismissed tribe as honky-driven false consciousness.

Except for the small cultural groups highlighted on the BBC website, Tribes, most African tribes appear to be fuzzy-edged, disorganized collectives that serve as proof of my professor, Ronald Cohen's, methodological maxim: "Tribes do not do anything; they cannot act and they cannot make decisions; only individuals have the ability to make choices and act on them."

Of course, 'tribe' and 'race' are likely to persist in popular use as intuitively self-defining terms. In contrast to the various anti and reoccurring notions of tribe, however, analysts of contemporary warfare are now citing the tribe as a specific form of organization—and a model unit for waging what they define as Fourth Generation Warfare (or 4GW).

I found the 4GW concept of tribe appealing because it identifies compact entities defined by their primary loyalties that display a highly adaptive organizational capacity to act in concert and coordinate with other Tribes and actors to pursue collective goals. These tribes may be traditional or synthetic; students of 4GW gravitate to the ability of a tribe like Hezbollah to protect the tribe's interest, which is an extension of their success in providing services and promoting their people's welfare.

In Africa, where the rise of the state never submerged the tribe, tribal organization rarely appears to benefit the people, even in circumstances of group solidarity galvanized by war or oppression.

FOURTH GENERATION WARFARE AND THE NEW TRIBALISM.

Fourth generation warfare is based on a combination of new and old tactics used by contemporary non-state combatants who are confronting the state in a variety of settings. The tribe of the 4GW analysts refers to tightly knit groups based on primary loyalties; they claim effectiveness of these tribes in a range of theaters commonly associated with 'the war on terror,' are rapidly making conventional military and guerilla strategies obsolete.

The 4GW concept derives from the basic theory behind the evolution of warfare articulated by Sun Tzu in 400 BC. Sun Tzu observed that there are asymmetries present on any battlefield and inherent to all conflicts; successful leaders devise innovative stratagems that exploit the asymmetrical aspect of an enemy's strategy.

Historians of modern war identify three major shifts in organization, technology, and maneuverability that exploited asymmetries in conventional warfare to change the way war is waged. Briefly summarizing the overlapping succession of these 'generations' helps clarify why analysts argue we are witnessing the emergence of a new, fourth evolutionary stage of warfare.

The large armies raised by centralized states of antiquity marked the rise of First Generation Warfare (1GW). Superior organization and logistical support saw the elite warriors and cavalry that formerly dominated the battlefield become incorporated into forces dominated by battalions of foot soldiers.

Warfare's second generation came about through technological advances in weaponry that allowed smaller forces with superior firepower to prevail over large 1GW armies; 2GW armies are associated with the emergence of Europe's modern states.

Third Generation Warfare came about through a synergetic combination of enhanced intelligence and mobility. 3GW was perfected by the Nazis, whose blitzkrieg tactics exemplified the capacity to quickly maneuver and penetrate enemy defenses at their weakest points, resulting in the Third Reich's series of rapid conquests at the beginning of World War II.

In 1989, two US Marine Corp officers stressed the efficacy of 'low intensity' guerilla forces in modern times to predict that the emergence of a new Fourth Generation mode of warfare was imminent. The unexpectedly easy defeat of Saddam Hussein in the first Gulf War of 1991 probably hastened its arrival. Instead of inaugurating the coming "American Century" of Washington's neo-cons, the enormous gap between the US led forces and any potential state-based enemy is redefining the field of battle.

The East African embassy bombing was a dramatic harbinger and 9/11 a confirmation of the shift to a whole new array of methods of resistance and attack by combatants who do not fight under a flag. Al Qaeda's Afghan-Arabs provided the first example of what the 4GW analysts refer to as the "networked tribe." Subsequent developments underscore the illusory nature of the victories declared after 3GW campaigns in Afghanistan and Iraq.

Fourth Generation Warfare blends the tactics of terrorist attacks and guerilla insurgency within a considerably more sophisticated approach. 4GW combatants launch attacks on symbolic and strategic targets while incorporating smuggling, counter-narcotics operations, cyber-terrorism, and other techniques not usually associated with war—including use of political, economic, social, and military networks. The strategy involves attacking the enemy simultaneously on three levels to increase the physical, moral and mental isolation of the enemy; the objective is to attain political goals by convincing opponents' leaders that their strategic opposition to these goals is either unviable or too costly to sustain popular political support.

While 4GW methods are often violent and disruptive, for the most part, they reflect the clinical use of bloodshed to target existing grievances and long-standing aspirations of oppressed and threatened groups. The analysts' concept of 'tribe' begins with qualities of the traditional ethnic societies, which they transpose to contemporary entities that may differ in origin and form, but operate according to the same tribal logic. David Ronfled of the Rand Corporation, for example, describes the 'tribe' as:

> ...the oldest and most successful organizational type ever devised. Its main purpose is to create a sense of social identity that strengthens the ability of the individual and the collective to survive. Traditional tribes rely on kinship ties (families, clans, etc.) and share a common mythology (lineage and place). Manufactured tribes promote brotherhood ("fictive kinship") and create their own mythology (anything that sets them apart).
>
> All tribes are based on mutual defense, respect, and honor. Tribes old and new share a strong primary loyalty to the group. The tribalism attracting the analysts' attention stems from some important insights into organization and decision-making, and they cite a range of empirical phenomena to support their observations.

The advantage of traditional and 'manufactured' tribes stems from their ideologically embedded, unified sense of purpose and commitment to the group's defense. As the statement above indicates, one important asymmetry the 'tribe' exploits is the unwavering obligation that induces its members to fight harder and under conditions that professional soldiers find difficult– while enduring high and even massive losses that undermine political commitment to wage war in democratic societies.

The tribe's re-emergence in the context of 4GW is also predicated on built in methods of communication allowing them to act in concert while rapidly responding to threats in decentralized ways that gives them an advantage over hierarchical structured military units, where information and orders have to travel up and down the chain of command, resulting in a slower decision-making and response cycle.

Tribes are also seen to posses a natural capacity for networking– one of the adaptive traits of 4GW insurgencies. This extends to another quality of 4GW: its ability to catalyze the process of reproducing itself within other 'ethnicities' or sub-national 'tribes' who are threatened by outside threats in a manner energizing their need to adapt. 4GW blogs are constantly identifying new 'tribes' actively evolving along these lines.

One military document states that 4GW, "involves not only many different players, but many different kinds of players, fighting for many different kinds of goals (from money through political power to martyrdom)."

This defines the networked tribe as a hybrid of Pareto political types: it is both the fox who knows many things, and the hedgehog who knows one thing very well. Hezbollah and the Pashtun-based Taliban are ranking exemplars of new and old ideologically networked tribes that have demonstrated their ability to thwart the superior firepower and technology of states. During the latest insurgency in Kandahar, NATO generals claimed progress on the basis of enemy body counts, and pleaded for reinforcements while their soldiers, reporting exceptionally intense Taliban resistance, retreated from their forward positions.

Hezbollah is a highly decentralized organization. The fighters who resisted the Israeli incursion into Lebanon are also service providers integrated into civilian populations. Its contraband networks span the Middle East, operate in Brazil and Uruguay, and sell smuggled cigarettes in the southern USA. In southern Lebanon, Hezbollah proved to be a largely invisible entity that was able to increase the salvos of Katyusha missiles raining down on northern Israel even while the Israeli army expanded their territorial occupation, and neutralized ten per cent of the invaders' tanks.

Victory in 4GW is not about sustaining the offensive or holding territory. To achieve their goals, 4GW combatants willingly accept the trade-off in land and casualties for the damage and disruption inflicted on enemy systems and negative publicity generated by their military response. The Hezbollah leader Sheikh Narullah said as much at the onset of the Israeli offensive: "If we survive, we win."

Indeed, this goes to the essence of military historian Martin van Creveld's paradox of modern warfare: those who fight against the weak and loses, lose; those who fight against the weak and win also lose.

Like tribe, 4GW discourse adapts an eclectic range of concepts and metaphors from disciplines ranging from conventional military science to anthropology, biology, and astronomy to explain the phenomenon. John Robb, is a military analyst whose Global Guerillas blog provides a particularly rich array of perspectives on 4GW that are illustrated through Robb's colorful and specialized terminology. Robb displays a knack for matching 4GW phenomena with existing concepts, like his application of 'open source' to warfare. Black swans, cascading system failure, open source war, stigmergic learning, swarming, long-tailed insurgencies, and oort clouds are other examples of this vocabulary.

If many of these concepts represent ideal types that may only partially describe individual cases, the concepts and terms are precisely defined and as explanatory, problem-solving constructs they achieve a tight fit with the subject matter.

Open source war, for example, refers to insurgencies based on "a resilient network made up of small, autonomous groups." The tribes in this case are able to "combine and recombine to form a viable network despite high rates of attrition," and as a result are "virtually immune to attrition and decapitation." The more important aspect of 'open source', however, is the rapid replication and modification of technologies and tactics across the globe.

A black swan is an anomalous unpredictable event, ostensibly named after Karl Poppers principle of falsification. Falsification holds that the truth of a statement like all swans are white is contingent upon proof that a black swan does not exist. The embassy bombings is a black swan in 4GW parlance because authorities in Washington refused to give credence to intelligence trickling in, warning from the

Government of Kenya, and Ambassador Bushnell's repeated requests to improve the embassy's security prior to the explosions that echoed across the world on August 7, 1998.

The systemic impact of such an event contributes to tribal strategies by giving rise to the somewhat jargonistic but analytically useful term, stigmergy (derived from the greek words stigma "sign" and ergon "to act"). Stigmergy identifies environmental mechanisms for coordinating the work of independent actors; like the way ants use pheromones to create trails, or how people use web links to establish informational paths.

Its application to 4GW is based on the footprint and trails left by the actions of actors (especially large organizations) that assist actors in decentralized networks to coordinate decision-making; an "attack signaling an increase in security in one area... directs actors to select other targets that will be more vulnerable as a consequence." Tribes use stigmergy to outsmart states.

It is important to remember that the return of the tribe is linked to the decline of the state. The decline of the state is the result of the failure to adapt to changes proceeding within the increasingly dynamic global environment. The state's decidedly unstigmergic propensity is to ignore critical signals within the environment and signs 'of the times'.

The 4GW crowd's bible is Van Creveld's 1999 work, *The Rise and Decline of the State.* Van Creveld predicts that state decline will lead to a variety of non-state organizations replacing its functions, but he refrains from saying exactly how. His military aficionados are connecting the dots.

4GW analysts' focus on modern tribalism and its proto-historical antecedents assumes that weak and failing states are encouraging segments of populations to regroup on the basis of primary loyalties. As Robb states, primary loyalties based on "gang, tribe, clan, ethnicity, religion, and more can power a much more cohesive organizational alternative to that of the nation-state." These primary loyalties are resurfacing in conditions that make for a potent organizational hybrid:

The tribalism we face today is a combination of these ancient mindsets and modern systems of thinking (economics, networks, communication, etc.). It's a very dangerous combination made stronger by the forces of globalization—which has leveled the playing field in the competition between tribes and states. Today, networked tribes thrive economically (particularly as participants in the multi-trillion dollar black economy) and project power globally. Implications of this new tribalism that may initially seem rhetorical or self-serving in fact appear more commonsensical and relevant to a spectrum of policy issues with each passing day. The 4GW discourse identifies organizational trends and activities that are entirely consistent with the general institutional shift to participatory development, indigenous knowledge and technologies, information and connectivity, and supporting private sector initiatives in place of foreign aid.

4GW analysts deem conventional counterinsurgency as doomed to failure. They argue that the inability to resolve conflicts through nation-building and collapsing rogue states (e.g. Iraq, Afghanistan) indicates that western states should deescalate conflicts wherever possible rather than ignite them. As one author states, "escalation is a false God that promises a return of the motivational clarity found in the wars of the 20th Century. It cannot deliver this."

Although the 4GW analysts stress the efficacy of networked tribes based on primary loyalties both in waging conflicts and in providing services for their constituencies, they never refer to the problem as one of tribalism. The same cannot be said for Africa, where concerned citizens and distinguished persons (like Barrack Obama during his recent visit to Kenya) alike lament the fact that tribalism remains the continent's primary socio-political pathology.

AFRICA: TRIBES OR TRICKSTERS?

The problem of tribes and tribalism in Africa has been examined extensively, generating analyses incorporating perspectives like those indicated by the titles listed in the following sample: *The Illusion of Tribe* (Aiden Southhall), *The Ideology of Tribalism* (Archie Mafeje), *Tribal Survival in Modern African Political Systems* (Colin Legum), *The Tribe as Fact and Fiction in an East African City* (David Parkin), *The Social Organization of Cultural Differences* (Frederick Barth), and *The Politics of Cultural Pluralism* (Crawford Young).

These authors represent a formidable collection of scholars, yet their combined acuity seems to have changed little on the ground. Tribe is a natural archetype and tribes are political tropes that continue to create conceptual confusion and civic strife across the continent.

The region's low level of development and globalization should dilute the 4GW concept's relevance for Africa: the rise of the state never wholly submerged the tribe, yet tribal organization rarely appears to benefit the people, even in circumstances of group solidarity galvanized by war or oppression. Some 4GW insights and lessons are nonetheless relevant to issues of tribe and conflict in Africa.

Consider, for example, how this quote [the inserts are mine] from a document entitled *The Manual of Fourth Generation Warfare* captures the correspondence between 4GW and the fuzzy aspects of ethnic competition in Africa's political arenas: "...the distinction between war [politics] and peace [development] will be blurred to the vanishing point. It will be nonlinear, possibly to the point of having no definable battlefields or fronts. The distinction between "civilian" [citizen] and "military" [tribesman] may disappear..." Also, where politicians exploit terrorist attacks by portraying them as crimes of hate, the analysts objectify terror as one in an arsenal of tactics targeting symbolic or system nodes in order to achieve calculated goals– and not to maximize collateral damage (which is counter-productive over the long-term). Though demonizing or dehumanizing the 'other' is used to incite communal violence in Africa, this kind of tribalism invariably serves instrumental objectives.

MEND, Nigeria's Movement for the Emancipation of the Niger Delta, is one of John Robb's pet case studies, updated by this entry on Global Guerillas of May 31 (2006):

> The list of people with big influence over the $2 trillion-a-

> year global oil market has long been an exclusive one, topped by Saudi princes and American presidents. This year, someone calling himself Jomo Gbomo emailed his way into the club. Since January, the obscure Nigerian rebel group that he claims to speak for has battled Nigeria's military, blown up oil facilities and kidnapped foreign oil workers. All the while, Mr. Gbomo has fired off emails to the international media taking responsibility for the attacks or threatening new ones -- and often roiling global oil prices in the process.

The rebel's bombing of an army barrack in Port Harcourt in September contributed to a five dollar spike in crude prices; Mr. Gbomo's insurgency is no doubt making Nigerian leaders rue the execution of Ken Saro Wiwa. Where such examples of African 4GW are still relatively rare, struggle between tribes and other vehicles for primary loyalties and the state is the norm.

In Kenya, ethnic mobilization and communal violence do not target military objectives, but are political tactics for waging "war by other means." The polite language of public discourses in Kenya camouflages and obscures, but does not conceal tribal motivations and ethnic arithmetic central to the nation's political wars. Everyone knows the score: victory is not about democracy and reform. It's not about respect and honor; it's about tricksters using tribes to capture the state, access to land, or valuable resources.

WHAT ARE THESE TRIBES AND WHO BENEFITS FROM THEIR TRIBALISM?

In Kenya and other African nations tribe is an unbounded entity defined according to system scales and context. A Gikuyu on one level is a Mundia in Kirinyaga, and transplanted Akamba when in Kitui. Are they linguistically wired clans? Not really: the Atangwa in Machakos are Masela in Muranga. Some Rendille are Arialle, who are also Samburu, while there are 'pure' Rendille who speak Maa but not their own tongue. I discovered our Luhya neighbours spoke Swahili and English at home; they could not communicate in the husband's Samia and wife's Maragoli dialects.

How are these tribes organized? Where terms such as mbari, jilib, mwiriga, ukoo, and mlango are examples of vocabulary describing clans or clan-type units — I have yet to encounter an authentically indigenous term for tribe. Clans were and often still are corporate entities that regulate access to land, resources, and control membership in the group. Like companies, clans also maintained cooperative and risk-spreading relations with other clan 'companies' participating in the regional economy. The Swahili term *kabila* substitutes for tribe because where the 4GW tribes are revitalized collectives emerging in the context of state decline, most tribes in this region are a product of state imposition.

Tribes are rigid where clans were mobile, spatially and in terms of identity.

Tribes don't do anything, but tribal leaders and the political clans they head do. The perks that come with capturing the state circulate mainly within a small elite comprised of the ruling clan and allies from other political clans. Their tribal rank and file rarely displays overtly tribal behavior, but politically, the overwhelming percentage follows the tribal line.

The caption of a picture accompanying a Sunday Standard essay by Dominic Odipo captured the situation: a large crowd is seated on the grass during a rally at Uhuru Park; the caption reads, "Are these Kenyans? No, they belong to Kenyan tribes." Although exiled corruption-buster John Githongo obviously meant to convey the magnitude of the Anglo-Leasing scandal when he observed, "I betrayed my government, and I betrayed my tribe," he backhandedly confirmed the same point.

Tribalizing the struggle among elites and clans leads to distinctions between democracy and mobilization, transparency and due process, accountability and empowerment, leadership and ethnic chauvinism becoming as muddled as the blurred categories of 4GW. Fomenting polarization amidst such murkiness serves the interests of the tricksters in the vanguard.

In the end, the military guys' emphasis on tribes as vehicles for primary loyalties, and as compact and efficient units for waging 4GW is misplaced. Their networked tribes have little in common with traditional tribes, but are actually networked individuals operating within political clans. In one 4GW analysis of how tribes actually work, the linkage between networked combatants and society are likened to the dynamics of the oort cloud to describe the way tribal insurgencies work.

The Oort cloud, named after the Dutch astronomer who first posited its existence, is an immense spherical cloud surrounding the planetary system and extending approximately 3 light years from the Sun. Oort clouds are believed to consist of molecular particles with a relatively dense core. The core gives rise to stars and planets of a solar system and continues to spawn comets that exhibit a weak gravitational attraction to the sun. Comets zoom around in irregular orbits and exert tidal forces that can create pertubations when they pass through a solar system (many societies associate the appearance of comets with disasters).

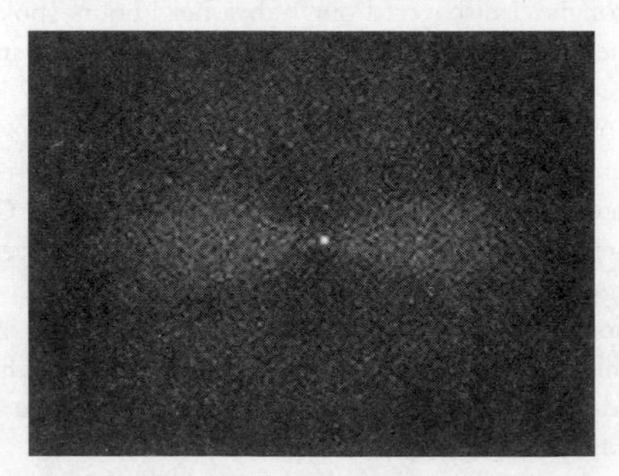

The Oort Cloud: Can You See the Tribes?

In the 4GW oort cloud, primary loyalties are initially concentrated within a core of relatively few ideologically united actors. They exploit a variety of criminal and licit methods to capture the resources and create conditions that attract a secondary band of sympathizers to their cause. These leaders and their clans coordinate with other 'tribes' to create circumstances that polarize the much larger body of neutral particles. In the oort cloud metaphor, the tribal core generates 'comets', erratic agents that largely disregard conventional societal gravity to stage black swans (an attack on a target, e.g. the embassy bombings and World Trade Center). The strategy of terror uses attacks on symbolic targets to engender systems and perturbations– creating conditions enhancing the tribe's stygmergic capacity to disrupt strategic nodes with a view of fostering cascading system failure.

This big picture analogy is engaging, even fun, but the application of scientific concepts invokes technical caveats. On his blog of March 9 of 2006, Robb reports that the "strategy of combining warfare, disruption, and criminality makes it not only possible for these groups to survive, but to thrive." He cites this as a classic indicator of "a dynamically unstable system," but does not locate the term within its dynamic systems context.

The turbulence of such systems on 'the edge of chaos' is a function of the non-linear dynamics engendered by high levels of feedback. This instability is not a permanent state. Feedback generated from the multiple centers usually present can either dampen or aggravate the system perturbations: the system either retreats back into the rigid state or undergoes phase transition. Turbulence and conflict on one scale are often a force for restoring equilibrium within the larger system. To use the oort cloud metaphor again, one astronomical description of oort clouds observes that, "the structure of the cloud is believed to consist of a relatively dense core that... gradually replenishes the outer boundaries, creating a steady state."

Humans have imposed upon the planet a multi-scaled political system that is clearly undergoing transition. The process was sufficiently advanced for Daniel Moynihan to use his 1988 study, *Pandemonium*, to illustrate why managing ethnicity and regional sub-nationalism will be the greatest governance challenge of the coming century. And in an article entitled, "The State in Lenticular Perspective," published around the same time, my own Professor Cohen outlines how after several hundred years of expansion, these pressures from below together with the expansion of supra-national organizations operate in tandem to shrink the political space long occupied by the state.

During the run-up to the new millennium, voices of progress were unanimous on the need to restructure the architecture of the international system. Before anyone acted on the premise, the 'tribes' kick-started the project by expanding into the opening political space. It is nevertheless important to remember that groups and other networked collectives coalescing around 'primary loyalties are just one element in the uneven, non-linear, regionally differentiated, and very complex process we are witnessing as it unfolds on different levels and different parts of the world.

Kenya, which hosts an ethno-cultural diversity greater than Europe's in a country the size of France, is obviously one of the more important laboratories for managing the impact of the forces from below problem. Because alternate civil structures are still young, the tribes are, in different ways, playing a critical role in mobilizing citizens' demands for reform. Large tribes are doing this via ethnic political mobilization. Smaller tribes, like the organically constituted Pokot and the essentially synthetic Laikipia Maasai, which emerged in the context of the ranch invasions marking the 100 year anniversary of 1904 British-Maasai agreement, use more violent methods to prosecute their rights to alienated land and resources.

These ethnic-based strategies are driven by instrumental goals, thoroughly modern aspirations that have little use for ancient mind-sets. The distilled wisdom based on African phenomena underscores that tribal identities and behaviors manifest across a wide phenomenological spectrum—and that loyalties are multiple, crosscutting, and ephemeral over time. Gunter Schlee's 1994 study of pastoralist clans, *Identities on the Move*, captures the fluid quality of tribes that many post-independence historians like Bethwell Ogot also identify in their work.

While scholars have yet to compile such insights into a comprehensive model that can be applied to contemporary variations on ethnicity, assembling the accumulating knowledge on the subject could easily end up as a very unwieldy and unparsimonious construct. The Bible gives us the tower of Babylon story and the Q'uran states, "we could have made you as one community, but we made you as many in order that you may understand." The tribe may appear to be a safe haven and a protective cocoon from the vantage point of mass industrial society; but in Africa's multi-ethnic patchwork of large, small, and medium sized communities, the tribe alone is a ghetto, an incubator for moral, mental, and physical isolation. Complexity theory luminary Robert Kaufmann coined the term "spontaneous internal organization," to help us understand adaptive qualities of complicated systems.

I have witnessed spontaneous internal organization emerge out of the chaotic run-up to Swahili weddings, contribute to the resolution of explosive disputes brokered by third parties, and on the Kenya side of the rubble pile created by the bombers who struck Nairobi on August 7 of 1998. It really works, but I don't think I could explain how to George W. Bush.

The 4GW notion of tribe derives from the embedded tendency in the West to define tribes in monocultural terms emphasizing their honorable warlike qualities. Maybe this is why leaders of the Western world bear much of the responsibility for unleashing the extreme tribal forces described in 4GW discourse.

AND THE CARAVAN MOVES ON

One of the more interesting aspects of the 4GW phenomenon is how critics operating within the school of military history and applied analysis are emerging as a most unexpected source of a trenchant and searing critique of the neo-conservative agenda. Where many liberals' reaction to ideas associated with a martial mind-set is to reject them based on the source, the radical shift in orientation demanded by the arguments generated by military scholars, bloggers, and students of 4GW pose a considerable quandary for the neo-conservative political clan.

In a 1997 article that has enjoyed remarkable wide circulation on the Internet, Major R. Peters categorically declares that America's open and information-savvy society will prevail in a fragmenting world of 'constant conflict' by exploiting the same asymmetries that 4GW tribes are currently using to their great advantage — superior knowledge of the enemy, their culture, and their thought processes. He nevertheless avers: "this will involve a good bit of technology, but the relevant systems will not be the budget vampires, such as manned bombers and attack submarines, that we continue to buy through inertia, emotional attachment, and the lobbying power of the defense industry." *Global Guerillas* and linked sites describe sophisticated weapon systems in the pipeline as dinosaurs that are already obsolete.

The Iraqi debacle is fueling a growing American lobby for radical military reform. The privatization of some military functions as previewed in Iraq and post Katrina New Orleans is prompting postings on the blogs referring to a future where the wealthy and political elites operate out of insulated cocoons protected by private security services, and everyone else remains exposed to the pandemonium and tribal demons Moynihan described.

The sum of these views represents a direct threat for the warlords of democracy and their special interest clans. Poor little honky devils: lurking within the oort cloud, I see the dragon of Chinese cosmology biting its tail.

PAUL GOLDSMITH was born in New York City in 1952, grew up in central Florida, studied literature at Tulane University in New Orleans, helped build Disneyworld, and financed his first trip to Kenya in 1974 by winning a workman's compensation case against Mickey Mouse. Following two years of regional field studies, he returned to Kenya in 1978, working in a number of different capacities and studying diverse local domains since that time. Upon completion of a Ph.D. in anthropology from the University of Florida in 1994, he renewed his quest to explore the asymmetrical complexities of African society and environment via an eclectic range of research, consultancy, civil society activities, and unplanned experience.

Hairdresser

Phyllis Muthoni

We both have conspired to create
a star and a sensation.
(I can see the lights
and feel the crowd's admiration.
I hear thunderous applause).

The person I'll be for the next five hours
is slowly coming into being.
The birth, by his dextrous fingers
aided by his instruments of power
dangling at his side in a black pouch
is now complete.
I hear music in the tresses.

After visiting him
I can be anyone I want to be.

All Others

Phyllis Muthoni

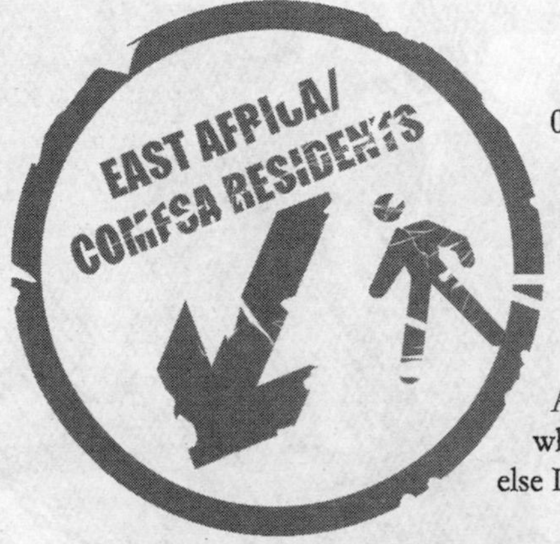

0735 hrs.
The whole world has been poured out
into Heathrow Terminal 4
The EU and Swiss counters are a breeze.
The 'All Others' queue meanders like
a river in its old age,
complete with little ox-bow lakes.
An hour and half later I reach the counter,
where it seems my every hair has to be in place
else I won't be let through.

Three weeks later
at Entebbe airport
it takes only a few minutes
to get through 'East Africa and COMESA.'
I notice, for the first time,
a modest queue for 'Others'.
I smile to myself, thinking,
There's some balance in this life after all.

PHYLLIS MUTHONI is a freelance writer of both prose and poetry, though poetry is her first love. In January 2005 she relocated from Nairobi to Kampala to work for a humanitarian organization. For her, Uganda has been a great source of inspiration in its geography, history and society. There is so much to enjoy and write about!

Illustration: Ray Gicharu

Dirt People

BY BRIAN COOPER

On a highway of rain-rutted and sun-baked earth, they drove fast enough to shake every loose bolt. A young woman sat between the lorry's drivers. For her passage from Isiolo to Marsabit, she had agreed to pay them a little more than those passengers who rode with the cargo. "Because," she explained, "I hate that wind and I hate getting so dusty like those who are used to it."

They reached a security checkpoint and stopped at the slab of spiked metal lying across the road. A police officer with an AK–47 rose from his chair under a solitary acacia tree. Yawning, he took their identification cards and, from Mugo, the current driver, a folded 100-shilling note. After he'd recorded their personal information, he returned all three cards to Mugo, and went to check the back of the lorry.

Mugo read the woman's name out loud "Alice. Akoth. Otieno. You are a Luo. I told my brother that you looked like a Luo."

"And you were right," she answered, taking her card. "So?"

Karanja, darker and smoother than Mugo, said. "You know, we are also Luos."

Alice laughed, and ignored Mugo's unnecessary correction: "Of course we are not Luos, we are Kikuyus." When Mugo joined in the laughter, everyone shook hands, including the two brothers with each other, another joke for Karanja.

The policeman returned and he told them they had to wait for other vehicles to reach the checkpoint. Then they could proceed north as a convoy, a less vulnerable target to bandit attacks. Karanja made a show of rolling his eyes, but Alice gave her attention to the officer's warning. "Once you pass this police station," the officer said, pointing at the flag flying behind him, "you won't even feel like you are in Kenya anymore."

They were nowhere. Besides the policeman at the roadside under the acacia, and a second officer in the doorway of the cement block police station, there were no visible people. The jumble of wood and metal behind the station might have been a deserted settlement, or just random debris. The dots beyond might have been goats or camels, and their herders, or they might have been rocks or depressions in the earth.

The passengers disembarked from the cab of the lorry, the brothers to change drivers, Alice to "have some little look around."

She glanced at the passengers riding in back. The men, by their faces, looked like Somalis; they lounged on the sacks of grain like they were in their own sitting room, and chewed their leaves of *khat.* The women wore the black *bui-bui* and veil and sat huddled so closely that they looked like a single giant spider. Alice found herself staring too long and forced a smile; the women stared back at her with eight icy eyes. Instantly, Alice regretted the unintentional mockery of pulling up the hood of her black tracksuit, but decided taking it down again would be worse.

When she reached the corner of the police station, Alice stopped to look back at the road. Mugo was talking to the policeman and Karanja was joking with the men in the back of the lorry, sharing their *khat.*

When the policeman noticed her, he cut short his conversation with Mugo, snapped his fingers at his partner, and walked towards her with long strides. He was a large, well-fed man, and he wore a clean uniform; his trouser cuffs showed little dust, and his shiny black shoes showed none. Karanja came strolling after him.

The policeman said to Alice, "Excuse me, madam, where are you going?"

She shrugged, and put one hand on the wall of the station. "I don't know, just around!"

He frowned. "The toilets, they are just over there." He pointed at a pair of cement latrines.

"Okay, thank you."

The policeman started to say something else, but he had nothing; he walked away, and Karanja approached. "If you're hunting a place to buy a magazine," he waved at the jumble of scraps, "you won't find it here, not *Parents,* not even *Hot Desires."*

"I'm just looking around."

"Okay, welcome, but you know that guy, this is his home area. So he is somehow sensitive, like maybe you will think the people are so poor." His voice took on a whine of complaint.

"Okay."

"But still, we can just walk a bit."

He prodded her with his eyes toward what started to suggest more than a pile of junk. A scrap village, mainly raw branches lashed together with plastic and daubed with mud and dung, lay at the bottom of a small escarpment, with only the roofs—also usually sticks and mud, but sometimes a sheet of plywood or tin—visible from the road. The children, naked, stared at them. The women, wrapped from head to toe in tattered *khangas,* looking like walking balls of rags, grabbed their children and ducked inside their houses.

Karanja started humming a pop song, louder and louder, until Alice looked at him with a confused frown. Then he caught her by the arm. She pulled away.

He smiled, "Where are you going? Don't be nervous." He put himself in the way of her path back to the road.

"I'm not." She made her voice loud and cheerful, and said it again. "I'm not nervous, I just thought we should go back to the vehicle."

"Maybe. If you want to talk to my brother. But we aren't leaving until we are many. It's good for people to stay together. At least you have time to use the toilet. Also, I have a question. You know what people say about Luos?"

"No, not really."

"Yes you do! They say you people really like sex. All the time. Even the women."

"I don't know."

"Oh yes, it's true. But is that only the people living around Lake Victoria? What about a girl from Nairobi like you?" He took a step toward her, reached for her arm again.

"I don't—stay there."

"Just come and we can find out." He unfastened his trousers.

"Mama, you know, at the next holiday I want to take a trip." In the kitchen, chopping up *sukuma* on the old table, the sound of Papa's car driving away, the quiver in her own voice.

"Yes, of course! Grandmother, Mary, Esther, all of your aunties, of course, we will go." The laundry girl outside crying a hymn, Alice's mother's subtle perfume.

"No Mama, I don't want to go on that trip to Nyanza, I want to go on my own trip. To Marsabit. I have a friend." The juice of the *sukuma* staining the edge of her T-shirt green, the television's bright song for margarine.

"What? What? She doesn't want to see her old grandmother and her aunties? She wants to go to—go to where? Isiolo and those sides? Your friend is a Somali, isn't it? No. You cannot go." The slap of her mother's broad palm on the table, smoke from the roadside corn roaster blowing in through the window.

"I have money."

How much? Not enough to get there except with Mugo and Karanja. What about sitting in the back? The men and the women in the back of the lorry watched her walk out from behind the police station, watched her like they knew what had just happened. Like they'd known even before it happened, when they saw her walking by herself. Like they didn't believe she hadn't known it, too.

The well-fed policeman didn't look at her.

Another vehicle drove around hers, and then another. They were waiting, Mugo waving for her to hurry. She didn't hurry, she just walked, and got into the cab between the two brothers, making her body even smaller so as not to touch either one of theirs. She held her head down, not wanting to see her reflection, the deep, round eyes that no man who'd touched her before hadn't first praised as beautiful, the cheekbones that made one man think of "God, shaping your face from the smoothest, richest clay."

Mugo said, "See what you've done? We're going to be at the back. Didn't you hear me beating the horn?"

"Easy brother, easy with the lady. Remember what I've told you about a lady, never rush a lady." Karanja, now driving, pushed the lorry to catch up with the convoy.

Mugo grunted.

"You know, a lady, she will come in her own time."

"How about you just take care of the driving. I want to sleep, okay?"

"That's true. You might not get much sleep tonight, right? Even you, lady," he nudged her with his elbow, "get some sleep, okay?" Karanja started singing to himself in Kikuyu.

She didn't sleep. She sat in the darkness of her eyes closed, her hood pulled down low over her face. Likewise in the mass of noise, of the lorry's rumbling and coughing engine and creaking body, the rushing wind, Mugo's snoring, even Karanja's singing and her breathing, she heard no distinct sounds but those in her head.

She thought about Stephen, her friend in Marsabit, a white, an American, a priest. Okay, not really a priest, but what did he call it while he learned to be a priest, a seminarian? So, for now, he could even have a girlfriend. For her "for now" was over now. For him?

A scream woke her up a few hours later.

"Easy, lady, easy, I have everything under control."

She screamed again.

They were slowing for another police check. Karanja slammed the brakes and Mugo twisted his whole body to scowl at her. "What is your problem woman? What is your problem? You don't have to act like a little girl."

"Take me home, where are we going you—" Alice cursed him in Luo.

Mugo answered, "We're going to Marsabit. We don't know where your home is. You can go with us to Marsabit, or you can leave us anytime. You can just go."

Karanja said, "No listen, you are home. You are with us, lady."

"Stop saying that!"

"Saying what, lady?"

The police officer, a woman, took their registration, asked them to sign her book, and then let them drive on. The road climbed a steep grade, winding towards the peak of a green hill.

Small trees and scrub grew on the lower slopes and the road brought them into higher zones of tall trees carrying vines and pale green moss, with smaller plants growing along streams and around pools, or from the sides of a sunny cliff. The trees broke up the desert wind; moist air drifted into the cab, carrying a slight chill.

Alice took off her hood and shivered. She heard birds chirping, an axe or machete chopping up a tree. The brothers rolled up their windows.

Karanja said, "Why are you going to Marsabit?"

"To see a friend."

"A friend? I think he must be a boyfriend."

She shrugged.

"Perhaps he hasn't arrived and you will have to wait with us? Perhaps you will even have to wait until tomorrow."

They reached Marsabit. Alice walked through town, asked for, and found the Marsabit Hotel. She waited outside in the shade of the awning, leaning against the wall.

The town sat in the sun, on top of the hill, and the street's brightness hurt her eyes. Camels, goats, donkeys, cattle, and people passed by her, but no vehicles. All the people were somehow funny, either Muslims, or very poor wearing rags, or very traditional wearing maybe some skins and beads. Alice didn't like Marsabit. She did not like waiting, standing alone and wearing trousers. In her bag, she had a long skirt and a *khanga,* but she just stood and waited in the shade of the awning.

"Excuse me, Alice Otieno?" A woman of about her age, wearing a skirt and blouse said, "Excuse me, are you Alice Otieno?" She was speaking English. "Your friend has called on the telephone."

The woman led Alice through a lobby, empty, but not spacious, with murals, red and brown and reddish-brown, of the same Rendille and Galla tribes people that she'd just seen outside, to an office where the woman pointed at the phone. Alice picked up the receiver, but didn't say anything.

"Hello? Alice, how are you? It's Stephen."

His voice sounded funny, like someone speaking through his nose. He always sounded like that, but usually she forgot.

Mugo and Karanja walked into the lobby, but they didn't see her.

Alice spoke in a sharp whisper, "When are you coming? I thought you would be here."

"Soon, soon."

"Soon?"

"Tomorrow. I'm sorry. I've already spoken to Nancy. You can stay there tonight and I'll pay tomorrow."

Mugo and Karanja were walking around the lobby; their footsteps, and even their breathing, echoed in the empty room. Keys for the rooms were hanging on the wall of the office. Twelve rooms, none of them taken. Karanja called out, "Nancy, we have come."

"One minute." She stood with her arms crossed, waiting for Alice to finish talking.

Alice pressed herself into the corner to hide from the brothers. She said to Stephen, "You want me to stay here? No."

"The rooms aren't so bad. Really, it's the nicest place in town. I stay there."

"But the people, I don't like them." Nancy coughed and walked out of the office.

"You couldn't mean Nancy."

She waited to answer and the line went dead. "Hello? Stephen? Hello?"

She held the phone and listened to the people in the lobby. Karanja apologized to Nancy for his brother's bad temper. "You know, he doesn't know how to behave around a nice lady. I am doing my best to teach, but no, he just can't learn." Alice hung up the phone as quietly as she could.

"Just give us a room," Mugo said.

"Two beds," Karanja said, "one for my brother and—"

"Yes, yes—"

"One for you and me."

The phone rang. Alice expected Nancy to come back and answer. When it had rung three or four times, Nancy returned to the office, but went to the wall with the keys. She said, "If it's for you, you can just answer."

The phone rang again, and Alice answered. "Hello?" Listening for the men's reaction to her voice, she didn't hear the person on the line. "Stephen?"

The line went dead again. Alice put the phone down and slumped against the wall.

"Sorry," Nancy said, "this place is just like that. You're from Nairobi? So am I. Imagine, I have to live here for this job. But at least you talked to Stephen? He said to give you a room."

Alice answered in a whisper, "I don't want to stay here."

"Okay? But it seems like you do not have a choice. Oh, sorry, but he isn't coming until tomorrow, isn't it?" She scratched the back of her neck.

"But—" she gestured toward the men outside.

Mugo leaned over the front desk to peer into the office. He saw Alice, but showed no reaction.

Nancy shrugged. Her left hand was shaking, jingling the charms on her bracelet. She tore a key off the wall and returned to the brothers.

Alice listened to Karanja's laughter, then their footsteps on the creaky wooden stairs, Nancy's light and quick, Mugo's heavy and sullen, and finally Karanja's, shuffling. She heard the soft-metal key wiggling in the simple lock, a lock like the one used for interior doors in her parents' house in Nairobi. Nancy was putting the brothers in room eight.

When Nancy returned, Alice was still studying the wall of keys. "It's your choice," Nancy said. "If you want a nice view, I think you should go for seven, nine, ten, or eleven. Maybe eleven is the best. Me, when I stay here, I stay in eleven."

"You're not staying?" She reached out, as if to cling onto Nancy by her hand, or the sleeve of her blouse, but Nancy said, "No," and Alice crossed her arms over her chest.

Nancy said, "I can leave by seven. That is when the night clerk comes."

"Just give me room nine."

"Room nine? Okay." She pointed at the wall of keys. "Just take it, that one."

Alice frowned. "I'm not the one who works here."

"What? Okay fine, no problem." Nancy yanked the key off its hook. "So now we can go?" She led Alice through the lobby and up the stairs to her room. Nancy opened the door and gave Alice the key. "Room nine." She went back downstairs.

Alice entered her room, and closed the door, but didn't lock it. She sat in a chair next to the window. She could watch the people outside without them watching her and she could see the thick misty forest beyond the town. Her room faced west, away from the dry valley and away, she thought, from Stephen's mission. She listened to the brothers talking, and couldn't tell them apart. They both spoke softly, with neither levity nor sharpness.

The sun set. The mosques made their call to prayer. Dogs barked. The wind threw dust and grit against the window and it rattled the panes.

Someone knocked on her door, three times, hard. "Come in." The door opened. It was Mugo. He stood in the doorway and stared at her. He closed the door, and walked across the room to stand over her, still staring.

Slouched in her chair, she resisted conflicting urges both to straighten and to curl into a ball; she spoke without lifting her head. "Say."

"You are sitting here in the dark, alone?" His voice was harsh and accusing.

"Waiting." She made her voice slow, making each syllable a word.

"Waiting for who? For Karanja, isn't it, you—" He seemed to say all his words at once.

She stared at the floor—not at his shoes, so worn as to show the bony shape of his feet inside—but at the floor, crumbling cement, still flecked with red paint in some places. "For you."

He seized her arm. "Okay, for me."

She willed herself not to pull away, but said, "Let go. Sit down on the bed."

He did. He continued staring at her. A minute passed. Mugo lit a cigarette. Alice scratched the wood of her chair with the nails of her first two fingers. They sat in the darkness and listened to each other's breathing.

Alice could see Mugo's face when he drew on his cigarette. She knew he could see hers when she nodded her head toward the window.

"So," she said at last, "do you love your brother?"

He rubbed his nose. "He's my brother."

"He's your brother so you love him or hate him, which is it?"

He coughed. "I cannot lie."

"You hate him."

"I hate him."

"So why don't you kill him?"

Again, they sat in the dark for a few minutes. Mugo crushed his cigarette on the cement floor and lit another one. Alice scratched the chair with her thumbs.

They listened to the room next door, to Karanja singing; he sang, with obscene raspiness, Christian songs from the Revivals. He was pacing the room, moving the few pieces of light furniture. Downstairs, they heard Nancy saying goodbye to the night guard. Alice felt Mugo's eye on her. She looked at the window and, when the breeze stirred the curtains, caught glimpses of outside: the black squares of low buildings, a stunted tree, someone else's window glowing in the light of a candle or lamp, and the sky, dark but not black.

Mugo stood and let himself out of the room. Alice closed the window. She pulled the bed away from the wall. It was heavy, and stuck on the uneven floor. She got behind the bed and braced her feet against the wall; she squatted and, in rising, pushed the bed until she'd jammed it against the door. Without even removing her shoes, she got into the bed, and pulled the covers over her head. Thinking about morning and her own bed in her parents' house—but listening to voices of men, angry, desperate, or angrily, desperately amused, from the room next-door or from the street below—Alice passed into sleep. She slept until morning, thrashing in her sleep when someone cried out and when someone banged on her door, but not once truly waking up.

She rose late. The sun had come up and, shining through the window curtains, had begun to heat the little room. From next door she heard a moan. She had slept in her clothes and had never unpacked her small bag; she was ready to go.

Stephen, a tall, soft-bodied young man with dark stubble, arrived in his Land Cruiser, his eyes wild with contrition, anticipation, and hurry. He almost jumped when he saw her, sitting on the steps outside the hotel.

"I got here as quickly as I could," he said.

"Good. I am happy to see you." They shook hands and he lightly kissed her, without noticing when she flinched.

"I hope you had a good night. The rooms here, they aren't bad really. But they're really—well, just beautiful at the lodge. Have you checked out? Is that everything?"

"I want to go back to Nairobi."

"What?"

"I hate this place."

"You—well, of course this place, but when you see—I thought we had planned—okay, if you can't stand to leave Nairobi, I could've just driven down and saved us both a lot of trouble, but if that's what you want, let's go now."

Stephen drove fast. Alice lay back in her seat with her hood up and her eyes closed, but she didn't sleep. When Stephen put his hand lightly on her knee, she didn't speak, but only slid it up to her crotch, pressing it against her. They had to slow down for a police checkpoint; Alice stiffened and huddled against the seat as Stephen drew his hand away. He had to downshift as they dodged the barrier, but the officer didn't make him stop.

When the sun had risen high enough that it wasn't shining directly across Alice and into Stephen's face; he took off his sunglasses. "Beautiful day for a drive, isn't it?"

Alice bobbed her head, but stayed well inside her hood.

"I bet the air feels good, too." Stephen cracked open his window and put his fingers out to feel the air. "It does, it does feel good." He darted a glance at her. Only the smooth triangle of her chin stuck out beyond the edge of her hood. "It feels good, I said, really good."

She emerged from the hood enough to see him with one eye. "Good? How does it feel good?"

He squinted at her, waiting for her to say something else. She nodded at the road ahead of them, indicating the dry stream bed where the occasional downpour had worn a marked dip in the road. "I know," he said, slowing down, and approaching the crossing at a slight angle, "I saw it a mile back."

She dropped her head against the back of the seat, showing her full profile.

"It just feels good," he said. "You asked me how the air feels good. And I'm saying it just feels good." He put his sunglasses back on.

The inside of Stephen's vehicle felt smaller than it did in Nairobi. Driving there, she sometimes felt embarrassed to see people walking and thought that she should offer a lift to someone, maybe to an old lady, wearing her headscarf in the Luo fashion and carrying a tall bucket on her head, or maybe to some school children, pushing and playing too close to the road. Maybe to some girls her own age who didn't have boyfriends, walking in pairs. But now she liked having room, with no other bodies pressing hers. She tried stretching out one leg, then the other, and then pulled them back tightly against her. And no one could sit in the back. Besides Stephen's black suitcase, it was filled with loose hunks of firewood and dirty tools. They reached another police checkpoint, where a couple of vehicles sat waiting. Stephen started to swerve around them, but the police officer blew his whistle and pointed to the space at the back of the line. It was the first checkpoint Alice had encountered with the brothers where she had gotten out to have a little look around.

The healthy, tidy policeman stood up from his post under the acacia tree, and crossed the road behind them. Stephen unrolled his window all the way as the man, idly swinging his long, thin baton, came around to his side. Stephen greeted the policeman and asked why they had to stop.

"Bandits. The ones we call the *Mashifta.*" He held up his hand pointing his fingers to make the shape of a gun.

"Has there been some trouble?"

"What?" The policeman took an exaggerated step backwards. "No, no trouble."

"With the *Mashifta.* That's why we're stopping."

The police glanced up the road for any more approaching vehicles. "Okay," he said, "I cannot lie, there has been a killing."

"A killing," Stephen repeated to Alice. Then to the policeman, "That sounds like trouble."

"Not there," the policeman said, waving ahead of them, "not on the road." He leaned over, braced his elbows on the vehicle and put his head halfway inside, trying to look at Alice, who dodged his gaze. Stephen shrugged in apology. The policeman shook his head. "I think I saw her yesterday. But okay, a guy was killed in Marsabit."

"We're just coming from Marsabit." Stephen put his hand on Alice's shoulder. Making no reaction, she remained a featureless form, legs curled up on the seat with her.

"Yes, that is why we are stopping all vehicles coming from Marsabit." The policeman stayed there another moment, watching Alice, then stepped away, noticing with a frown the dust his uniform had picked up from the side of Stephen's Land Cruiser.

He walked away, brushing himself off, and crossed to his own side of the road. Alice watched him, but when he turned on his heel, she dropped her head– and found Stephen also trying to catch her eye. Stephen put his hand out, right below her face. Black hair covered his hand, from just behind his knuckles to where his rolled-up sleeve covered his arm. On his face, hair made him seem manly, but on his hand, it made him seem like an animal that lives in small places.

She had told him this before, and made him laugh. His hands had tried to crawl up her sleeves and then she'd laughed so much that she cried.

He wanted her to say it again, so she said it: "Your hands are like a monkey's, get them away from me." She meant to say it like a joke, but she said it with cruelty.

Still, he laughed like she had made a joke and reached into her hood, darting his fingers under her chin, around her neck. "Monkey, monkey, monkey!"

They were caught by surprise when the policeman again appeared at Stephen's window, clearing his throat. "I have spoken to my colleagues in Marsabit," he said.

Stephen tried to remove his hand from Alice's neck, but she stayed with him, pinning his fingers between her chin and her collar bone so that he had to pull hard to free them. In reaction, Alice tossed her body against the door.

The policeman averted his gaze and addressed the steering column. "I have spoken to my colleagues in Marsabit and they want me to ask. Okay, they want me to be asking everyone. You people know something about the killing? Because you are coming from Marsabit?"

Stephen put his hands on the steering wheel. "We're coming from Marsabit, but we don't know anything. Alice?" He glanced at her; she made no gesture. *"Hakuna."* He said to the policeman in Swahili, "We don't know. Nothing." He shrugged, trying to push out more words, "Nothing. Okay?"

Alice listened, studying the policeman's reaction. "It was at the hotel," he said, locking his gaze with Alice's.

Stephen switched back to English. "The Marsabit Hotel? That's where she stayed."

"It was a guest at the hotel," the policeman said, raising his voice and rapping his baton against the side of the vehicle. "A Mr. Gitonga. One of the two brothers who carry relief food to the North." He stared so intently at Alice that Stephen had to look at her, too. "I even have his first name. Do you want to know it?"

Alice's eyes flickered.

"Karanja."

Alice released her breath at once and took another one.

"His throat. It was cut. Like he was a goat."

Stephen reached for Alice's arm. "In the hotel where she was staying?"

"Yes. So I am asking if you know anything about it."

"No," Stephen answered.

The policeman stepped away from the window. "Thank you, sir. *Sawa sawa."* He walked behind the Land Cruiser, but he didn't go back to his side of the road, instead stepped up to Alice's window. "And you, just to confirm, you don't know anything about it?"

"No."

He put his hand on her face to turn it toward his. He spoke to her in Swahili, "Karanja was very black and he laughed so much."

"Yes."

"His brother is saying there was a small Luo girl traveling with them." He held her chin firmly.

Stephen opened his door, and got out, "Hey what are you doing?"

The policeman ignored him. "He said her name was Alice Akoth Otieno."

She closed her eyes.

"But I think your name is something else. You're a pretty little Luo girl, but I think your name is something else."

Stephen slammed his door.

"I don't even need to check your identification. I don't even need to tell them I saw someone like you. Isn't it?" He let go of her and she dropped her face into her hands.

Stephen pushed himself in front of the policeman. "What are you doing?"

The policeman pointed down the road with his baton. "You can go."

Stephen hesitated, and then got back into his Land Cruiser. The policeman signaled to his partner to remove the barrier.

Stephen drove quickly, soon overtaking the sluggish lorries.

Alice rode with her forehead resting against the side window, with only the fabric of her hood to cushion her against every bump and jolt of the rough road. She watched the wavering line that followed them, the faint shadow cast on the road by the dry plants that grew alongside it. Each plant cast its own shadow, three or four times longer than the plant's height; sometime she thought she could distinguish the shadow of a particular plant, the frayed end of a single stunted strand of grass. Otherwise, she saw only a wavering line, rising and falling with the rise and fall of the road, with the height of the plants, even it seemed, with the Land Cruiser's proximity to the edge of the road.

Inside the car, the trim on the door had started to come loose. Alice slid her fingers between the wood-grained plastic and the metal of the actual door. As the vehicle bounced on the road, she let her fingers stretch and break the threads of glue.

"Stephen." At the restaurant two months ago in Nairobi, fingering the silverware, the iridescent smudge of her sweat on the blade of the knife. "Stephen, I want to come to those sides, to see where you stay. Even during the holiday, if I can get a little money." The tingle in her throat and in her fingers when she says money, the cool air descending in ribbons from the ceiling fans, her mother's subtle perfume.

"I hope you're not even thinking of taking a bus. I'd have to arrange a flight for you. Let me look into it." A gap in the hard chatter of the white people all around them, a tone shift in the low hum of the waiters.

"Please, that would be too much." Reflected candlelight, the shine of water glasses, knives, eyes, the smell of half-burned onions, of fat that should come from a fruit or a flower.

"I don't know what Father Douglas would say... I mean all the excitement and commotion of someone coming in by plane." Their own waiter's voice, the wall of his white tuxedo jacket, the plate of fog and steam set before her, Stephen's hands.

"Never mind. If I come, it will be a surprise." Her voice, a clod of red clay, dropped in waters churned by an afternoon thunderstorm.

They reached Isiolo and the tarmac, slowed down for the speed bumps and local traffic. Vehicles of all sorts—from donkey carts to pick-ups to buses to heavy lorries—idled through town, making small adjustments to their cargo, dropping sacks of grain, taking passengers, unloading bright orange plastic bowls, loading an uncooperative goat.

Every activity involved noise. People shouted at both their animals and their machines, and at each other whether they argued or agreed. *Matatu* touts banged on the sides of their vehicles, calling out destinations. Drivers honked their horns and revved their engines.

Stephen rolled up his window. "Are you okay?" He asked.

"I'm okay." Her voice sounded tired and creaky.

"What did he say to you?" He nodded behind them. "At the checkpoint."

"Oh. He said I should stay there and marry him." She scratched harder at the glue inside the door.

Stephen braked for a young goat. "He said what?"

"He said you wouldn't care."

"Wouldn't care?" He pressed on his horn, adding a few drops to Isiolo's auditory deluge. The goat's herder, a nearly naked boy with a slender stick and an angry grimace, whipped the goat's back. "Well what did you say?" He hit his horn again.

"I didn't say anything. I wanted to go back to my parents."

"To your parents?" Stephen swerved around the goat, bumping its hindquarters with the back of the Land Cruiser. The goat jumped out of the road, and the boy whipped the vehicle.

"To my parents."

They passed through Isiolo and joined the road to Nairobi. The traffic thinned a little and increased its speed. Stephen had plenty of room to pass. When they had only open road in front of them again, Stephen said, "Sorry."

Alice retracted her hand from the door and held her breath, hoping for something.

He nodded without taking his eyes off the road. "I'm sorry. That sounds very frightening to be in a place where someone is being killed. You are probably feeling many things that I can't appreciate." He reached toward her and again, looked at her, or rather, at his own hand. After some hesitation, he set it on her shoulder.

"Yes." She didn't flinch, and she didn't lean into him.

His hand slid off by the force of its own weight. He said, "Did you know about it this morning when I picked you up?"

She leaned into her corner.

"You don't have to tell me, of course." Again he raised his hand, this time to settle on her thigh, but only by the fingers, and they slipped off almost immediately. "I mean, it's not like I expect just fun all the time. But if you don't talk to me, I feel useless."

They gained altitude by a succession of gentle hills. The peaks of Mt. Kenya sometimes appeared, many kilometers away. More often, Alice saw cows grazing on large fenced ranges of long grass.

Stephen said, "I know if I had been there, you wouldn't have had to stay there, but what would be different? You didn't know him, and he would still have gotten killed."

She shook her head, frowning to herself. Whatever she'd been hoping for, she wouldn't get it.

"What?" Stephen pressed. "He wouldn't? You think you would have saved his life?"

She shook her head harder, hard enough that it hurt, in a dull way, and had to hold her breath so as not to cry. "You are driving too fast!"

He braked, and she lurched forward. He held her by her shoulder. She opened the door and, as the vehicle stopped, jumped out. She landed on her feet, bending her knees to where her fingers touched the ground. She walked into the grass, grabbed a fence post, and threw her head forward to vomit.

She had a scant mouthful of dull yellow. Stephen parked the vehicle and turned on his hazard lights. He ran to her, stopping a foot behind her. "You know I'm sorry."

She turned around. "I did know him. They were the ones who gave me the lift."

"Oh." He reached for her face, but drew back without touching it.

"Now I want to pray."

"Yes, good." He planted his feet and reached for her hands.

"Not with you. Just alone."

He smiled, stunned. "I think this is one thing I can do." He shuffled closer to her, tried to grab her hands, but she pulled them away and lifted her knee into his crotch. He shrank away.

"I'm sorry. I want to pray alone."

With a deep breath, he took a decisive step towards his vehicle. "I–"

She crossed the road and walked along the shoulder and let herself cry a little. When she heard Stephen's vehicle creeping up behind her, she turned and glared at him. He stopped and turned off the car. When she'd walked far enough that she could look back and not see anyone inside the vehicle, she heaved a loud, low moan and leaned her head against a fence post. She whispered, "Please, please God–"

And she asked for nothing.

She cried some more, but stopped when she heard another vehicle approaching. The vehicle passed without stopping, but she didn't cry any more. She stood with her head pressed against the fence post and listened to the wind.

Finally, she raised her head and said, "Amen." She wiped her face, and started to walk back to the vehicle.

When she crossed the road, Stephen started the engine. She waved for him to come.

When Stephen reached her, he leaned over to open the door. "Do you feel better?"

"Yes, I do. I'm glad that man is dead. It is the punishment of God for him to die and go to hell and burn and burn."

Stephen gave his full attention to the road.

They drove through Nanyuki, then Nyeri, then Thika, each town seeming successively more like a place where people should want to live, with less wind and more green, less noise, and more cash. Outside Thika, they visited the shop outside the Del Monte farm and bought pineapple juice. Alice drank a one quart packet by herself, and Stephen bought another one for her to take to her mother.

When they returned to the vehicle and started driving again, she said "Thank you." Then she took a deep breath and said, "If I become pregnant, you cannot be a priest."

Stephen looked at her while keeping one eye on traffic. They rode on a divided highway, two lanes in each direction, and packed with Peugeots, *matatus*, and mini-buses, all driving their fastest, eager for the start of rush hour.

"You could not be a priest, isn't it?"

"Alice, there's nothing—" He stopped, loosened his grip on the steering wheel and softened the tone of his voice. "Right?"

"Can I put on the radio?" She did. Capital FM was playing American rock songs from the early 60s.

Stephen lowered the volume.

"You don't love old school?"

"Is there a way you could be pregnant?"

She slumped in her seat. "I was only curious to know what could happen."

"How could I make you pregnant?"

She mimicked his voice, crudely exaggerating its nasal quality. "How could I make you pregnant?" She shrugged. "In the usual way. That a man can make a girl pregnant."

He spoke through his teeth (and inadvertently, his nose), "But we've never done that and we're not going to do that."

"And why not?" She held out her palm to offer her own explanation. "Because you want to be a priest instead."

He released his breath. "Yes, that's right."

"It's just a little fun for you." She put her hands up. "Like the young people used to do in the villages. And maybe you are also afraid of AIDS? You should be, after all I am a dirty African."

"Alice, if—" Approaching a roundabout, he had to decelerate.

"I should get the—ni ni— the leather . . . " She daintily placed her hands over her crotch. "I don't know, *kama* leather panties? But it's not my tribe—"

"Alice! What are you trying to say?" He glared at her.

She stared back at him, suddenly no frivolity in her eyes.

"Alice, why did you say that about being glad that man was dead?"

"Because he was bad." She folded her arms as she spoke, and let her voice drop. Stephen started to respond, but was distracted by traffic. He gassed the Land Cruiser into the roundabout and joined the flow of traffic into the City Centre. He had to switch lanes frequently just to keep moving.

Alice said nothing until they'd passed through the City Centre and she had to tell him the way to her parent's house in Lang'ata. "Left. Right—no, straight. Okay, here." She continued to pick at the glue under the loose trim on the door.

Stephen looked at her, "What are you doing?"

"Sorry," she said, and pulled her hand back. "Is this your vehicle?"

"No. It belongs to the mission."

"So why do you care? They can just fix it tomorrow."

Stephen forced a smile. "I do like this one," he said, pointing with his elbow at the radio, which was playing something with lots of jangly guitars and multiple voices.

Alice's parents lived in a two-storey stone house inside a walled compound shared with three other houses. A full-time *askari* sat in the guardhouse next to the gate. He came out to open the gate as they approached, but Alice waved for him to stay.

Stephen put the vehicle in park and reached for her hand.

"Sorry, I want to go." She shook free and opened her door to get out.

"What, you mean you want me to go? Can I meet your parents?"

"Why? They know I am a modern woman, and have some boyfriends, but that doesn't mean they want to see them." She slid out. "Goodbye."

She walked toward the gate without looking back. The *askari* opened the small door and saluted her. She said, "Thank you, and don't let that man come in."

She ducked through the small opening into the compound and closed the door behind her. Listening for the sounds of Stephen driving away, she waited between the wall of the compound and the house of one of her neighbours.

She heard the sounds of the compound, children playing, housegirls cooking; the TV. A mobile phone rang, and she lowered her shoulder to take off her backpack. But she'd left it in Stephen's Land Cruiser. She heard someone inside the house answer his phone and begin laughing. Outside she heard a vehicle, maybe Stephen's maybe another passing by. She walked toward her house.

Her father greeted her from inside. "Alee-alee, you've come back. Mummy said you were going away to Lake Naivasha."

She ran toward him, shaking her empty hands in the air, and crying. "Daddy! Daddy! They stole my purse, they stole my phone! They stole everything from me!" Wrapping her arms around herself, she fell into the cool washed darkness of her parents' house.

BRIAN COOPER and his wife Joan lived in Nakuru from 2000-2002 and worked as Peace Corps volunteers. He and his family, including a two-year-old son, now live in Washington, D.C. Although he makes his living as a writer, he pays for it by working as a consultant for local NGOs.

Illustration: JNK

Reflection

Steve Partington

The sky can not contain itself.
The low sun's heartbeat pulses, once,
and ruptures through the firmament.
A cluster round the one bus home,
but someone - look - is moving from the crowd
and looking upwards for an instant.
If you could, you'd see her heart
does not contain itself.

STEPHEN PARTINGTON is a poet. He has just realised a book of Kenyan poetry titled 'SMS and Face to Face.' *He is a school teacher and makes bad tasting fruit wines.*

Women To Women Marriage

BY WAIRIMU NGARUIYA NJAMBI AND WILLIAM E. O'BRIEN

EDITOR'S NOTE:

Studies of women who marry women in Africa are relatively few in number and generally dated, with few recent contributors. Based on interviews in central Kenya with Gikuyu women involved in "woman-woman marriages," this study critiques the extant literature, focusing on two key issues. Most authors have perceived narrow conditions and functionalist purposes for explaining woman-woman marriages. Our interviewees typically express complex reasons for marrying women, suggesting that woman-woman marriage is a flexible option within which women may pursue a range of social, economic, political, and personal interests. We also critique the concept of "female husband," suggesting that while the "husband" role can be male or female, the term is not so easily separated from the male connotations it implies in western contexts.

I ask myself, 'What is it that women who are married to men have that I don't have? Is it land? I have land. Is it children? I have children. I don't have a man, but I have a woman who cares for me. I belong to her and she belongs to me. And I tell you, I don't have to worry about a man telling me what to do.'

–Ciru, married to Nduta

Introduction

The practice of women marrying women is somewhat common in certain societies in West Africa, Southern Africa, East Africa, and the Sudan (O'Brien 1977). Yet, besides a total lack of discussion in the popular media, what is typically called woman-woman marriage is the subject of a very small body of academic literature.[2] Early scholarship is limited to the margins of several colonial-era ethnographies such as those of Evans-Pritchard, Herskovits, and Leakey. Leakey ([1938] 1977), for example, writing on Kenya's Gikuyu over six decades ago, devoted only two pages to woman-woman marriages out of a 1,400-page, three-volume ethnography.[3] More recent work remains equally marginal. Precious few writings address woman-woman marriage practices exclusively (e.g., Amadiume 1987; Burton 1979; Krige 1974; Oboler 1980); within others the subject remains little more than a footnote (e.g., Davis and Whitten 1987; Mackenzie 1990; Okonjo 1992). Since O'Brien's (1977) call for field research into woman-woman marriages more than two decades ago, there has been no study of Gikuyu woman-woman marriages, and few studies anywhere else. Our study attempts to revive this dormant discourse in relation to the Gikuyu.

Based on interviews with members of households containing woman-woman marriages, we attempt to provide images of this institution as practiced in central Kenya. Relying upon these women's voices, we present these Gikuyu woman-woman marriages in relation to major themes in the literature.[4] On the one hand, we critique what appear to us as narrow and deterministic accounts of the circumstances under which woman-woman marriages take place, as presented by some authors. Particularly challenging to such accounts are these Gikuyu women's expressed reasons for marrying, all of which go beyond the limited scenarios previously suggested by others. Leakey, for example, in his work on the Gikuyu, provides only a single circumstance in which such marriages can occur. Conversely, our attention is on the ambiguities and flexibility inherent in women's decision to marry women. In addition, we point to the strong emotional bonds to one another expressed by these women, shedding critical light on the omissions of purely functionalist perceptions of woman-woman marriage relationships. We also challenge the generalized conceptualizations of women who initiate such marriages as "female husbands." That term, used by Leakey and virtually all other authors on the topic, regardless of cultural context, imposes a "male" characterization upon a situation where none necessarily exists. Emphasizing a term such as "female husband" prompts sex-role presumptions that do not fit these Gikuyu women, who bristle at the implied male-identification regarding their roles.

This study is based on interviews with women in eight households in a small village in Murang'a District in central Kenya. This case study approach does not attempt to portray a generalized picture of woman-woman marriages, but relies upon the women's situated words to explain why they have married women, allowing them to present their own illuminating perspectives (see Smith 1987). A more comprehensive survey of woman-woman marriages would be welcome as a means of answering questions regarding the prevalence of the practice as well as general demographic characteristics of such households, but was beyond the small scope and limited resources of this project.[5]

The Gikuyu are the largest ethnic group in Kenya, generally occupying the administrative unit of Central Province. "Kikuyuland," as it is commonly called, is bounded by Nairobi to the south and Mt. Kirinyaga (Mt. Kenya) to the north, the Rift Valley and Nyandarua Range (Aberdares) to the west, and the Mbeere Plain to the east. The Province is subdivided into three administrative districts: Kiambu District on the northern outskirts of Kenya's capital Nairobi; Nyeri District in the environs of Mt. Kenya; and Murang'a District, considered the spiritual heartland of the Gikuyu, in the center. Typically referred to as the Central Highlands region, the topography of much of the province is characterized by a series of ridges and valleys. This landscape has influenced the relatively decentralized customary political organization and land tenure rules among the Gikuyu, though such customary arrangements now co-exist with national political and state land tenure regimes (Mackenzie 1990; Muriuki 1974).

Most of the woman-woman marriage households in the study engaged in peasant farming for a living, dividing their agricultural production between cash crops and subsistence crops—a pattern typical of this rural setting. However, some of the women were engaged in other occupations including shop ownership, market trading of small commodities, and, in one case, matatu (mini bus) driving. The initiators of these relationships, who are called *ahikania*, were all landowners, and the households all had modest living standards similar to most others in the locality. Though the interviews took place in a rural setting, two of the subjects were residents of Nairobi, while another lived and worked in a nearby small urban center.

The majority of the *ahikania* were middle-aged at the time of marriage, and two were in their early 30s. All of the *ahiki,* the women who accepted the marriage offer, were between the ages of 20 and 30 when they were married. Education patterns of the subjects shows that most of the initiators of the marriages were educated through the traditional Gikuyu educational system of *githomo gia ugikuyu:* one had a high school education, one primary school. Almost all of the women who accepted the marriage offer had at least a primary school education. The wide range of age and education suggests to us that woman-woman marriage continues to be a relevant potential life-option for Gikuyu women.

Kuhikania, the process of getting married, and *uhiki,* the marriage ceremony, takes place in the same manner for woman-woman marriages as with woman-man marriages. In fact, there is no separate term to differentiate a woman-woman marriage from a woman-man marriage. Even the term which describes the marriage initiator, muhikania, is used to describe a woman or a man.[6] As woman-woman marriages are not sanctioned by the various Christian churches in the region, *kuhikania* and *uhiki* continue to be performed through customary guidelines. The woman seeking a marriage partner, the *muhikania,* announces, either through a kiama (a customary civic organization) or through her own effort, her desire to find a marriage partner, or muhiki. Once the word is out, interested women go to visit, and once a suitable partner is found the muhikania's friends and family bring ruracio (gifts associated with uhiki) to those of the future wife and vice-versa. *Uhiki* takes place after this gift exchange and is performed with ceremonial blessings, termed *irathimo,* by elders of both families as the new wife moves into the muhikania's house.

Woman-Woman Marriages and Family Definitions

While woman-woman marriage may be familiar to most anthropologists, at least in passing, the topic remains relatively obscure to most people outside Africa. In family studies discourse, the topic is pushed to the extreme margins by an historical fixation on western nuclear families as a universal ideal. This normative presumption of nuclearity makes it very difficult for particular non-western family forms, such as the woman-woman marriages in this study, to be evaluated as anything but bizarre novelties. As Skolnick and Skolnick argue:

> The assumption of universality has usually defined what is normal and natural both for research and therapy and has subtly influenced our thinking to regard deviations from the nuclear family as sick or

perverse or immoral. (1989, 7)

Several features of western nuclear family ideology go to the root of its alleged functionality: the notions of monogamy and permanence, compulsory heterosexuality or opposite-sex relationships, and the perceived need for a father figure (Scanzoni et al. 1989). The Gikuyu woman-woman marriages we studied challenge this thinking on all counts. Not only are the adults involved in these marriages of the same sex, but also there may be more than two, and the form of the family is not necessarily permanent (as an ideal) once a union is made, but may change periodically. Furthermore, men are often absent from such relationships, though they may be involved in married relationships as spouses of women who initiate woman-woman marriages.

One example of such a relationship in our study is Kuhi's household. In this complex case, Kuhi (a woman) and Huta (a man) were originally married to each other. Later, they decided together that Huta would marry a second woman, Kara, creating a polygamous marriage.[7] Later still, Kuhi entered into a woman-woman marriage with a woman named Wamba. Wamba came to that family as Kuhi's marriage partner, and to assist in raising the children of that household. In this particular case, Wamba could have a sexual relationship with Huta (whom she also informally regarded as a husband), and was not restricted from having sexual relationships with other men outside their household. Later in her life, while still married to Kuhi, Wamba married a woman named Wambui. The result is that this single household contains four marriages: two woman-man marriages and two woman-woman marriages. Such complex relationships do not break any "rules," expectations, or ideals of woman-woman marriages, but are an accepted aspect of such relationships in Gikuyu contexts.

Krige (1974), a central figure in the woman-woman marriage literature, focuses her critique on the common presumption of opposite-sex partners as the basis for all marriage. She suggests that definitions of marriage, even when accounting for cross-cultural difference, tend to emphasize the male-female relationship as paramount. Some authors have attempted to incorporate woman-woman marriages into this universal presumption by suggesting, as does Riviere (1971), that the woman who initiates a marriage to a woman is playing the role of a man and can therefore be counted as male. Hence, Riviere (1971) rejects the notion that woman-woman marriages prove exceptions to the idea of opposite sex partners as the basis for marriage. Krige argues, however, that the woman she refers to as the "female husband" has no necessary male characterization: to count "female husbands" as "men" imposes a western assumption that "husband" is automatically associated with maleness (1974). As we suggest later, in these Gikuyu woman-woman marriages, the so-called "female husbands" do not identify their roles with maleness, providing support for Krige's position. Unlike Krige, however, we question even the use of the term "female husband."

The idea of same-sex relationships has spurred discussion of the sexuality of women in such marriages. A few texts imply that there may be sexual involvement in these marriages. Herskovits, for example, suggested that Dahomey woman-woman marriages sometimes involved sexual relations between the women (1937). Davis and Whitten go so far as to state that the main issue in explaining these relationships generally is over whether reasons for such partnerships are in fact "homoerotic" or strictly socio-economic (1987, 87). While sexuality was not directly discussed in our interviews, we can glean from the experience that this dichotomy makes little sense.[8]

In our Gikuyu locale, women in these relationships did not talk about sexual involvement with one another, although some did indicate sharing the same bed at night. However, in South Africa, Lovedu woman-woman marriages imply no sexual involvement according to Krige's (1974) suggestion, while in Kenya the Nandi eliminate even the possibility of a sexual relationship in such marriages according to Oboler (1976). At best, given the ambiguity in this Gikuyu context, one might borrow Obbo's assertion regarding the Kamba of Kenya that while there may be no clear indication of sexual relations among women in these marriages, we simply cannot dismiss the possibility (1976). We agree with Carrier that this possibility has been too quickly dismissed by some authors, and suggest that the subject deserves more careful investigation (1980). At the same time, we question the assumption that sexual contact is the only factor that determines whether one should be considered as "homosexual" (see Martin 1991).

On the other side of the dichotomy, to suggest that such relationships are based solely on socio-economic factors like access to land and other resources or lineage ignores the close emotional ties experienced by these women. Such functionalist views have strongly influenced historical, and still-held stereotypes of African marriages generally. African family relations, compared to the privileged, western nuclear family form, are often portrayed as relatively primitive since they are presumed to be based on practical considerations alone, such as access to resources—as opposed to having a significant emotional aspect (e.g., Albert 1971; Ainsworth 1967; Beeson 1990; Kilbride and Kilbride 1990; Le Vine 1970). The women interviewed help undermine such rigid notions, demonstrating clear emotional commitment to the women they marry. For example, one participant, Nduta, proclaims her feelings for her muka wakwa, or co-wife, Ciru:[9]

> No one dare to disturb my co-wife in any way, and especially knowing what I would do to them. No one dares point a finger at her. I tell her to proudly proclaim her belongingness to me, and I to her... What I hate most is when people come to gossip to me about my co-wife's whereabouts or whom they have seen her with. I don't care as long as she is here for me now and even after I am gone... Regardless of what she does, she is here because of me. Then why should I tell her what to do and what not to do. She is a free woman. And that is what I want her to be. So, when they come here to gossip, I tell them to leave her alone. She is mine and she is here on my property, not yours... She who sincerely loved me and I

loved back, let her stay mine. It is she who shall enshrine and take over this household when my time comes. (in interview)

In addition to expressing love (wendo) for Ciru, Nduta also alludes to the fact that Ciru is not restricted from having sexual encounters with men outside the woman-woman marriage relationship. Such liaisons, however, in no way undermine Ciru's reciprocated love and appreciation for Nduta. In a separate interview, Ciru, who has been married to Nduta for over 25 years, presents her deep feelings for her marriage partner:

> I know that some people do talk negatively about our marriage. Although honestly I have never caught anybody personally. But I ask myself, "What is it that women who are married to men have that I don't have? Is it land?" I have land. "Is it children? I have children. I don't have a man, but I have a woman who cares for me. I belong to her and she belongs to me. And I tell you, I don't have to worry about a man telling me what to do. Here, I make all the decisions for myself. Nduta likes women who are able to stand on their own, like herself. I do what I want and the same goes for Nduta. Now I'm so used to being independent, and I like that a lot. I married Nduta because I knew we could live together well. She is a very wonderful woman with a kind heart. (in interview)[10]

While functionalist interpretations perceive African family relationships in terms of the purposes they serve in the functioning of a society, our interviewees highlight the complex and intertwined aspects of relationships that one would expect to find in a discussion of any committed, caring marriage partnership, undermining prevailing notions of the non-emotional African "Other."

One other point in the ideology of the nuclear family that remains strong, even among scholars, but is challenged by the woman-woman marriage data, is the alleged need for a father figure to maintain "functionality" (Cheal 1991). Regardless of how diversified family lifestyles become, the presence of a father, whether played by the biological father or a father figure, is very much preferred and privileged over his absence. Long ago, Malinowski (1930) wrote that "in every society a child must have a socially recognized father to give the child a status in the community" (in Skolnick and Skolnick 1989, 8), and "illegitimacy" was considered to be a sign of social breakdown. Illegitimacy still is regarded as such by many, and there is a resurgence of this ideology in the family studies literature, as well as in popular family discourse (Scanzoni et al. 1989). The presence of a father is apparently not so important in many woman-woman marriages. During interviews, some women downplayed the importance of men in their households. Of the eight households in our study, six did not include permanent relationships with male partners.

Among these six households, it seemed clear based on our interviews that male involvement with children, beyond procreation, was restricted, even identities of designated male genitors could not be revealed. Ciru's comments support the view that males are viewed principally as friends and/or sex partners with no claim on children or property. What does she desire from men? Not much, apparently, except perhaps sex, and she can get that when she wants on her own terms:

> I have freedom to have sex with any man that I desire, for pleasure and for conceiving babies. And none of these men can ever settle here at our home or claim the children. They can't. They are not supposed to, and they know that very well. They come and go. (in interview)

Nduta's comments present the same lack of interest in having a man around as the ideal situation, expressing the independence provided by keeping men out of the household:

> We have no interest with a man who wants to stay in our home. We only want the arume a mahutini (men met in "the bush," a term for "male genitors")—meaning those who are met only for temporary needs. The meaning for this is for a woman to be independent enough so that she can make her own homestead shrine. Ciru sees also that I myself do not keep a man here. What for? To make me miserable? If I kept a man here who will then start asking me for money to buy alcohol, where would I find such money? No, I won't agree to live like that. It is better for one to look after oneself. It is better for one to look after oneself. (in interview, emphasis added)

Another case that downplays the importance of a male presence is that of Mbura, who had been married to a man, though he had died over 40 years ago. She was more recently married to a woman, Nimu, who subsequently left after a couple of years. Mbura was later married to a woman named Kabura on the last day of this fieldwork. Mbura responds as well to the question of the place of men in the woman-woman marriage household, adding that, to her, men are not trustworthy, though she still appreciates their temporary presence:

> Men, even the good friends, know that they are not welcome here. They are here just for a visit and to leave. Whatever they come here to do, they must leave. They cannot be trusted. That is not good. One is given respect and that's all. (in interview)

Despite the fact that the other two households in the study did have men present as partners of one of the ahikania, or marriage initiators, the need for a "father figure," an ideal of most heterosexual nuclear families is clearly not a universal reality for all family situations.

Beyond Common Explanations

An overview of the literature on woman-woman marriages in African societies might tempt a reader to make three intertwined cross-cultural generalizations. The first generalization regards access to children. Sudarkasa suggests that the basis for woman-woman marriage, as with African marriages generally, is the desire "to acquire rights over a woman's childbearing capacity" ([1986] 1989, 155). That is, the woman who initiates a marriage seeks access to children that she herself does not have. Rights over childbearing capacity are often linked to a second general theme: that children are desired by such women as a means of transferring property through inheritance. Krige suggests that woman-woman marriages contracted "as a last resort in raising a male heir to perpetuate the name and inherit the property of a man . . . seems to be its most common form" (1974, 29). Connected to both general circumstances is the third common assertion that women's "barrenness" is a fundamental factor prompting woman-woman marriages. In fact, one of the most widely held general assumptions, as Burton points out, is that woman-woman marriages must involve women who cannot themselves have children (1979). Evans-Pritchard's account of the Nuer suggests that almost exclusively it is "barren" women who make such marriages (1951). Langley, speaking of the Nandi, said that three types of women practiced woman-woman marriage: those childless married women who are too old for childbearing, childless widows, or a childless wife unable to conceive (1979; see also Talbot [1926] 1969, and Oboler 1980). Finally, Leakey asserts that among the Gikuyu it is childless widows beyond childbearing age who marry women in order to continue their husbands' lineages ([1938] 1977).

Leakey's description of Gikuyu woman-woman marriage practices encompasses all three generalizations ([1938] 1977). He claims that woman-woman marriages occur when a man leaves property to a widow beyond childbearing age, when no other male inheritor is present (such as a brother, half-brother, son). This widow is then expected to marry a woman who would bear her a son with the help of a designated genitor, who has no rights over the children or property.

By offering such a narrow scenario, Leakey denies flexibility and variation regarding the circumstances under which Gikuyu woman-woman marriages take place. Positing such limited "rules" for woman-woman marriages can be hazardous not only when applied across cultures, but also when applied within a single culture or locale, as our Gikuyu examples demonstrate. Gikuyu women in our relatively small study sample, living within a very proscribed spatial setting, expressed multiple and heterogeneous reasons for marrying women, defying the circumscribed explanations provided by Leakey, as well as others across the African continent. The women initiating these marriages pursued various objectives: companionship to appease loneliness, to be remembered after death, to have children to increase the vibrancy of the household, to fulfill social obligations in accordance with indigenous spiritual beliefs, and not least to avoid direct domination by male partners in a strongly patriarchal society, including men's control of both the women's behavior and household finances.

Our study does not deny the inability to bear children, inheritance, or lineage as partial explanations for some, or even many, Gikuyu woman-woman marriages. Expressed reasons for marrying women in our study did often include the desire for the muhikania to have a child to inherit property and/or to perpetuate her family lineage. However, such explanations are never offered as the exclusive reasons, nor are they offered by all women. Such women appear to have much greater latitude in choosing how and why they participate in woman-woman marriages. For example, situations that defy Leakey's account include those in which women who are already married to men (who are still alive) and have their own children then initiate uhiki, or marriage, with a woman, as in the above described case of Kuhi (married to Wamba).

Mbura's explanation for kuhikia, or marrying a woman superficially, resembles Leakey's account, since she expresses a desire for children that she herself cannot bear, as indicated in the following statement:

> I married Nimu because I could never have children myself. I did not even give birth to children who later died, nor did I experience any miscarriage. I remained the way I came out of my mother's womb. And now I'm getting old and there is no way I can sit, think and decide to have a baby because my time is over, unless Ngai's [God's] miracle happens to me [she laughs].[11] I think a lot about how my husband left me and how I can't have a baby. That is why a cry of a baby makes me happy and sad at the same time. One has to realize how special a child is. . . . So, when I think about all these things: how I can't have a child, how my husband died and left me nothing, and how I have this illness, I ask Ngai wenda mdathima na mutumia ungi [God, please bless me with another woman]. . . . "Won't you please send that woman here to my home?" Who knows, that woman might . . . give me a child. . . . Don't you see when I die I will be satisfied that I have left somebody in that home, who shall continue and revive that home? (in interview)

While she seems to portray a conventional account—marrying a woman to have a child to continue a lineage—Mbura's explanation is more complicated, indicating a desire for children beyond their role as inheritors of land and name. This is not to suggest, however, that lineage is not important in Mbura's decision to marry a woman. But the lineage she seeks to perpetuate is not necessarily her husband's, as Leakey and others would argue. Rather, Mbura is most interested in being remembered herself, as she indicates in the following statement:

> If I were to die even as we speak, that would be the end of it. I would be completely forgotten. No one would ever mention my name. That is simply because there would be no one to carry on my name. Since my husband died he is still remembered by many. But the key reason why he is still remembered is because of me.

> Someone may pass through here and demand to know "Whose home is that?" Then turn around and ask, "What about the next one?" One would reply, "Did you know so and so? This is his wife's home." Now do you see that the reason he is being remembered is because of me? Because I can be seen. But if I were to die, who will make me be remembered?. . . That is why the idea of marrying another woman came to me. Even now as we speak, if Ngai would bless me with another woman I would appreciate her.

Mbura continues, suggesting that companionship to appease loneliness is another strong motivation for marrying a woman:

> Let me tell you, I'm not the only one or the first one to marry a woman. And certainly, there are many others out there like me. I'm all alone just like that. No husband, no child. Just poor me. No one is here to keep me company or even to ask me "Did you sleep well?" except for occasional visits by some people like those you met here the other day. (in interview)

While Leakey's explanation may partly account for Mbura's case, Nduta's case clearly has emerged under a set of circumstances not fully considered by Leakey. First of all, Nduta's decision is the result of women's collaboration, namely between Nduta and her mother-in-law. Nduta married a man named Ndungu with whom she had three sons and a daughter. However, early in their marriage, her husband and their three sons were poisoned to death by some people in her husband's clan who wanted their land. After their deaths, Nduta's mother-in-law advised her to marry a woman as a way of protecting their family and land from male relatives who were trying to take her land, a sign of the tenuous hold that women have over land in Gikuyu society (Mackenzie 1990). Rather than being victimized by men within their family, Nduta's case shows how women collaborate to look out for one another to protect women's interests:

> When a woman is left alone, she should not be frightened, but must be brave. You must make yourself a queen, otherwise, be a coward and everything you stand for will be taken away from you by those who are hungry for what you have. . . . If you were a woman, and you had properties, you will be the first one to be stolen from by the men who thought they were more important than women. So, she must act. . . . I had a lot of properties and if it were not for *karamu* [the "pen"] that cheated me out of many of them, I would still have a lot.[12] I lost many of them because I was a woman and I had no sons. So my mother-in-law advised me to marry my own woman because all my people had been finished [i.e., killed] except for my daughter. And that is the piece of advice

> that I myself chose to follow. So I married her. When I married her [Ciru], she said "It is better to live with a woman. I'm tired of men." I responded, "Is that so?! I love that." We became good friends and partners and thereafter I gave ruracio to her family. (in interview)

Mackenzie, in discussing gender and land rights in Murang'a District, also describes woman-woman marriage as a strategy for Gikuyu women to prevent male relatives from stealing land from them (1990). She suggests that such women who marry other women appropriate custom as a source of legitimation, attempting to manipulate customary tenure rules to their advantage. Gikuyu land tenure is complex, given the coexistence of customary and state rules. Customary tenure in Murang'a District is based on the *mbari*, or sub-clan system in which local mbari elders control and allocate use rights to land. While during the 1950s and 1960s, colonial and independent governments implemented a system of individual land ownership; individual title did not fully supplant the mbari system. Both tenure systems are utilized based upon circumstance and interests, and are often manipulated to the advantage of men and detriment of women (Mackenzie 1990).

Compared to both Nduta's case and Mbura's, Mackenzie discusses a woman (referred to as "WG") who, "being without sons, chose to 'marry' a woman on her husband's death to prevent her brother-in-law from snatching their holding of 5.6 ha" (1990, 624). Mackenzie's account acknowledges these women as agents who are able to resist the strong patriarchal tendencies of their society. However, despite this important contribution, Mackenzie's brief account describes the circumstances of woman-woman marriages largely in terms provided by Leakey, limiting the option to widows who marry women to provide male inheritors. Thus, Mackenzie does not present other factors expressed by our interviewees, such as Mbura's emphasis on loneliness, desire for children, and a wish to live in a vibrant household.

While Nduta does not claim loneliness as a factor in her decision, her explanation also diverges somewhat from Mackenzie's, as well as Leakey's, scenario. Nduta's case is similar to Mackenzie's and Leakey's images of woman-woman marriage presented by those authors in that she had been married to a man who died and she had no sons (they died as well). However, upon marrying a woman after her husband's death, she asserts that she could have passed her land to her daughter, Ceke. Indeed, Ceke was given half of Nduta's land. While Nduta explained that she could have left all of her land to Ceke, she decided against doing so because she did not want to constrain her daughter with the social expectations that "staying at home" entails:

> ...I didn't want my daughter, Ceke, to stay here. I gave her freedom to fly and land wherever she wanted. That is the same freedom that brought me here. So why would I want to hold her here? Women like to go far. They don't like to be held down at their birth home. (in interview)

While the issue of inheritance is important in Nduta's case, related to her difficult struggle as a woman to maintain control over land resources, Nduta adds an important dimension drawn from Gikuyu mythology. This reason becomes clear when we hear Nduta, who is about 90 years old, speak of her dead sons who, she says, visit her in her sleep to thank her for marrying a woman:

> *Roho wa anake akwa makwrire* [the spirits of my dead sons] come to visit me to show appreciation for what I have done for them. One time they came and told me, "Thank you, mother for marrying Ciru for us. We are very grateful for bringing us dead people back home again. We are grateful indeed. For that we will always be watching over you. Nothing will ever harm you. We will take care of you." And then I would say, "If I didn't marry Ciru for them, who else would I have married her for?" Then the other day they came to tell me that I have got only five years to live; that I'm going to die soon [she laughs hard]. I said, "Is that so? Thanks a lot and may Ngai be praised!" That is fine for me. I need rest. (in interview)

Nduta's sons died long ago, very young, and had not been able to accomplish much in their lives. Some Gikuyu still believe that if someone dies suddenly, his or her life activities can be carried out as if they are still alive so that their opportunities would not be denied. Thus, when their mother married Ciru, she married her in the same way her sons would have married had they lived. In this sense, even though these sons were already dead, they feel quite at home because of Ciru's presence.

While Nduta's and Mbura's cases push the limits of Leakey's narrow inheritance-focused account of woman-woman marriage, the case of Nduta's daughter, Ceke, falls largely outside the scope of his scenario. Ceke's decision to marry a woman appears to be heavily influenced by the example set by her mother, who acted as a role model. However, unlike her mother she was at the same time still married and living with her husband, Ngigi, together with her daughter, Wahu, along with Wahu's six children. Having grown attached to Wahu's children, Ceke was insecure about whether Wahu would move away with them, leaving Ceke in a household without children. Ceke's marriage to a woman (Ngware) was thus viewed as a way Ceke could have more children. Ceke's intention was that her wife, Ngware, would have children with her husband, Ngigi. After having a child, however, Ngware left the household. Ceke and Wahu (her daughter) then reached an agreement that the children would be welcome to remain with Ceke even if Wahu decides to leave:

> Although my daughter was living with me at the time, and had all these children that you see here, I did not know what to expect from her. I did not know whether one day I will wake up and find her gone with all her children that I personally have raised and who actually call me maitu [mother], or whether she had already

> made up her mind that she will never leave. I made that move of wanting to find out when my wife [Ngware] left us. After that, my husband and I made an agreement with Wahu that she will live with us permanently and that if she will ever feel like leaving, her children that we have raised as our own will be welcome to remain with us where they are already guaranteed good care as well as land settlement when they grow up. In any case, this is her land too, you know. Since we have got no other children, everything we have belongs to her and her children and to my other son borne by my wife before she left. (in interview)

While this example supports the general claim that women marry women to acquire rights over childbearing capacity (Sudarkasa [1986] 1989), Ceke's decision is not linked to property inheritance, "barrenness," or widowhood: the three essential criteria for a Gikuyu woman-woman marriage, according to Leakey. Like Mbura, Ceke's strong desire for children was an important factor in her decision. The option of woman-woman marriage as a means to fulfill this desire was immediately apparent, given the influence and example of her mother, Nduta.

Finally, we have already alluded to the more overtly political motivations for marrying women expressed by some of our interviewees. The relative freedom from male control, which appears to be built into Gikuyu woman-woman marriages, is expressed most forcefully by Ciru and Nduta in previous quotations. Recall, for example, Nduta's conversation with her then wife-to-be, Ciru, who commented, "I'm tired of men," to which Nduta responded, "I love that." And Nduta's comment about why she doesn't live with a man, stating "What for? To make me miserable?" Recall also these women's comments regarding the sexual freedom they find in these relationships. And finally, recall the opening quote in which Ciru states that her woman-woman marriage allows her to avoid having "a man telling me what to do."

These examples demonstrate that flexibility, heterogeneity, and ambiguity appear as guiding principles in explaining such marriages, rather than being governed by somewhat rigid social rules, as the literature so often implies. However, contributions to the woman-woman marriage literature have continually, since the early-twentieth century, presented these relationships in functionalist terms. Cheal suggests that functionalist explanations continue to be perceived as having a "subterranean" influence on the study of families, describing such relationships in terms of "the ways in which they meet society's needs for the continuous replacement of its members" (1991, 4). Our alternative has been to present the institution of woman-woman marriage, at least in the Gikuyu context, as a flexible option available to women within which they may pursue any number of interests: political, social, economic, and personal.

What's in a Name? Rethinking the "Female Husband"

Another area of concern for us in the literature is the unquestioned use of the term "female husband," the general term used to describe women who initiate woman-woman marriages. Mackenzie (1990), in the above section, uses the term to describe such women in the Gikuyu context, as did Leakey ([1938] 1977) many decades earlier. Regarding the Nandi in Kenya, Oboler defines the term "female husband" as the woman who initiates the woman-woman marriage, as a woman "who pays bridewealth for, and thus marries (but does not have sexual intercourse with) another woman, and by doing so, becomes the social and legal father of her wife's children" (1980, 69). Evans-Pritchard (1951), Herskovits (1937), and Seligman and Seligman ([1932] 1965) all connect the female husband to these gendered characteristics. More recently, Oboler opens her paper with a quote from one of her female informants:

> No, I don't [carry things on my head]. That is a woman's duty and nothing to do with me. I became a man and I am a man and that is that. Why should I assume women's work anymore? (1980, 69)

Oboler argues that among the Nandi, male and female sex-roles are so strictly divided, especially regarding property management issues, that female husbands are literally defined by others and themselves as men in order to resolve the sex-role contradiction.

Not surprisingly, the major debate regarding the term "female husband" is over the male social traits often attributed to such women. Some have criticized the emphasis placed on gendered assumptions regarding sex-roles. For example, Krige suggests that one cannot assume that female husbands generally are taking on male roles (1974). Rather, one must carefully study sex roles in particular societies. For the Lovedu, Krige points out that numerous roles involve both males and females. Oyewumi, writing about the Yoruba, argues that local terms for both "husband" and "wife" are not gender-specific since both males and females can be husbands or wives (1994). As a result, as Burton (1979, 69) contends, the assumption that "husband" and "male" are automatically connected "confounds roles with people" since "husband" is a role that can be carried out by women as well as by men. Amadiume (1987), Burton (1979), Krige (1974), Oyewumi (1994), and Sudarkasa (1986) all suggest that in many societies, "masculinity" and "femininity" are not as clearly defined categories as they are in the West; presuming that "husband" automatically connotes "male" and that "wife" connotes "female" imposes western sex-role presumptions on other societies, ignoring local ambiguity regarding these roles (Sudarkasa [1986] 1989).

While our study supports views that women initiating marriages are not characterized as "male,". we question the continued use of the term "female husband" to describe such women. Burton (1979), Krige (1974), and Sudarkasa (1986), while criticizing those who confuse social roles with genders, implicitly suggest that the term "female husband" is adequate and that the only task is to transform its connotative meaning.

We argue that the term "female husband" should be reconsidered on the grounds that the male connotation of "husband" cannot be so easily disposed of; just as the term "wife" conjures an association with "female," so does "husband" with "male." Especially in contexts where gender roles are ambiguous, this implicit association will easily mislead readers to impose western presumptions upon woman-woman marriages. Thus, in our view, efforts to theoretically disassociate gender from such role-centered terms--like "husband" and "wife" in this instance-imposed originally by western researchers in colonial contexts, will in a practical way continue to impose a male/female dichotomy.

Some early colonial-era ethnographers might be interpreted as ambivalent and uncomfortable in the application of the term "female husband." Talbot ([1926] 1969) and Herskovits, for example, both write the concept as female "husband" (1937). That approach to the term "husband" (in quotes) seems to acknowledge that the term applies only imprecisely, even problematically, to women who initiate marriages to women, and is used only for lack of a more appropriate term. Others' use of the term, such as that of Evans-Pritchard (1945; 1951) and Leakey ([1938] 1977), shed the ambivalence of previous ethnographers, thereby legitimizing the term female husband as a concept for use by future researchers.

For most, however, the male connotation of the term was with little doubt intended in most early writings, given the apparently widespread presumption of male identification with the roles of such women. The functionalist perspectives of the times presumed a clear, gendered division of roles in family settings, making it difficult to apply any concept but "husband" to what appeared to them as the dominant role in these relationships. We acknowledge that there is nothing essential about the term "husband" that necessitates domination and control. But we also acknowledge, as does Oyewumi, that historically the term "husband" in most western contexts is normally associated with the role of "breadwinner," "decision-maker," and "head of household" (1994). We feel that the use of the term "female husband" serves to mask the relatively egalitarian woman-woman marriage relationships we encountered. Sudarkasa even acknowledges that, generally, there is no necessary subordination in woman-woman marriages, and that in many societies many aspects of decision-making and control over resources are parallel and complementary (1986).

The relative absence of domination, for example, is evident in the terms the women used to describe one another. The women interviewed never used the Gikuyu term for "husband" *(muthuri)* to describe their partners. Instead, they consistently referred to each other using the terms *mutumia wakwa* and *muka wakwa,* which when used by these women translates as "co-wife," or muiru wakwa, which translates as "partner in marriage," indicating the mutual respect and relative equality between them. While most women in our study who initiate the marriages tended to be women with social influence and/or relatively greater material wealth, within the marriages both women interpreted their relationship as semiotically and materially equal.

Furthermore, women in our study rejected any male-association with their position of initiator of the marriage. None of the women interviewed indicated that they aspired to be like "males." What follows is Nduta's perception of herself in relation to the seeming "maleness" of her marital position:

> I stayed at Nairobi for three weeks at my daughter's house, and when I came back they were joyfully shouting "She is back!" And because I brought them bread just like other men who work in the city do around here, the children started shouting, "Here comes our baba [father]! Our baba has arrived! Our baba has arrived!" (she laughs). I called them ndungana ici.[13] "Who told you that I am your baba?" (she laughs again). So I asked them, "Is that what you see me as? I'm not your baba. But thank you for appreciating that I can also bring bread home." Therefore, even when you see me quarrel with them sometimes, I don't store those quarrels in my heart. I brought this family together not to destroy it but to care for it. (in interview)

Nduta is being teased by her children, who called her baba, because of the bread she brought from the city, just as men with urban jobs do when they visit their rural homes, not because her position as initiator of the marriage automatically connotes male characteristics.

As a tentative alternative to "female husband" we have been using the phrase "marriage initiator" to describe women in that position. However, we acknowledge that such description can be problematic, especially if it is used to focus more attention on the "initiator" at the expense of the agency of the one "initiated" into the marriage. We also acknowledge that descriptions of such concepts will differ from one culture to another.

Avenues for Future Research and Conclusions

This article addresses the neglected topic of woman-woman marriages in Africa, relying upon Gikuyu women to speak about issues that have lain dormant for a number of years. Our effort has been to challenge researchers on the topic to rethink the ways in which such relationships have been represented up to this point.

Future research must rely more heavily on the voices of Gikuyu women to investigate this subject, not necessarily as a "better" and "authentic" way to tell these women's stories, but also as a constant reminder that these women have typically not had opportunities to speak and tell their own stories. Research must become sensitized to the idea that local voices relate the complexities, ambiguities, and heterogeneity involved in practices of woman-woman marriage, and in the analysis of how these practices take place and how the women involved perceive them. We do not suggest that because these Gikuyu examples suggest flexibility, ambiguity, and heterogeneity that all African woman-woman marriages are the same. Rather, we raise the possibility that earlier explanations import assumptions that obscure different interpretations.

A number of issues regarding Gikuyu woman-woman marriage remain. Our study did not investigate, for example, the prevalence of such marriages among the Gikuyu. Early in the twentieth century, Leakey simply stated that such relationships were "not uncommon," while our own sampling in the early-1990s (perhaps surprisingly) uncovered eight households within a small locale ([1938] 1977). A census of these households might show woman-woman marriages to be more common and persistent than the silence in the literature would imply. Oboler's survey among a Nandi community in Kenya's Rift Valley suggested that three percent of households contained woman-woman marriages (1980). However, her small sample does not necessarily mean that this rate of woman-woman marriages is the same for Nandi society generally nor does it say much of anything about other societies containing woman-woman marriages.

Another issue that needs further exploration is the emergence and transformation of Gikuyu woman-woman marriages during the 500 year history of the Gikuyu. Muriuki offers evidence that the matriarchal origins of Gikuyu society had been superseded by patrilineal and patrilocal social and political organization by the mid-seventeenth century (1974). It is certainly not clear, but perhaps Gikuyu woman-woman marriage is a remnant of a matriarchal past. While nothing has been written of origins, more recent twentieth-century social transformations have without doubt profoundly impacted practices of woman-woman marriage. As with other indigenous practices, Christian churches have severely and unfairly questioned the morality of woman-woman marriages, and have, in turn, shaped public opinion. For example, recent baptism guidelines from the Catholic Church in Kenya include their policy on, in their words, "women who 'marry' other women:

In regard to this traditional practice, the first step is to insist that this arrangement be given up completely and that meantime [sic] all those involved, plus any other persons directly responsible for the arrangement, be denied the sacraments. After the women have separated completely, each one will be helped separately and any infants will be baptised. (Kenya Catholic Bishops 1991, 21)

Such official condemnation impacts public perception by suggesting that such marriages represent an affront to Christian values.14 To our knowledge, no opinion poll has been conducted among the Gikuyu, a predominantly Christian ethnic group, which might give a clear indication of public attitudes. Such a poll has been conducted in Nigeria, where Okonjo suggests that 93.5 percent of 246 Igbo women surveyed disapproved of woman-woman marriage, a perception undoubtedly influenced by decades of Church pressures (1992). Similar disapproval in our study locale might be evident in that at least some households appear to face a certain amount of open hostility coming mostly in the form of teasing. For example, Nduta complains about the teasing she sometimes endures from neighbors, some of whom refer to her as a "man" (muthuri) simply because she is married to a woman:

> . . for these people laugh at me saying that I am a man. I'm not a man. I'm neither a man nor a woman. That is who I am, like a

decent being. So I tell them. I have to be strong. Well, I'm not a man. (in interview)

Perhaps twentieth-century social changes, which have seriously dislocated, though not completely eliminated many indigenous institutions, fosters an ambivalence toward woman-woman marriage as a practice that is simultaneously acceptable, yet also incurs hostility. The acceptability of woman-woman marriages is evident in the fact that despite some hostility, these Gikuyu woman-woman marriages are in no way secretive or hidden. All of the women in the study underwent a marriage ceremony to affirm their relationships, a ceremony no different than that for an opposite sex, indigenous (i.e., non-Christian) Gikuyu marriage. Like other marriages, woman-woman marriages are facilitated by clan elders from both womens' families (rather than priests or ministers), and involve an exchange of gifts between both families as well as dances and food. Such marriages are clearly not "underground" in any way.

Silence among feminists regarding the issue of woman-woman marriages is another issue. By now, it has been well documented that well-meaning feminists from western contexts have often represented "Third World women" in problematic ways. A common view is that of a linear women's emancipation, suggesting that societies have moved through evolutionary stages from women's oppression toward liberation, with western feminists having made the greatest progress and "Third World women" still mired in more overt forms of oppression. As a result, Third World women, a problematic category in itself, are often described by feminists "in terms of the underdevelopment, oppressive traditions, high illiteracy, rural and urban poverty, religious fanaticism, and 'overpopulation'" that appear to rule their lives in relation to those in the relatively liberated West (Mohanty 1991, 5). Such a linear view ignores what in many cases are long histories of women's empowerment and resistance, demonstrated here by woman-woman marriages.

By marrying women, these Gikuyu women are clearly radically disrupting the male domination that operates in their everyday lives. Their stories may begin with land and struggles over material resources, but they are also stories of love, commitment, children, sexual freedom, vulnerability, and empowerment. The "implosion" of all these things makes these women's stories unique and all the more compelling to feminists who are constantly searching for unique practices of feminism that resemble, but are not engineered by, western feminism (Haraway 1997).

NOTES:

1. "Gikuyu" is the indigenous spelling of what is commonly referred to as "Kikuyu."

2. Other terms include "woman-marriage" and "woman-to-woman marriage."

3. Moreover, he apparently did not even get his information on the topic from women involved in such relationships. Discussing his data-collection strategy, Leakey indicates that he relied solely upon male informants to learn about the topics discussed, presumably including woman-woman marriages.

4. The names of interviewees have been changed to protect their identities.

5. This research was originally part of a graduate thesis project in Family Studies. The interviews took place between May and August of 1992.

6. Note that multiple Gikuyu terms seem to describe the same concept. Choice of term depends upon the context in which the concept is employed. For example, while "marriage initiator" in one context is expressed as muhikania, the plural form of the concept is ahikania.

7. It is important to acknowledge that in most cases polygynous marriages among the Gikuyu come as a result of negotiation between the first wives and husbands.

8. While the sexuality of the women involved in woman-woman marriages is clearly one of the most interesting unresolved issues on the topic, the Human Subjects Review Board reviewing the research proposal decided that the topic was too sensitive, and therefore declared such questions off limits.

9. Interviews were conducted in the Gikuyu language and were translated by the primary author.

10. Miario miuru, or "negative talk," that is mentioned by Ciru in this quotation points to fundamental changes that have occurred in Gikuyu society over the course of the twentieth century with colonialist religious and educational training. These changes are reflected in complex local attitudes toward indigenous practices and are discussed briefly in the last section of this paper.

11. Ngai commonly translates as "God," although the Gikuyu term carries no gendered connotation.

12. Karamu, or "the pen," refers to the use of title deeds (by those who could read and write--mainly men) that conferred private ownership of property since the 1960s. This private ownership was started under colonial rule and undermined (though it did not eliminate completely) more customary land tenure rules (Mackenzie 1990).

13. Ndungana ici is a derogatory term that translates most benignly as "You Stink!" However, the term also has sexual connotations, and is only used by elders to criticize misbehavior of younger people.

14. Related to condemnations of woman-woman marriage practices are official condemnations of homosexuality as expressed in recent homophobic statements by Presidents Moi of Kenya, Museveni of Uganda, and Mugabe of Zimbabwe, who referred to homosexuals and homosexual practices with terms such as "scourge," "abominable acts," and "lower than pigs and dogs" respectively. Some in Africa argue that the lack of local African terms for "homosexual" is evidence that homosexuality is foreign to Africa. However, in the Gikuyu language there is no term for "heterosexual" either. Should this be taken as evidence that sexual relationships between women and men do not exist? Among the Gikuyu, male-to-male sexual contact is traditionally prohibited; but prohibition suggests to us that such practices are already in place.

WAIRIMU NJAMBI is originally from Kenya. Her current research and teaching interests include social/cultural studies of science, technology, and medicine, feminist studies of technoscience and medicine, critical studies of race and sexuality, postcolonial studies, and the theorization of women's bodies.

WILLIAM O'BRIEN is assistant professor of Geography at Radford University, where he teaches the regional geography of Africa and Asia and Environmental Studies. His research and teaching interests include issues of postcoloniality and globalization, discourses on third world environments and development, and participatory sustainable development planning in Africa.

Subira

Ukoo Flani MauMau

Ni step by step haijalishi mguu gani
Ulistep chini ulipotoka kitandani,
Right ama left uka jilaani,
Unadhani mafanikio yana kawia
Yatafikia, tabasamu unapo shuhudia
Majaribio kwa njia
Sahani mezani ndani imani
Tushibe wewe nami
Tupande hizi ngazi

Tunaweza teleza
Anguka maswali kuteketeza
Huwezi kosa njia bąda ya nia
Kumbuka hizi ngazi tunapanda
Hazipandwi kwa tashwishi
Hakuna cha labda, hakuna cha kuweza
Nikujua kawaida miujiza
Ghetto maisha kukaza
Sikitu kwetu sima brother
Tunatangaza ufalme
Wa-sanaa za kuungaza
Kwanza kabisa
Kufufua ma soidier wote wale kufa vitani

Malaya Ama Mpenzi Bado Ni Hip Hop

La-balaa

First Chapter

Penzi lako ni machungu mateso
Shida na njaa labda kesho
Nitapata so …
Futa machozi, damu na jasho … Ume …
Nipa mapozi kuniumiza muscles … Niki …
Zunguka na wewe …
Ukanifungua macho
Kila metaphor methali kwangu ni kama Kiss
Mistari safi ni lips zako na miss
Vina silabi instrumental ni figure yako miss
Kama twagombana uanga ni track yaku-diss
Kama twazozana uangani ni track yakuplease
Niki-enda show aleti ushenzi
Niki-rusha show uangatwafanya mapenzi
Aki-chezwa kwa radio mimi ulengwa na machozi
Video clip ikiwa kali mi ukula mapozi
Nimempenda mi sioni
Binti siwezi mweka mfukoni
Hivyo chakututenganisha labda kifo
Ndivyo nakupenda vilivyo

Second Chapter

Mimi na wewe ni Adam na Eve
Bila wewe mimi siwezi believe
Naeza ishi bila mimi kuona wivu
Nakile nimeachieve
Ni hii poem na kiss
Hii poem na huu miss
Mimi ni belong na huyu Miss
Yule mmoja
Mtoto ambaye kapenda soldier
Mtoto ambaye kuoa mimi siwezi ngoja
Yeye kwangu ni wifie sometimes pia mboch
Saa I… ngine malaika
Saa ingine uanga bitch
Niki-enda studio napata mapozi
Niki-anza kurecord twafanya mapenzi
Niki- fika club mimi sitaki gozi gozi
Mii nataka sauti yako … Initulize
Nifunge macho nibaki nikusikize
Umenishika mbaya hata usiulize
Hii ni crucial
Labda twende out iwe track commercial
Juu boy lazima niile langu jasho … So
Futa machozi kwa macho

UKOO FLANI

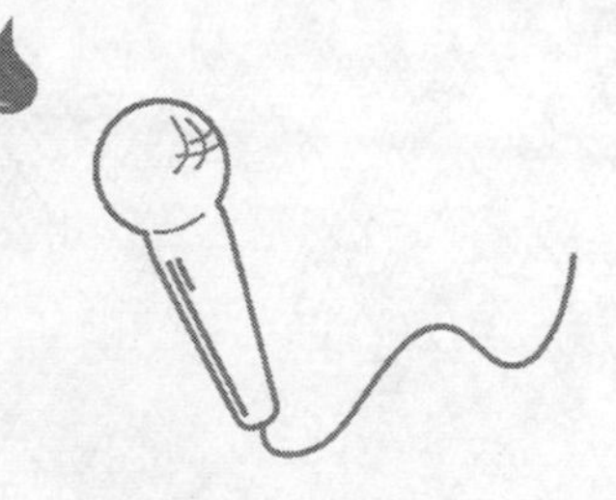

Mau Mau suspects arrives at detension camp

Detainees on arrival for screening

Families waiting to be screened in Nairobi

Thompson Falls detention canp

Operation Jock Anvil- Screening

Hatua

Kang'ethe Ngigi (MC Kah)

Mwafrika imani mlimani tengeneza altar
Punguza majeneza ,magerezani
Omba jah jah malcom x
Custom za ethias, bomb gomora na Sodom
Burn burn ma sheriff wa town
Ma clown wenye crown za gold
Bila wisdom ya old
Namuomba mungu,mumba earth na mbingu
Nauliza mbona minyororo za chuma hamna
Na bado tabu?
Ananijibu ukoloni mambo leo tangu
Uafrica kukosekana, kwa vitabu za kizungu
Na share hili jibu na ma interlect
Wa university
Wanao jali economy, technology
Zaidi ya humanity, acha niwakumbushe humility
Karibu mau-mau university
Elewa wisdom ya mababu
Freedom kujivunia mila bila aibu
Ku-realise kujitemea culturewise
Kujitengenezea black man paradise

B Blogguy™ GET YOUR OWN BLOG | FLAG? | NEXT BLOG>>

Ghetto Livity

I have read of the Beauty of the African Sunset
but I never saw it beyond the shanty line.
I never heard a lion roar—what I hear is,
M.C. Bingi toasting over a heady reggae track:
"... sauti ya Simba!"
Sweaty bodies. Gyrating.
Foot shuffling. Groins bumpin',
a loud groan...
"... he coming, huh?"
No, Komo got stabbed... Blood on the Dance Floor!
But who cares?
Play on... *D.J. weka tracki!*

I never smelt bush fires, or the coming of the rain;
but I can smell the Herb burning.
Dinda sits behind a pillar of smoke...
suddenly, he is transfigured.
"Oh, I see Moses!" he says.
"Oh, fuck it!" say I.
Moses never lived to see Canaan!

In the backroom, Aaron's rod is budding.
But Bobo has no time to marvel.
(Tayari amecheki ya Musa, Firauni, labda hata Yesu!)
She just scratches her crotch and waits for the next;
the line is seven deep...
... I hate this shit!
Not the HIV—hell life is short anyhow.
I am thinking superfecundation—Multilateral Fertilisation!
Seven kids, in the ghetto, and no daddy;
shit, pass me that bar of Geisha—
"Oh baby... call me Onan!"

In the Main Bar, now, with Morio.
He has 300 grand, in cash and a HK-11;
(Ex- GK... si u jua!)
He smells of blood and cordite.
But the Tuskers he buying don't smell...
... of... of blood and cordite;
of lives lost and families ruined!
Soon the sun will rise in the east—
Who cares?
I cannot see it passed out under the table, FUBARed—
(Fucked Up Beyond Any Recognition)—
enough to escape my demons;
at least for today... today!
and today is all I live for...
...and that is Ghetto Livity!

posted by POTASH at 17:47 | 5 comments»

Al Qaeda

Beverly Nambozo

I am an Al Qaeda
Metal scanners are my foes; my friends,
The scanner rubs me up and rubs me down
It makes a sound,
I take off my metallic belt willingly,
Your scanner rubs me up and rubs me down again.
This time it is my metallic bra.
Please help me undo the clasp,
Your scanner is glowing red
As it rubs me up and rubs me down again
The scanner makes a sound.
It is the metal in my garters
Your scanner begins to bulge.
You take me to a room
The scanner beeps and beeps and beeps
I am an Al Qaeda.
Metal scanners are my foes; my friends.

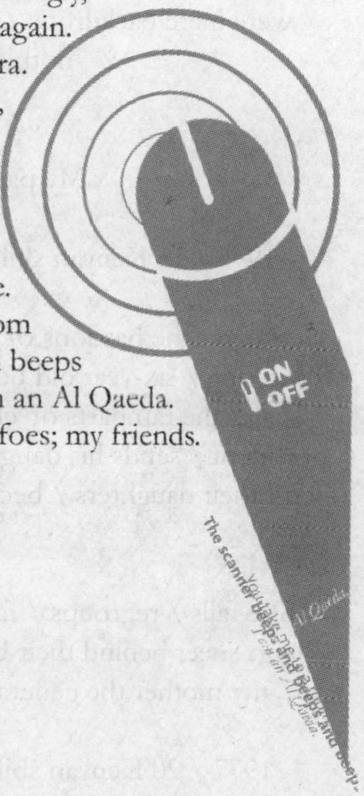

shilling love

Shailja Patel

Part 

They never said / they loved us
Those words were not / in any language / spoken by my parents

I love you honey was the dribbled caramel / of Hollywood movies / Dallas / Dynasty / where hot water gushed / at the touch of gleaming taps / electricity surged / 24 hours a day / through skyscrapers banquets obscene as the Pentagon / were mere backdrops / where emotions had no consequences words / cost nothing meant nothing would never /
have to be redeemed

My parents / didn't speak / that / language

1975 / 15 Kenyan shillings to the British pound / my mother speaks battle

Storms the bastions of Nairobi's / most exclusive prep schools / shoots our cowering / six-year old bodies like cannonballs / into the all-white classrooms / scales the ramparts of class distinction / around Loreto convent / where the president / sends his daughter / the government ministers, foreign diplomats / send their daughters / because my mother's daughters / will / have world-class educations

She falls / regroups / falls and re-groups / in endless assaults on visa officials / who sneer behind their bulletproof windows / at US and British consulates / my mother the general / arms her daughters / to take on every citadel

1977 / 20 Kenyan shillings to the British pound / my father speaks / stoic endurance /
he began at 16 the brutal apprenticeship / of a man who takes care of his own / relinquished dreams of / fighter pilot rally driver for the daily crucifixion / of wringing profit from a small business / my father the foot soldier, bound to an honour / deeper than any currency / you must / finish what you start you must / march until you drop you must / give your life for those / you bring into the world

I try to explain love / in shillings / to those who've never gauged / who gets to leave who has to stay / who breaks free and what they pay / those who've never measured love / by every rung of the ladder / from survival / to choice

A force as grim and determined / as a boot up the backside / a spur that draws blood /
a mountaineer's rope / that yanks / relentlessly / up

My parents never say / they love us / they save and count / count and save / the shilling falls against the pound / college fees for overseas students / rise like flood tides / love is a luxury / priced in hard currency / ringed by tariffs / and we devour prospectuses / of ivied buildings smooth lawns vast / libraries the way Jehovah's witnesses / gobble visions of paradise / because we know we'll have to be /
twice as good three times as fast four times as driven / with angels powers and principalities on our side just / to get / on / the / plane

Thirty shillings to the pound forty / shillings to the pound / my parents fight over money late in the night / my father pounds the walls and yells / I can't– it's impossible– what do you think I am? / My mother propels us through school tuition exams applications / locks us into rooms to study / keeps an iron grip on the bank books

1982 / gunshots / in the streets of Nairobi / military coup leaders / thunder over the radio / Asian businesses wrecked and looted Asian women raped / after / the government / regains control / we whisper what the coup leaders planned

Round up all the Asians at gunpoint / in the national stadium / strip them of whatever / they carry / march them 30 miles / elders in wheelchairs / babies in arms / march them 30 miles to the airport / pack them onto any planes / of any foreign airline / tell the pilots / down the rifle barrels / leave / we don't care where you take them / leave

I learn like a stone in my gut that / third-generation Asian Kenyan will never / be Kenyan enough / all my patriotic fervor / will never turn my skin black / as yet another western country / drops a portcullis / of immigration spikes / my mother straps my shoulders back with a belt / to teach me / to stand up straight

50 Kenyan shillings to the pound / we cry from meltdown pressure / of exam after exam where second place is never good enough / they snap / faces taut with fear / you can't be soft / you have to fight / or the world will eat you up

75 Kenyan shillings to the pound / they hug us / tearless stoic at airports / as we board planes for icy alien England / cram instructions into our pockets like talismans / Eat proper meals so you don't get sick / cover your ears against the cold / avoid those muffathias / the students without purpose or values / learn and study / succeed / learn and study / succeed / remember remember remem-

ber the cost of your life

they never say / they love us

Part 

I watch how I love / I admonish exhort / like a Himalayan guide I / rope my chosen ones / yank them remorselessly up / when they don't even want to be / on the frigging mountain

like a vigilante squad I / scan dark streets for threats I / strategize for war and famine I / slide steel down spines

I watch heat / steam off my skin / when Westerners drop / I love you's into conversation / like blueberries hitting / soft / muffin dough / I convert it to shillings / and I wince

December 2000 / 120 shillings to the British pound / 90 Kenyan shillings to the US dollar / my sister Sneha and I / wait for our parents / at San Francisco's international terminal

Four hours after / their plane landed / they have not emerged

And we know with the hopeless rage / of third-world citizens / African passport holders / that the sum of their lives and labour / dreams and sacrifice / was measured sifted weighed found / wanting / by the INS

Somewhere deep in the airport's underbelly / in a room rank with fear and despair / my parents / who have travelled / 27 hours / across three continents / to see their children / are interrogated / by immigration officials

My father the footsoldier / numb with exhaustion / is throwing away / all the years / with reckless resolve / telling them / take the passports / take them / stamp them / no readmission EVER / just let me out to see my daughters

My mother the general / dizzy with desperation / cuts him off shouts him down /
demands listen to me I'm the one / who filled in the visa forms / in her mind her lip curls
she thinks / these Americans / call themselves so advanced so / modern but still / in the year 2000 / they think it must be the husband in charge / they won't let the wife speak

On her face a lifetime / of battle-honed skill and charm / turns like a heat lamp / onto the INS man until he / stretches / yawns / relents / he's tired / it's late / he wants his dinner / and my parents / trained from birth / to offer Indian / hospitality / open their bags and give their sandwiches / to this man / who would have sent them back / without a thought

Sneha and I / in the darkened lobby / watch the empty exit way / our whole American / dream-bought-with-their-lives / hisses mockery around our rigid bodies / we swallow sobs because / they raised us to be tough / they raised us to be fighters and into that / clenched haze / of not / crying

here they come

hunched / over their luggage carts our tiny / fierce / fragile / dogged / indomitable parents

Hugged tight they stink / of 31 hours in transit / hugged tighter we all stink / with the bravado of all the years / pain bitten down on gargantuan hopes / holding on through near-disasters / never ever / giving in / to softness

The stench rises off us / unbearable / of what / was never said

Something / is bursting the walls of my arteries something / is pounding it's way up my throat like a volcano / rising / finally / I understand / why I'm a poet

Because I was born to a law / that states / before you claim a word you steep it / in terror and shit / in hope and joy and grief / in labor endurance vision costed out / in decades of your life / you have to sweat and curse it / pray and keen it / crawl and bleed it / with the very marrow / of your bones / you have to earn / its / meaning

KADENGE NA MPIRA,
JOE KADENGE NA MPIRA,
ANACHENGA, MOJA,
ANACHENGA MBILI,
ANAKUJA KATIKATI,
ANAENDA UPANDE HUU,
ANARUDI UPANDE MWINGINE,
ANAKIMBIA,
ANATEMBEA,
ANATAMBAA,
ANAMVISHA KANZU,
ANAPEPETA MPIRA,
AMEMCHENGA MCHEZAJI
WA KWANZA,
AMEMPITA SWIPA,
ANAMHEPA FULLBACK,
MTIZAME,
NDIYO HUYO,
NDIYO HUYO,
ANAENDA,
ANAENDA,
ANAANGALIA HUKO,
ANAANGALIA KULE,
ANATIZAMA KUSHOTO
HAONI MTU,
ANATAZIMA KULIA, ZII MTU,
ATAFANYA NINI,
SASA MWANGALIE,
ANAAJIITAYARISHA,
ANAVUTA,
ANAPIGA TEKE,
ANAPIGA SHOOT!
ANAPIGA SHOOT!
ANAPIGA SHOOT!

KADENGE WITH THE BALL,
JOE KADENGE WITH THE BALL,
HE CUTS ONE,
CUTS TWO,
COMES TO THE CENTER,
HE GOES THIS WAY,
HE GOES THE OTHER WAY,
HE RUNS,
HE WALKS,
HE CRAWLS,
HE JUGGLES THE BALL,
HE DODGES PAST THE FIRST PLAYER,
HE HAS GONE PAST THE SWEEPER
HE ESCAPES FROM THE FULLBACK
LOOK AT HIM!
THAT'S HIM!
THAT'S HIM!
HE IS GOING
HE IS GOING
HE LOOKS THIS WAY
HE LOOKS THAT WAY
HE LOOKS RIGHT, HE DOESN'T SEE
ANYBODY
HE LOOKS LEFT, NOBODY.
WHAT WILL HE DO?
NOW LOOK AT HIM.
HE IS GETTING READY.
HE PULLS IT
HE KICKS!
HE GIVES IT A SHOOT!
HE GIVES IT A SHOOT!
HE GIVES IT A SHOOT!

Author: INTERNET ANONYMOUS

MPIRA IMEIPITA MOJA KWA MOJA KATIKATI YA MIGUU YA GOLKIPA MAARUFU JAMES SIANG?A IMEIINGIA NDANI NA KUPASUA NETI...
THE BALL HAS SHOT STRIGHT AHEAD, AND THROUGH THE MIDDLE OF THE ESTEEMED GOALKEEPER, JAMES SIANGA'S LEGS, IT HAS GONE IN AND TORN THROUGH THE NET?

WASIKILIZAJI, WANANCHI, MASHABIKI, NI....
LISTENERS, CITIZENS, FANS, IT IS A....

TATU BILA!! THREE ONE!
MAYOWE!! SCREAM!
KELELE! NOISE!

MASHABIKI WA ABALUHYIA WAMEFURAHI!
ABALUHYA FANS ARE HAPPY.
MASHABIKI WA GOR MAHIA WAMEZIRAI!
GOR MAHIA FANS HAVE FAINTED.

Illustration: Kwame Nyongo

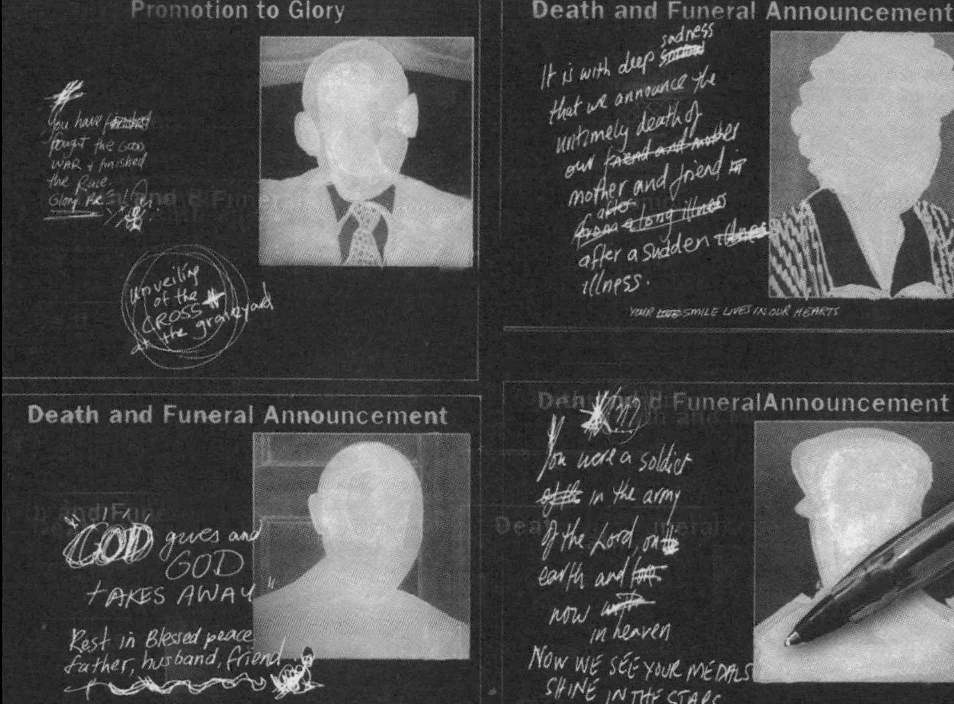

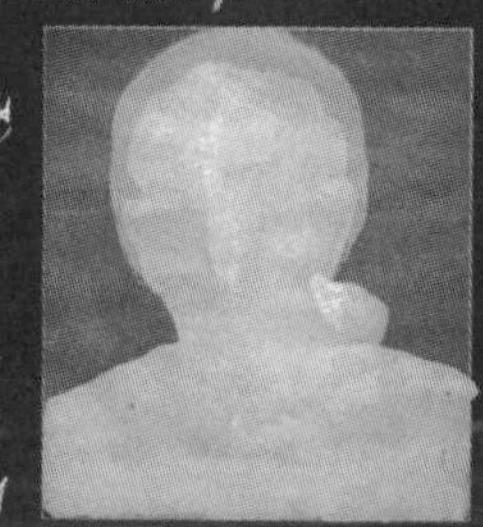

Illustration: JNK

Obituary Man

BY MUTHONI GARLAND

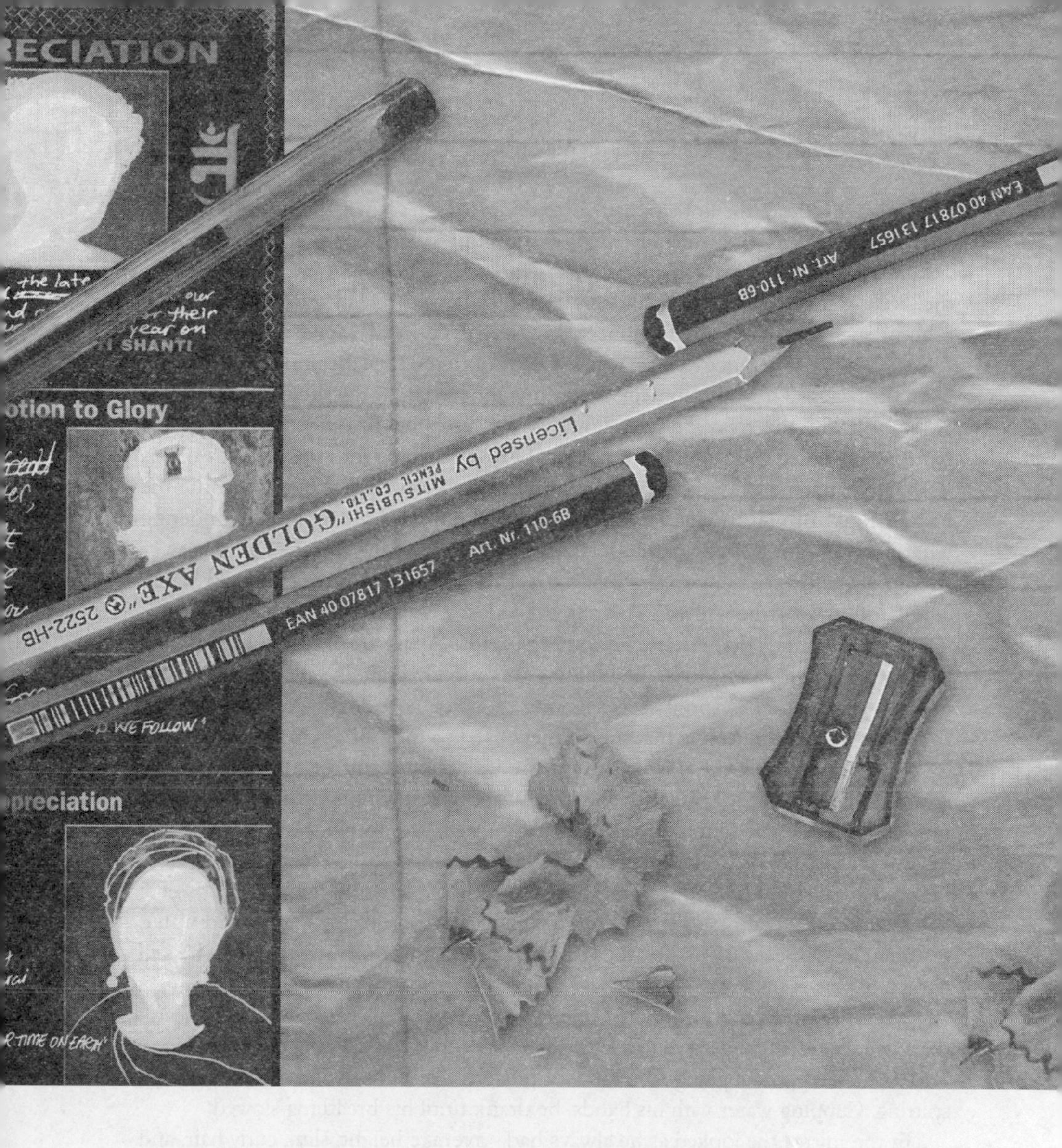

Wacha Dev designed and edited obituaries for *The Kenya Gazette.* On his desk lay printed proofs. He studied each dead face, testing himself as to whether he felt a connection. Only a full-page Hindu businessman from Thika raised a tingle. They shared the same surname—although in the garden of names, Dev was a common weed. After verifying that his dead faces were each contained in the rightful place, Wacha Dev sprawled his initials at the bottom of the page. About to put down his pen, he spied a three-line notice that he hadn't put there:

Tomorrow at seven, I will appear

At the Nairobi National Museum to
have some part of me cut off.

Unlike his dead, the notice wasn't boxed in. It wasn't labelled or embellished. It revealed no clue as to the identity of its author, but lodged like a red stain between a Funeral Announcement for a Sister-in-Christ, lay-elder, and choir member of the New Redeemers Church, and An Appreciation for twin girls—the beloved grand-daughters of a retired engineer once involved in the building of Kenyatta International Conference Centre. Wacha Dev wondered how the notice had sneaked onto his pages. For a hot moment, he even wondered if he'd written it himself. He copied out the three lines on a yellow post-it slip, stuck it onto the back of his hand, and studied the wording for a while before reaching into the recesses of his desk. He extracted a nondescript brown bottle and shook his AZT tablets onto the notice. Pink. Brown. White. He'd been taking them for four months. Wondering what part of him each colour addressed, he swallowed the tablets, and put away the bottle before heading to the men's toilet to wash them down with tap water. The faint buzz of the television blaring in the large reception area upstairs filtered down, highlighting the absence of other sounds. Apart from a few editors and reporters filing in late stories, the building was mostly unlit and deserted. Metallic odours of ink and newsprint seeping along the wide corridors were swallowed by the tingle of pine antiseptic that the cleaners used to mop floors in the bathroom.

Wacha Dev stuck the post-it slip on the wall-to-wall mirror in the bathroom and attempted to see through the words. Without knowing why, they frightened him, as though it was him facing an amputation; as if the announcement was about his own dying. He broke into a sweat. His fingers shook. When he tightened them into a fist, they felt dry and rubbery. He splashed his face until the panic subsided, and then used a wad of toilet paper to dry himself. Too quickly it absorbed water, disintegrated. Specks of tissue caught on his stubble but the mirror verified he still had all his bits.

Wacha Dev opened his mouth wide, wider, checked his throat—a deeper pink than usual, and shiny with saliva. He hacked an experimental cough. It developed into a full fledged coughing fit, rich with phlegm. He bent his head into the sink, spitting. Cupping water with his hands, he drank until his breathing slowed.

In the mirror, he looked as he always had - average height, slim, curly hair, and long-lashed eyes that his girlfriend, Tichi, often described as 'bedroom,' particularly when he was tired. Like now. Maybe he'd go home and catch the late night news at eleven. Maybe he'd face her, accuse her, nail her.

As though reading his mind, Tichi flashed him on his mobile phone. In a sing-song voice, she dragged out the last letter of her words.

"So-o?"

"So what?"

"Are you coming-g? I've cooked for you a big *ugali-i."* Tichi's girlish giggle implied something else.

To play along, he bared his teeth in a mock growl. Tiredness turned it into a yawn. He hadn't slept properly since the diagnosis. "I'm coming. I'm coming."

"What are you doing?"

"Waiting for the messenger to collect the proofs."

"But even you can take them up."

"Consider this. A guy is employed to fish leaves out of a swimming pool. It's a hot, sweaty job. Seems to him the more he fishes, the more leaves shed. He gets a bright idea. He offers to cut down the trees. Boss says okay smart guy, go ahead. Guy cuts trees. Guy is out of a job."

"Silly-ee. How can you lose your job by taking things upstairs?"

"One, they might expect me to do it all the time. Two, it might cost the messenger his job. Three, I'm not silly."

"No, it's just me you're avoiding." She paused as though waiting for him to deny it. Then she giggled to soften the awkwardness. "Wacha, it's not going to work. I'm not going anywhere."

"That's what I'm afraid of."

She released a long sigh. "Please" she said. "Life is not fair or easy for any of us."

He'd once leaned towards proposing marriage to Tichi. That was before they'd gone for the HIV test (at her prompting); before he'd listened to her cry as she confessed to a fling, "Before," she claimed, "I'd committed myself to you."

Now it was his turn to stay uncommitted. Suppressing his panic meant not dealing with the issue of what to do about her. He resented her pressuring him. He wanted to hang up, cut her off, but she'd only call back, and call back. She'd be there at home waiting for him. He hoped she wouldn't beg, wouldn't go on about how much she loved him, loved him, loved him.

She didn't. "The landlord just came by."

"Shit. What did you tell him?"

"That you'd be home soon."

"How many times do I have to warn you not to open the door at night?"

Maybe the landlord, the old bastard, infected her.

In the background Wacha Dev heard the soap opera playing on the 32-inch TV on which he'd blown an entire pay cheque, and then he heard nothing.

Mistakes happen. Obituaries might merge with classifieds and convert the back pages into haphazard islands of flotsam and jetsam. Words might lose their way, take a wrong turn, attach themselves where they don't belong. A farmer from Muranga had once threatened 'to sue the *braday* newspaper and its *braday* foreign shareholders and their *braday* mothers because his *rate* wife was not a *braday* eighteen-year-old-man from Kisumu who'd perished after A *Braday* Short Illness!'

Someone had screwed up - switched the photographs of two death announcements. Strangely, even though the newspaper wrote to offer a make-good, the eighteen-year-old's family never showed up. In any case, that Someone had been fired and Wacha Dev hired. Because he was half-Indian and his boss believed Indians fed on detail.

With a red marker, Wacha Dev circled the three-line notice and stuck a question mark beside it. Since he'd found out his status, he didn't trust himself. But he'd not authored these three lines. And there were no jokers left in the department, not since the company embraced the global slogan, 'Profits Above All' and let loose its twin-headed ogre—Redundancies and Retrenchments.

Perhaps the notice was a trap. His positive status might have leaked. Perhaps this was nothing but a corporate search for any other reason—An Other excuse—to *redund* and retrench him. Wacha Dev double-checked every damn line, comma and full stop. The dead looked blankly back at him.

The test theory lost its sting when Wacha Dev considered who might have set it. He doubted that his immediate boss, Mr. Ernest Simiyu, had the imagination.

But if the notice wasn't a test, what was its relationship to the dead?

Perhaps the museum, in a desperate effort to seek attention, intended to offer an extreme biology class—a dead body cut up for public consumption. Not that Wacha Dev could blame them, what with the typical Nairobi dweller's perception of the museum as a superfluous national mausoleum.

Perhaps the notice was one of those clever advertising teaser campaigns. Like the one in which a girl removed an item of clothing every day. By the Thursday, she'd united the Kenyan religious fraternity in condemnation and its male species in admiration. Papers sold out. On the Sunday she'd dangled a lacy petticoat from her fingernails. Below her shoulders her 'perfect body' was revealed to be the engine of a car. Wacha Dev couldn't remember the make.

But if the advertisement was for the museum, the only stated object in the notice, this idea rubbed up against an old stone. The place was run by the government. And when had government ever taken a creative risk?

Besides, this had the whiff of something more personal, more desperate. More like the manoeuvres going on beneath his skin. Wacha Dev underlined 'some part of me'. His mind leapt to an obvious conclusion. After all, A Whole Penis was an endangered species. In its vicinity, somebody was always sharpening a knife.

Just before he'd gone to high school, his mother had taken him for circumcision. In their crowded Jamhuri estate, they'd been much talk, elbow-ribbing and finger-pointing about circumcision—who had done it, who was a coward, who was a boy/man/girl/strong African/weak Foreigner/wrong tribe. The uncle who lived with them then assured him that circumcision would make him whole. But nobody provided details, and he'd been too embarrassed to ask. On the way to the clinic, Wacha Dev had been terrified that it would all be cut off.

The messenger entered the basement office to collect the proofs. A long service award, in the form of a silver pin, shone on his navy-blue uniform; a uniform that hung on him, echoing the dry looseness of his skin—as though he'd shed a bucket of weight all at once.

"Mu Hindi," the messenger said in greeting.

"Wacha," Wacha Dev corrected.

He didn't like to be referred to as an Indian. Wacha, either intended to mean 'leave it,' or 'you've got to be joking,' was clearly what his Indian father had told his

Kikuyu mother—a sales assistant in his carton manufacturing concern—when she confessed her pregnancy to him twenty-six years ago. He'd fired her, of course.

Wacha Dev had never met his father, but his mother had managed to extract enough from him over the years to educate Wacha.

"Kesho, Tomorrow," the messenger said in goodbye. "Wait." Wacha Dev indicated the three-line notice that he'd circled.

The messenger read it out loud, enunciating each word:

Tomorrow at seven, I will appear

At the Nairobi National Museum

To have some part of me cut off.

"What is this? Somebody advertising a haircut?" Wacha Dev faked a laugh. "Or a nail-trimming service?"

"You think of it as a joke?" The messenger shuddered, shaking his drooping jowls. "He was on television upstairs. With my own two eyes, I saw the place where his finger had been cut off. The finger floated in a glass container full of liquid. It sat on the desk in front of the interviewer."

"Who was this person?"

"Maybe a djinni."

Wacha Dev let that one go. "What reason did he give for cutting off his finger?"

Within the mountain of uniform, the messenger's shoulder blades rose up like two narrow peaks. "Who can understand the ways of ma-djinni?"

He might have exaggerated, but in the time that Wacha Dev had known the old messenger, he'd told no lies. Still, the notice was clearly in the wrong place.

Tichi flashed him again.

"Anyway," she said, as though continuing an ongoing conversation, "what's so interesting there?"

"Not obituaries." Wacha Dev laughed without really laughing. "Obituaries bore me to death."

An irritation at the back of his throat felt like a tribe of safari ants crisscrossing his tonsils. He started to cough.

"Then pleeeease come home."

She disappeared off the line just as suddenly. But something in her voice resonated. Fear. Though he couldn't have said why, he was glad she was afraid.

The elevator doors pinged open.

The day was done but that didn't stop Mr. Simiyu from giving the impression of being a busy man. He strode into the basement.

"I don't know how you work in this mess."

The basement accommodated back issues, ancient files, and the kind of broken office paraphernalia—printers and fax machines—that someone from IT or Technical would rescue one day because they were too valuable to throw away.

"It looked no different when I got here, boss." Wacha Dev replied, wondering about the purpose of this late visit. "I haven't made a mistake. Have I?"

"Well..." said Mr. Simiyu, frowning. "That's not the point, young man."

From behind his back, Mr. Simiyu produced a printed strip and stretched it in front of Wacha Dev. "Step Up. Be Counted," he said, as though Wacha Dev couldn't read the bold print for himself.

Wacha Dev had worked in obituaries for two years. Mr. Simiyu had taught him the standard layouts and wordings himself, urging him to pay attention to title, photo, content. Wacha Dev had caught on in half an hour, but knew enough to keep asking questions. Wacha Dev became so adept on computer graphics that the other clerks started handing him their raw copy to input. He didn't mind. It was easier to type and design than to deal with customers, especially the single girls that his colleagues referred to him. Girls who blinked back tears, in need of comfort, while he doggedly probed for details of their bereavement. Giggling and digging elbows at each other, his colleagues watched him, whispering loudly enough for him to hear.

"Will the Mu Hindi be lucky tonight?"

He knew they wanted him to date one of them so they could box him, label him, move on. But it seemed too intimate and binding to tell them about the girl he had at home. In any case, Wacha Dev was shuttled downstairs. Mr. Simiyu called it a promotion, and even matched it with a raise in salary. But he later admitted that Wacha Dev's *point-five* looks and clever ways disturbed the girls upstairs and confused customers.

"New corporate slogan, young man," said Mr. Simiyu. "Because competition is seriously eroding our revenues."

"The alternative press is snatching more dead people?" Wacha Dev sniggered. "Grave Robbers!"

"Eh? Exactly. And each of us must do our part to reverse this situation. When I spoke with the directors today..."

Wacha Dev stopped listening. As part of a general sweep of his desk, he ran his eyes over the three-line notice before planting them back in the space between Mr. Simiyu's sparse eyebrows. That, and a judicious nod every now and then, delivered the impression that he hung onto every kernel of clever corn planted by senior management into Mr. Simiyu's porous topsoil.

A black stain ringed Mr. Simiyu's hairline. He dyed his patted-down afro with Easy Black. Despite that, and the fact that his shiny two-slit suits flapped over his bottom when he walked, Wacha Dev liked Mr. Simiyu. His vanities seemed so modest. Mr. Simiyu was the kind of man he'd have liked for a father; the kind of father who'd treat Wacha Dev as a worthy young man on whom to press his wisdom. A father who'd never cut off his son, although it could be construed that since Wacha Dev had never made any effort to contact him, he'd also cut off his father. 'Cut off' as an omission, a minus, a lacking. A circumcision, of sorts. All this cutting, he thought.

He wondered if the me (in some part of me) intended to represent more than the physical self, and if so, where me began and ended. Of course, the part of himself that Wacha Dev most wanted to cut off coursed his whole body, invisible, and indivisible. But he also wanted to cut off Tichi, and her bloody 'life is not meant to be fair' approach to this business of living with the dying.

Mr. Simiyu stopped talking, looked at Wacha Dev.

Extracting his handkerchief, Wacha Dev blew his nose before guessing. "Step Up. Be Counted. Right?"

"Very good, young man."

Wacha Dev indicated the notice and his question mark beside it. "That's why I want to know what this is doing in my obituaries."

"Where else do I insert it?" Mr. Simiyu blustered. "Better buried here than the back page."

Perhaps this was the real reason for the late visit.

"Frankly, the idea of someone travelling all over Africa having bits of himself cut up for display in national museums is crazy." Mr. Simiyu spoke as though arguing with himself. "I'd prefer not to run it, but there is no legal basis to deny publication... and the customer paid top rate and..."

'Profits Above All,' Wacha Dev finished the sentence in his head. He asked, "Who dealt with the customer?"

"He sent it in by courier, and provided only a general post box address and a mobile phone number. But *mteja hapatikani kwa sasa*—the subscriber cannot be reached, is all you get when you call this number."

"You think the joker is for real?"

"Didn't you see his nose sitting on the interviewer's desk?" Mr. Simiyu gestured around his nose. "Didn't you see the holes on his face?"

Wacha Dev lied. "I didn't look further than the finger, Sir. I didn't know what to believe."

"A crew rushed to KBC TV to interview him. By the time they got there, he'd vanished. As we speak, reporters are combing the city. The story is holding up the front page. I'd better go up and see if anyone has news. In fact, I suggest you go home. You don't look like yourself."

Mr. Simiyu marched out with the same urgency with which he'd come.

So who or what did he look like, Wacha Dev wondered about himself. Did he appear to others like a man intending to be cut or a man already cut?

Images lie. Once, a lady in a jaunty little hat, dragging along two young boys, bulldozed her way into the newsroom.

"I am not dead," she declared.

The photograph definitely looked like a younger, plumper, happier version of her. Yes, she was the wife of the man stated in the obituary, had these two children, and originally hailed from Meru. But no, she was no longer Catholic, didn't sing in any choir, didn't belong to a Mothers' Union and most of all, didn't care even one fingernail for the husband who'd chased them out five years earlier.

"I've certainly not died of tuberculosis or short illness or suddenly," she'd said. "Obituaries only spell out the truth when it's cancer and other respectable diseases that filthy husbands don't give their wives! But, I am not dead, so no way will I be buried on Saturday. Not unless someone intends to kill me in the next two days, in which case I am here to expose that plan!"

Of course, the paper published a correction, and at the woman's insistence, accompanied it with a photograph of her in her jaunty hat grasping the hands of her boys in their neat school uniforms.

Wacha Dev remembered how he'd flicked his fingernail as he demonstrated the woman's dramatics to Tichi. Remembered how the two boys smiled in the photograph, the corners of their lips turned down as though forced to display bottom teeth to a dentist.

Since he'd submitted the 'final' edit, Wacha Dev was only supposed to mark changes on the proofs, but he overrode the password and called up the obituary pages on his computer screen. The three-line notice screamed its presence. To match its neighbours, he drew a border around it. To further blend it in, he changed the type from italic to standard, and the colour from red to black.

'Step Up. Be Counted' rang in his ear. Perhaps he wouldn't tone it down. Perhaps he'd tone everything else up. While the editors upstairs waited for their breaking story, he'd reposition the obituaries as advertisements for the dead.

Title. Photo. Content.

He drew a red border around each entire obituary page, and in loopy italic script titled the top, Our Dearly Departed. On the funeral notice of the Sister-in-Christ he upped the emotional texture by changing the wording from, 'Announcing The Death...' to 'Promoted to Greater Glory...' On a similar one, he inserted, 'Risen To Join The King...'

For the twins, 'Sad to Announce...' became, "Grieves Us to Mourn... prematurely snatched from the loving bosom of family..."

On another, he underlined, 'and his wife, a teacher who'd once taught the Vice-President.'

The Hindu's obituary was padded enough. It even specified that he'd passed away at the exclusive Princess Zahra Ward of the Aga Khan Hospital.

When the Aga Khan's daughter had visited Nairobi to commission the ward, Wacha Dev had tagged along with a *Kenya Gazette* crew. But she'd been surrounded by so many dark-suited company and security men that he'd only glimpsed a halo of dark hair and a silky pink trouser suit that probably cost a fortune but looked like pyjamas to him. More impressive were the hotel-like rooms of the new ward. Now he wondered if their carpeting, floral colours, dim-able lighting, and mounted television were actually intended to assuage the guilt of those left behind rather than comfort the dying. His forehead burned. His stomach made an oozy noise. It seemed to him that dying was a ratty business that could not be assuaged at all.

Sucking an antacid tablet, Wacha Dev left the building. He stuck the post-it slip with the three-line notice onto the solid centre of his steering wheel. So somebody was cutting off bits of himself. Why, why, why? He waited for meaning to land. It buzzed like a mosquito searching for the most-tender spot of him to bite. He wanted to slap it against his brain, watch it bleed its reason for appearing in his life.

He loosened his tie, released the top buttons on his shirt. The ants seemed to be marching down his neck and along his spine. At a follow-up visit, the lady at the clinic had warned that his CD4 count had dipped since the news of his status, and since he was on ARV, then it was probably a mental thing going on.

"Watch out for opportunistic infections," she'd warned.

A snivelling irritation might develop into pneumonia or tuberculosis or even a brain oedema. What started as an upset stomach might be the pre-cursor to kidney failure or liver crises or a bloody malfunction of his spleen. What appeared to be a man cutting up himself might turn out to be a sign—of what?

"Exactly when did... the mistake happen?" was the only question he'd asked Tichi after her confession.

"More than a year ago," she'd said, as though that somehow mitigated the harm.

The post-it slip on the wheel seemed to vibrate, deepening Wacha Dev's conviction that its message was intended for him. Tomorrow at seven I will wake up, he silently mocked it, in my flat on Church Road, beside Tichi who sentenced me.

He decided to pass by the Museum.

On approaching Museum Hill, Wacha Dev ran into a traffic jam. Cars, matatus, outside-broadcasting vans, cameramen, and people clogged the road and lined the driveway leading to the museum. Jacaranda trees along the perimeter fence offered viewing platforms for the enterprising. A number sat atop the decorative canopy over the museum gate. It creaked every now and then as though it would break. This didn't seem to disturb the policemen manning the gate. Watchmen in neighbouring buildings charged people who wanted to warm their hands or faces on their charcoal fires. Vendors plugged their oranges, bananas, sodas, *miraa* and Tropical Sweets. A turbaned preacher screeched, "Repent! Repent! The time is hee-arrr!' and begged people to heed this manifestation of the awaited sign. On an amplified stereo of a yellow souped-up car, Suzanne Owiyo boomed her famous ode to Kisumu City. On another, Marvin Gaye promised sexual healing.

Of the amputee, there was no sign.

As though participating in a curtain raiser to the main event, people laughed and gossiped. A few danced to the disparate tunes, jerking onto the road, and only jumping back to avoid the determined *rungu* of a neon-coated policeman.

As he slowly drove through the jam, Wacha Dev rolled down his window to better hear the speculation.

"Did anyone see the creature go inside?"

"What is he going to cut off this time?"

"Stop pushing me. If I'm run over by a car, will you pay my bill?"

"*Si,* in Philippines, men are nailed to crosses?"

"Tongue went in Egypt, I hear. A protest against the Nile Water Treaty..."

"Me, I have to see for myself with my own two eyes."

"My sister said her friend said her Uncle said it was a White man spreading a curse throughout Africa."

"New technologies, my dear. That thing called computer that carries messages in the air from one computer to another. Explain that."

"I missed! I wish I had a TV."

"But the skin didn't look white though it's hard to tell because my TV is not a colour one."

"Nigerian juju for sure. Didn't I warn against Nigerian witchcraft movies?"

"This thing is about money. A hungry man will sell anything—even his organs, even his children."

"Politics, man. You know how it is. A disgruntled candidate, a crooked judge..."

The idea that this could be a money-making or attention-grabbing charade annoyed Wacha Dev. He wanted the amputations to happen for a reason, to make sense to him. He wanted the amputee to be a person like himself, unable to deal with the prospect of dying. A person who'd discovered something so vile in himself that he had to get it chopped off bit by excruciating bit.

Tichi flashed him.

"I'm in the car," he said.

"So what's that noise in the background?"

"Music to my ears," he said, and hung-up.

He could have chosen to be Indian, he thought, living within its safe, steel-wire cocoon. When he was six or seven, his mother's car had broken down on a busy street as she drove him to school. After abusing two mechanics who mushroomed out of nowhere offering to fix it, she'd grabbed Wacha Dev's hand and taken him in a matatu to the industrial area. He'd never been in a public minibus before. They'd had to alight and walk for a long time into the interior. His mother was hugely pregnant, and complained about the heat and the distance, but refused to answer his questions about where they were headed. They reached a factory surrounded by high walls.

"We are here to see the boss, the big boss," she'd demanded of the uniformed man guarding the towering gates.

The guard took his time emerging from a wooden cubicle. "Who are you?"

Gripping Wacha Dev by the back of his collar, she thrust him towards the guard. "I'm bringing him to his father."

Wacha Dev wondered why his mother wasn't afraid of this big, dark man. The guard studied Wacha Dev's shiny, curly hair. He studied Wacha Dev's mother, lingered over her belly. He clicked his tongue.

"Do you have an appointment?"

His mother shrieked, "Open the gate. Open the gate. If he won't talk to me on telephone, he will address me face-to-face."

"Madam, without an appointment, there is nothing I can do." The guard re-entered his cubicle.

"Did I create him by myself?" she cried, "Can't you see the Dev in him?"

Her crying upset Wacha Dev more than her anger. And he wasn't sure about this Dev in him.

"You men are all the same!"

The guard ignored her.

"Why should I struggle so much by myself when his father can provide the life he deserves?" She turned to Wacha Dev, ruffled his hair. "It is your right!"

With a last feel of his hair, she pushed him towards the guard.

"Tell him his son is waiting outside," she shouted, before waddling back in the direction they'd come from. "I have to fix my car, go to work, pay for this, pay for that, buy this, buy that, while the father does what?"

When Wacha Dev called her, she shouted, "Don't cry. Your father will open the gates for you."

But the towering gates stayed shut.

When he got tired of crying, and hot and bored of drawing stick figures in the dust, the security guard allowed Wacha Dev into the cubicle. He fell asleep sitting on a hard chair. Late afternoon, the security guard asked him if he had money, and if he knew the way home. Wacha Dev shook his head and sniffled. Only then did the watchman call reception from the black phone.

"He calls himself Wacha Dev," the guard said. "What am I supposed to do with him?"..."I'm going off duty."... "He looks like an Indian to me, but what do I know?" The guard had to repeat the story several times to several people, and afterwards clicked his tongue and grumbled, "They talk as if they don't insist I chase away anyone without an appointment!"

Eventually, a dark, elderly lady emerged from the pedestrian gate. She gave Wacha Dev a glass of milk and sugary biscuits with NICE written on them.

"Who is your father?" she asked, while he ate.

Not only was this old woman not the father he'd expected would open the gates, but she also didn't seem to know who he was. Maybe they'd come to the wrong gates.

"My mother told me that my father is Dev," he said, invoking the authority of his mother.

It seemed to settle something in her mind. "Mr. Dev said he'll meet you on one condition."

Wacha Dev pretended to be busy chewing, but inside fear ate at him again.

"Mr. Dev said he doesn't want you to fall in the crack."

Wacha Dev eyes scampered over the ground. "What crack?"

She answered in the same memorised way he did to a question from his teacher. "The crack between two cultures."

Wacha Dev stared at her.

She shrugged, moved her lips about. Her eyes lit up. "Mr. Dev is a rich man. He can pay for a top school. Wouldn't you like to go to a top school?"

When Wacha Dev still didn't answer, she added, "He drives a Mercedes. And he can buy you as much milk and biscuits as you want."

Now he was certain this condition would be another towering gate, one that required a long boring wait, one that involved his mother crying and walking away.

"I want to go home," he said, trembling.

She told him not to cry, that she would take him home. She asked him to wait while she fetched her bag from inside. She returned much sooner than expected. Shaking her head, she exclaimed, several times, *"Hawa ma-tycoon!* A child is better off with its mother."

And she ensured he had a seat on not one, but two matatus, paid his fare, and escorted him right to the door.

His mother hugged and fussed over Wacha Dev as though she'd never expected to see him again. Wacha Dev pushed her away. The lady handed over a padded brown envelope, and refused to stay for tea. Thereafter, she dropped off a padded brown envelope every month. His mother never mentioned his father again. Wacha Dev was certain he'd made the right choice.

The choice was consolidated in high school. An Indian friend invited him to the new five-star Sanatan Dharam Sabha temple for a Diwali celebration. He admired the intricate carvings of twenty-four deities and forty-six saints, the gilded over-pinks and over-blues in the marriage hall, the fireworks display and the long banquet tables of food in the social centre.

Unused to the quizzing, probing and kidding along, he inadvertently leaked to his friend's mother that he was of the Devs of a carton factory in industrial area. The lady ogled her black-lined eyes at him before gathering other ladies in silk saris. They pressed food on him, asked and chattered with and about him, pinching his cheeks and touching his hair as though he were a puppy. They were so kind and concerned that it seemed easier to let them conclude that his own mother was a simple-simple, poor-poor, helpless, uneducated African woman than to fight against the tide of their prejudices.

"Shame-shame!" they said about his father, dipping and nodding their heads, and jingling their bangles. "Bit dark skin, but you can see the Dev in the shape of his nose."

"Shame-shame!" they said, looking down at him. "The poor thing knows nothing about Diwali, nothing about his gods, nothing about his family or sect or Punjabi customs, nothing."

"Shame-shame, only!" they said, tweaking his dark Dev nose. "We should adopt him. No?"

And hot with shame, Wacha Dev extricated himself.

Africans asked fewer questions. In fact, his looking different opened their gates for him. And since he'd been circumcised, at home and in the estate, they allowed him space to be himself. So he'd consolidated his choice by studying African literature at Kenyatta University. He'd chosen what seemed the easier life and now he'd die for it.

Tichi had fallen asleep on the living room sofa, clutching her mobile phone. A white t-shirt rode high on her slim thighs.

"Malaya," he said, under his breath, his head throbbing. The Slut.

Lights blazed. On television, a judge on *Vioja Mahakamani* banged his gravel in a courtroom of people who continued to argue amongst themselves.

He'd been rather pleased that Tichi had dragged him to the clinic, not because he suspected her of infidelity—far from it, but because his mother had warned him to be careful, particularly of *hoi-hoi* Nairobi girls. A clean bill of health would have fit in so well with his plan to introduce Tichi to his family as his future bride. Now Wacha Dev stared at her as he had at the clinic, after the test, as she'd babbled on about a 'mistake.'

"Look at you," he sneered. "Who would know, baby, who would know those great big eyes are nothing but a window to a virus factory?"

Her braids stood out in all angles as she sat up, rolled her shoulders.

"I should have placed an adwertisemint in Bombay Times, only," he said, with an exaggerated Indian accent. "Wanted, wirgin to appear at Yomo Ken-yatta Airport to how hersilf Curt By Me!"

"*Kwani* you think they don't have AIDS in India?" Tichi's voice was snarled with sleep.

He paced up and down. Her eyes followed. Wary.

"What do you want?" she asked.

Wacha Dev raised his fists, brought them down on the coffee table. The glass on top of the wooden frame broke, fragmenting into irregular pieces.

"You're bleeding." Tichi scrambled up, stood behind him and wrapped her arms around him.

He shook her off. She fell.

His head felt like it would splinter and scatter sharp, rough, painful pieces of him all over the place. "Close your legs! Close your legs!"

He kicked...at nothing, kicked without breaching the gap between them.

She drew her legs together and pulled down her t-shirt.

"Go," he said. "Get out."

He staggered to the bedroom.

He woke up naked.

His swollen hands throbbed from multiple mini-cuts and abrasions. The buttons sewn into the mattress had pressed their pattern onto one side of his body. A waft of the cocoa butter Tichi rubbed on her skin rose from the bedding dumped on the floor. In the living room, he saw the broken table and scattered glass.

Tichi was curled up on the sofa in the shape of a question mark. She'd changed into day clothes as though to communicate that she'd only stayed the night because it was too late to leave.

"Shit, shit, shit." As the roar of last night rang in Wacha Dev's ears, it occurred to him that what he'd really like to cut off were the parts of himself making him sink into her.

Pouring antiseptic into a sink of water, he washed his hands. They probably had bits of glass embedded, but Wacha Dev was suddenly in too much of a hurry to bother with that. Wincing at the sting, he wrapped each hand with a dishcloth, leaving only the tips of his fingers to wiggle free. With these, he somehow managed to start his car, and drive.

To dissipate the smell of antiseptic, and his depressing thoughts, he rolled down his window by pressing the electronic button. It was still dark. Few cars were out on the streets, and the streetlights, though recently rehabilitated, were few and far between. He pulled up at the traffic lights at the Westlands roundabout. A hawker thrust *The Kenya Gazette* under his nose. The paper rustled as though it were alive.

Wacha Dev jerked the car forward. The hawker jogged alongside.

"Open job-o for me. I need to eat..."

"Get it out of my face unless you want to donate."

"Mu Hindi," the man said, twisting his mouth, "how much did your car cost?"

Wacha Dev jabbed the electric button with his bandaged hand. As the window wound up, the paper slid off the steering wheel onto his lap. But the hawker didn't pull back. Instead, he let his hand obstruct the closing of the window.

The light turned green.

The hawker didn't look particularly frightened. In fact, he stared at Wacha Dev as if ready to accept whatever happened, even if that 'whatever' involved pain. Maybe the guy was bluffing. Too easy to assume that a guy in humble circumstances suffered a shortage of brains as well. Wacha Dev pressed the button again. The window inched up another notch.

A flicker of something—hate or pain or surprise—temporarily cracked the man's martyr-like expression. Like most hawkers, he was muscular in a ropy way. A short-fade haircut merged with the contoured lines of beard ringing his well-defined cheekbones, and an equally thin moustache underlined his wide nostrils.

Perhaps the danger in those three lines lay in interpretation. To have (in to have some part of me cut off), might imply the power lay in someone else's hand - a Wacha Dev at the Nairobi Museum, who'd somehow coerced the amputee into having his parts chopped off.

A car hooted, roared past.

Wacha Dev jabbed the button again. The window squeaked against its human barrier. The man didn't flinch. Instead, he frowned at Wacha Dev's bandaged hands. Then, slowly and deliberately, he raised his other hand, and placed his fingers on the edge of the window. A thin gold band glinted on his third finger. He pushed down. The window squeaked. The man leaned into the window and grimacing with the effort, pushed harder. The window gave, and gave until it was all the way down.

Wacha Dev wondered at the depth of a man's strength. Clearly no Wacha Dev, or God for that matter, at any museum had power over a person's choice as to whether or not to have part of himself cut off.

"Open it for me." Wacha Dev jabbed at the newspaper. "Open the obituaries."

Despite, or because of their history, the hawker obeyed. He laid the pages across the steering wheel.

Our Dearly Departed, in red, seemed appropriate. The dead faces, oddly identical in expression, seemed resigned to their fate. But who were they? Were the twin girls budding Sheng rappers re-made to sound like choir angels? What had the lady who'd taught the vice-president taught her own children? Was the Sister-in-Christ really another Mother Teresa or a lonely spinster with a crush on her preacher? Were his homebound brothers and sisters less important to the man whose obituary was peppered with distant cousins living in the USA? Had the man whose cute childish photograph belied his age actually been a carjacker butchered in a shootout with the police? Was the businessman's family secretly celebrating his demise so they could take over the shop? Did the Hindu man, incidentally or accidentally, have a secret son?

The hawker leaned into the window, folded and lifted the newspaper. He spoke in a surprisingly gentle voice. *"Umeifiwa? Pole baba."* You're bereaved? Sorry, brother-man.

Despite the chill of a crisp dawn, the crowd at the museum who'd waited at the gate all night, generated heat, sweat, and noise. The police had cordoned off the area. Raising his bandaged hands, Wacha Dev made his way through to the gate. The security guard eyed his bandages and his curly, shiny hair as though they were related to the strangeness of the occasion. He directed Wacha Dev to the great hall where a lady's voice on the microphone urged the crowd to respect the rules and refrain from taking photographs. But the people flashed cameras and jostled for position as though fighting for a share of a national treasure.

They circled a ringed dias, in which, Wacha Dev imagined, the amputee sat awaiting the clock to strike seven. This muscular circle of bodies repelled his advances. No matter how hard he stretched or pushed or jumped, Wacha Dev could not break through. As the woman on the microphone instructed, "Order, Order," he wondered if the amputee was frightened at what was to come, or exhilarated at taking charge of his future.

But would people note anything, Wacha Dev pondered, apart from the fact that the amputee had himself butchered and displayed across this unforgiving continent? Was it enough that one or two people, like Wacha Dev, might wonder why? Unless, that is, the amputee intended his message for a particular person. Was it possible that he had offered the first gesture, a finger, maybe, to prove the serious nature of his intent, and when that had been ignored, matters got out of hand?

No formal presentation or commentary explained or built up to the main event. But, as the time approached, the people stilled, talking in fearful whispers as though anticipating a religious or other-worldly experience. To ease the tension, Wacha Dev edged his way around the fringes. That is when he noticed the jars displayed on a ledge running along the walls of the hall. Above each jar, a card written in red italic described the item, and the capital city in which it had been cut off - Kigali, Harare, Lagos, Cairo, Dafur, Freetown, Kinshasa. Nairobi was a blank. And in the jars filled with urine-yellow liquid, floated a finger, a nose, an ear, a tongue, a toe, a nipple and a chunk of meat that proffered to be a slice of buttock. Amazing how extraneous they seemed to the core of a man.

"What is the man doing now?" a breathy voice enquired.

Wacha Dev answered. "Directing attention to his core."

Somebody clicked his tongue. "Does he think God gave him a mouth for decoration?"

Wacha Dev answered, "I bet the tongue was the first he had cut off."

Eyes and cameras swivelled in Wacha Dev's direction. Puzzled looks dwelt on his hair and bandaged hands, and darted over the contents of the jars immediately behind him before lingering again on his hair and hands. The wall of bodies silently parted open to admit him.

Wacha Dev stepped forward, flashlights dazzling him as he searched for the amputee.

"This must be the one who is going to do the cutting..."

"How come nobody is arresting him?"

Wacha Dev caught sight of the amputee—a man, or rather, a mutilated body of a man with a short, striped *kikoi* wrapped around his waist, seated in the centre of a dias, incisions and slashes marking his face and torso. Bar the missing bits, a black man of average height and weight. He pointed a stump of a finger at Wacha Dev. His eyes burned.

Wacha Dev spoke. "I'm the obituary man."

"Why is this one talking about obituaries?"

"Are obituaries written while you're still alive?"

"If the *jamaa* wants us to know him, *si* he writes a book."

A lady touched Dev softly, and whispered, "Please don't cry."

"Haiiiiya!" said the voice over the microphone, "Even the other one is crying."

"Ashindwe! The devil be defeated!"

"They know each other?"

Knowing. Nodding.

"Is he going to cut or not? I've got to get to work."

"Me, I never even have time to read the Gazette in the morning..."

"Don't call me sister. My mother doesn't know you."

"Si you push even you..."

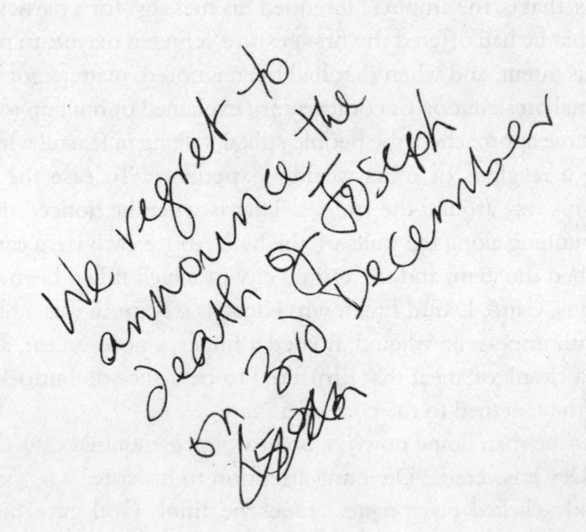

MUTHONI GARLAND is a Marketing consultant of many years standing. She is also a writer, and recently won a BBC award for her short story. She lives in Nairobi, where she writes. She has been published in various journals around the world. In 2006, she was shortlisted for the Caine Prize for African literature.

Illustration: JNK

The Purpose Of The Blindfold

BY PETER TRACHTENBERG

What is just?

We'd heard the announcement on the radio that people weren't allowed to leave their homes, and we thought, Okay, no problem. We heard gunshots around the neighborhood, we heard yelling. The house was surrounded by soldiers. I saw the commanding officer; he was one of our neighbors. He beat down the door. He said, "You, K–." my husband's name was K–. "What are you doing here when everybody else is outside being checked by security? Come out with your identity card." My husband went outside with his card, and then from April 7 till the 14th they held him at the roadblock, right nearby. So he would have seen them torturing other men and young people, young boys. They cut off men's genitals and fed them to the dogs. They hacked people to death with machetes. He watched all of it. And at two or three o' clock one morning it was his misfortune to be tortured, too. He died on the fifteenth, very early in the morning.

Not "he was killed," but "he died." Rwandans often used that innocuous phrase when speaking of loved ones they'd lost in the genocide. I took it for an attempt at normalization. During World War II the Nazis had committed most of their crimes away from eyewitnesses, herding their victims to remote killing grounds or sequestering them in death camps whose function was betrayed only by the pillars of smoke that rose from their chimneys. Afterwards it was possible—if not particularly credible—for people to say they hadn't known. In Rwanda, though, the killing took place in public. Everybody saw it. All you had to do was look out through your garden gate. All over Kigali bodies lay piled on the roadside like sacks of refuse until they were picked up by garbage trucks; Hutu office girls in white dresses picked their way to work between spreading puddles of blood. General Roméo Dallaire describes seeing one such girl slip and fall. She got up quickly, but still, he writes, "it was as if someone had painted her body and her dress with a dark red oil. She became hysterical looking at it, and the more she screamed, the more attention she drew." What need was there for anyone to be more explicit? I hadn't been in Rwanda long before I was taking it for granted that when anyone spoke of a death ten years before he meant a death by violence. Murder had become a natural death.

On the eighteenth, at nine in the morning, a group of soldiers and militiamen came to my house. They told me, "Give us the money your husband left you." My husband's body was being dragged through the street, no one had buried him. They formed mountains, the bodies of all the men and boys they'd killed. And I said, "I don't have any money. We don't have any money." They carried me from the living room and took me into a bedroom; my mother-in-law was shut up in another room. And from that day until the end of the war, the soldiers raped me. They were at it day and night, day and night, all of them. They came in all together, they dropped their pants at the same moment, and they raped me, jostling each other. There was always another group waiting in the living room. If one man left, another one came in to take his place, one after another. In the fifth month of my pregnancy, I aborted. They took me to the hospital for the abortion, and they told me, "We killed your brothers and sisters with machetes, but you, we're just going to rape you till you're dead." That whole time I was naked, I never had clothes on. I was completely swollen. I had infections, I kept vomiting. I couldn't even cry because I wanted to die and I couldn't die.

In the midst of violence, especially if that violence is prolonged, a relationship sometimes forms between perpetrators and victims. It is not a true relationship, in the sense of a free association of individuals, only the simulacrum of one or, more accurately, a parody. It may come into being because the victims implicitly understand that their survival depends on winning the good will of their captors or because even killers—maybe especially killers—need to feel that they are good people and will seek validation of their goodness from the very ones they are about to kill. It may simply be that when human beings are forced together over time they fall by inertia into the lulling rhythms and protocols of society. For such reasons a group of soldiers and militiamen might interrupt months of rape and sexual torture to take their victim to the hospital for an abortion; it's startling to realize that at the height of the genocide Rwanda's hospitals were still functioning, treating old people with pneumonia, children with broken arms. And, of course, delivering babies.

What was the meaning of that gesture? On one level, the abortion was a continuation of the violence these men were inflicting on their captive, an intensification of it, a rape committed in the deepest parts of her body. As a Catholic, the woman would experience it as a murder of the life within her, of her husband's life, because it was his baby they were killing; they were killing him all over again. And at the same time she would know that she was being spared, since it wasn't uncommon for génocidaires to terminate the pregnancies of Tutsi women in other ways. And so at some point in the procedure, perhaps only for a moment, she might feel a tremor of gratitude, and in recollection this gratitude would be the most terrible thing of all.

If I go before the court, if I tell them what happened, if I say what was done to my body, people will mock me. All I want to say is that they made me suffer. I want to tell the story of my suffering. And I want the one who raped me to understand that he tortured me, that he's guilty. I want him to understand what he did—freely, without being forced—I want him to admit his blame.

The woman who told me this story was named Athanasie M. She was forty-five, with a handsome oval face that had begun to soften with age and very large dark eyes that looked even larger because of the dark circles beneath them. The whole time she spoke she held my eyes with hers. Once she had been a girl on one of the thousands of haystack-shaped hills that make up the Rwandan landscape—Rwanda, *pays des milles collines*—destined for a life of farming beans and sorghum. Against all expectations she had gotten an education and become a gym teacher at a polytechnic in Kigali. She had married, borne children. And then the life she had won for herself had been torn asunder and she had been turned into a sort of domestic animal, naked and speechless, kept alive only to be abused until it would be time to kill her. It seemed a miracle that she could speak. But she could write; she had a journal that she had written about her ordeal. "Each page," she said, "is a thousand tears." Now Athanasie worked at a women's center counseling other survivors of rape and sexual torture, many of whom were sick with AIDS. In this regard, she considered herself fortunate. As a result of what had been done to her she could no longer perform any kind of physical labor, not even sweep a floor, but she didn't have the virus and could look forward to a long life. Perhaps it's better to say that she could anticipate a normal life-span, which for a Rwandan woman in 2002 was 46.8 years. I had been recommended to Athanasie by someone in the States, and when our interview was over she told me, "When you see David, you must remember to tell him how fat I've gotten." The pride in her voice took me aback until I remembered the possible connotations of thinness.

The clinic was a complex of low grey cinderblock buildings decorated inside with the drawings of the clients and their children, crude productions of crayon, glitter and construction paper mounted on the walls with yellowing tape. When I left, a group of women was dancing in the earth yard. They were welcoming some visitors from a Canadian aid organization. The dancers' movements were fierce, strutting; they held their arms out from their sides, their fingers splayed and quivering, and lifted their knees high, like wading birds. Drums sounded. The women dipped, took a step forward, a step to the side, a step back, each pent inside her square of an invisible grid drawn on the red earth. Some of them looked very old, their faces seamed, their eyes dim. Their limbs might have been made of twisted rope. One woman had only one leg, on which she hopped unceasingly, as if trying to pound a stake into the ground. Up and down she leapt, grinning and triumphant and terrible. I suppose she was trying to proclaim victory over her disfigurement, but to me she seemed like a reproach to the world of the whole.

A few weeks before this, at a cocktail party at the American Club in Kigali, I'd been introduced to a man who worked for a Christian conflict-management organization. He was running reconciliation workshops. Reconciliation was a word you heard a great deal in Rwanda. You heard it from government officials, including employees of the eponymous Unity and Reconciliation Commission, and the spokespersons of victims' groups, from *ex-detenus* and, more rarely, from *rescapés.* You heard it from taxi drivers. Depending on your point of view, the unanimity with which the word emerged under certain lines of questioning could be moving or creepy. I was curious as to how one would go about teaching reconciliation in a country that was already pursuing it as single-mindedly as China had once pursued five year plans. My acquaintance said his workshops were based on scripture and geared toward local pastors, who were then supposed to pass on what they'd learned to their congregations.

"Which is what?" I asked. "I mean, what are you teaching them?"

Insects were keening in the brush. I had walked a half mile up the steep slope of Avenue des Grands Lacs in the heat of the late afternoon and was disheveled and sweaty, while the man I was talking with looked as well-pressed as a cruise ship captain. But when I asked my question his face flushed; maybe he thought

I was being provocative. "We tell them to think of Rwanda in terms of a family quarrel."

Of course Rwandans needed to reconcile. Ten years before they had suffered a genocide comparable to the destruction of the Jews of Europe. Hundreds of thousands of Tutsi and moderate Hutu had been killed; thousands more had been raped, tortured, maimed, made destitute. Because these horrors had been perpetrated by members of the Hutu majority, ostensibly in the name of their ethnic brethren, surviving Tutsi viewed almost all Hutu with bitterness and suspicion. But the official rhetoric treated reconciliation as something that could be brought about by fiat, hurried along by government bureaus and pastoral committees. And it skipped over certain essential preliminaries. Before Rwanda's people could reconcile, some of them would have to be held accountable for the crimes they had committed against the others, and make penance for them. "Held accountable," "make penance": the very insufficiency of these phrases suggested how hard it would be to do either. For their part, the survivors needed assurance that they wouldn't be victimized again. The soldiers of the current government constituted one kind of assurance, but one that was only partial and provisional; unaided force always is. True reconciliation depended not on force alone but on force allied with, subordinated to, justice: on principle. Such justice would have to satisfy the genocide's victims without irreparably alienating the majority population, which feared that as administered by a regime that was dominated by Tutsi justice would turn out to be nothing more than revenge. At civil rights demonstrations in the U.S. you used to hear the chant, "No justice, no peace." In Rwanda at last it made sense.

From a purely material perspective, other needs were more pressing. Rwanda was poor and nobody there was poorer than the *rescapés.* They had lost everything; looters had stripped the very roofs from their houses. Thousands of Tutsi women were dying of AIDS, which the rape squads had deployed as a weapon of delayed biological warfare, the object being not only to defile victims in the present but kill them slowly in the future. There were families—and this was a country where families were big and endlessly ramified, everybody related to everybody else—made up entirely of children, the older children caring for the younger ones, valiantly, hopelessly. What could these children know about raising children? Their parents had died before they could teach them. And yet it often seemed that what survivors wanted most was justice. In Rwanda the word had even more connotations than it does elsewhere. A spokeswoman for Avega, the association of widows of the genocide, defined it as being able to bury your own dead, a right especially resonant in a country where the most common memorial was a heap of unclaimed bones. (Actually, a lot of bones were being claimed by the ruling Rwandan Patriotic Front, without undue consideration of whom they had originally belonged to. When government workers opened a mass grave at Gisozi, they dug up tons of skeletons, leaving behind the identity cards that had been buried with them. Witnesses who sorted through them afterward said that many of them designated their bearers as Hutu. It didn't matter. When the bones were later put on display at the national genocide memorial, they were all Tutsi.) Many of these crushingly impoverished people equated justice with financial reparations. But beyond that I sensed a widespread desire for something that resisted definition. It was as if in the back of their minds the survivors held the idea of a Platonic justice of which all known instrumentalities—all laws, statutes, courts, tribunals, settlements, penalties—were only shadows. "What I need is justice itself," Athanasie told me. "True justice."

I thought I understood this, and not just because what had happened here suggested a Platonic archetype of injustice, a crime so immense as to make any response to it seem pathetically, even insultingly, inadequate. (Hannah Arendt was speaking of genocide when she said that we "are unable to forgive what [we] cannot punish [and] we are unable to punish what has turned out to be unforgivable.") In the hierarchy of human needs, justice may be only a tier below shelter or mother-love. Maybe it represents father-love, a love that, unlike the magnanimous, blanketing kind mothers give us, is based on distinctions, boundaries, equivalency—one thing for another. One symbol for such love is a staff, which leads some people to think of it as merely punitive. But a staff is also used for pointing. Human justice, in Büber's formulation, is each person getting what he deserves, while divine justice is each person getting what he is. And also, presumably, each creature, plant and stone: to them, too, a nature is given. Divine justice began on the first day of creation, when God parted the heavens from the earth. When He cast Eve and Adam out of paradise, He wasn't punishing an act so much as decreeing that this, henceforth, was what it would mean to be human—that is, mortal, homeless, and ashamed.

Human justice is human; It applies to relations between human beings or between human beings and the man-made artifact of the State. The afflictions sent by God or nature don't trouble us the same way wrongs committed by other people do. The very word "wrongs" is indicative, since it isn't used of nature. A tidal wave may kill a quarter of a million people and a man with a knife only one, yet it's the murderer who inspires not just horror but outrage, and it's the murderer we seek to punish. King Xerxes flogging the sea is only an image of the folly of power. I do not think this difference stems solely from the human capacity for malice. Eichmann appears to have sent millions to the gas chambers without feeling much of it. Men know that God and nature are bigger and more powerful than they are (though in our time this knowledge may be fading). But we think of other men as our equals, not in the social but the creaturely sense, as beings moved by the same desires and aversions as ourselves and subject to the same laws of pain and death. Every crime shatters this equality. When one man kills another man, he declares that he is big and the other is small, is nothing. If the victim's wife and children are forced to witness this, they too are made nothing. When a chemical plant discharges poison gas that wipes out a village, all its people are made nothing and their annihilation is compounded when the officers of the chemical company are allowed to live on without consequence. Among the things I heard during my time in Rwanda, one of the most painful was uttered almost incidentally by a *rescapée* after I asked her if she believed Tutsi and Hutu could ever truly reconcile. "It is impossible," she began, and I think she meant to explain, methodically, impersonally, why this should be so. But suddenly she clutched her head and blurted, *"J'étais très abaissée."* I would translate it as "I was so degraded" or "abased," except the French more clearly expresses the idea of being lowered. At that moment everything that had been done to this woman snapped into focus with such clarity that I could no more stand to look at her directly than if she had been the sun.

From the state's perspective justice has multiple functions, from ensuring that the criminal cannot harm others to deterring future wrongdoers (when the latter is carried beyond a certain point, it becomes a form of mass terrorism with the threat of jail or execution held at the throat of an entire suspect population). To victims of crime, however, or to their survivors, the purpose of justice is to restore the equality between themselves and the persons who wronged them. That this equality is spiritual is evident from the fact that it may be restored even to the dead. It's precisely when justice is denied that people most long for it, even if they can only imagine the world in which it exists. Hell was invented because on earth men commit crime after crime and grow fat while their victims' children go hungry. And perhaps the belief in hell—hell even more than heaven—was enough to console entire nations during the thousands of years in which they suffered at the hands of others without redress, without even the acknowledgment that a wrong had been done to them.

Personally, I doubt it. And I think that societies that fail to address the great crimes in their past remain blighted by them. The long backwardness and impoverishment and brutality of the American South, conditions that afflicted whites as well as blacks, must have had something to do with the unburied corpse of slavery, a corpse that wasn't a corpse at all because in some ways it was still alive, the haint at the crossroads, the hellhound on everybody's trail. Russia may have emerged from the eighty-year sleep of communism but it is still dreaming of the crimes that were committed in communism's name; only in dreams can it name the crimes out loud. You could say that the Southern states remained poor and ignorant and violent because so many young men had been killed in the war; or because they remained dependent on farming; or because slavery—or its kinder, gentler successor, sharecropping—became the paradigm for all the region's labor relationships; or because as long as poor whites were reassured that they were better than blacks they would allow themselves to be treated almost as wretchedly as blacks were. You could find equally rational explanations for Russia's lawlessness and inanition. But you would be ignoring the fact that people who have committed terrible crimes feel guilty or simply afraid and they pass their fear down to their descendents, while those who have survived such crimes, even their children and grandchildren, have a coal burning in their stomachs, which is the desire for justice. Or, if justice is not forthcoming, for revenge. "Do you think it is going to stop because we are safe now?" one *rescapée* asked a foreign observer. "So much death, so much grief, so many families wiped out, and we are to forget about it. The fire is out; but not the fear. And what about the fire inside?"

To assuage the survivors' need for justice—and to address the plight of some 120,000 detainees crushed inside its prisons—the Rwandan government had embarked on a legal experiment. The experiment owed something to South Africa's Truth and Reconciliation Commission and something to traditional Rwandan jurisprudence, or rather, to the idea of such jurisprudence as it had come down through the accounts of European civil servants and anthropologists and the stories of old people. It dispensed with most of the mechanisms of adversarial law. It would, for instance, move the settlement of the genocide from courtrooms to the villages where so much of the slaughter had actually taken place. Instead of legal professionals, the alternative system would use volunteer judges elected from the general population, contemporary counterparts to the elders who had once been the arbiters of the nation's moral life. In place of the skirmishing of rival attorneys, the impugning of witnesses, the dismantling of facts, there would be the stately unscrolling of collective memory. Who knows this man? What are his crimes? Who saw him commit them? And if, in the western model of criminal procedure, the defendant is mostly silent, here he would have a chance—would be urged—to speak; his fate would hinge on his speaking. In a sense the new procedure would be a dialogue between the survivors and the accused, with a role, too, for the witnesses: an entire country telling the story of its wound and coming to agreement about who and what had made it, the agreement being the prelude to the wound's healing. That, at least, was what was supposed to happen. The name for this experiment was *gacaca,* the Kinyarwanda word for "lawn" or "grass."

On one of my first nights in Rwanda I came back to the hotel to find the desk clerk watching a movie on TV. A crime picture: in a clearing in the woods one man was kneeling before another, who was deciding whether to kill him. The kneeling man groveled for his life: "Tommy, look in your heart, Tommy, look in your heart." I'd seen the movie before. The character was a double-crossing scumbag and the actor played him that way, making him sly even in his terror, a being unworthy of life. I wanted him to get it. And very soon Tommy, having looked in his heart, would oblige me. I looked over at the clerk, but couldn't read his expression. "Miller's Crossing," I told him uselessly. *"Dirigé par les frères Coen."*

Kigali is shaped like a bowl, or rather, a group of bowls, the hills forming a rim around a central basin. As in other cities, the heights belong to the wealthy while the low ground is occupied by the poor. The streets in this part of town are unpaved and ungraded. They yaw and pitch and subside into craters that might have been made by bombs. Four-wheel drive is obligatory. Amid the omnipresent red dust even new structures resemble ruins (one exception was an incongruous glass-fronted office tower that turned out to be the property of Laurent Kabuga, a prosperous *génocidaire* who fled Rwanda when the RPA took Kigali and whose present whereabouts are unknown). The combination of topography and history yields a metaphor– the city as mass-grave, as offering bowl filled with bones and blood. Yet at the time of my visit Kigali was a boomtown. For this it could thank the genocide. Everywhere you saw the Land Cruisers and Pajeros of the donors: UNICEF, Oxfam, the World Food Organization, Save the Children, Christian

Aid, whose vehicles bore the slogan, "We believe in life before death." The aid organizations had snapped up the choicest real estate in Nyarugenge, big walled compounds shaded by violet-blossomed jacaranda and patrolled by guards armed with AK-47s. The sidewalks outside were often planted with a surreally purple ground cover called St. Cresa whose triangular leaves made me think of the tips of devils' tails—cartoon devils, maybe. The journalists had spilled out of the Intercon and the Mille Collines into the cheaper hotels, like the one I was staying in on the Rue du Deputé Kamuzinzi, which had no fax service or Internet connection and power that blinked out several times a day. And there were the evangelicals, Americans mostly. They had come to Rwanda for the same reason the donors had: because they saw a vacuum that they felt called upon to fill. And like the journalists, they were in the business of storytelling. Not for nothing did they call themselves bringers of good news.

Rwanda was still mostly Catholic, but ten years after the atrocities the old loyalty was frayed. Too many clergy had collaborated. The U.N.'s International Criminal Tribunal for Rwanda had charged the former rector of Christ-Roi College in Butare province with four counts of genocide. A priest in Kibuye was accused of having murdered 2,000 Tutsi by bulldozing the church in which they had taken refuge. (The holocaust was ecumenical, the list of *génocidaires* also comprising a prominent Seventh-Day Adventist minister.) As a result, Rwandans were migrating to the *"nouvelles églises,"* which were intimate, boisterous and egalitarian and whose doctrines stressed not just the remission of sins but the sloughing off of the self. Well, who wanted to stay the same person who had seen his sisters gang-raped and sawed in half and then hidden for days beneath their corpses? Who wanted to stay the same person who had done such things? Given a choice between being absolved and being reborn, who wouldn't choose to be reborn? To be reborn is to become a baby again, and a baby knows nothing and is loved by everyone (the desire for radical self-renewal may also explain why so many Rwandans were converting to Islam, which according to *The New York Times,* was now the country's fastest-growing religion). After a few weeks in the country, I could spot the evangelicals, and not just because they were white. They were usually heavier than the aid workers, and on the whole they seemed happier. It was the evangelicals who kept telling you how much they loved the Rwandan people.

April 7 would mark the tenth anniversary of the onset of the genocide, and a number of events had been planned in commemoration. The government was holding a march through the center of Kigali, and for a while it was rumored that the U.N. was planning to sponsor one, too (given the often strained relations between the ruling Rwandan Patriotic Front and the U.N., the second march might be seen as a gesture of solidarity, even of atonement, or as one-upmanship. As it turned out, however, the U.N. held its commemoration at its headquarters in New York, and it did not include a march). There would be conferences and symposia. There would be concerts and art exhibits. The remains of an unspecified number of victims would be unearthed from mass graves and formally re-interred on the grounds of the new genocide monument in Gisozi. On a pre-opening visit

I had seen the rows of coffins that would receive them, stacked like crates in a warehouse but decorously covered with strips of lace. At midday the entire nation would observe three minutes of silence. Official guests would include delegates from dozens of countries, 250 from Belgium alone; Pierre-Richard Prosper, chief prosecutor of the ICTR; Philip Gourevitch, the journalist who had written the best-known account of the genocide; and the Canadian general Roméo Dallaire, who as commanding officer of the U.N.'s peace-keeping contingent had tried to avert the catastrophe and, failing, had stayed on to be its witness. Failure and witnessing had weighed on him so heavily that in the years since leaving Rwanda he had on several occasions tried to kill himself. Kofi Annan may also have been invited but chose instead to attend the U. N. ceremony in New York which, all things considered, was probably a good decision. In the spring of 1994 he had been in overall charge of the U.N.'s peace-keeping operations, in which capacity he had vetoed Dallaire's plans to intervene in the bloodletting. If the general could be seen as one of the genocide's collateral casualties, Annan could be seen as one of its many negligent step-fathers.

The world's tendency to treat the genocide as a one-time occurrence irritated many Rwandans. They reminded visitors that Hutu political parties and Hutu-led governments had been orchestrating the mass-murder of Tutsi as early as 1959, maybe not continuously, but with sufficient frequency that somebody should have spotted a trend. Instead, confronted with mounting evidence that certain elements (politicians, military officers, ideologues, street thugs) were preparing a final solution to what someone in those circles may have called 'the Tutsi question'—confronted with General Dallaire's chillingly detailed intelligence of how that solution would be set in motion—the U.N. had not only failed to act but barred Dallaire from acting, cutting his forces from 2,600 to 450. There was plenty more blame to go around. You could blame the U.S, which, dreading a reprise of its humiliation in Somalia the year before, had pressured the U.N. into withdrawing troops. You could blame France, which having succored, equipped—and on occasion fought beside—the Rwandan army through years of human-rights abuses, had continued to protect the génocidaires. Reminding the world of past derelictions was something Rwanda's new leaders were very good at. The exploitation of guilt is a classical Rwandan political skill, denoted by the phrase *akebu kajya iwamugurarura*—"one makes the borrowed basket return." And perhaps, knowing that anniversaries are occasions for strong feelings, including feelings of guilt, the RPF had chosen to mark the genocide as if it were a discreet event that had begun on April 7, 1994 and ended in July of that same year, one hundred days in which close to a million Tutsi and moderate Hutu were killed, at approximately five times the rate at which Europe's Jews had been exterminated under the Third Reich.

A few weeks before I had gone to a village an hour and a half from Kigali to interview a *rescapée* named Jeanne D'Arc M—Joan of Arc M. One of the striking things about the country was how steadfastly it preserved certain remnants of its colonial past, names in particular. Jeanne D'Arc, Dieudonné, Athanasie, Faustin—had anybody in Belgium or France given children such names since World War

II? The village was bleached, dusty, walking through it was like walking through a faded photograph. Even the banana trees seemed leached of color. Jeanne D'Arc's house was built of mud and cow dung and was surprisingly cool inside. It had no windows; light streamed through open doors at the front and back. The only furniture was a bench, a low table, and three high-backed chairs. On one wall was a sampler embroidered with the Kinyarwanda phrase, "Zaburi 143:1." The Biblical reference meant that the family was probably Protestant rather than Catholic.

Jeanne D'Arc had large, deep-set eyes that were the chief source of energy in her face, which was narrow, triangular and distorted by tension, as if it were being pulled in several directions at once. She was forty years old but had the unlined skin of someone much younger. That and her smallness, which was exaggerated by her outsized tee shirt, gave her the look of a pinched child, a child forced to live like a grownup in a world without protectors, and angry about it. We think of people as being aged by suffering but I find that the opposite is often true, perhaps because in extreme pain, as in severe illness, time seems to slow down. Ten years before this woman had seen the genocide sweep through her village. Her husband had been killed; her in-laws had been killed; her sisters had been raped and then killed. She and her two children had survived only by fleeing into the marshes, where she had hidden until the Rwandan Patriotic Army, the military wing of the RPF, had rescued her. She said this without emphasis, but afterwards I realized that she had lived in hiding for three months, amid mud and reeds, tormented by stinging insects, not knowing if she and her children were the only Tutsi left alive. This happened often during the genocide. At a symposium in the States I met a woman who had spent those hundred days huddled with thirty others in the tiny bathroom of an Anglican church. She too seemed oddly youthful.

Jeanne D'Arc lived in an isolation that was almost absolute. Apart from her children and brother, who had hidden separately in the bush, there were no other Tutsi left in the village. Her relations with her neighbors were minimal. The people across the road—the road in question was barely ten feet wide—were "criminals." That is, the husband was in jail for things he'd done during the genocide and in Jeanne D'Arc's eyes his guilt extended to his wife. Still, she tried to get along with her for the children's sake; if anything were to happen to her, she'd need someone to take her to the hospital. It had been suggested in official circles that the ten-year commemorations would provide the country's thousands of rescapés with what Americans call "closure." I don't remember what word Rwandans were using. Jeanne D'Arc had no plans to attend any of the ceremonies, neither the big one in Kigali nor the smaller one in her district capital. "It just brings everything back," she told me. "The thoughts turn in my head. I look at pictures of my family and I relive all those years before. I'd like to tell the government to stop the celebrations. They're for the people who are happy, not for the ones who still grieve."

I was working with a translator named Geneviève and a Dutch journalist, and the latter asked Jeanne D'Arc how she envisioned her future. "I can't say anything about my future. The only thing that's important to me is my children. Let them grow up safe and healthy. As for me, there is nothing." She folded her arms defiantly across her chest, as if someone had suggested otherwise, then said it again, almost spitting. "Nothing."

"Zaburi" means "Psalms." It wasn't until I got back to the States that I had a chance to open a bible and read the verse in question: "Hear my prayer, O Lord, give ear to my supplications; in thy faithfulness answer me, and in thy righteousness." The next verse goes, "And enter not into judgment with thy servant: for in thy sight shall no man living be justified."

To see the contours of the genocide you had to squint through a haze of misrepresentations so dense that in comparison mere facts seemed gauzy and unconvincing. Some of the misrepresentations were products of ignorance and laziness and some were deliberate. It was ignorance and laziness, together with racism, that led the American press to initially characterize the killings as 'ancient' and 'tribal', words that connoted a spontaneous upwelling of essential African savagery, drums beating in the background. Of course such characterizations proved useful to interests, primarily but not exclusively American, that opposed intervening in Rwanda. This was just what those people did to each other every few years, what could anybody do about it? The aforementioned interests sometimes argued that the killings weren't really genocide, they just looked like genocide. (As I write this, much the same arguments are being made about the atrocities in Darfur.) This distinction was necessary in view of the 1948 U.N. convention that treats genocide as a trip-wire requiring an immediate response from all member states. To watch footage in which a Clinton administration spokeswoman tortuously skirts the g-word is to get a premonition of Clinton himself, four years later, saying "It depends on what you mean by 'is.'" It's also to have incontrovertible proof that history really does replay tragedy as farce. The French, for their part, seized on the RPF's killings of Hutu civilians to make the peevish case for a "double genocide," a term they found so apt that they were still using it ten years later.

In this manner the whole of Rwandan history became debatable, as did the very nature of categories like Hutu and Tutsi. (A third group, the Twa, is too small and marginalized to figure significantly here.) The old wisdom, promulgated by German and Belgian colonists and in time accepted by the colonized, spoke of tribes. The Tutsi were tall, attenuated, elegantly sharp of feature; the Hutu short and thickset. They were Eloi and Morlocks. Dazzled by the Tutsis' physical beauty and their docile, tidily centralized kingdom, Europeans insisted that they had to come from somewhere else, Ethiopia or Tibet or, most daffily, Israel, an origin suggested by their intelligence and 'love of money.' (Years later, recalling the Ethiopian theory, a Hutu propagandist would promise to send the Tutsi back there "via the Nyabarongo," a river that flows north.) Wherever they came from, they weren't really black. The Europeans saw that the Tutsi ruled and decided that they were born to do so. They saw that Hutu served and decreed that serving was their biological destiny. They didn't notice that only some Tutsi ruled while others were quite as lowly as their Hutu neighbors, or that the two groups' ties of clientage and subjection were fairly recent, dating only to the 1860s. That was history and the *abazungu,* the whites, didn't believe Rwanda had history. It had race. And in the years that followed their subjects came to think so too. Under colonialism even the most wretched Tutsi prided themselves on their noble blood, while after independence an entire ideology sprang up around the importance of being Hutu. By the time of the genocide the ranters of Radio Television Libre Mille Collines were claiming that the Tutsi fighters of the RPF had tails, cloven hooves, and red eyes that shone in the dark. And many Hutu were believing them.

However, unlike any of the other groups that anthropologists recognize as separate ethnicities, Hutu and Tutsi lived together, spoke the same language, observed the same customs, ate the same food. In addition, the two populations had been intermarrying for so long that they were often difficult to identify on sight. And since 1994, of course, the talk about race had come to seem not just unsound but sinister. In its place one now spoke of class, the word "Tutsi" designating aristocratic herdsmen and "Hutu" peasant farmers. The *mwami,* or divine king, was a Tutsi , as were most of his court, but elsewhere the social boundaries were said to be so porous that Hutu could become Tutsi by acquiring cattle and Tutsi who lost their herds "fell" into Hutu-dom. If the tribal model advanced the interests of the colonial authorities, the discourse of class served the purposes of the RPF. Because most of its leaders were Tutsi, the only way it could pass for democratic was to blur distinctions between the rulers and the ruled.

For similar reasons it promoted the fiction that the two groups had lived together in prelapsarian harmony until the *muzungu* came slithering into the garden. Like the first serpent, he had tempted the garden's inhabitants with knowledge, not the knowledge of good and evil but the knowledge of Hutu and Tutsi. In post-genocide Rwanda it was bad form to use those labels; in some instances it was illegal. Everybody was now just 'Banyarwanda.' Foreign observers were saying so too. An American journalist assured me that the difference between Tutsi and Hutu was no greater than that between people from Brooklyn Heights and people from Bensonhurst. "You can tell if somebody's from Bensonhurst just by looking at him, but that doesn't mean that Bensonhursters are their own ethnic group."

I tested this theory on a cab driver named Alphonse. He was a Tutsi, who had escaped the genocide by fleeing to Burundi and returned to find that more than thirty of his relatives had been killed. "No, that's not right," he said briskly. "Tutsi and Hutu are different. Tutsi are tall, they're thin, they have long noses—*comme les blancs,"* he added. "Hutu are short and very strong and they like to eat a lot. Also they have flat noses with big nostrils." He flattened his own nose with a finger. "Their nostrils are ten centimeters wide!" Here I should add that Alphonse was quite short, no more than 5'6", and had a very broad nose.

What all this reminded me of was the old debate about Jews: Were we a religion or a race? I used to brood about it as a child, not the actual question—none of the Jews I knew were all that troubled by phenomenological uncertainty—so much as the fact that some gentiles were so intent on classifying us. Even as a ten-year-old I intuitively understood that classification was a kind of mastery and that it might be a prelude to other kinds that were less conceptual. Having classified the Jews as a race (though not, as Goebbels liked to say, a human one), the Nazis snapped the constraints that had hampered the Inquisition and were free to destroy Jews who had never set foot in a synagogue, Jews who had turned Christian, and—in the case of children of gentile mothers—Jews who by Jewish standards had never been Jews at all. To know that *goyim* were still trying to figure out what we were after all that was to sense what a cow might feel if it were somehow to see a butcher's diagram of cuts of beef.

Many Tutsi I met felt a kinship with Jews. "The Tutsi and the Hebrews," a Pentecostal minister mused, as we bumped down a paved road that wound around one of Kigali's hills. "Two peoples who have suffered so much for such tiny countries." Once I was interviewing Benoit Kaboyi, a spokesman for Ibuka, an organization of Tutsi genocide survivors whose name means "Remember!" We were speaking at cross-purposes, every question I asked seemed to offend him, until it finally came out that I was Jewish and my father's mother had been killed at Auschwitz. "Oh, then you understand," he said, with the peremptory triumph of a man who has just succeeded in getting his point across to someone very stupid.

But of course I didn't. I had never known my grandmother or any of the other relatives who vanished in the camps. I had never seen my people rounded up for slaughter. I had never been forced to live next door to their murderers.

In the initial interview the police officer is deferential while the subject speaks in monosyllables. Her voice is not just flat but oddly stifled, as if she were speaking through some obstruction, as for example a mask or a blanket that she had pulled over her head.

> You understood your rights?
> Yes.
> OK, I'm going to read them to you again for the purposes of this tape recording, OK?
> OK.
> You have the right to remain silent and not make any statement at all and that any statement you make may be used against you and probably will be used against you at your trial. Do you understand that?
> Yes.
> Any statement you make may be used as evidence against you in court. Do you understand that?
> Yes.
> You have the right to have a lawyer present to advise you prior to and during any questioning. Do you understand that?
> Yes.
> If you are unable to employ a lawyer you have the right to have a lawyer appointed to advise you prior to and during any questioning. Do you understand that?
> Yes.

And you have the right to terminate this interview at any time. Do you understand that?

Yes.

Are you willing to waive those rights that I've just read to you and continue to talk to me about this?

Yes.

This was June 20, 2001, at one in the afternoon. The interviewer was Sergeant E.S Mehl of the Houston Police Department; the subject's name was Andrea Pia Yates. She was 36 years old. In her mug shots she is thin, lank-haired, with a heavy jaw and a wide, sensitive mouth. She stares at the viewer so intently that her eyes seem lidless, and their expression is at once fearful—terrified, really—and grief-stricken, though it's possible that she was too dazed to feel much of anything. She may not have known what day it was or why she was being made, gently, by deferential Houston police officers, to stand in front of a wall-chart marked with lines and numbers, first face-on and then sideways, while somebody took her picture. My sense is that the police were treating her delicately, as one treats the victims of particularly ghastly crimes, but also with horror and even awe, which is not something policemen often feel. She may have sensed the complexity of the feelings that crackled around her. Maybe she thought she was in hell. She'd been thinking of hell a great deal and she would later tell doctors that she had done what she had that morning with the purpose of saving her children from it.

Newspaper reports would describe her as a nurse, though it had been seven years since she'd last worked in a hospital. Since then she had devoted herself full time to the care of her husband, Russell and their five children: Noah, aged 7, John, 5, Paul 3, Luke 2, and a girl, Mary, aged six months. Rusty Yates was a deeply, if narrowly religious Christian, who took certain scriptural injunctions literally, among them the ones concerning man's dominion over his wife, and testimony suggests that it was he who wanted a large family and insisted that Andrea school the children at home.

Following the birth of her fourth child, however, she fell into a severe depression, refusing to eat or bathe or speak and twice attempting to kill herself. She was hospitalized and put on the drug Haldol, which relieved her symptoms, but her psychiatrist warned the couple that having another child could precipitate further episodes of what had been diagnosed as not just post-partum depression but psychosis. This was in August, 1999. In November of 2000 Andrea Yates gave birth to a daughter, Mary. The following March her father died after a long illness and her symptoms began to recur. Her mother-in-law found her agitated and unresponsive. "If I asked her a question, she often whispered a delayed answer or did not answer at all. She would stare into space. Her arm trembled. She would tap her foot and scratch her head until it was bald in spots. She bit her lip. She didn't eat." Twice more she was hospitalized and released. Rusty's response was to ask his mother to help with the housework and childcare. On the morning of June 20 he left their house in Clear Lake for his job at NASA. Andrea was to stay alone with the children until his mother arrived. Sometime after that she called 911 and asked the operator to send the police. She would not say what the problem was, which prosecutors would later cite as evidence of a guilty conscience.

When officers arrived at the Yates' one-story Spanish-style house on Beachcomber Drive, she was waiting for them, her hair wet and tangled. She ushered them into a bedroom. Here four of her children lay side by side on a bed, their bodies covered with a blanket. One of the officers followed a trail of water to the bathroom, where the fifth child, Noah, was lying face down in the bathtub.

> Um, after Rusty left, you filled the bathtub with water, is that correct?
> Yes.
> How many bathtubs are in your home?
> One.
> OK, so it's just the, uh, the master bath I guess you would call it?
> Yes.
> OK, is it a regular sized bathtub or is it a big one?
> Regular sized.
> How far did you fill it?
> About three inches from the top.
> About three inches from the top, um, after you drew the bath water, what was your intent? What were you about to do?
> Drown the children.
> OK. Why were you going to drown your children?
> Here the transcript reads, "Fifteen seconds of silence."
> Was it, was it in reference to, or was it because the children had done something?
> No.
> You were not mad at the children?
> No.
> OK, um, you had thought of this prior to this day?
> Yes.
> Um, how long have you been having thoughts about wanting, or not wanting to, but drowning your children?
> Probably since I realized I have not been a good mother to them.
> What makes you say that?
> They weren't developing correctly.
> Behavioral problems?
> Yes.
> Learning problems?
> Yes.
> So after you drew the bath water, what happened?
> I put Paul in.
> OK, and when you put Paul in the bath water, was he face down or face up? He was face down.
> And he struggled with you?

Yes.

How long do you think that struggle happened?

A couple of minutes.

And you were able to forcibly hold him under the water?

Yes.

By the time you brought him out of the water, had he stopped struggling?

Yes.

There was no more movement?

No.

This happened four more times. Yates testified that only Noah tried to run from her. But the medical examiners found a strand of her hair in John's fist, which suggests that there was a struggle.

To read an account of an actual crime—what book publishers call a "true crime"—is to experience several different kinds of tension. One has a sense of time moving unswervingly toward a predetermined end, the moment in which the crime is committed. The closer it draws to that end, the more swiftly it seems to move. Yet even as it approaches the terminal moment time is pared into finer and finer slices, no longer months or weeks but hours, minutes, seconds, and each of those slices is dense with incident. The husband gets up from the breakfast table and kisses his wife and children; the door clicks shut behind him. The mother clears the breakfast things, stacks milky bowls in a sink. A little boy whines to be let out. The baby waves her spoon, and a soggy bit of cereal flies off and sticks to the baseboard. The mother stoops to wipe it off, then straightens as if remembering something. She goes into the bathroom. She turns on the bathtub faucet. She tests the water temperature on her wrist. This tension between speed and slowness is one of the chief characteristics of suspense.

In the last moments everything is documented. Here, as in some grotesque dance chart, are all the actions the perpetrator and victims took on their way to their fatal intersection, down to the last flailing struggle in two feet of filthy bathwater. We owe this density of detail to the courtroom and forensic technologies that unpack entire narratives from a spray of bloodstains or the dried saliva on a pillow. So in addition to the tension between speed and slowness, there's a tension between the known and the unknown, between what is witnessed (for true-crime writing makes the reader a witness to acts that in reality occurred in darkness) and what can only be imagined. No matter how much information we are given about the crime, we never know what passed through the victim's mind in his last moments, nor, for that matter, through the killer's. At least a killer of a certain sort, an amateur. For even when such a person confesses, my guess would be that she holds something back, out of cunning or guilt or because she has walled off the part of herself that experienced the murderous impulse and has no more access to the thoughts of that other self than she would to any stranger's. Such a killer might be described as innocent, not because she is blameless but because she knows nothing.

In turning the reader into a witness, the true-crime narrative places him in a moral quandary, for someone who witnesses a crime is supposed to intervene. The more immediate and detailed the account, the more urgently one feels this pressure. Who wouldn't want to save five small children from being killed, or their deranged mother from killing them? But it's too late to save anybody. The children are in the earth; the mother is in a cell. The dream of the present dissolves like a bridge of sand and we remember that we are reading about the past, which we cannot change. The result is a third sort of tension, that between the reader's fantasies of power and his recognition of his powerlessness. The same tension is at work in what might be called true-crime's prototype, Greek tragedy, which also dramatized terrible misdeeds whose outcome the spectators knew by heart:

> CASSANDRA: Alas, O wicked! Is thy purpose that?
> He who hath shared thy bed,
> To bathe his limbs, to smile—how speak the end?
> The end comes, and quickly:
> A hand reaching out, followed by a hand again!

Cassandra has the ambiguous gift of predicting the future, but in *Agamnenon* the horror she prophesies takes place in real-time, as if she were watching it unfold on a video monitor. In another moment she too will become its victim. One of the distinguishing features of the violence in Greek tragedy is that it is fated. "What is happening cannot be otherwise, cannot not happen." Apart from all the appeals to moral or ritual obligation, the commands of the gods or the strictures of kinship, the characters kill because they have to, out of a necessity as implacable as the laws of physics or mathematics. Imagine Agamemnon's murder as the product of a quadratic equation whose first term is the crime of his father Atreus and whose second is his own sacrifice of his daughter, Iphigenia. That Atreus is a monster who butchered and stewed his brother's children and Agamemnon merely a warlord trying to appease a goddess is irrelevant. When you see an equation written on a blackboard, there's nothing to indicate whether the numbers denote apples or severed heads, and either way the answer is the same.

A few contemporary press accounts suggested that the Yates killings, too, seemed fated, citing their hum of portent and particularly the warnings of the psychiatrist who treated Andrea after her last suicide attempt. (Rusty Yates reportedly tried to have this doctor charged with criminal negligence.) But fate was a pagan invention. Christianity has always had problems with it. It was bound to be uncomfortable with a force the Greeks had placed even above the gods, which is why Boethius spends so much of *The Consolation* trying to demote it. Fate reduces free will to the papery thrashings of a moth in a bell jar—a moth that thinks it is gliding through the open sky. And from a fundamentalist perspective, fate is particularly dangerous because it makes it harder to assign blame. How do you blame a killer who is obeying the compulsion of destiny? Such a person is not an actor but a weapon—say, the shears of Atropos, the last and most dreadful of the moirae. What do you a call a killer whom fate obliges to slay her own child or spouse or parent? Perhaps another victim. As she stands trembling before her son's sword-blade, even Clytemnestra becomes an object of pity. The chorus declaims, "I weep for both and for their double pain." As earlier, watching her slay Agamemnon, it asks, "What here was not sent from heaven?" In the eulogy he delivered at his children's funeral, Rusty Yates declared that everything that had happened had been God's will.

Gérard Prunier, the most eloquent chronicler of the Rwandan genocide, notes that it, too, seems to have been fated. The equation is more complicated than the ones that yield the deaths of Agamemnon and the Yates children, but it makes sense that a nation's fate would be more complicated than any individual's. For centuries Hutu and Tutsi had a relationship that was partly exploitative and partly symbiotic. Under King Rwabugiri the relationship tilted further toward exploitation. The Tutsi accrued more power and the Hutus lost it. One or two days of every six they had to perform the humiliating *corvée* labor known as *uburetwa*. Tutsi were exempt from it. First the Germans and then the Belgians, with not a little guidance from Catholic missionaries, wrote these inequalities into law; the latter introduced identity cards so that everyone would know who was Hutu and who Tutsi. The cards translated colonial fantasies of race into the realities of class. People who carried one kind of card got educations and jobs in the civil service. Those who carried the other sort had to be content tilling their stony plots on those green hills as perfectly conical as the hills in a child's illustrated fairytale. Both groups learned to see themselves the way their colonizers saw them: as clever, lordly, quasi-Caucasians or as stolid, pious, rather dull-witted sons of the soil.

Beginning in the 1950s, however, the authorities underwent a change of heart. Rwanda was to be democratic. Democracy meant majority rule. The Hutu were the majority, then as now some 85 percent of the population. Therefore they would rule. In preparation for that day, the Belgians ushered select Hutu into schools and government and encouraged the formation of Hutu political parties. The prevailing ideology of the latter could be summed up as, Now it's our turn. This was understandable and in a more prosperous country might not have been a bad thing. But in Rwanda there was little to take a turn at, and so the ideology came to mean getting back at the old oppressors—not the Belgians, who were on their way out, but the Tutsi. The massacres started even before independence and continued at intervals throughout the presidency of Grégoire Kayibanda. One outbreak in 1963 claimed 10,000 victims in four days. In 1973 the pogroms spread into the schools, where Hutu students killed their Tutsi classmates with impunity. One *rescapé* recalls that the President's response to protests was, "Oh, those are just children playing."

The man who told me this story was a researcher named Isidore Munyakazi who had come to America to do his post-graduate work in theology and peace studies.

Physically he was an archetypal Tutsi, tall and thin even in middle age, with cautious, deep-set eyes. When I met him (incredibly enough, while I was raking leaves on my front lawn and he was canvassing the neighborhood for the phone company), he struck me as vain. He was going bald but disguised it with a sporty wool cap that he wore indoors and out. His people came from the East, near Kibungo. His father had owned a great many cows, the traditional measure of wealth, and used to spend hours standing on a tall termite hill on his land, watching them graze below. But during the pogroms of '73, Isidore told me, Hutu came and, not content with stealing cattle and beating the herdsman, destroyed the hill. "Destroyed it, for no reason. And I cannot forget the time that the chief of police came to our house and shot our dog. He did it only because it was a strong, brave dog. It would bark and bark to protect us. There was no other dog like this one. And so the chief of police"—he aimed an imaginary rifle and squeezed its trigger—"shot him."

I was struck by how calmly he could speak about what he'd seen during the genocide. He would describe crouching in the pews of the Church of St. Paul, trying not to attract the attention of the Interahamwe who were prowling its aisles in search of victims, and his tone would be placid, even proud. He had survived a calamity that had swallowed almost a million other people and saved his family as well, partly through luck or providence but partly because of his courage and resourcefulness. Yet when Isidore spoke of the shooting of the family dog, his voice was filled with wondering grief. He sounded almost childlike. Maybe it was because our love for animals is rooted deep in the earth of childhood. And maybe he sounded that way because the gratuitous meanness—the spite—of those attacks was enough to make any grownup cry out in childlike incredulity, the outrage of a child who has seen something he loves destroyed by another child. In mythological terms Hutu and Tutsi often resemble warring twins; it's an odd coincidence that their traditional occupations, farming and herding, are the same respectively as Cain and Abel's. Over the years the Hutus' hatred has become ingrown and baroque—during the genocide it seemed that they would give Tutsi extra organs for the pleasure of ripping them out—but from time to time they revert to slaps and pinches. And weak as these are, they still draw blood.

Isidore told me that his brother and the police chief were now neighbors, and friendly. 'They drink beer together, and my brother says—,' his voice became teasing, 'I still remember what you did to my father's dog, don't think I don't remember.' And the chief of police says, 'I didn't do this thing. They made me do it."' I would like to know if Isidore's brother believes him, or if the chief expects him to.

Juvénal Habyarimana, the army general who overthrew Kayibanda in a coup in 1973, cast himself as a protector of Tutsi: Just so in Hebrew school we used to hear about "good tsars" who sheltered the Jews. He seized power on the pretext of restoring order after the pogroms, and during the early years of his presidency there were fewer outbreaks of violence. Relatively speaking, Rwanda prospered. But over time the economy deteriorated. The World Bank, which had loaned the country a great deal of money during the good years, began its familiar disastrous tinkering in the social machinery, deepening inequalities and creating a new class of dispossessed and idle young people. These would eventually find employment in the ranks of the Interahamwe. In 1990 an army of mostly Tutsi exiles led by Major Paul Kagame invaded the country from neighboring Uganda. The response of the Habyarimana regime was to seize on the methods of its predecessor and lash out at the Tutsi under its control. Over the next four years a pattern emerged: paroxysms of ethnic violence leading to defections to the rebel forces, whose advances justified further violence.

As money dried up and the RPF pushed deeper into Rwanda, the Hutu power structure began to fracture. Moderates wanted an accommodation with the rebels. Hardliners simply wanted to crush the Inyenzi—the "cockroaches." In the journal Kangura one found the "Ten Commandments of the Hutu." (Number Eight: "Hutu must cease to have pity on Tutsi.") Not content with bloodthirsty rhetoric, some of the factions acquired militias. A death squad called Reseau Zero carried out massacres of Tutsi and hits on members of the Hutu opposition; its leaders included several of the President's notably ambitious in-laws, who were beginning to turn on their patron. If Habyarimana had been content with a semi-totalitarian Rwanda, the new extremists, in Prunier's formulation, aspired to "absolute power through absolute terror." Part of the awfulness of the genocide is that it emerged from a rivalry between Hutu factions. It was a ploy in that rivalry. As if someone, sensing that he is about to lose a high-stakes game of cards, were to take out a gun and shoot, not the other player, but a stranger at another table. The philosopher René Girard writes: "In some societies whole categories of human beings are systematically reserved for sacrificial purposes in order to protect other categories."

On the evening of April 6, 1994 the presidential jet was shot down shortly before it landed in the capital, killing Habyarimana and the newly-elected president of neighboring Burundi. For all the mystery attending the assassination (furtive white men seen fleeing the vicinity; a recent French inquest that pins the blame on Kagame) there's no question as to what it signaled. As soon as he heard of the crash, Isidore Munyakazi began telephoning foreign acquaintances to see if any of them would shelter his family. One man, a Belgian, agreed, but shortly afterward called back to say that he couldn't come to fetch them. The city was already full of roadblocks.

For the next three months Rwanda gave itself over to a single national project, the annihilation of the Tutsi and their Hutu "allies." The project was organized from above, and its orders were passed down as if by a bureaucratic bucket brigade, from the Presidential Palace and the Ministry of Defense down through the prefectures and districts to the individual cellules. There were meticulously compiled lists of victims. There was a specialized killing apparatus. The militiamen who came to cull the refugees in the churches of St. Paul and Ste. Famille came bearing signed authorizations. All this was in accordance with the country's reputation as the Switzerland of Africa. Yet the genocide was also a popular project, one that enlisted—implicated—a broad swath of Rwandan society. It appealed not just to people's fears and resentments but to a spirit of license. The image that comes to mind is a carnival, one painted by Breughel, with revelers waving bloody scythes and bonfires that have real bodies burning in them. Goaded by the Interahamwe, ordinary farmers became murderers, timid at first, but increasingly skilled and enthusiastic. "The whole village would go out and come back, and the whole village would celebrate in the evening, and the whole village would split up the booty," a foreign researcher told me. "And the women would be eager for their men to come back and bring as much as they could. Suddenly they were rich. They could only do this for a while, because they could only leave the soil for one season. So instead of harrowing the soil, they harrowed humans."

For the normal Tutsi life ceased to exist. One of the problems attending post-genocide legal proceedings is that so few of the *rescapés* can compose a coherent narrative of what they lived through, the typical survivor's story consisting of a primal scene of cauterizing horror followed by months of flight or hiding, the world shrunk down to the dimensions of a false ceiling or a fetid bathroom where you and thirty others made yourselves as small and quiet as you could, knowing that even breathing too loudly might draw the attention of people who had made it their business to kill you. How to distinguish one day of this from the next? Narrative does for time what geometry does for space, it makes events make sense, but some events will not be made sense of. A woman interviewed by the filmmaker Anne Aghion recalls looking out her doorway one morning to see the people on the next hill methodically butchering their neighbors. "At first," she says, "you'd think they were cutting down banana trees. People feel no pity when they cut down a banana."

From above the genocide was ordered and even logical; on the ground it was chaos. This division is familiar from accounts of war. Generals see one thing and foot-soldiers see another, and before they lose the power of sight the ones the soldiers kill see something else again. Almost fifteen hundred years ago Boethius struggled to reconcile the divine order that rules the universe with the heartless randomness of the real, which was about to make him one of its casualties. He pictured a series of concentric circles with a tower rising from its center and God at the summit. Where the outer circles described their grinding revolutions, all was noise and motion and smoke. But at the center it was still, the air was clear. Atop His tower, God looked down on creation and instead of mindless colliding and pullulating beheld the stately working-out of Providence. Perhaps that is how the genocide looked to its architects: its gods. Rwanda is a very small country, with many high places, and you can imagine the *génocidaires* standing on a hilltop, surveying their work—the industry and ingenuity of the killers, the plenitude of the dead—and seeing that it was good.

I'm not a trained journalist, and I have to admit that it was a while before I could bring myself to ask Rwandans to talk about what had happened to them in more than general terms. I was afraid of sounding prurient and I was afraid of compelling traumatized people to excavate the traumatic past. Here is part of an interview with Beata Mukamazimpaka, a proud employee of the pharmaceutical company KiPharma and a volunteer gacaca judge, in her late fifties, dignified, softly wattled, with half-glasses dangling from a chain about her neck. It was difficult to picture her hiding beneath a false ceiling while Interahamwe storm-troopers sacked her house and murdered the members of her family who had been unlucky enough to remain below:

> It was evening, towards nine o'clock. We had closed up the house because we were afraid... People came, I don't know who. They were Hutu. They told me, "Open up!" I asked them, "Are you Tutsi?" They said, "Open up! If you don't open up, we'll do it ourselves and then you'll see." Again and again I asked, "Are you Tutsi?" Somebody tried to beat the door down. My son, who was sitting in the living room, they caught him. Then they tried to cut off the lights, the electricity. The imbeciles, may their mother cut out their hearts! They began to take things out of the house. They broke things. My grandfather said, "Run for your lives!" He yelled, yelled, yelled. But. . . . they killed my son. Later we heard noises. Maybe they were climbing [up to the roof] to pry off the tiles. I was agitated. . .I told Giselle—the daughter of my niece who was killed—"Be quiet, because they're trying to pry off the roof tiles. Be quiet! They're going to kill us all!" . . . They left around two in the morning. . . . Finally we parted the curtains a little and saw that there was nobody outside. They were gone. The children went to the neighbors' house. I also went to a neighbor's. But they'd killed him.

When I listen to the tape, what leaps out at me are the questions I failed to ask. When and how did the intruders actually enter the house? Why did Beata's son stay downstairs in the living room instead of climbing to safety in the rafters? Did he sacrifice himself to protect his mother? Did she hear him being killed or only discover his body when she came down from her hiding place? As Beata recounted her exchange with the thugs at the door, I had a sudden image of the Big Bad Wolf saying, "I'll huff and I'll puff and I'll blow your house down." At the time it seemed shamefully inappropriate. But of course even a cursory reading of the Brothers Grimm reminds us that the old fairy tales are awash in blood. She answered my questions in French, but toward the end of the interview she summed up her predicament in English: "I can say that we have survived, but survived dead because we are all the time dead."

Nobody disputed that Andrea Yates had killed her children, and so any defense would have to hinge on her sanity. Most observers agreed that she was severely mentally ill. For days on end she sat in her prison cell, seemingly unconscious of her surroundings. She shook and picked at her scalp. When her husband entered her holding cell, her first words to him were, "You will be greatly rewarded." To an examining psychiatrist, she amplified the explanations that had so plainly baffled Sergeant Mehl. The children had to die because she was a bad mother. She knew she was a bad mother because they kept misbehaving. "They didn't do things God likes," she said. "They stumbled because I was evil. They were doomed to perish in the fires of hell." The reason she knew that was because Satan himself had told her so. He had also told her that the only way to save them was by ending their corrupted lives. Then, presumably, the state would end hers. Here was somebody who wanted to die, wanted it so badly that she may have seen her children's murder simply as a means to that end. The psychiatrist Lucy Puryear, who diagnosed Yates as schizophrenic with post-partum psychosis, testified that she was the sickest person she had ever treated.

In August, however, the Harris County District Attorney's office announced its intention to charge Yates with multiple counts of capital murder, and to seek the death penalty.

The State of Texas defines insanity in accordance with the 1843 M'Naghten Rule, which excuses a defendant from criminal responsibility only if his mental impairment made him ignorant of the nature and quality of his act, at the time he committed it, or incapable of distinguishing right from wrong. It would apply to someone who stabbed a man to death thinking he was stabbing a wild beast or the devil or that the knife in his hand was a rose. It would apply to someone who believed that there was no moral impediment to his stabbing anyone he pleased. It does not apply to most of the people we usually describe as mentally ill. The M'Naghten rule belongs to an age when insanity was simply the binary opposite of sanity and lunatics belonged to the same conceptual class as midgets and Siamese twins. In most of the country it has been replaced by more nuanced diagnostic standards. Texas is one of the few states that still uses it. Texas law also stipulates that criminal defendants are sane and places upon them the burden of proving otherwise. You might educe this as a further example of a judicial rigor that has made the state the U.S.'s perennial leader in executions; since 1976 it has killed 289 inmates, more than the four runner-ups combined. You could also argue that the Texan attitude toward insanity reflects an ethic of individualism that nails each person squarely to the cross of his actions. Among the nails used is a state law that bars a judge from informing a jury that a defendant it finds not guilty by reason of insanity may still be incarcerated for the rest of his life. I have tried repeatedly and fruitlessly to rewrite that last sentence to make it clearer and am convinced that its tortured syntax reflects something tortured in the law itself. As any carpenter will tell you, the best way of making sure a nail doesn't come loose is to bend it as you drive it in.

Still, even in Texas seeking the death penalty for a woman—moreover, a white, middle-class woman—was unusual and politically risky. Before filing charges, Joe Owmby consulted not just other district attorneys but members of his church. Owmby is African-American and goes to an African-American church where most of the people he canvassed, he says, "had this opinion: They had the suspicion that if Andrea Yates had been black, we wouldn't be having all this attention in the first place." His voice held a playful snap of impatience. Maybe he was enjoying twitting a white liberal—there was no use pretending I wasn't one—for his squeamishness.

"The black people that I know are not opposed to the concept of retribution. A lot of them are opposed to the death penalty because of the way they feel it is carried out, but the principal underlying concept of the death penalty being right for certain crimes, not a lot of African-Americans are opposed to that. And a lot of people I talked to strongly felt that justice would be served if Yates received the death penalty." During this time, Owmby told me, he'd been listening to a radio talk show in which most of the discussion had to do with the Yates case. One caller had said: "'You know, I can understand how a mother can be under pressure psychologically and kill a child. I can understand that. But,' and he put it this way, 'I think she ought to be coming to herself around that third child.' His point was, What are we debating? This woman killed five children. Even a crazed person would have time to consider. And from the newspaper accounts, this wasn't some frenzy."

The Greeks, too, equated madness with frenzy, the violent overthrow of reason and the senses, usually inflicted by the gods. Frenzy is an amalgam of ecstasy, terror and rage. Its victims cannot distinguish between one thing and another, between one person and another, or between persons and animals. In their delusion they become like animals themselves. Maddened by Dionysus, Queen Agave mistakes her son for a lion and, with her fellow Maenads, rips him to pieces as a lioness might. People in a frenzy do hideous things but are rarely punished for them. What punishment could be more terrible than Agave's realization that she has killed her son? Frenzy itself is the punishment.

But Andrea Yates had killed her children methodically. "It takes a while to kill five children," Owmby told me, "And it takes some thought." Because she had thought, because she had waited to act until there was no one in the house to stop her, because she had drowned her children one by one instead of laying about her with a knife—an option she had considered but dismissed as too bloody—she couldn't be insane. Most criminal trials may be seen as a contest between two opposing sets of facts, but the Yates trial, which began eight months after the murders, pitted two opposing definitions of madness. Andrea's attorneys and psychiatrists cited her suicide attempts and hospitalizations, her catatonic symptoms, the Satanic voice that tormented her with descriptions of her children's eternal suffering. Owmby and his colleague Kaylynn Williford kept reminding the jury that Yates hadn't acted in a frenzy. And when the police came to her door that day, she didn't tell them that she had saved her children but that she had killed them.

Their star witness was Park Dietz, a California-based forensic psychiatrist who had honed his reputation on Jeffrey Dahmer and the Unabomber, on which basis he was said to command fees of five hundred dollars an hour. He claimed that Yates had been sane at the time she committed the crimes and only become psychotic afterward: Killing her children had driven her crazy. Throughout, she had known that what she was doing was wrong. Otherwise, Dietz argued, "I would expect her to try and comfort the children, telling them they are going to be with Jesus or with God." She had not tried to comfort them. And afterwards she had covered their bodies with a blanket, which the psychiatrist read as evidence of a guilty conscience rather than of maternal solicitude or a pathetic wish to turn dead children into sleeping ones. The most damning piece of evidence, though, was an episode of the TV show "Law and Order" that had aired some time before the killings. The plot concerned a woman who drowned her child in the bathtub and got off on an insanity plea. Dietz said that Andrea must have seen the episode and been inspired, and his interpretation had a certain persuasiveness since, in addition to his other credentials, he was one of the program's consultants. But when Yates's counsel George Parnham tried to verify these claims, he discovered that no such episode of "Law and Order" had ever been broadcast or even taped. Confronted with the inaccuracy, Dietz conceded that he had been mistaken. Parnham, whose air of gentle, somewhat baffled decency seems almost out of place in a criminal lawyer, asked for a mistrial. The judge refused to grant one. On March 12, 2002, after deliberating for three and a half hours, the jury found Andrea Yates guilty on two counts of capital murder.

What decided them, in the end, may not have been the contradictory and confusing assertions about the defendant's mental state, but the evidence of what the victims had suffered before they died. That did not have to be interpreted. Williford reminded the jury that it takes a drowning child some three minutes to lose consciousness. Noah had died in water that contained his siblings' vomit and feces. "Is this the act of a loving mother?" she asked. One commentator shrewdly observed that this was the prosecution's covert theme, one that made any debate about intent and insanity beside the point: Andrea Yates had been a bad mother. It followed that her children had to be taken away from her. In her closing argument, Williford repeatedly claimed to be acting on their behalf, to be demanding the justice they could not ask for, a justice whose central provision was that their mother be put to death. These claims were unverifiable, the children being dead. Still, many people believed that this would be what they wanted. After the jury pronounced Yates guilty, the president of a victims' rights group called Justice for All told reporters, "I believe it was the absolute perfect verdict. In all of this, we didn't have someone to speak for the children. But [the prosecutors] spoke for the five children, and the jury heard them."

If the prosecutors had wanted victims who could speak for themselves, they could have found them in the courtroom. There was Rusty Yates, compulsively playing Tetris on his Palm Pilot and trying to ingratiate himself with reporters. He was that difficult thing to like, a needy sadist, and many onlookers felt that he was at least partly to blame for his children's deaths, but his grief was unmistakable. His cluelessness made it more awful, the way a child's grief is, except that his cluelessness was willed. Also present was Andrea's elderly mother, who in two years had lost her husband and five grandchildren and was now faced with the prospect of losing her daughter. She was sometimes seen weeping alone outside the courtroom. Yet the prosecution chose not to speak of these people as victims. This was probably because neither of them—nor, for that matter, any of the other people directly affected by the children's deaths—wanted Andrea found guilty. Indeed, Rusty insisted that she was the case's real victim.

Well, what is a victim, actually, and how should such a person be treated? The law often seems not to know. Not knowing, it treats them like members of some fractious, well-connected minority, impossible to satisfy yet impolitic to ignore. Only in the last twenty years have federal and state governments passed legislation that funds counseling for crime victims and their families or gives them the right to be notified of a criminal's impending release or, for that matter, the right to attend his trial: In the past, the defense would often subpoena victims as witnesses solely in order to keep them out of the courtroom, where their presence might cast a shadow over the deliberations. It's only lately that victims have been allowed to testify during a trial's sentencing phase so that their suffering may be weighed into the fate of the condemned. Defense attorneys dread such testimony, which completes a circuit between criminal, crime and victim, reminding juries that every major crime is a crime against somebody, that what has been violated is not just a penal code, but a human being.

Defendants' advocates sometimes argue that the campaign for victim's rights is actually a covert war on the rights of the accused, one waged, as it were, by irregulars, but prosecutors have their own problems with victims. And victims are often less than happy with prosecutors. Most D.A.'s are pragmatists; their budgets and case-loads make them so. They want to get as many convictions with as little effort as possible. In practice, this means plea bargaining. Victims, however, are idealists. What they really want is something impossible: that their losses be undone. Failing that, they want verdicts and sentences that are commensurate with those losses—sentences that repair the shattered equality between the perpetrators and themselves. But this desire places victims radically at odds with most of what actually goes on in the courtroom. They are like pilgrims standing horrified in the marketplace where they expected to find a temple. Or maybe any temple will look like a marketplace to them. Because what kind of punishment is commensurate with the murder of the person you loved most in all the world? With months of rape and sexual torture? With the extinction of an entire people? A thousand years ago the Norse and Anglo-Saxons made murderers pay wergild to the families of people they'd killed, a practice that was revived after World War II when Germany agreed to pay restitution to survivors of the Holocaust. My father received such wergild; my step-mother still does. But neither of them would say that it made good their losses, or adequately punished the guilty.

In May 2003, shortly after the invasion of Iraq, U. S. District Judge Harold Baer ruled that there was sufficient evidence to show that country had supported

Osama bin Laden's terror network and must pay millions in damages to families bereaved in the terrorist attacks of September 11, 2001. The decision outlined nearly $104 million in damages and named as liable the former Iraqi government and Saddam Hussein, along with Osama bin Laden, al Qaeda, the Taliban and the former government of Afghanistan. The judge acknowledged that, in making their case, the lawyers representing the families of two 9-11 victims had relied on "classically hearsay" evidence but said that such evidence was nevertheless sufficient to convince a jury of Iraq's culpability. An attorney for the plaintiffs called the ruling "a significant victory." Yet that September, Judge Baer barred the plaintiffs from collecting any funds from Iraqi assets frozen in the U.S., on grounds that President Bush had earmarked those monies for the country's post-war reconstruction. And in July 2004 the Senate commission investigating the 9-11 attacks concluded that there had never been any cooperation between Iraq and Al Qaeda. It's too early to say what bearing this will have on the judge's ruling, or on the victims' search for restitution.

The Oresteia tells the story of a series of revenge killings. To avenge his sacrifice of Iphigenia, Clytemnestra kills Agamemnon; Orestes—with some prodding from the god Apollo—kills Clytemnestra. You picture them, father, mother and son, standing in a row, each poised to slay the one before him. Having murdered his mother, Orestes is pursued by the Furies, abominable crones whose eyes weep blood, an apt metaphor for sorrow distorted into wrath. He seeks refuge at the temple of Pallas Athena and begs her to judge his case. There follows a murder trial— the world's first— in which the facts are even starker than those in the Yates killings; that Orestes has committed murder on a god's orders doesn't mitigate his guilt so much as extend it to the god who, appropriately, stands beside him in the dock (few things about this story are more alien to a modern Christian reader than the idea of a guilty deity. We may believe in a god who dies for man's sins but not one who actually takes part in, or even instigates, them). Instead, the trial hinges on whether it is permissible to kill a mother in order to avenge a father and, by extension, on which parent has a greater claim on one's loyalty: which parent is the "true" one. Athena, who has no mother, having sprung from Zeus's forehead like a thought made flesh, casts the deciding vote in favor of the father. Orestes goes free.

Apart from its psychological undercurrents, its themes of father-love and mother-hate and mother-love deformed into hate, the Oresteia is a myth about the origins of justice. Justice comes into being to put an end to the reign of universal vengeance. Each of the killers in this drama is paying back an earlier killing; each claims to be acting in the right. The violence extends deep into the past, to the primal atrocities of the brothers Atreus and Thyestes and, with the arrival of the Furies, threatens to overflow the confines of the family and inundate the realm of the gods. The Furies are old deities, residing not on Olympus but in the vaults and tunnels of the underworld. Nobody likes them. "No house is this to be approached by you," Apollo scolds them, when they invade his temple,

> But rather go where heads fall from the block,
> Where eyes are gouged, throats slit, and boyhood's bloom
> Blasted by gelding knife...
> Such festivals
> Are your delight and fill heaven with loathing.

Yet even he and Athena, the respective embodiments of reason and wisdom, seem intimidated by these infernal agents of pure, unreasoning retribution, and when Athena acquits Orestes she promises them their own shrine in her city for fear they will otherwise blast it with plague. In the formula made familiar by fairy tales, she has to repeat the offer three times before the Furies accept. Once they do, they are magically transformed into guardians of civil peace.

We know this story. Before there was justice, there was only vengeance, the unmediated reciprocity of offense and counter-offense, outrage and retaliation. If your neighbor stole some of your sheep, you stole some back from him. If he killed your son, you killed his; maybe you simplified matters and killed the neighbor himself. Maybe you killed one of his cousins. You could do what you wanted, within limits, as long as you adhered to some loose idea of what was right, though "right" might be only your name for the vessel in which you stored your bile (even today, when people on the street talk about doing the right thing they are usually talking about killing). Your other neighbors might frown on theft and murder, might view them as breaches of ethics or propriety, but they wouldn't get in your way as long as they didn't feel personally injured. Everything was personal back then, the fuming intimacy of grievance. The Oresteia doesn't play out among strangers, it takes place in a family, because who inspires greater hatred than the enemy in the house? In his variation on the myth, Sophocles gives us the following exchange between Orestes and his sister:

> ELECTRA: And yet you see but a small part of my pains.
> ORESTES: And how could there be any more frightful to see?
> ELECTRA: This: that I live among murderers.

But there's always the danger that vengeance will burn on forever, consuming not just the original combatants but their children and grandchildren. Much of the world still lives and dies this way. In certain countries it is as if every man received on his father's death a box containing a sword or gun and instructions on whom to use it, this being his sole inheritance and the only thing he will leave his sons after him. Vengeance doesn't just propagate vertically, but laterally, through the surrounding population. It makes no exception for neutral bystanders; the concept of neutrality is alien to it. Stripped of their ideology and profiteering, their Milosevices and Charles Taylors, what are Ulster, Bosnia or Liberia, Sierra Leone or the West Bank, but vendettas that jumped the fuel break and became firestorms, sucking everything into themselves, no matter how old or young or inoffensive or defenseless, using babies as tinder and children barely big enough to carry a gun as soldiers, prizing such soldiers above all others because they are too young to know fear or repress their cruelest impulses? A child knows that once you have sliced open a pregnant woman the next thing to do is eat the fetus inside her. The examples of Atreus and the vivisectionists of the Interahamwe suggest that men know this as well. Meanwhile the normal aspects of communal life are neglected or subordinated to the exciting demands of the blood-feud. The fields go untilled, the classrooms are empty. We might be on the Island of Lost Boys. In the frenzy of reciprocal slaughter entire societies regress to a state of enraged, bereaved childhood from which they may never emerge.

Justice, the story goes, arose as a means of forestalling this eventuality. It replaced personal grievance with a rationalized system of offenses and penalties. For universal vengeance it substituted a single act of reprisal, carried out against a victim who had been judged guilty—not a victim at all, but a criminal. The criminal, too, was an invention, and evidence of his newness is the fact that thousands of years passed before judicial systems knew quite what to do with him, their deliberations at first being concerned less with what the defendant had done than with what the victim wanted as restitution. Aeschylus devotes as much time to Athena's negotiations with the Furies as he does to the debate over Orestes' guilt. At the end of negotiations the Furies don't go away, but remain in Athens to be honored by its people. Justice doesn't banish vengeance but subsumes it. This may be why in most representations she bears not just a scales but a sword: Kafka's court portraitist paints her to look like the goddess of the hunt. And perhaps her blindfold is necessary to disguise the fact that her eyes once shed tears of blood. For similar reasons, we speak of people "taking private vengeance" or, the obverse, "taking the law into their own hands."

I imagine that all this took some time, an almost geological shift from custom to code, tribal or village councils to established courts with permanent retinues of judges, bailiffs and recorders. In the beginning justice would have functioned as a referee, weighing the arguments of rival claimants and trying to arrive at a penalty—not even a penalty but a settlement—that was more or less acceptable to both. Even execution might be acceptable, given the choice between sacrificing a single kinsman to losing dozens to unchecked violence. But in the course of thousands of years justice evolved the same way other systems do, toward increasing differentiation and complexity. It classified acts as legal or illegal; it classified persons as victims or wrongdoers. And instead of serving as a buffer between those categories, it increasingly defined its role as protecting the former from the latter—or, if its protective measures failed, avenging the victims. In this way justice became the guardian of the wronged: further, their surrogate. Criminal trials in the U.S. are designated "The State vs." Perhaps this, as much as any concern for defendants, is why actual victims were more or less exiled from the courtroom. They had become redundant. In their name justice pursued the malefactor, proved his guilt, took his life in pieces or one great gulp. In everything it did it expressed the outrage of its charges, and it did so it more effectively than they ever could. Yet crime victims feel other things, as well: grief, shame even, at times, compassion for the ones who injured them. These may be beyond justice's power to express.

On adjoining pages of a book called *Justice and Gacaca,* one finds two statements about the character of justice in pre-colonial Rwanda:

"The goal of the rule of law was not the repression of the guilty person, but his socialization."

"Vengeance was a religious obligation for every male."

Rwandans I asked kept assuring me that the apparent contradiction was no contradiction at all; it was just the difference between microcosm and macrocosm. Minor disputes, say, quarrels over land or cattle, were brought before the village elders, who would hear out the claimants and, instead of ruling in favor of one side or another, try to work out a compromise both could live with. The disputed land would be divided, or one party would cede some of his land in exchange for a share of the other's crops. The elders made their deliberations while seated on the grass: hence, *gacaca.*

There was some disagreement about what the system covered. Geneviève Told me that *gacaca* were used in cases of rape, with the offender usually being pressured to marry his victim and the two families celebrating the union with a vow of amity and ceremonial draughts of beer. But a Dutch anthropologist named Klaas de Jonge thought this would only be true if the victim were of low station. "If a Hutu man raped a Tutsi girl, there would be some killing." In his view the *gacaca* had been Rwanda's equivalent of civil courts, and any genuine offense—in the language of western law, any crime—could only be resolved by violence. It wasn't just honor that made this necessary, it was fear. The spirits of murder victims cried out for blood and if left unappeased might turn on their relatives. Every violent death was a debt that had to be repaid regardless of who had originally incurred it, and behind the culture of revenge lay the unspoken calculation that it was better to collect from the living than to stand surety before your own dead. Sometimes the state, in the form of the god-king, would intervene. Tharcisse Karugarama, a former vice-president of the Supreme Court justice who was one of the moving forces behind the new *gacaca* law, told me that the *mwami* would hear the combatants' grievances and then grant the offended group leave to slay one of the offenders; this might not be the original killer but simply a kinsman of the same status as the murdered person. "They would come and bring somebody and make as if to kill him—take a spear and put it here." Fixing me with a hypnotic stare, he held an imaginary spear-point against his throat. He'd once been a prosecutor and still knew how to create a sense of drama. "But they would not actually do the execution. They would go through all the rituals of killing but they would not kill. They would do a mockery of killing. And the community would clap, cheer, beat their tom-toms, drink their gourd of beer, and say they have reconciled."

De Jonge had doubts about the mockery part, but he was, after all, a European and afflicted with the European disease of skepticism. Most Rwandans preferred to believe that before the white man justice had been relatively bloodless, a spear held briefly at someone's throat and then lowered while the onlookers laughed and shouted their approval. Over time I came to connect this with the belief that

Hutu and Tutsi had lived together in harmony until third parties—colonialists or bad leaders—taught them to hate each other. There was some truth in this, though it struck me as odd that the people who blamed the genocide on their leaders passed over the fact that most of those leaders had been as Rwandan as themselves. I remember a young man who, when asked his thoughts about the catastrophe, declared, "Our politicians back then were very, very, very bad!" He spoke with the theatrical vehemence of someone scolding a child. But the *génocidaires* had been men.

The exact workings of the traditional justice system would be of mostly academic interest had that system not been refurbished to deal with the genocide. This became necessary because Rwanda's devastated criminal courts had proven incapable of dealing with it. By 1998 they had handed down only 1,274 judgments, out of more than 100,000 cases awaiting trial. Each of those "cases" was a detainee sweltering in an overcrowded prison so scarce in amenities that he depended on his family to bring him the food he ate. Many of the people convicted had been tried without counsel. Some had been executed. "I had so many prisoners, the numbers were so high, and I was working very, very hard to process their files. And I thought I had failed," Karugarama recalled. "I couldn't move at the pace at which you were expected to render justice in a reasonable time, couldn't prepare the files in a reasonable period of time. I would never live to do the work, my children would never live to see it done."

People had higher expectations of the ICTR. It enjoyed advantages Rwandan courts could only dream of, including a large staff of distinguished jurists and the cooperation of the international community. It was also very well-funded. By the beginning of 2003 it had spent five hundred million dollars. However, in the eight years since its inception it had handed down only nine decisions. In fairness to the tribunal, it does provide defendants with attorneys. Moreover, it has succeeded in convicting some of the atrocity's chief architects, including former Prime Minister Jean Kambanda, the first head of state ever to be found guilty of genocide. Still, most Rwandans I spoke with had little good to say about it. Even the ICTR's location, not in Rwanda, but in Arusha, Tanzania, seems like a breezy insult. Some of its staff have been exposed as *génocidaires*—including one man who took part in the massacres while working for the UN, on which basis he was able to claim compensation for the pay he lost when he was finally fired. Women testifying about being gang-raped have been harassed by defense counsel and ridiculed by judges. Women infected with HIV during their ordeals have been denied the anti-retroviral drugs the court routinely gives HIV-positive defendants. "Where would we draw the line?" a spokesman explained. "If you want to treat one witness, you have to treat all the witnesses."

When I asked Athanasie Mukarwego what she thought of the ICTR, her response was, "Those people in Arusha, if a bolt could come down from heaven and destroy them all, it would be enough."

"You mean the planners, the big fish?"

"The big fish, the small fish, everyone." Her tone suggested that 'everyone' included judges and attorneys, maybe even recorders and bailiffs. In her eyes, and I suspect in the eyes of many Rwandans, an institution set up to bring justice to the moral chaos of the genocide had instead become identified with that chaos, an insult placed on top of the obscene injury of the one million like a party hat propped on a skull. The UN had failed them again—not just the UN but the entire legal edifice of modernity. Before the ICTR there had been the courts of the Kayibanda and Habyarimana years, which declined to punish murderers of Tutsi, and before them there had been the courts of the colonial administration, which allowed *abazungu* to treat Africans as they pleased. Who could blame Athanasie for seeing the apparatus of western law the way so many westerners do? As a vast con game designed not to satisfy victims but dupe them, its judges and attorneys only shells that when turned over are always revealed to be empty?

And so the country reached into the memory of its past, not worrying for the moment how reliable that memory might be. In September 1999 a group of officials held a workshop to determine the goals and procedures of an alternative justice system centering around *gacaca* jurisdictions. Such a system, they agreed, should uncover the truth of what had happened during Rwanda's murderous three-month fugue. It should punish all those who had taken part in the crimes—in the term that had become almost as common as "reconciliation"—"put an end to the culture of impunity." The new system would relieve the burden of the criminal courts so that neither victims nor detainees would have to wait decades for their cases to be settled. Perhaps most important, the *gacacas* would be a participatory project, enlisting *rescapés*, witnesses and even suspects in a debate whose goal was not only justice but, again, reconciliation. One practical implication was that great value would be placed on confessions; defendants who did so promptly and with convincing remorse could reduce their sentences by half. At best, this was plea bargaining and depending on how skeptical you were you could see it as a tacit admission that without such confessions the tribunals would be unable to convict anybody. Alternatively, you might see it as a grand gesture from the state to the detainees: Confessing would be their way of taking an active part in the proceedings, of elevating themselves from the objects of justice to its subjects. Presumably, subjects of justice would have an easier time accepting its verdicts—accepting that these were in fact justice—than people who saw themselves as powerless, maltreated pawns. Just so the genocide's survivors might one day have an easier time forgiving those who had acknowledged their guilt before them. I remembered what Athanasie had said about the men who raped her: "I want him to understand what he did—freely, without being forced—I want him to admit his blame." How closely the *gacacas* approximated this idea of justice would depend in part on what their various participants meant by "freely."

In March 2001 these principles were enacted into law. In many ways the most impressive thing about it was its specificity, for in it the great amorphous body of the genocide was subjected to a Linnaean scheme of classifications. At the top of this scheme were Category One offenders: those who had planned or organized the killings, those who had incited others to kill, those who had committed rape or sexual torture or murdered with "excessive wickedness." They would continue to be prosecuted in the magistrates' courts, which reserved the option of putting them to death. Beneath them, the law envisioned a Second Category of ordinary killers, people who had followed orders rather than given them. There was a category for man-slaughterers and batterers; there was one for looters and vandals. Each of the lesser categories was subject to a different penalty, ranging from twenty-five years in prison to restitution and community service. Each level of crime would be tried in a different gacaca jurisdiction: Second Category offenders in the 106 district tribunals, Third Category in the 1,550 sectors, Fourth Category in the nation's 9,500 cells.

The scheme's precision was practical, to be sure, given the number of detainees awaiting trial and how loose and improvisational those trials were likely to be: the instructions for judges stipulated only eight rules. But it also had a philosophical dimension. Genocide resists all ordinary kinds of apprehension. It has an impenetrable event horizon. Hannah Arendt describes the concentration camps as "holes of oblivion," so shut off from the world of the living that every report from them has an air of unreality and even their survivors doubt what they lived through. A perfect genocide would leave no surviving members of the victim-class. It would destroy the memory of that class or poison it forever. This was why the Interahamwe infected rape victims with HIV; it is why they didn't just cut off the genitals of baby boys but buried the severed parts beneath the doorframes of burned houses. Similar reasoning may have lain behind the *génocidaires'* decision to enlist the entire populace in the butchery. For as long as there have been gangs, they have secured the silence of new members by requiring them to make their bones, and the idea that somebody someday might even attempt to bring so many people to justice would probably have been enough to make the genocide's planners burst out laughing. "Where all are guilty," writes Arendt, "nobody in the last analysis can be judged." But the *gacaca* law insisted that judgment was possible. It would count each victim, categorize every act; it would name each perpetrator. Slowly, deliberately, it would pace around Rwanda's hole of oblivion and measure its exact circumference.

That October the country elected more than 250,000 volunteer judges called *inyangamugayo*— "persons of integrity". Under the law, they had to be of good character, "exempt from the spirit of sectarianism and discrimination." They could not, it went without saying, have taken part in the genocide (to my surprise, they could be genocide survivors. Of the handful of judges I interviewed two were *rescapés* who had lost several family members, and one had fought in the RPA force that first marched into Kigali. "We called it," he remembered, "the place of devils"). Before they began serving, the judges received thirty-six hours of training in the gacacas' procedures. It seemed like very little, considering that many of them were barely educated and the procedures had never been tried before. Still, the *inyangamugayo* I met, four men and one woman ranging in age from the late thirties to late fifties, appeared neither cowed nor jaded by their responsibilities. They didn't remind me of judges. Their gravity and modesty made them more like deacons in a church, members of the congregation who have been elevated to perform a sacred function, but not too high. When I asked them if they thought it would be hard to judge people who might literally be their neighbors, none displayed even a flicker of doubt.

The government had gone to great lengths to insure a turnout at the trials, employing everything from radio talk-shows to pop songs, as well as the sorts of veiled coercion that go unremarked in a society where the smallest administrative unit has its own "self-defense committee." I'd read an account of a preliminary *gacaca* hearing—the reporter had described it as a cross between "the Salem witch trials and a Mississippi Christian revival" —and so I thought I recognized villages where the jurisdictions were taking place: the stream of foot traffic along the main road or in the narrow paths between fields; the men and women sitting patiently on hillsides so steep it would be risky for someone to doze off. Outside one village in the south people stood in a great circle in a cow pasture. They were waiting for something, I thought, perhaps for the truck from the prison, with its cargo of pink-jumpsuited detainees. But I was told they were praying. And every other gathering I witnessed turned out to have a different purpose. With the exception of a few pilot jurisdictions in selected districts, the *gacaca* were still in their pre-trial phase and consisted solely of fact-finding sessions. The most dramatic of these sessions was a presentation of prisoners, at which those who wished to could confess and witnesses could exonerate those who'd been wrongly arrested. But by the time I got to Rwanda this stage of the proceedings was over. The pre-gacaca I attended was in a disused schoolhouse in the center of Kigali and the judges on the scene were just sorting dossiers, with no audience in attendance. The persons of integrity sat in twos or threes on scarred benches, their folders stacked at their feet. They were trying to decide whether a particular suspect had killed with intent or just in passing; whether another's crimes were so hateful as to place him in the First Category and transfer him to the regular courts. A few weeks before I'd been introduced to a man who had confessed to killing three people in his village, two of them children, yet he had been classified in the Second Category and released from prison after six years. The judges discussed their dossiers calmly—even Beata Mukamazimpaka, who had hidden in the rafters as her son was murdered in the room below, was calm. They were just dossiers.

This was the last of the pre-gacaca sessions. No one could tell me when the actual trials would begin: in August, maybe, or October. The system had entered a holding pattern.

Another story from the Greeks, by way of Sophocles: Oedipus is king of Thebes, raised to the throne by marriage to the widowed Queen Jocasta. And also by the people's acclaim, for it was he who liberated the city from the Sphinx, another one of the Hellenic nightmare females, half lion and half human, by answering her riddle. Years later he is still understandably proud of this:

....I came by,
Oedipus, the simple man, who knows nothing—
I thought it out for myself.

And so years later when Thebes is stricken by plague, it's natural that his subjects should ask him to rescue them once more and he agrees, out of pride, certainly, but also because, like a good ruler, he shares their misfortune:

I know that you are deathly sick; and yet,
Sick as you are, not one is as sick as I

Simone Weil was fascinated by classical anticipations of Christianity, but as far as I know she never remarked on the parallels between Oedipus and Christ. For Oedipus also takes on the burden of others' suffering. In time, of course, it will become clear that the burden was really his all along, something he set down once—maybe at a crossroads between Corinth and Thebes—and then forgot but that has been waiting for him to claim it or to let it claim him. It is, after all, his. But all he knows in the beginning is that the plague is the result of a pollution, and soon an oracle declares that its source is the murderer of the old king, Laios, who was killed around the time of Oedipus's arrival, by unknown persons evidently still present in the city. Up until then one might have wondered what the king was supposed to do about the plague; he's not a physician. But now his fitness for the task is clear: "Once more I must bring what is dark to light."

Oedipus Rex, then, is a detective story, probably the world's first. Its protagonist is both the investigator of a crime and its perpetrator, an unwitting perpetrator but no less guilty for that. The winding-spool of the drama's suspense is the opposition between his desire to know and his desire not to know. Or between seeing and blindness, a metaphor the characters take turns blurting like children charged with a grownup secret: "Your own eyes must tell you." "You cannot see the evil." "But I say that you, with both your eyes, are blind." As the shards of evidence cohere, Oedipus increasingly suspects that what he's piecing together is his own destruction. What could be simpler than to just stop seeking answers? Even the queen begs him to stop, but still he keeps asking, summoning witnesses from the ends of his realm, prising answers from them, he needs to know, to see, just as having seen he will gouge out the eyes he saw with. The act is at once self-punishment and a horrified renunciation of the faculty of sight. Who can blame him for never wanting to see anything again?

Much has been made about the psychology of Oedipus Rex; in our time he's the punch-line of a shrink joke (a dated joke at that: shrinks don't believe in complexes any more, they believe in neuroreceptors). Most such glosses place the emphasis on the hero's crime. This, we're told, is what every man wants to do, deep down. But Sophocles will have none of it. Oedipus kills his father because he was fated to kill him. All his efforts to avert that fate have only brought it closer: not just his efforts, but poor Laios'; this was his fate, too. We are in a moral universe where calamity is both random and inexorable, a heat-seeking missile that tracks its target through every evasive maneuver. In such a universe what can Oedipus be guilty of, and what is guilt at all except a kind of bad luck?

> If I was created so, born to this fate,
> Who could deny the savagery of God?

The Talmud has a story in which God reproaches Cain for slaying his brother, and Cain in turn accuses God of having set him up for it by creating him with the inclination toward evil, the Yetzer ha-Rah. There's no mention of what God replies, which suggests that the Talmudists never meant Cain's argument to be taken seriously. Even back then the Jews believed in guilt because they believed in free will. Their worldview had no place for fate until Freud brought it up from the basement and started calling it the unconscious.

This isn't to say that fate obviates guilt. Clytemnestra doesn't die an innocent. What fate does is contribute to a more nuanced vision of human responsibility, an intricate bitmap of freedom and unfreedom in which there are many shades of doubt and pity. Cain is unequivocally guilty of Abel's murder, though God still shields him from the retribution of other men. Fate moves Oedipus to kill his father and bed his mother, but ignorant and powerless as he is he bears the consequences. He has the doubleness of somebody who is simultaneously innocent and guilty. It is a modern doubleness, and it makes him pursue the truth about Laios's death and shrink from it, with that combination of drivenness and dithering that every neurotic knows so well. And it's why, when he finally accepts the necessity of knowing what he did—and beyond that, knowing who he is—and suffering for it, that he becomes heroic. To fully appreciate how heroic, try to recall the last time you heard of a criminal taking full responsibility for any crime, that is, without pleading for clemency or citing extenuating circumstances or promising that he's really learned his lesson and is really, really, really sorry.

This insistence on bearing up under fate, of playing the hand that was dealt him, makes Oedipus an early stoic, maybe stoicism's first literary type after Job. In many ways he's a more complete stoic than his successors because he shoulders not just his suffering but his guilt: in Christian terms, his sin. To make a virtue of this may seem unproductive, given the long, poisonous tradition of blaming sufferers for their suffering. The Book of Job remains subversive because it portrays a righteous man afflicted by a god who is supposed to be just. Even more than his misfortune, Boethius is troubled by what his misfortune may say about his character—or what the world may think it says—and one can practically hear him sigh with relief when he learns that his greatest failing is ignorance. Both the Job author and Boethius propose that the good suffer in spite of their goodness. This is a step up from the Calvinist idea that those who suffer, suffer because they are wicked and therefore deserve whatever they get. But Sophocles dramatizes the suffering of a man who is flawed, even sinful—proud, impulsive, quick-tempered, violent—but still doesn't deserve what happens to him; a large part of the history of the world can be packed into that word still. It seems to me that Sophocles' formulation most closely describes the way reality works. Most suffering, even that of the crooked and aberrant, is undeserved. Think, again, of those embezzlers in the gas chambers. Now add to them the gossips and cheats, the bigots, the adulterers, the grasping landlords, the sly tradesmen, the wife-beaters and shrews, who were hacked to death in Rwanda. Who among them got what was really coming to him?

The question arises—who are the victims of Oedipus's crime? Put another way, who has been diminished by it? Laios, plainly, but at the play's outset he's been dead a long time. The king's survivors? That would be Jocasta, but she's come to terms with her first husband's death and is happy with her new one. There are the surviving families of Laios's servants, whom Oedipus killed along with their master, but this story takes place before a servant's life was worth much and perhaps those who were that small to begin with could not be made any smaller. By the ancient standards of the blood feud, the case of Laios is settled, or rather, forgotten. But the gods have not forgotten. Years after the old king's death they still smell the mineral stench of his blood and demand justice, even if justice brings misery to the victim's entire line, wife, son, grandchildren. What do they matter? Their lives are to the gods what the lives of servants are to kings. The story of Oedipus gives us a glimpse into the mythic past of the law at an intermediate stage between the indiscriminate savagery of feuding clans and the systematized intervention of society. And what it reveals is the reason for that intervention: not the anguish of victims but a principle that on close inspection turns out to be the wrath of the gods.

Following sentencing, Andrea Yates was transferred to Rusk prison outside Houston. In the spring of 2004 she was residing in the Skyview Unit, where she was being seen by two psychiatrists and getting a daily cocktail of anti-psychotic and anti-depressant medications. According to her attorney, this is more or less the same treatment she'd receive in a state psychiatric hospital, the main difference being that her new home has bars on its windows and barbed wire on the walls below. She's a popular inmate, and the warden has given Parnham informal assurance that she won't be transferred into general population on his watch. "You want to know what he always tells me?" Parnham said. "He tells me, 'I don't know what that little girl was like before, but I can tell you she's not the same person today.'" There was pride in his voice. He might have been speaking about a child of his own, a difficult one who'd caused him great worry in the past but was finally doing all right.

Rusty Yates was visiting Andrea every other week and making public professions of his continuing support. In private, I was told, he was trying to persuade her that she wanted a divorce. Evidence suggests that Yates was still smarting from some of the media coverage he'd received during the trial, and he may have shrunk from being the one to end their marriage. It would make him look like a bad guy. That summer, as the third anniversary of the murders approached, Andrea took a turn for the worse. She stopped eating. She reported talking to her children and seemed not to realize they were dead. Eventually she became so debilitated that she was placed on suicide watch and rushed to Galveston prison hospital. Here she responded to treatment, and a few weeks later she was judged well enough to return to Skyview. Shortly after that Rusty Yates announced that he was seeking a divorce. People who know the case say he's anxious to start another family.

What happened to Andrea Yates wasn't vengeance. Her victims' survivors viewed her not with anger and revulsion, or at least not primarily so, but with horror and pity and asked that she be treated as a sick person rather than a depraved one. Part of this, of course, was because they were her family. But maybe they also felt that there was no point in compounding her suffering. Parnham thinks that one day Andrea will be cured. My immediate thought on hearing this was that for her sake I hope not. For Andrea Yates to be cured would be for her to grasp, fully, what she did: to know what Oedipus knew. Actually, this may already have happened, briefly. She once told her attorney that what she found most painful was thinking of how her children must have felt when they realized that she was trying to kill them. A while after that she retreated once more into psychosis.

Horror and pity, incidentally, are the classic responses to tragedy, the feelings it is supposed to arouse in spectators. Aristotle writes about this.

My own opinion is that Yates went to prison because of a principle. I'm not sure what the principle is: maybe, crudely speaking, that a mother shouldn't get away with killing her children. If in modern justice, the state functions as a protector of victims, this is doubly true when the victims are children. Over centuries, justice, like some very old people, has grown august and detached, serenely impersonal in its blindness. But sometimes, as when a child is murdered, it reverts to its earlier ferocity. The blindfold is removed; the eyes beneath weep blood. The Furies, we know from tragedy, are sharp-sighted and scry the guilty person no matter how far he may run. But the blood in their eyes may keep them from seeing the exact nature of his guilt. Then again, Texas may be right in asserting that justice is supposed to punish acts, not wring its hands over a killer's mental state. Every time Andrea Yates' attorneys brought up what was going on in her mind, Owmby and Williford had only to remind the jury what must have been going on in her children's. And maybe it's fanciful to characterize the law as an enraged Nemesis. It's just as likely that the blindfold stays in place regardless of who the victim is, child or grownup, it doesn't matter. The principle remains rigidly intact. It has to, since it's all that stands between us and an eternity of universal vengeance, a hell in which we ourselves are the devils. Really, who would want it to be flexible?

"Why do we seek justice?" Joe Owmby asked me. "Why do we hold people accountable for what they do? What right does Andrea Yates have to take away from us the potential of those children? We will never know what she has taken, but we know she's taken something. One of them was interested in insects, he wanted to be an entomologist. And I don't know what he would have discovered.

I don't know what music she's taken, what literature she's taken, but she's taken something from society, and there's no justification for what she did. Through the ages we have always valued human lives, and this is what we will do to those who take them without justification. If you look, that is when we become more civilized. We have these punishments to stop Clan A from killing all the people in Clan B just because their brother was killed. That's where the death penalty comes from. So it's civilization that moves us toward the death penalty—not our uncivilized nature, but civilization."

Later I asked him if he ever applied what he heard in church in the courtroom. He chuckled. "I had one case, the defense argument was—and they started this line of argument—that Cain was exiled for murdering his brother, and that was enough. He was just exiled. And my response was—" he half-rose from his seat, as if making an objection. "'That wasn't capital murder!'" Texas defines capital murder as multiple homicide or homicide committed in the course of another crime, for instance, during a robbery or rape. Cain, of course, only killed Abel, in a moment of childish jealousy. And as far as the Bible lets us know, he lived out the rest of his days without doing further harm, set apart from his fellows by the mark God had placed on his forehead.

In spring 2004 the state of Texas tried another woman who'd killed her children, this time in Tyler. Her name was Deanna Laney. Her victims were her sons Joshua, age eight, and six-year-old Luke. She stoned them to death, a method she must have chosen for its Biblical connotations, though the way she did it probably had no precedent in the Bible, at least not in regard to children: She picked up a heavy stone and smashed their skulls in with it. Unlike Andrea Yates, Laney was acquitted by reason of insanity; The M'Naghten rule came down on her side. Owmby told me that her madness was evident even to a lay person. On the 911 tape her voice is a hair-raising sing-song, and when the operator asks her to describe her emergency, she coos, "I killed my kids." She proudly told the investigating officers that she and Andrea Yates were messengers, and that they would meet in heaven. One of the expert witnesses who testified on Laney's behalf was Park Dietz, who had done so much to put Andrea Yates in prison. He told the jury that his client believed God had commanded her to kill her children, and so naturally she'd obeyed Him. In the end Laney's acquittal may have had less to do with the jury's opinion of her sanity than with the fact that it could, broadly speaking, relate to her. And Yates's whole problem may have been that the voice she heard was the devil's.

Up in the hills on the eastern edge of Kigali a group of ex-prisoners and *rescapées* was building houses for the *rescapées* to live in. This was under the auspices of the Prison Ministry, an international program whose executive director in Rwanda was a Pentacostal minister named Déo Gashagazi. He was tall and heavy and wide in the hips, ungainly-looking when he wasn't preaching, and his profile was almost Mayan, the fleshy nose forming a continuous line with a high, bumpy forehead.

We drove to the site in a land cruiser, following a cobbled road that wound around the hillsides and narrowed as it climbed. Toward the summit the cobblestones gave way to hard-packed dirt. Most of the buildings in the neighborhood were made of earth, with thatched roofs and maybe a wooden door if the owner was better off. Shops were identified by the minimal displays of merchandise arranged out front, three girl's dresses or a few cans of palm oil or a jumble of dusty machine parts. Churches had crosses on top; mosques had rickety plywood minarets. We passed children solemnly driving goats.

The Prison Fellowship's primary purpose was to spread the Gospel among the incarcerated, but in Rwanda it was also playing an instrumental role in the justice system, encouraging suspected *génocidaires* to confess and repent their crimes, not just in the privacy of worship but before the law. The spiritual benefit to the detainees was matched by the practical advantage to the courts and *gacaca* jurisdictions. For this reason, Déo and his fellow ministers had been given virtually free run of the prisons. Often they worked with prosecutors. Detainees who had seen the light would get their cellmates to confess, and they in turn would pass the message on to others. The penitentiaries were being swept by an epidemic of penitence. "These men," Déo said, "have lived with such a great weight on their spirits. Confessing is a relief for them." It could also be a reprieve. Detainees who had already spent eight or nine years awaiting trial had only to sign their confessions to be set free, time served.

If they were Déo's men, though, they had to build houses. Near the top of the hill the car stopped, and we got out and began to climb. The slope was steep; once or twice I would have fallen if one of Déo's assistants hadn't steadied me. The house was maybe thirty feet up from the road, with others like it set farther up the slope. It was a shell of mud brick, no bigger than a one-car garage. A dozen men and women were laboring inside it. The men wore trousers and undershirts, the women wrap skirts and headscarves, and all of them were daubed and spattered with mud, their hands caked with red mud to the elbow. Two or three men shoveled earth from the slope behind the house; some women soaked it with buckets of water. It was stirred into mud and scooped onto plasterer's hawks and slapped onto the brick in handfuls. Both the men and women did this. The sound of slapping was ceaseless. I assumed that all the women were *rescapées* and the men ex-detainees, but there was no way of being sure short of asking, and I'd been in Rwanda long enough to know better than to ask. Déo had introduced his assistants, Benoit and Faustin, respectively, as a Tutsi who'd lost family in the genocide and a Hutu who'd spent time in prison. He'd broken the etiquette of ethnic silence, and the men had allowed him to break it, to show me how the two groups could reconcile in Christ. By groups, he meant Hutu and Tutsi, but also, implicitly, perpetrators and victims.

Yet later it emerged that Faustin, a short man with thinning hair and a burst blood-vessel in one eye, may not have been a perpetrator at all. He said he'd been railroaded into prison. Before the war he'd been a baggage-handler at the Kigali airport, a good job, the kind you didn't throw away, especially not with eight children to feed. He'd always kept out of politics. During the trouble he'd stayed home like everybody else; everybody was afraid. It was only afterward, when it was all over that somebody, a jealous co-worker, said some things about him, for which he was arrested and sent to prison. Now he was free, he'd found God, he bore nobody ill-will. That was the gist of it. Asked what the charges against him were, Faustin said he was supposed to have killed people, though he wouldn't say what kind of people or under what circumstances he was supposed to have killed them. When he spoke of the events of '94, he said "the war" or "the trouble" rather than "the genocide," which may or may not have been significant. And his claim that he'd stayed out of politics was disingenuous. People who stayed out of politics didn't get jobs as baggage handlers. The whole time we were together, I noticed, he kept exchanging looks with Benoit, who was sitting with us at the table. He'd told his story earlier, using language almost as noncommittal as Faustin's. I had a strong sense that the two men were in collusion, each assenting to the other's version of the past and abetting the other in his reticence. I could understand why Faustin would want to leave certain things unsaid but Benoit's wariness perplexed me. Then I thought of something Geneviève had told me when I first met her: "There are people who accept what happened. They are healed. From their point of view ten years have gone by, they cannot keep crying forever. There are others who forgive but don't forget. And then there are those who do not accept, who will never accept. They will never recover. And they will not talk to you."

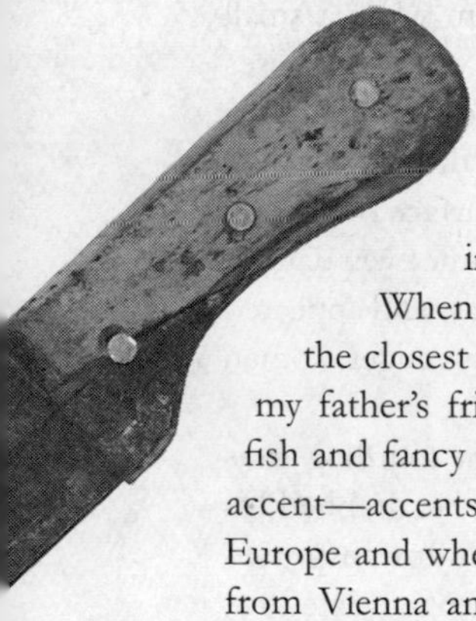

I thought as well of the older people I'd grown up with, in New York City fifteen years after the liberation of Auschwitz. When I was a child I called them my aunts and uncles though, really, the closest of them were no more than second cousins and many were only my father's friends or business associates, men who dealt in yarn or smoked fish and fancy provisions, and their wives. What they had in common was their accent—accents—they came from a number of countries in eastern and central Europe and when I was older I could make out the difference between the ones from Vienna and the ones from Prague and Riga. They were like my parents' accents, only foreign. It was through that foreignness that I eventually came to realize that my mother and father were foreign, too, in what may have been my first independent use of deductive reasoning. Part of what I felt for them most of my life—that baffling mangrove tangle of tenderness, anxiety, pity, contempt and guilt—probably had to do with the sense that as foreigners they were vulnerable to certain kinds of misfortune from which Americans were immune. And I, of course, was an American.

The other thing these people shared was the numbers tattooed on their wrists. The ink was blue, the ciphers were thick and faded; the sevens had a slash through them. As a child I was fascinated by those markings, and it occurs to me that when, as a teenager, I started embellishing my sevens with a short diagonal bar I may have been unconsciously imitating them. Of course I knew what the tattoos meant. My father had told me. "They did that to him in the camps." Later I would see documentary footage of inmates getting their numbers, getting numbered, as part of the industrial process whose end product was not even corpses but plumes of smoke, as if the whole point was to subsume human beings into the landscape of hell. For all that I grew up among survivors of those holes of oblivion, (a term Arendt eventually retracted, since people had managed to crawl out of them), most of what I learned about the camps comes from books or movies. I remember one "uncle" telling me that he'd met my "aunt" in Treblinka, where he'd lost his first wife and she her first husband; they must have married very young. But otherwise what had happened in those places remained unspoken. People didn't talk about it; it was better not to, why bring it up all over again? I heard this often during my childhood, from many different people, though always uttered in the same tone. It was the tone of someone who had suffered greatly and wanted to avoid further pain, even if such pain might somehow be salutary, as in the case of someone with a blasting migraine who refuses to get up from bed to take a painkiller. But there was also shame in it.

That weekend I attended a service at Déo's congregation. It was made up of genocide survivors, former prisoners, and women whose husbands were still in prison, and in its noise and exuberant melodrama it was typically *nouvelle église.* When I entered, a parishioner was slapping time on a hand-drum while a small man who appeared to be blind—the meeting hall was dim but he wore sunglasses with thick black lenses—led the worshipers in a hymn. He shouted the verses in a fierce, hoarse voice and hopped up and down to the beat of the drum, pumping his fists and thrusting out his chest like a swimmer breaking the surface of a pool. The congregation was infused by his energy, made reckless by it. Some even danced themselves, but the moment he stopped they subsided into their seats and appeared to age ten years. The men's faces were grey and somber. Even the younger women in their bright head-cloths looked fatigued.

They revived some when Déo began to speak. Even through the muffling arras of a foreign language, it was clear that he was a terrific preacher. He grabbed his listeners by the scruff of the neck like a cat seizing its kittens and calmly transported them from one emotional state to another. A tiny girl named Juliet translated for me, so I know he told the story of the Fall, turning it into a parable of evasion, with Adam blaming Eve for giving him the apple and Eve blaming the serpent and none of them asking for forgiveness. He told of a woman—he didn't say if she was Tutsi or Hutu—who was taken hostage by a militia, also unspecified, and asked if she wished to say anything before she die. "So she is telling him that she believes in God," Juliet whispered, "and now when I say it, it is fine if you kill me." She was not afraid to die. The woman's faith struck terror into her executioners. Déo popped his eyes and ran in place, as graceful as any of the massive comedians of the silents. Everyone in the room laughed, even the men who ten years before might themselves have belonged to militias and if so were unlikely to have asked their prisoners if they had any last words. Prunier tells of a milicien who was so moved by the faith of a Catholic lay worker that he asked her to pray for his soul before he shot her. Still, he shot her. And more often you hear of Interahamwe telling their captives, with gloating thoroughness, precisely how they were going to rip the life from their bodies.

The thrust of all these parables was the importance of speaking out and taking responsibility for one's actions. It was a message tailored for an audience that was poised—or, more likely, braced—for a nationwide campaign of truth-telling. The only way the *gacaca* will succeed is if Rwandans tell the truth. The *rescapés* will do that, but they may not have much to say if they were in hiding, out of sight of the perpetrators but also unable to see them. Many detenus will confess, but some of their confessions will be suspect. You hear of people pleading guilty to lesser crimes to avoid being prosecuted for more serious ones, and of persons already convicted taking the fall for relatives and friends, secure in the knowledge that their sentences are unlikely to be increased. Because of the premium placed on confessions and the looseness of standards of evidence, innocents who refuse to speak may end up serving more time than chatty murderers.

The great unknown is the third parties, the Hutu who watched and saw and until now have remained silent. Reports from the pilot *gacaca* have been unpromising. Part of the problem is that, from a practical perspective, the procedures are a nuisance. Most Rwandans are subsistence farmers who work every day in the fields. In addition, they have to contribute labor to the commune; they have to attend political lectures and go to church. Who would want to spend one or two more days every month squatting on the ground in the rain or sun, straining to hear people talk about the horror of ten years before and knowing that you too may have to say something and that it will probably get you in trouble? Rwandan society is tightly enmeshed, with the ties between extended family members replicated in ties of social and political obligation. In such a society no one ever feels truly alone. The corollary is that no one ever feels completely free to tell the truth.

The other problem, according to Alison DesForges of Human Rights Watch, is that the *gacaca* fail to address an entire category of crimes, the ones committed by the new government and its soldiers. Some of these offenses took place during the chaos of the war and others afterward, as the RPF was raking in the last chips on the table. Some of them could be attributed to the indiscriminate use of firepower and a few were unflinching massacres of unarmed civilians. Almost all the victims were Hutu. The government has ruled that these killings qualify as war crimes or crimes against humanity, but not as genocide, and has declared them outside the gacacas' purview. A recent addendum to the law of 2001 fails to mention such crimes at all, effectively dropping nearly a hundred thousand victims into a juridical oubliette. But in Rwanda memory is reinforced by kinship. At every *gacaca* a certain portion of the witnesses will have relatives whose death they blame on the state, which denies responsibility or insists that it must be determined elsewhere. Now that same state is asking these people to tell the truth about other deaths that it deems more important, the deaths of Tutsi. But in the new Rwanda Hutu and Tutis don't exist. There's just Banyarwanda. DesForges gave me the strong impression that the reason for the halt in the *gacaca* is that witnesses aren't cooperating. The government, in the meanwhile, has been floating rumors that it's about to charge a large number of new *génocidaires*, maybe as many as a quarter million. I asked her if this was a McCarthyesque ploy to terrorize people into testifying, but she said it was an exit strategy. "The government will announce this preposterous figure and make noises about prosecuting them all. But really this is the government's way of admitting that it's impossible to try the lower levels of the genocide. And after a while it will throw up its hands and declare a general amnesty."

Hannah Arendt thought the reason some of the Nuremberg defendants seemed so smug during the trials was because they knew exactly what they'd gotten away with.

The sermon was nearing a close. Rwanda, Déo was saying, was like a truck loaded with prisoners. Some of the people on the truck were judging the others, saying, "This one has stolen. This one is a killer." But they too were in prison. He was serious now, his voice accusing. "In this room there are no killers," Juliet translated. "There are no thieves. There are only servants of God." I tried to ask her what he meant by that—it seemed to contradict everything he'd said earlier about responsibility—but the fierce little choirmaster burst out in another hymn.

The emotional high point of the service had occurred earlier. It was a laying-on of hands. People who wanted to be saved came up to the front of the room, and one by one the reverend placed a hand on their foreheads and told the devil to leave. Sometimes he coaxed and sometimes he bullied. He pushed one docile man down the entire length of the aisle. At times he spoke, or shouted, in tongues. "Ra-ba-ba-ba, RA-ba-ba-BA!!" Juliet said he was calling down fire from heaven. Few people were immune to these ministrations. They rocked or wept silently or quaked with sobs. In the pews babies slept imperturbably against their mothers' breasts. Abruptly one woman began to shriek. My immediate thought was that this was the appropriate response to all that had happened in this country, but it quickly became evident that she wasn't just crying out of grief. Her shrieks grew louder and higher; she convulsed. She was in a frenzy. Déo came over to her and placed his hand on her head, but she was not comforted. She didn't want to be comforted, or the thing inside her did not want to be. Her screams mounted and Déo had to pray more loudly to be heard over her. Soon he was bellowing in her face. "RA-BA-BA-BA-BA!" The woman lunged away from him, was held back by other worshipers, broke free. She fell to the floor and thrashed there, still screaming, until some women ushered her to another room where her cries grew fainter until they ceased. Some time later one of these women returned, bearing aloft a little piece of cloth with something dark and wet wrapped in it, like a used teabag. "Is that a bad spirit?" I asked Juliet. The question didn't surprise her. "No, this is something she has been using, like a cigarette. But now she is giving it up."

I could understand. When I'd quit smoking I'd wanted to scream all the time. Exorcism is an appropriate model for Rwandan justice, or a model for the Rwandan substitute for justice, just as possession gives Rwandans a way of explaining the horror that befell them. The truth is that some of them designed that horror and inflicted it on the others, but everyone prefers to speak of it as something that came from elsewhere, like a pestilence or a fire from heaven. Prunier himself, the most rigorous of judges, often speaks of "killer victims" or "victim killers." What happened in Rwanda will never be adequately punished. The ICTR may somehow get around to trying the entire pantheon of monsters, the Bagoseras and Bizimanas and Ntabakuzes, but even if it succeeds in convicting them before the last of their surviving victims die, they will be vastly more comfortable in prison than most of their victims are in freedom. As for the ordinary people who became monsters, most of them too are beyond the reach of justice. There aren't enough jails; there aren't enough prosecutors. Even 254,000 *gacaca* judges may not be enough. Viewed against the enormity of the genocide, the crimes of Rwanda's new government seem very small: one would be tempted to call them misdemeanors if murder weren't always reckoned a felony. However, in excluding them from the sphere of justice, the government may end up shrinking the sphere's circumference to zero.

Sophocles is right. For those who have escaped being murdered the most frightful pain may be knowing that they live among murderers—one reason why so few Jews who lived through the Holocaust returned to Germany. This is the predicament of most surviving Rwandan Tutsi. And so many of them tell themselves that their neighbors were not murderers, not really. They tell themselves the same things the murderers themselves do: that those who killed, killed out of ignorance or fear. They blame the genocide on outside forces, if not on the *abazungu* then on leaders who in the telling somehow cease being Rwandan, and if not on the leaders, why not on demons? Traditional Rwandan religion also believed in possession by spirits, good and evil. What might such a spirit look like? And what happens to the people it once lived inside?

In one of their pretrial interviews Park Dietz asked Andrea Yates why she thought it would be right to kill her children. "If I didn't do it, they would be tormented by Satan."

As you drowned each one," he continued, "Did you think it was the right thing to be doing?" Andrea nodded yes. She explained that as she held the children under the water, she prayed that their souls would go to heaven. It was only afterward that she realized how her acts might be perceived by others. Satan had left her.

Dietz asked why Satan would leave her after she'd obeyed him.

To this Yates replied, "He destroys and then leaves."

In the same village where I met Jeanne D'Arc Mukamukenga I was introduced to a murderer named Stefano Kayinamura. Actually, the meeting took place in Jeanne D'Arc's house, which she'd consented to let Lola, the Dutch journalist, and myself use for our interview. On the eve of the tenth anniversary of the genocide such events had become routine. The *rescapés* got some money, the *ex-detenus* got some—less, ideally—the translators and facilitators got some, and so did the ministry that sold permits to foreign journalists and researchers. The payments violated the rules of both journalism and academic research, but some people made them anyway. Imagine a country so broken as to depend on the proceeds of atrocity tourism. We didn't ask Stefano into the house until Jeanne D'Arc had finished talking with us. He was forty years old, a small, wiry man in a soiled shirt that he wore unbuttoned, not out of sexual bravado but because it was hot and he'd been working. There were traces of red earth on his shirtsleeves. He came in slowly and looked over at Jeanne D'Arc, but when she avoided his gaze he did the same and for the rest of the visit barely looked at her again. He didn't look at us much, either, but answered our questions while staring fixedly ahead, like someone giving an interview by remote hookup on the TV news. The TV people always warn guests to keep their eye on the camera, and the inexperienced ones take it literally.

During the genocide Stefano had killed two children and a woman; the woman had been pregnant. On his return from a refugee camp in the Congo he'd been arrested and spent six years in prison, winning an early release after he confessed at a pilot *gacaca* hearing. He was among the first beneficiaries of the new justice system, and he was grateful to it. Confessing had cleared his conscience. When he came home people had welcomed him, not just his family but *rescapés*, because they felt justice had been done. The *gacaca* worked. People could live together without feeling afraid. "When you've committed a crime," he added—and for a moment he dropped his gaze from the imaginary news camera and looked at us—"You're filled with fear."

Lola asked, "If the government pressured you, would you kill again?" Stefano became agitated. "Look, even if it happened, the genocide wasn't our idea. It was the authorities. They gave us the idea and made us do things. If they gave the same orders again, I'd never obey them, because today I know it's wrong to kill a schoolchild." He sounded less guilty than exasperated, as if he'd put up with all the high-minded badgering he was going to take.

The whole time he was speaking Jeanne D'Arc stared at the ceiling or at the floor or at her clenched hands in her lap. She too had been to a *gacaca*, to testify against the man who'd raped and murdered her sisters, but it had gone badly. She was alone; the defendant was related to the head of her cell, and either for that reason or because he'd named other perpetrators he was let go. A while afterward, he'd come to her and asked for pardon. She shrugged. "I gave it to him, there was no choice."

Writing this, I imagine someone protesting that that's what the *gacaca* are all about: Forgiveness and reconciliation. And I recall a scene from Anne Aghion's *gacaca* documentary, a conversation between two women who are peeling cassava. One of them says, "I can still see how he grabbed my baby off my shoulder and flung it on the ground." She takes a piece of cassava from the basket at her feet and flips it across the room, making a trilling sound with her lips. "Then he beat it to death. And now he would come and tell me, 'Forgive me, because in fact I did you a big favor.' And I'm meant to reply, 'Thanks, I forgive you.'"

At the end of the interview Stefano made to leave, but Geneviève stopped him. She's a handsome woman in her early fifties, with the soft, leonine features and world-weary voice of a Simone Signoret. She and her family took no part in the genocide, but like millions of Hutu they fled Rwanda in advance of the RPF and spent some time in a refugee camp in the Congo. The camp was run by *génocidaires,* which didn't stop Geneviève from telling everyone she met that all Hutu were guilty of a great crime and should be praying for God's forgiveness. She continued to speak like this even when her life was threatened. Now she blocked Stefano's path and asked him something that he seemed to find astonishing. Ignoring his answer, she went on addressing him, her voice both teasing and scolding. Once or twice she touched him on the chest. When she was finished she joined Lola and me outside by our hired taxi.

"I asked him," Geneviève explained, "If he had ever asked this lady to forgive him. He told me, 'Why should I ask her? I never did anything to her.' He is being a typical man, it makes me lose my patience. I told him, 'Only think of what this poor lady has been through! Put yourself in her place! If what had happened to her had happened to you, wouldn't you want her to say something? Now go to her.' And so he did." By now Jeanne D'Arc and her neighbor had left the house and were standing together in the shade of the thatched roof. They spoke hesitantly and often looked away from each other, but a half-hour before they'd seemed miserable at having to breathe the same air. Geneviève said "I'm not sure, but I think I may have accomplished something."

I was grateful to her for not using the word "reconciliation." It was too early to say if these people were reconciling. They might only be coexisting. Lion and antelopes are known to coexist as well, beside water holes, in the brief interval before one pounces on the other.

In the apartment building where I grew up there was a woman from Hungary who'd come back from one of the camps. She was short and buxom and had a broad, flat face framed by a coif of black hair, so black it might be described as Asiatic, with bangs rolled in the style of the 1940s. I don't think she spoke much English. She wouldn't acknowledge you when you greeted her in the lobby; she wouldn't hold the door for you. And if you made the mistake of getting into the elevator with her, she'd start screaming.

Postscript:

In February of this year, the verdict against Andrea Yates was thrown out on appeal, in recognition of the flawed nature of the prosecution's psychiatric evidence. On George Parnham's recommendation, she still resides in the prison psychiatric unit. This may be a good idea, given that the personnel know her and feel protective of her. "I don't know what that little girl was like before, but I can tell you she's not the same person today."

In March, Rwanda convened the first *gacaca* tribunals.

PETER TRACHTENBERG is the author of Seven Tattoos: A Memoir in the Flesh (Crown, 1997) and of fiction and essays published in the New Yorker, Harpers, Bomb, "T": The New York Times Travel Magazine, tricycle, triquarterly, The Columbia Review, Chicago, and bookforum. He is currently at work on The Book of Calamities, a nonfiction exploration of suffering and its narratives that will be published by Little Brown in 2007 and from which this chapter is an extract. Trachtenberg is a recipient of the Nelson Algren award for short fiction and an artist's fellowship from the New York foundation for the Arts. He lives in upstate New York with his wife, the writer Mary Gaitskill.

Crater Lake
Naivasha
Food for Thought.....
the Venue for the
'Sir Michael Caine Literary Workshop 2005'
..... Setting for Inspiration
Safaris
CORDON BLEU
P.O. Box 312, Naivasha, Kenya Tel: +254 (50) 2020613
E-mail: crater@africaonline.co.ke Fax: +254 (50) 2021372

Girl's HIV infection blamed on father

Amos Kareithi

A girl who was allegedly infected with HIV by her father is living at the Nyeri Provincial General Hospital for fear of punishment.

The eight-year-old girl from Naromoru refused to go home after she was discharged, saying her father, who was arrested on Wednesday, had threatened her with death if she exposed her ordeal.

"He sneaks to my bed at night. He does bad things to me after removing my clothes. He told me that if I ever tell anybody, he would slash off my hands and legs and then kill me. Please take me to a boarding school," the girl said amid tears.

Her stepmother confirmed that the minor cannot walk properly because her husband, 40, has been defiling her. The girl's mother died in 2002 from HIV-Aids related complications.

Relatives have pleaded with the hospital authorities not to release the girl.

Illustration: JNK

Ruler Of The Roost

BY SOSPETER SHAKE

It was a warm Friday afternoon. Mdamu, his wife Tenge, their son Chrispine and their other four children were seated outside their two mud and corrugated-iron houses having a simple lunch of ugali and sukuma wiki. Save for Mdamu, the rest were eating from a large wooden tray which was placed at the centre for easier access to all. Mdamu, a lean, gaunt man with sparse, greying hair and rheumy, sunken eyes sat a short distance away on a low, smoke-blackened stool, quietly munching his food with a detached, abstracted air about him. He seemed oblivious of the others just as they also studiously avoided eye-contact with him just while conversing desultorily among themselves.

Suddenly, from behind the kitchen-house there emerged a fleeing hen with a rooster in hot pursuit. The hen, in desperate cackling noises, fluttered and dodged and tried to fly, but the determined rooster finally caught up with it and, propping itself by holding the hen tightly with its beak, made a few hurried thrusts and then released it. The hapless hen calmly ruffled its feathers, and then looked this way and that way for its chicks. The chicks promptly surrounded their mother and together went foraging off, leaving the victorious rooster taking a different direction in disdainful nonchalance.

Tenge picked a potsherd and flung it at the rooster, but it ducked and flapped away in the direction of mother-hen and her chicks.

Chrispine, a student in a nearby secondary school and who was still clad in his full school uniform, appeared to derive a lot of vulgar pleasure from this momentary spectacle, and sniggered impishly as he furtively stole glances at his parents. The younger children seemed to pity the poor hen for being brutally assaulted by the heartless assailant, and were sorry that their mother's missile had not landed on its target.

"Don't be stupid—eat your food and go to school !" Mdamu snapped at his son. The boy promptly turned to the food, affecting an aggrieved, self-deprecatory mien. Silence ensued for a short moment until Tenge decided to break it: "We shall eat this cock when my sister Julia comes next week," she announced to no-one in particular.

The children looked at her hopefully, with beaming faces. She was a small, brown woman whose pretty near-cherubic face belied her many years of hardship and adversity. She was heavily pregnant, and with her cheap maternity dress she cut a vulnerable picture.

Mdamu arched his eyebrows and looked at her. "Is that so? Then why did you want to kill it just now?"

"Who wanted to kill your lovely cock?" countered Tenge, visibly chafed. "I was simply chasing it away. Or did you want it to join us for our little lunch?"

"And haven't you just said you will kill it when your sister arrives?" demanded Madam quietly, his voice tremulous with emotion.

"Yes; when Julia comes we should welcome her properly. She has always been very helpful to us. A mere rooster will not increase our poverty."

"And why, may I ask, won't you kill one of the hens instead of the only rooster we have in our home?"

"I know it's the only cock we have—yes. But it's already past its prime—it's now old...and useless. You have been refusing with it for a long time now. Are you waiting for it to die of old age? I don't think there's any harm in eating it now. In any case, there are many other cocks in the neighbourhood for our hens."

The children's eyes silently appealed to their mother to be quiet. They knew their father's unpredictable outbursts of anger, and could sense this was about to happen. Mdamu wearily leaned back on the wall and emitted a deep sigh. "Old... and useless," he muttered. "It might be old and useless, but nobody is going to kill it, Julia or no Julia." With his sunken eyes now closed, Mdamu appeared to be brooding over some distant problem which made him forget about his food.

Chrispine, who never missed an opportunity to flaunt his seniority to his other siblings, ventured to break the silence like his mother had done a short moment ago. "Mother, this food is not very delicious. At least we should have killed one of the rabbits which are breeding too fast," he announced pertly.

Mdamu sprang up like a leopard, his face contorted with fury as he glowered at the insolent boy. "What? Did I hear you right? Can you repeat what you have just said?"

Chrispine inwardly flinched from his father's overreaction, but because he did not want to appear effeminate by being brow-beaten over what he considered an innocuous remark, he irritably riposted: "I was talking to my mother."

With incredible swiftness and agility Mdamu picked a plank of wood lying on the ground and savagely hurled it at the boy. It caught him smack on his back as he tried to duck, and he fled away screaming in pain.

"Yes I know!" Mdamu shouted after him. "You're always talking to your mother and planning things behind my back! Why are you running away then? Come back and face me squarely if you think you're man enough. Bastard!"

"Wuui...wuuii...!" Tenge was screaming in alarm. "Come and help me please! My child has been killed! Wuuii!" Her hands were clasped behind her head and her bosom thrust out in helpless resignation. Mdamu menacingly ordered her to be quiet.

Tenge gauged the mood and instantly stopped wailing, her bosom convulsing with rapid intakes of breath. "If you want to kill someone today you had rather kill me, but please leave my innocent children alone. Oh, my God. What did I do to deserve all this? I think I was born under an unlucky star. No peace at all in this house these days!" She smacked her lips in exasperation.

"Nonsense! You and your children no longer respect me!"

Tenge had also lost interest in the food and was now washing her hands with water in a small sufuria. This, together with the children's accusing glances, tended to soften Mdamu, but he stubbornly clung to his pride and refused to make amends.

"This son of yours does not respect me at all these days, and you know it. In fact, you are to blame for all this because of your excessive pampering. And these days he echoes everything you say. You talk of killing a cock and he immediately pipes about killing rabbits. What's all this? Just a small thing and you start yelling 'My son, my son.' I'm sick and tired of all this nonsense. Is he not my son too?" He paused for breath, and when his wife's response was not forthcoming he went on: "Yesterday after he came home from school, what happened? I told him to go and cut some grass and herbs for the rabbits and what did he do? He brought very little grass, hardly enough for three rabbits. And he now has the cheek to complain that the rabbits are breeding too fast. Is this boy really normal?"

Cocking her head in gesture of defiance, Tenge finally retorted: "It's because when you sell the rabbits you take the money to your Mama Pima and leave us starving. Do you think the children can enjoy working for nothing - never seeing the fruits of their labour?"

Mdamu averted his eyes, a trifle abashedly. "Well... if you want to spoil the boy the way you spoiled Eunice, go ahead." He abruptly turned and strode into the bigger house, entered their bedroom, put on his tight-fitting leather sandals and left the compound without another word.

As he trudged along the footpath, his mind was a turmoil of untidy and conflicting thoughts. At one point he would see himself as a self-righteous champion of his dignity and at another moment his mind would veer towards self-reproach and a disconcerting feeling would creep over him.

However, he firmly stifled the latter intrusion and gave himself a clean bill of health as one not deserving of blame for, according to him, the major culprit in the numerous domestic squabbles was none other than his wife Tenge, who had taken it upon herself to be the ruler of the household and to rally the children against him. This boy and his mother, he thought painfully, believe that I am useless just because I can no longer provide for them as I used to. But I still have some land and my two houses, humble though they are. If I decide to sell them, what will they do? That's when they'll know I'm not a person to be taken lightly.

He tripped over a stone and quickly reached out for some brushwood by the wayside to check the certainty of an undignified fall. "Shit!" he muttered under his breath as he collected himself. "I'm not a man to fall that easily." Back onto the narrow, sloping footpath he now walked with a bit more caution to avoid the small jagged stones jutting out of the hard earth as they made his movement rather laborious, what with the tight-fitting sandals he was not accustomed to wearing. He only wore them on special occasions such as this when he was going to his son's school to see the principal about the boy's behaviour.

When his mind drifted to his son, some fear tensed his body as he wondered whether he had hurt him badly. Was the boy in school or not? Could he have gone to the chief, or even the police? You never know with youngsters these days. He characteristically denied any fault on his part. A boy who believes he is man enough to stand up to his father deserves some hard tackling. And this woman Tenge...

The harsh clang of the school bell snatched him out of his reverie. He was already in the vicinity of the school. He could see the students in their blue-and-white uniforms merrily trooping back into the school compound with the boundless jauntiness of the youth, and he envied their zest for life. As he neared the Administration block, he had the uneasy feeling of a trespasser in alien territory, an intruder into unfamiliar domain. With his threadbare clothes and ill-fitting sandals he felt out of place and utterly overwhelmed by the orderly ambience of the school compound. He briefly entertained the thought of turning right back and abandoning the whole issue. But some courage stood by him and he marshalled his inner resources of self-respect and knocked the door, albeit a trifle feebly.

The youthful school typist courteously welcomed him and directed him into an inner door that led to the Principal's office. He timidly knocked and went in when he heard the words "Come in, please."

The Principal, a plump, youthful-looking man in a maroon suit, cream shirt and yellow tie, greeted him amiably and waved him to a chair. As he sat, Mdamu marvelled at the numerous books and files in the office, and wondered whether the Principal had read them all.

"I'm Mr. Mavu," said the host, shaking the visitor's hand warmly.

"What can I do for you, please?"

Mr. Mavu's easy bonhomie melted Mdamu's diffident stiffness and he relaxed somewhat. "Thank you very much, Mr. Principal. I am Johnstone Mwamela Mdamu, and I come from Machi village. I'm sure you know the place."

"Oh yes, I do. I'm rather new in this place but I've made an effort to know the area as much as possible. As you know, proper knowledge of one's environment will certainly make one's work easier. This is the village next to the M.P.'s ranch, isn't it?"

"Y-y-yes...that's the village," drawled Mdamu, rather dispirited because the mention of the M.P.'s ranch brought back bitter memories of the past.

"Please continue," urged Mr. Mavu with a benign expression. Mdamu promptly enumerated Chrispine's latest misdeeds and suggested that the boy's nascent insolence should be nipped in the bud. He explained that he was not shirking the responsibility of correcting the boy, only that the boy's mother was proving to be an unhelpful partner and as two heads are better than one, he had decided to come for the assistance of the principal who was the boy's surrogate parent.

"Is Christine Mdamu the boy in Form Two Green?" asked Mr. Mavu after Mdamu had completed his narration. Mdamu was cornered. He squirmed and fidgeted uncomfortably on his seat, completely at a loss for words. The fact was that he could not answer the principal's question because he did not know which form the boy was in, let alone the stream. He finally managed to blurt out some incoherent noises to evade the question.

The principal fiddled with the computer on his desk and confirmed what he had said. "Yes, Chrispine Mdamu is in Form Two Green." Mdamu nodded in ignorant perplexity, intrigued by the Principal's grasp of the technological wizardry which produced instant information. "The boy used to be among the top students in the class," continued the Principal, "but of late his academic performance has shown a downward trend."

"Is that so? The boy doesn't show me his end-of-term reports." Mdamu affected a deeply aggrieved tone, biting his lips and shaking his head.

"That's a way serious mistake. And what reason does he give?"

A wave of delectation coursed through Mdamu as he noticed the effect his words had on the Principal, and he decided to go for the kill. He railed at length against the boy's deteriorating conduct as Mr. Mavu nodded intermittently, his fingers a dove-tailed knot under his chin. When Mdamu was through, Mr. Mavu casually took a biro-pen from his coat pocket and started jotting down in his notebook the salient points that had emerged from the narration. He then raised his head and looked intently at his visitor.

"You have mentioned something that is very important for us in the school: you have informed me of the boy's poor behaviour at home. That could account for his poor performance in class work." He nibbled thoughtfully at the lid of the biro-pen. "You see, my friend, what is sometimes overlooked by some of us is the close correlation between discipline and academics. There is no gainsaying the fact that the two are directly related. Thank you very much for reporting to us the boy's poor conduct at home before it is too late to correct him. Here in school we have no problems with him, but boys of his age can be very sly. This is why working together—both parents and teachers—is of paramount importance in moulding the character of the child at this critical stage."

"Very true," nodded Mdamu.

"And because you have brought the matter to us in good time, I agree with you that we can nip the problem in the bud."

"Of course!" This time Mdamu nodded even more emphatically. "He should be taught a lesson once and for all!"

"It is our bounden duty to correct these youngsters, for if we do not do it now, they'll blame us tomorrow."

"That's very correct, Mr. Principal. We should never allow these youngsters to sit on us!" Mdamu's sunken eyes twinkled with malice. He was convinced the impudent brat was going to have it rough from his Principal, and he as witness.

"Some guidance and counselling would really be useful..."

"With some punishment!" volunteered Mdamu, his gaunt neck craned towards the Principal. Mdamu's coarse antics mere now getting out of hand and his irked Mr. Mavu.

"Well, everything should be done to bring him back on track," he averred, and to change the topic slightly, he said: "You also mentioned that the boy does not respect you, but respects his mother. Now that's very interesting, and I'd like us to address the matter without fear or favour so as to unravel the root cause of the problem. I hope you don't mind that, do you?"

Mdamu's face fell. He searched the Principal's countenance for any hint of a reprimand, and when he spoke his voice carried a subdued, faraway nuance. "My dear brother," he began, "I must be very frank with you." He paused. "In my house my wife has decided to be the ruler. I have no voice in my house. Whatever I say or do is of no consequence to her. She has also rallied the children against me, and they don't respect me now even the youngest. Can you imagine that, my dear Sir? I have tried to be good to them, but to no avail. Even the only son I have has decided to be on his mother's side. They're doing all this because I'm now jobless." He looked agitated.

Mr. Mavu pretended to be busy with the notes he had been taking so as to allow for ample time for the man to compose himself. "Oooh...now I get it...I get it now..." he temporized. "How—why did you lose your job?"

Mdamu managed to calm himself and coherently explained how he had been employed as a cow-hand in a ranch belonging to his Member of Parliament and how the same M.P. had charitably offered to pay school fees for his eldest child-Eunice—after she had done well in primary school and had been offered a Form One place in a reputable boarding school in Nairobi.

After only one year of secondary school the girl got pregnant and had to leave school, but the worse shock was when it came to light that it was none other than the magnanimous M.P. who was responsible for putting the young school girl in the family way. "And when, as the offended father, I made some noise, I was immediately shown the door and warned to keep my mouth shut. That is when I came to agree with the saying that the powerful should not be trifled with," Mdamu summarized.

A wry smile played on Mr. Mavu's face as he reflected on the cynical capacity of the poor to justify their impotence. "What happened to your daughter Eunice thereafter?" he queried.

"Of course she came back home, but to make sure that her poor example was not going to be followed by my other daughters, I gave her a thorough beating. She should have had the guts to say No! at whatever cost. I wonder what mothers teach their girls these days." He sighed, then eyed Mr. Mavu, pensively.

"As the boss of the house I made sure of one thing: she had to carry her own cross: baby, food, clothes and all. The only thing I allowed her was shelter." The man was now opening up, coming out of his cocoon. "I intended my orders to be followed to the letter, but like all women my wife tried to be clever by helping her secretly. When I came to discover it they both paid for their disobedience—I chased the girl and her baby out of my house. A man has to be respected in his own house as the head of the family."

"And where is Eunice now?"

Mdamu started. He stared blankly in front of him. "At first she went to stay with a relative at Voi where she quickly found a job as a house-maid, but I'm told she later escaped and went to work as a barmaid in Mombasa. From a housemaid to a barmaid!" he spat out, his face taut with indignation.

"Up to now I have not got over the shock."

The typist knocked gently and opened the door half-way. "Excuse me, Sir," she said to the principal. "The gentleman who wanted to see you yesterday has arrived."

"Oh, thank you. Tell him to give me just a minute. He released the older man and asked him to return when classes for were over for the day. Fortunately for Mr. Mavu, the visitor was of a brisk and formal bent, and did not take long to leave. Soon after, Mr. Mavu sent for Chrispine Mdamu.

The boy walked in timidly and stood in front of the principal's table. "Good afternoon, Sir," he greeted.

"Good afternoon, Chrispine," the principal answered suavely. "How are you?"

"Very fine, Sir."

"I've called you here, Chrispine, over a very serious matter. We have come to realise that you are not doing very well in your classwork, and naturally we are very concerned about it and would like to help you as much as possible. But that would only be possible if you fully co-operate with us, that is, if you help us to help you. And that is why I have called you here. Is there a problem that is affecting your studies?"

Chrispine's head whirled. He was skeptical about the warm sincerity of the principal's words, especially as one of his schoolmates had told him that he had seen his father entering the principal's office. What could have brought his father to the principal? Chrispine quailed within himself, but he decided to be candid. "Yes, Sir... there is," he mumbled.

"Please let me know about it," Mr. Mavu prodded gently, adopting the avuncular mien that disarmed most students, "unless, of course, it is something so private and personal you would not want to talk about it with your principal."

"I...I can talk about it, Sir."

"Good. Please do so without any fear."

The boy gained courage and volubly emptied his heart. When he finally released him and told him to return after classes, Mr. Mavu was armed with enough facts for impartial arbitration in this case between father and son, and he was sure this would not sit well on the former. However, he resolved to do the needful. When the bell to end the school day was rung, Mr. Mavu left the other assignments and started mulling over the problem which had invited itself to his table, but his characteristic geniality reasserted itself when the typist informed him that Mdamu and his son were ready to see him. The pair walked in cheerlessly, the father in front.

The father sat on the same chair he had sat on earlier, while the boy stood a short distance away, his left hand clasped round the wrist of the right hand behind his back, head and shoulders cast in a slouch of exaggerated humility. There was palpable tension between father and son, for each felt that the other was the aggressor.

Mr. Mavu broke the ice by asking, "Do you know this man, Chrispine?"

The boy stole a quick glance at his interrogator, somewhat bemused by the import of such a superfluous question. "I do, Sir," he nodded.

"Who is he?"

"He's my father, Sir." He did not raise his head.

"Thank you." The principal turned to the father and asked him to feel free and ask the boy any questions. Chrispine waited with bated breath for the killer punch.

"Thank you very much, Mr. principal." He turned to the boy. "You have told the principal that I am your father, and I bet that is true. Now my question is: Who is the boss of the house?" The boy was silent. "He is a rude boy who does not answer his father even in the presence of his principal. But to save time, I will go to the next question: Can you remember, Chrispine, the many good things I have done for you ?"

The boy could not readily remember anything worthwhile that the old man had ever done for him, but he knew it would be imprudent to utter the truth at this point. "Yes, I do," he answered tamely.

"Do you know why I was doing all that?"

Chrispine lifted his head slightly and stole another glance at his principal; wordlessly appealing to him to put an end to this rigmarole, but when he was met with an indifferent stare he lowered his eyes meekly and remained silent. Mdamu repeated the question but the boy still remained mum.

"You can choose to keep quiet for as long as you like because you are rude and stupid." Mdamu snapped, "but the truth is that I did all that because you are my child and I have an obligation to see to your welfare so that you can become a responsible citizen in future." He paused briefly to allow this important message to sink in. "And now my other question, and which you must answer or else I curse you right away, is this: Is it because I can no longer fully see to all your needs now that I have suddenly become a contemptible rag?" Mdamu's sunken eyes gleamed in their sockets and his lips twitched spasmodically. "Is that the reason why all of you at home no longer respect me?"

"No," answered the boy, averting his eyes from his father's harsh scrutiny.

"Then what is the reason? Answer me!"

To save the boy from further torture, Mr. Mavu asked what the boy's fees balance was. Mdamu suddenly recoiled and his anger was now replaced with a certain nervousness which gave him a hunted, washed-out appearance. "There is still a lot to be paid... since the beginning of the year he has not paid anything ... also he has some balance for last year," he stammered.

Mr. Mavu furrowed his eyebrows in bewilderment. He was sure Chripine Mdamu was one of the few students who had no fees balance; he had merely asked the question to defuse the growing tension between father and son. He was also puzzled by the older man's reaction to his straight-forward question. The man had given a slight start and seemed to cower within himself, a hunted look on his face. Why? He turned to the boy. "I'm sure you have paid all your school fees, Chrispine?"

The boy was tongue-tied. "Y-y-y-es, Sir," he whispered with trepidation.

Mdamu jerked up his head and stared at his son accusingly, his face bristling with fury. "Use your head, you silly boy! Answer the principal's question truthfully!"

Calmly, Mr. Mavu bade the man to keep his cool. The case was taking a very interesting turn, he believed. He again fiddled with the computer to ascertain the veracity of the boy's answer and his own statement, then primly announced that Chrispine Mdamu of Form 2 Green, admission number 2458, had paid all his school and owed the school nothing. Both father and son lowered their eyes, each engrossed in their own thoughts after the principal's startling revelation, and once again Mr. Mavu dispelled the cloud of tension by enquiring from the boy who had been paying his school fees.

Chrispine cleared his throat. "My ...my sister, Sir," he replied huskily.

"Who?" Mr. Mavu asked again.

"My sister, Sir." This time his voice, though husky, was quite audible.

"Your sister? Which sister?" "Mr. Mavu darted a glance at Mdamu who had now shrunk into a woeful slouch.

"Eunice, Sir," the boy said falteringly.

"Your own sister Eunice? You mean my ...my own daughter Eunice?" Mdamu asked rhetorically.

The boy was now close to tears.

"Now, Chrispine ... Why wasn't your father informed about this arrangement?" The principal came to his student's assistance again. "I mean...it was a good arrangement. She was helping your father, which is good. So... he ought to have been put in the picture, surely?"

"My ...my mother wanted it to remain a secret, Sir."

"But why? What was wrong with your father knowing your sister was doing such a good thing?"

"Because...because...I don't know, Sir!" He wiped his eyes with the back of his left hand.

"Your father has told you that you are no longer a child, young man, and that is very true. Do not waste our time," he firmly admonished, fixing his eyes on the boy.

With some circumlocution, the boy managed to explain that the secret was at hir mother's behest and it was meant to safeguard the money from his father who had lately taken to much drinking and idleness. "But Eunice has been bringing us some money after every end of the month," concluded the boy. After hearing all this Mdamu hauled himself up, bade the principal a stiff good-bye and hobbled out of the office. Mr. Mavu questioned the boy further then released him.

As he plodded along the footpath towards home Mdamu's mind was a whirlpool of confusion. What his son had divulged at the principal's office was the ultimate proof of the treachery in his household. So Eunice the barmaid had now become the adored bread-winner and he a mere parasite? he thought bitterly. I'll teach them a lesson they'll never forget.

Mdamu conjured up various methods of retribution but did not settle on any he felt was efficacious enough. Tenge was now heavily pregnant and so he could not beat her up for she could easily miscarry or even die. An evil thought flitted across his tortured mind. So what if she dies? He firmly repressed the savage thought. But ... oh yes! I've got it now! I'll go right in that house and kill myself after accusing them of driving me nuts with their mistreatment. They will be racked by guilt throughout their miserable lives.

My blood will be on their hands. Yes! He caressed the thought for a while, but slowly came to realise that he did not have the guts to take his own dear life. No. Then what? Good, I've got it now. I'll do something that will show them I'm not the useless, improvident fellow they think I am. I'll sell my house, land and all the other property and with the money I'll start a new life elsewhere—alone. That's it. He smiled darkly. His mind floated.

He could see his wife and children (including Eunice) crawling to him with tears in their eyes. They would prostrate helplessly in front of him and desperately implore him to bail them out of their misery. But he would remain completely indifferent, for he would now be settled elsewhere with a young comely wife who would bear him loving and well-behaved children. Mdamu's delirious fantasies would have continued had he not stumbled against a stone on the path and lurched forward, off-course. He nimbly avoided a dangerous fall by clutching onto the shrubbery by the wayside with both his hands, muttering imprecations.

He realised with a sinking heart that this was the same place he had nearly fallen as he was going to his son's school. This curious coincidence filled him with a vague, visceral dread, and he soon relapsed into an untidy assortment of thoughts which now took on dark wings of suspicion, soaring high with his perverted imagination. My wife cheated on me; there is no way Eunice and Chrispine can be my children, he thought. A daughter from my own loins can not turn into a prostitute; neither can my own son start behaving like a woman. Tenge has been cheating on me! I'll kill that woman! In fact, somebody else has been paying for the boy's school fees, not Eunice. It can't be Eunice. No wonder they wanted it to be a secret. Tenge's lover has been paying the school fees. She has been cheating on me. Even the pregnancy she is now carrying is not mine. Even the other children—Eunice has Tenge's prostitute blood, he concluded.

When he reached his home he entered his bedroom and soon came out, leaving the compound with a bleak smile. Tenge and the children who were engaged in various activities looked at one another questioningly, but did not speak until he was out of earshot.

Mdamu went straight to Mama Pima's place. Mama Pima was a cheerful, voluptuous woman whose quarters were a popular drinking den. Part of her popularity was that she also physically entertained her male clients who were willing to part with enough money. Mdamu absent-mindedly exchanged greetings with the other customers and politely accepted a few sips from some of them. He bought and drank three cans, and a pleasant heady sensation coursed through his entire body. This made him to start warming up to the others, his initial callowness loosening up. He bought his friends several cans as they chatted desultorily with the legendary conviviality of the drinking fraternity.

To the utter disappointment of the other drinkers, Mama Pima suddenly announced that there was no more beer, but not before surreptitiously signalling Mdamu to stay behind. After shooing off her grumbling customers, she assured Mdamu that there was enough beer and that she had only deceived the others because most of them were drinking on credit and she had noticed that they had taken advantage of Mdamu's generosity to fleece him.

She went into another room and reappeared with a jerrican full of the illicit drink. "Please drink and be merry. This is a special offer from me as you are my very good customer, okay? Please drink to your fill," and she wriggled off.

Mdamu drank abundantly; drowning his sorrows with every gulp, and was soon sailing on a wave of ecstasy. Even in his inebriated bliss he felt and smelt Mama Pima's presence before he heard or saw her. She sat close to him on the sofa, her soft arm across his shoulders, enabling his head to repose in the crook of her arm. Placing her right leg on his hips, she easily pulled the yielding man to her and smothered her with kisses and caresses which, together with the sweet fragrance of her heavily perfumed body, sent Mdamu giddy with sexual desire. The thought of Tenge's betrayal and her pregnant state crossed his mind and he willingly responded to Mama Pima's prodding as she shepherded him into her bedroom. It was a wonderful experience for Mdamu, and he slept soundly with a contented smirk on his face.

It was by sheer instinct that Mdamu woke up before dawn. The huge fluffy bed was strange to him. He wondered where he was. He shook his throbbing head and rubbed his bleary eyes with the back of his hands, then squinted through the gloom of the room to get some focus. He felt hungry, and the events of the precious day came flooding into his head. He looked at the sleeping woman and her luscious body, but decided against a repeat perfomance. Very cautiously so as not to wake her; he inched away from her and slid off the bed, searching for his clothes.

"Oh, so you're already awake ?" cooed Mama Pima sleepily. She had turned and was propping her head and shoulders on her elbows, smiling ingratiatingly at the outline of the naked man. "Please come back to bed."

"No, I must be going now," he quickly responded, yawning and stretching himself. He felt uneasy as this was his first act of unfaithfulness. He had to get back home as soon as possible. He found his clothes, quickly dressed up and hurriedly left the wheedling temptress without ceremony.

Mdamu reached his house in a very surly mood. He headed straight to the kitchen where he knew his food would be warming by the fire-place, making sure he was silent enough not to wake the sleeping girls. He decided he should bathe first before eating and he poured some water from a debe into a plastic basin and carried it outside to the makeshift bathing place just behind the kitchen. He liberally lathered himself with a hard piece of soap and vigorously scrubbed himself with a mass of sisal fibre as if to rid himself of any signs of illicit intimacy. After his toilet, Mdamu went back to the kitchen, drank three cupfuls of water, picked a plate and ladle from a wooden ledge under the window and turned to get his food.

Two sturdy logs were feebly smouldering between the three hearth-stones, but there was no sign of food next to the fireplace or anywhere in the kitchen. However, Mdamu knew his family had cooked and eaten because he could see some unwashed sufurias and plates. He drank two more cupfuls of water not so much to slake his thirst as to assuage his hunger. He pulled a mat next to the fireplace with the intention of resting awhile, but he soon slid into a slumber ...

The Mdamus were in a large, open canoe, leisurely heading for the shore. They were all engaged in animated conversation as Mdamu expertly guided the vessel in the placid sea. The cool breeze and the pellucid sky enhanced the joy and beauty of the excursion as they glided along. Soon some straggly clouds appeared in the sky, gradually thickening and darkening to cast a pall on the azure sea. This was followed by a kind of chilliness in the air, and a light drizzle which quickly turned into a torrential downpour. Mdamu paddled on robustly, with the others, especially Tenge, Eunice and Chrispine, trying to offer help with their hands so as to add speed.

The erstwhile calm sea was now growing turbulent , with strong surfing waves rocking the canoe, making it to list at times dangerously from side to side, nearly capsizing. Their carefree gaiety had now turned into a sombre, terror-stricken gloom because of the prospect of calamity. Mdamu turned his head, looked at his family and adjudged the situation as hopeless. He suddenly plunged into the sea and started swimming vigorously towards the shore, leaving his drenched and cowering passengers at the mercy of the elements. In his attempt to save his life he had forgotten to leave the paddle behind, making their situation even more perilous.

They called out to him, but to no avail. Mdamu reached the shore and turned once to look at his family. They had all formed a knot around Tenge, who was now praying fervently for salvation as the others called out for help. Mdamu looked away to avoid their accusing stares. He could clearly hear their plaintive cries as they cried desperately for him. He suddenly felt some invisible force pulling him up by his shirt-front, heftily hauling him up, and saw a gun aimed at his chest...

With a terrified scream Mdamu was up. He blinked rapidly, unseeingly, and could hardly make out the worried faces of his children. "Father! Father! Quick!" It was Chrispine's voice, and he was urgently tugging at his father's shirt-front. "Come and help mother!" he urged anxiously. He quickly regained full consciousness, and allowed himself to be led by his son to their bedroom, where his wife was moaning painfully. The labour pains were on her. "You can go; I'll attend to her on my own," he told his son. The boy obediently left, relieved to be away from his parent's exclusive domain.

Mdamu looked at his wife. Her pretty face was taut with pain. She urgently needed help. He instinctively dipped his hands in his pockets, foraging for any money left after the previous night's impulsive splurge, and a wave of remorse assailed him after discovering that what remained was very little. The unscrupulous temptress must have divested him of some of his money as he slept. Where would he get help now? Julia his sister-in-law was due to arrive the following week.

The nearest government hospital was four kilometres away and he had no means of taking her there, yet the slightest delay could prove fatal. There was a private clinic nearby, but he had recklessly squandered all the money he had been keeping for this emergency. To make matters worse, he was not in very good books with the neighbours as he had distanced himself from them by avoiding village communal work and activities. Mdamu was in a quandary.

Tenge groaned agonizingly. There was no more time to waste. Mdamu shouted for some water to be warmed, then with single-minded determination he applied his smattering of midwifery on his wife. In a short while the sharp cry of a new-born baby could heard, and the children outside looked at each other expectantly. Mdamu came out of the room, beads of perspiration on his face, and sent Chrispine to go for Aunt Julia. He then asked the eldest girl to bring some warm water in a basin. The other younger children who had been told by Chrispine and Martha to expect a new-born baby looked dismayed when they saw their father empty-handed, but he told them to be patient as he re-entered the room with the water.

Shortly afterwards, Mdamu came out with the blessed bundle in his hands safely covered with some homespun swaddling clothes. The children swarmed around him with eager curiosity, itching to touch the baby. "Here is our special visitor," he announced delightedly. "What name shall we give it?" The children came up with a number of names, all of which Mdamu politely turned down by playfully shaking his head. "Do you know why I have rejected all your suggestions?"

"No-o-o-o," they chorused in unison, warming up to their new, friendly Dad.

Mdamu allowed for a short pause to whet their curiosity the more. "I will tell you, my children. All the names you have suggested are female ones, but our visitor is a man!" The children now gazed at the sleeping baby with added curiosity, and unrolled a few other male names.

"We shall name the baby after your maternal grandfather because Chrispine is named after my father. Is that alright?"

They all agreed, delightfully applauding their father's decision with a volley of claps.

"Tonight," said Mdamu, "we shall all gather together after supper for thanksgiving prayers to God for guiding our new visitor safely. It is indeed a blessing." He regarded the children tenderly. "This is a very special day and we shall celebrate it in our own small but special way. Martha, go and kill one of the chickens. Your mother needs plenty of soup now."

"Father...which...? Should I kill a hen... or the cock?" The girl had with a touch of concern remembered the earlier exchanges between her parents.

"Kill the cock!" Mdamu said unequivocally. "And kill one of the hens too. We should all have enough chicken for lunch and supper, more so because your aunt Julia will be here tonight to help your mother." The children pranced about joyfully. This was a new person they were seeing, not the aloof, ill-humoured tyrant they had become accustomed to. Martha skipped off in search of the fowls, and the other children trooped after her. Mdamu went back to the bedroom where she found his wife, though exhausted, lying on the bed with a smile on her face. She had heard all. Wife and husband looked at each other, and love shone through their eyes.

Mdamu gently placed the baby next to its mother, glad that he had sent for his sister-in-law in case of any puerperal disorders later, especially as the baby had come a bit earlier than expected. He went for pen and paper and scribbled two short notes. "I have decided to invite Chrispine's principal next Sunday after church for a family get-together," he informed his wife, sealing one letter in a khaki envelope. "He struck me as a good chap. Any objections?"

Tenge shook her head. "The second letter," Mdamu continued with a mischievous wink as he picked another envelope from one of the card-board boxes, "is to a very special lady who must by all means come for the get-together. But I can only post the letter with your permission."

Tenge waited patiently, a puzzled expression on her face because she had heard Mdamu sending for her sister Julia, who was also included for supper

"I have written to our daughter Eunice. I hope you will kindly provide me with her address?" he enquired teasingly, carefully inserting the note in the envelope and sealing it.

"As for the pastor of your church, I will personally ask him tomorrow when I attend church to be with us next Sunday to lead us in the thanksgiving prayers."

Tenge silently turned her head aside and, gently stroking her new-born baby, smiled with genuine happiness in her heart.

Photography/ Illustration : J.N.K.

SOSPETER SHAKE is the headmaster of a small secondary school in Wundanyi Division in Taita. He studied Literature and Philosophy at the University of Nairobi. Mr. Shake is a literature teacher. Several of his short stories and a collection of poetry have been published by Forward Press (UK).

Estrangement

Gathondu Mwangi

This is how love dies,
not in outbursts,
or short spurts of hate.
Love dies,
in differences,
in indifferences,
and retreats irretrievably
into silence

Frankenstein's Lament

Gathondu Mwangi

If you let your mind stray would you follow it?
If you lost your mind would you search for it?
Once I let my mind wander far
I've never found it since
If you could run away from your mind where would you go?

Happiness is a Goat

Gathondu Mwangi

Happiness is a goat
skipping on three legs and a horn
playing hopscotch with a toad
tucked in its belly, a patchwork grin
visible through its goaty goatee.

Should you find it, tell me.

Illustration: Ray Gicharu

Holy Shit

BY DOREEN BAINGANA

We walk out of his house one sunny morning feeling all right. I am bursting with the happy-to-be-alive feeling that comes after a good night of lovemaking. Everything around me looks new; the clear morning sun just before it gears up for the midday heat, small birds twittering in the trees, a cute kid hiding shyly behind her mother's long skirt.

I hold my lover's hand as we walk down a small street towards Ntinda in Kampala. I am old enough to have a lover, but the word still gives me guilty pleasure. For a night, at least, our bodies joined together and became one moving bulk with a joyous myriad of tentacles and orifices. After adult conversation at dinner, debate over fish stew, *matoke* and beer, I was on my back, legs spread wide and flailing in the air in that ridiculous position women, be they High Court judges, little old ladies with funny yellow hats and moustaches muttering to themselves on the bus, or our very own Mothers' Union mothers, have ended up in sooner or later. We are spread out like roast chicken and poked and prodded and it is the most delicious thing there is.

My lover and I completely opened ourselves to each other; there were no secrets left. In bed, that is. He explored all sorts of places in, on and about me. Now he knows me better than I do myself. In bed. We screamed and giggled and growled together. We swam greedily in the exact same hot tenderness, fury, plunging pool, and finally, finally, languid fatigue.

But it's the next day. Now we walk down a dusty murram road that leads to the main highway into the city center. The road, a typical Ugandan small-town scene, is lined with uneven wooden kiosks selling *Ruwenzori* bottled water; *chapati;* chewing gum, plastic cups, plates and buckets in bright blue, green, red and yellow; cell phone cards. Amid the stray dogs, old worn bicycles leaning on tree trunks; fast-spoken news coming from a radio somewhere, and old gray men sitting in the shade, waiting for nothing but death, is a lone thin brown cow. Its legs are stretched out, taunt, straining to the point of tremors. I watch it. A cow with such a concentrated, stern, pained expression? Is it giving birth? No, it's not swollen with pregnancy. I can't take my eyes of it. I tug at my lover's arm to slow him down. "Look, look!"

A bright pink thing pushes out of the cow's thin behind. The muscular-looking piece of flesh stretches open, and out comes an army-green giant of a worm, out and leaning over. It hangs mid-air for a moment, tentatively. But, it is too long and heavy now, it breaks off and falls, flopping down onto the roadside and spreading out into a flat steaming green cake. Dust rises in a gentle applause.

"Did you see that!?" My voice is almost a yelp.

My lover's face twists in an eloquent grimace of disgust. "You! Stop your bad manners."

I giggle as we walk on, but he will not follow wherever my senses take me. A cow shitting is not a beautiful and moving symbol of pure eros, not to him. For me, that was last night all over again. The naturalness and dirtiness and honesty of the physical. The cow's indecent, innocent pink protrusion and smelly loud plop of shit landing is the brazen badness, rudeness, sliminess of sex. Does he not see this, feel this? Wasn't he there, last night, with me?

I had discovered and mapped his whole body. He gave it to me; I owned it. I deeply understood his mouth and limbs and scalp and cock. I saw his face go tender. He saw mine open-mouthed grotesque with sharp pleasure. But now, now, we are on the other side. Our clothes, these deceivingly thin cotton shields, are back on. Coffee is speeding through our veins and brains, pushing us to the next thing, a crash landing.

I let go his arm. We go back to talking newspaper headlines, using words as steps to back away from each other, from ourselves. I look into his face and almost recognize the eyes of my lover. Almost. Where is he? Who was that lusty me? We move further and further away, like memory does from reality.

DOREEN BAINGANA is a Ugandan writer, currently living in the US. Her short story collection, Tropical Fish: Stories out of Entebbe, was published in February 2005 as the winner of the AWP (Associated Writers and Writing Programs) Award in Short Fiction in 2003. Ms. Baingana also won the Washington Independent Writers Fiction Prize in 2004, and was a finalist for the Caine Prize in 2004. She has been a Writer-in-Residence at the University of Maryland, College Park. She has an MFA from the same university, teaches at the Writers' Center in Bethesda, Maryland, and works part time at Voice of America radio.

Illustration: JNK

The Other Side Of Knowing

BY DAYO FOSTER

The sudden change from the warmth of bodies, noise and gaiety to a brash ocean wind squeezes my skin closer to me. I rub my hands over my arms, flattening the landscape of hair tipped bobbles, only to have them peek up again in protest at the cold. My toes cling to each other for warmth as I crunch my way past the dread-topped coconut palms, past a few occupied benches shrouded in capsules of shadow. The bathrooms are at the back of the club.

A girl is leaning against the row of sinks. Her cigarette is tucked into a holder and her hair is pulled back off a face you would want to look at again. She holds and moves her body in a way that would make you want to look at her again. She drags her eyelids down, and keeping them closed, turns her back to me. Smoke wisps upwards and she says clearly, to the occupants of the first cubicle,

"You'd better hurry up in there. Someone's come in."

I had started the beginnings of a smile but now it's shrinking. What it would have been is paused and reversed, so I can regain my face, keep it to myself, carry myself past her to a cubicle at the far end of the room. I walk past tiny scuffles, and little unhs.

The door won't shut. My pee seems to come out all in a rush, too quick, too loud. The tap gushes out when I open it and splashes onto my dress. I look at the girl out of the edge of my eye. She has not moved. The cigarette is almost at the filter. The grunting has not stopped.

Outside, one of the capsules of shadow splits into two. I cannot see who it is at first. Then the girl says,

"It's getting a bit cold. Let's go back in."

Remi's voice.

He says, "Let's sit out here for a bit longer. I'll keep you warm. Stay close."

By the time I walk past them, they are locked into each other again, like a self-involved octopus. They do not notice me.

When I walk in, I cannot see anyone I know. I move into the shaded dark, edging along the wall, past clumps of people, with a few scattered pairs, all with parts of their bodies touching. The song changes and I hear Amina's whoop as she drags Yuan to the dance floor. It's not a tune that needs close contact.

Oh. I'm going to Barbados.

Oh. Going to see my girlfriend.

She flings her arms around Yuan's neck, pulls his head down, and kisses him on the lips. He's not pulling back. He's not struggling. They stay intertwined for a long time. My heart squeezes itself tight and my eyes drum. Sadness, anger, bitterness, rage, all flash by, strobing with the disco lights—black, shiny, acid blue, blood red. Using my hands behind me as a guide, I find the rough wall to lean on, to watch from.

I attract the attention of a few beer stuffed young men, who detach themselves from their gang, only to stumble towards me and my frosty cracked smile, and then stumble back towards a raucous re-welcome into their group.

The song ends. Amina drags Yuan off, leading him by the hand. Why? She can choose whoever she wants. Surely she must know. Why? He's told me before he doesn't fancy Amina. And today of all days!

I know what I have to do today. I will choose and I will do it.

Reuben can drive. I direct him all the way. Will you take me home? Why don't you stop here for a bit? Shall we move to the back seat? I have the good sense to take out the condom in my disco bag.

I sleep through much of the next day, getting up late afternoon to have a second shower. I think about taking a walk, but when I go outside, Osman is sitting there, on his little stool, with his radio pressed to his ear. The newsreader is announcing in Wollof,

"The president will be leaving soon for the second leg of his meet-the-people tour. He will be visiting Mansakonko..."

"Nanga deff," I say as I walk past him, towards the gate.

"Jama rek," he replies.

I catch his scent as I walk past—it's the roughness of old palm wine ground into stale unfiltered cigarettes. Reuben's had been straight out of a bottle. Outside the gate, the idea of trudging through the dust, up to the shop for a Coke and a breath of fresh air does not appeal any more. I turn around and go back to my room.

When Reuben rings, I don't want to speak to him. I don't want to speak to Yuan or Amina either. They leave messages with my sister Kainde:

"Ring Reuben when you get out of bed. He will be at home."

"Yuan rang to say he looked for you last night and that Amina told him you'd left. He waited for you anyway until they closed the disco, in case you came back."

"Amina says Yuan was looking for you everywhere yesterday. She left him at the party, waiting for you because he wanted to take you home. She says you should ring her back immediately."

Remi rings but does not leave a message.

While the phone rings and Kainde collects my messages, I stay in my bedroom. The curtains are still flowery blue. The walls are still yellow. And the stupid sun is still washing the air with heat.

"What's wrong?" asks my mother the next morning.

"Just tired," I reply.

"What's up with you?" says Taiwo.

"Mind your own business," I answer.

Kainde continues to write down my messages. She knocks with a murmur of explanation, and then shoves pieces of paper under the door.

"Thank you," I reply to each one.

I feel empty. Reuben has not brought knowledge.

Remi's reaction is what I would have expected.

"Lord have mercy! With Reuben!"

She shakes her head, covers her eyes with one hand. She opens her mouth, closes it again. She holds her chin with her left hand to ponder, and then asks,

"What was it like?"

I twist my mouth in response. Yes. With Reuben.

"When my dad came to pick me up, he thought you'd want a lift. He wondered who you went home with. And whether your mother knew."

"So what did you say to him?"

"That I didn't know." She pauses and scratches her nose, "But I thought Yuan was the one. How on earth did you end up with ...?"

She shuts up when she sees my face.

On one of the days when I spend more of my time in my bed than anywhere else, Aunt K comes around.

I hear her way down the corridor, talking to Kainde.

"Watin do am? What's wrong with her? Boy trouble? You say 'boy'? Let me go talk with her."

Her footsteps accompany her comments to Kainde. "There are certain things in life you shouldn't hurry along. Look at Aunty Beedi—it wasn't until she was in her 50s that she found someone to settle down with. That's the kind of thing that's enough to make anyone live long. Look at her, she's just like a young girl now. Her face is fresh, she's always giggling when I meet her out shopping."

She stops outside my door. "Which borbor dis? Which boy? You don't know? She didn't say? You're her sister—you should talk to her. I won't always be around you know."

She raps on my door, three sharp ones.

"Comut dooyah. Open up. I have something to say to you. Might as well let me in now, or I'll shout it out in the corridor. Right here where I'm standing."

I get up to let her in. My door has been locked, key-locked, all day.

After Aunt K leaves, my mother delivers two weak taps on my door.

"Yes, ma," my dry throat scrapes out as an answer.

She says, "I heard Kiki in the corridor. About you having boy trouble. I've talked to you about this kind of thing before."

Her voice sounds odd, a bit higher in pitch than usual. Ma breathes deep at the end of her sentence.

"I'm okay. It was just Kainde telling tales."

"So there's nothing I should worry about? Nothing I should know?"

"No, ma, nothing."

"Don't forgot what I've told you."

"I know, ma, men are only after one thing."

"That's right. And when they get it, they don't stay."

At the door, she grabs the handle. She goes out but her footsteps do not go away. How can she ever begin to understand what it's like inside of me? I scowl at the shadow of her legs falling in two thick lines on the little crack of air under my door. She stands there as I listen to her listening for me.

Amina barges into my bedroom the next day. "Why didn't you ring me back?"

Her arms move to rest on her hips, akimbo. I know what she's staring at. My hair is sticking up on end. My eyes are puffy and my cheeks ashed grey. I am in a pair of tartan flannel pyjamas.

"What's up with you? Yuan's going stirfry crazy. And here you are looking all rough."

"You're good friends now, are you?"

"We talk. He's pretty cool."

"I saw you kiss him at the disco."

"Oh. Is that what this is all about then?"

Her raised eyebrows. Her scrunched up face with the questioning look. Her you-stupid-girl shake of her head.

"I know you like him. There are lots of men and boys out there. I don't need Yuan."

I burst into tears.

"Look, you know I fool around. I kissed him on a dare that's all. It means nothing."

Amina throws herself on to the end of my bed, and leans on one elbow watching me sob myself into my pillow.

"Pull yourself together. It's not the end of the world you know."

Three days later, I start to come out of my room more often to face the world with its bright shining sun. Reuben calls on a day I'm closest to the phone and I pick up.

"Ha-hallo. That sounds like you Ayodele," he starts.

"Yes, it is."

"I've been phoning ..."

"And I've got the messages."

"Ah I wondered whether you'd like to go for a charwarma or something?"

"Not today, thanks."

"Perhaps another time?"

"Perhaps."

By Thursday the following week, my head is in a twist. I chose the guy I didn't want, and am now ignoring the one I did want. I feel stupid.

We are about to go for our end of year, end of school picnic party. This is our very last time together as a class. I am late on purpose, having asked Amina and Remi to save me a seat. Although we were all allowed to bring one guest, most of us haven't bothered. Remi has invited Kojo, her boyfriend, and he will be driving up to meet us later.

Reuben finds me as soon as I arrive and comes up to grin and mumble a few words. "You're looking nice," he says, but his eyes do not quite know where to look on my body. They jump from my face, to my boobs, then my feet. He stares at my leather flipflops while I think up an answer.

"Thank you," is the best I can do.

His eyes flicker back up to mine and then stare past my right ear towards the main school entrance, where our rowdy, chattering friends wait.

"Which bus are you going in?"

"That one. With Remi and Amina."

His hands find his pockets.

"Just wondered, whether. Um. You'd like us to sit together?"

"Thanks, but the others are waiting for me."

His eyes shift past my face to a spot beyond my left ear.

"See you then."

Most of us are wearing jeans, khaki trousers or shorts. Amina's version of our teenage uniform is tight, tight, dark, dark drainpipe jeans with a loose t-shirt screaming 'babe'. I see her clambering into the bus, squealing about something or other, as she usually does.

We are going to a tiny village up past Pirang. Mrs. Foon, a teacher at our school, has relatives who own a farm by the river. The buses have come to pick us up on the forecourt of our school. We are waiting for the drivers to be given final instructions. Everyone is trying to find someone they'd like to sit next to. Stragglers jostle for improved bus seats. An hour later, we're crammed into the two buses. They ease out through the front gate, past 'Coast High School' written out in red china grass against a patchy bit of lawn, onto the road to start our journey. We're taking everything we need for our party. There are plastic sacks of ice stuffed into metal bins for our drinks. A couple of car batteries to power the music and small speakers. Half a tin drum, cut lengthways, that will be our BBQ. Bags of charcoal. Lots of crates of soft drinks with a few stray ones of Julbrew beer—our teachers have acknowledged that we are after all, now officially Grown Up. We have cane mats and malans to spread out on the ground. There are vats of seasoned chicken, and half a sheep, potatoes, plantains, baskets of mangoes and drifts of lettuce leaves.

Moira, Remi and Yuan got into the bus early, and picked the best spot—the row of five seats in the back.

I sit next to Amina, who declares, "Could not find anyone young enough to invite who wasn't coming already, so I came on my own."

Remi says, "Why am I not surprised?"

"Yeah," Yuan says, "you mix in different circles, Amina."

"And those friends won't want to come to a boring Sixth Form party," Moira adds.

I know Yuan senses something is different about me. He leaves his eyes on my mouth when he looks at me. I find I cannot keep my eyes on his whenever they meet.

We drive past groyned beaches and sleepy casuarinas, past huddles of stalls by the roadside at Serrekunda, and newly built Amadiya mosques. The road is fine until we get past Brikama, when it becomes dusty tarmac with many generous pot holes, accompanied by two parallel lanes of laterite carved out on either side by weary drivers. Rain-worked ravines hurry across the road. The bus tilts over each bump.

There's talk of university, some drifting towards us at the back before being snatched away by wind through the open windows.

"I've had enough of studying," says Remi, "Kojo will have to earn all the money."

"So he becomes a doctor and you become a wife?" asks Amina.

"Any problem with that?" Remi asks, her voice sharp.

Moira sighs and asks, "And you, Yuan, what will you do?"

"I've applied to a couple of universities in America to please my parents, but as I keep telling them, Europe will be a lot closer. I'd rather go to England."

"I know I won't be able to go to England without a scholarship, even if I get the university place," I say.

"All this England, England. Why not try further afield? I want to go somewhere where no one else is going, like Italy or Singapore," says Amina.

"I want to work, start earning some real money," says Moira.

"I wonder where we'll all end up," I say.

Elsewhere on the bus, there are occasional bouts of laughter, raucous shouts across the aisle. "Pipe down," says Mrs Foon, "you're almost grown-ups."

We turn to stare out of the back windscreen. An outrider in a blue security service uniform speeds towards us flashing blue. It steadily gains on us, stirring up a blanket of red dust. It appears he wants us to get off the makeshift laterite road, and stop on the potholed tarmac. The driver turns the engine off in protest.

The outrider pulls up next to the driver. "Get off the road, the president's coming."

"I'm already off it, so he can stay in the middle."

"Don't be cheeky. The President needs a smooth ride. Get back on the tarmac."

"That's not so easy here—look at that huge hump at the side."

"Get off soon, and show proper respect. Or the next outrider will make sure you're sorry."

We crowd on the driver's side of the bus, gawping at the leather booted man in a moonscape helmet.

Amina stands up on her seat, her tight packed rounded bum hovering north of Yuan's spiky head. She yells out of the window, "Is Mr. Bojang in the car with the president?"

The outrider turns to her and replies, "What's it to you?" before gunning his engine and giving us a blast of processed petrol.

"How do you know a Mr. Bojang, in with the president?" Yuan asks.

"I get around."

It doesn't take long to get the story out of her.

"I met him at Landing's a couple of months ago. He happens to like school girls." She puts on her cheeky grin and her eyes spray sparks of merriment. "He thinks his power and money will buy him anyone."

"But you showed him otherwise, right?"

"You bet. Men are so stupid—not you Yuan, you are perfect. They think a flash of dalasi and a flag with the president's seal on it are all it takes to sniff a girl's underwear."

"You should be careful. What if he'd turned nasty?"

"Nasty? In a place as public as Landing's? No chance. I teased him a bit, let him buy me a drink and then went off to close dance with someone else. Soon enough, some skinny girls were on to him. They looked young, so I think they diverted his attention from me."

"All these stories, Amina!"

"I bet you have a few of your own. Go on, tell."

"I'm sure our lives will never be as exciting as yours," says Yuan, looking at me.

We have arrived at the farm, and hauled our communal picnic into the shade of an enormous mango tree, off season, with huge glossy leaves and coarse thighed buttresses off its trunk. Remi and Moira start to spread out mats and pillows, trays and cups.

A few fishermen are offering boat rides off a shaky looking jetty—built of planks from the insides of coconut palm, sodden with brackish water. Tongues of river lick the sides of the canoes, hollowed out trunks that can take three or perhaps four slim people at a time. Amina and Yuan dare me to join them. We leave the other two to the unpacking.

The boat trip itself is without incident. The fisherman uses a long pole to ease us away from the bank. Stretches of bare mangrove roots above the surface of the water breathe in air without a shudder. Once we are in the little tributary, with the mangrove on both sides, voices from our picnic site get rubbed away by our distance. All we can hear are bird noises. Clusters of river oysters have crusted onto the mangrove. The fisherman splashes his paddle past a group of women up to their waist in water. They wield large blades, prising the oysters off with hands thickened from years of doing the same thing.

Even Amina falls silent, letting her hand trail through the water.

"Watch out, it might be sweet enough for crocodiles," Yuan says to her.

"Don't be silly," she replies, but she takes her hand out, sprinkling the river water at Yuan.

She makes it all look so easy, this mucking about with boys, this ease at being around them.

When we get back to the jetty, the others get out first as they are nearer the front. When I stand up, the canoe suddenly tips to one side.

"Togall," shouts the boat man.

"Move your weight," yells Yuan.

Do I sit, stand, move or keep still? In the seconds it takes me to decide I don't quite know what to do, the boat loses its balance under me. I fall backwards, away from the jetty, into deep water. It is thickly brown. I cannot feel which way is up. I cannot see the bubbles I blow out. I thrash about at first, and manage to bring my head above water, but when I open my mouth, all it seems to do is swallow. I know I can swim, but it takes a full sharp-edged minute before I can convince my body it needs to let the water carry it. Then my foot touches something, hard and slimy. A scream boils free from my body. My arms start to punch the water again, my feet kicking.

"Try to get to the boat," instructs Yuan.

I see the long shape of the boat's bottom alongside me. Relief swamps the fear. The boatman who was also flung into the river appears next to me. My legs start to kick the water and my arms find a stroke. The jetty comes closer.

They help me out – Yuan and Amina each claiming an arm while the boatman tries to boost my feet with his hands.

I sit in a pair of borrowed malans all afternoon, one tied round my waist as a skirt, the other in a halter top. My clothes, which Remi wrings out, are lying on a nearby bush, drying in the sun.

Mangrove roots in the river can feel like the skin of crocodiles.

We stay in our tight little group, lounging in the shade. Mrs Foon waves a hand. Reuben walks by several times on his own, making a track to and from the jetty. Kojo eventually arrives in his father's old snub nosed Peugeot 504, his exhaust giving a little fart when he turns off the engine. He walks towards us.

"Here he is," Remi announces, "our ride home."

Yuan greets him with a, "Hey man, you've missed all the action."

"What action? Tell me more, but first get me something to drink. That road's a killer."

Moira says, "Ayodele got soaked." Everyone piles in to elaborate.

Yuan concludes, "She looks calm don't you think, for someone recently rescued from being crocodile food." Their heads all swivel round to look at me.

The barbeque tin drum is now with hissing with mounds of oysters piled on the ash-rimmed coals. I stand up to make a pretend curtsey. "I'll get us some river food to celebrate my watery resurrection."

Armed with a tin enamelled bowl piled with a mountain of barbequed oysters, I make my way back to the group, only to find they are still discussing the intricacies of how I lost my balance—how I looked flailing about in the water, my swimming technique, and my final last lunge towards the jetty. Fuelled by the empty green bottles beside them, Amina and Yuan are miming my actions, as if scripted.

"Why don't you talk about something else for a while? How come Amina knows someone who works with the President, for example?"

"That's not half as interesting as falling into a river when there's a perfectly good jetty to get off onto," protests Amina.

"Good point Ayodele," says Yuan. He shakes his index finger at Amina. "Girls like you should leave men like that alone."

"Why?"

"Go on, someone, fill me in," says Kojo.

With relief, I summarise. "On the way here, an outrider ordered us off the road. As he drove off, Amina asked about the whereabouts of a certain Mr. Bojang. Then she told us that she'd met him at some club. Which is worse? That or swimming with crocodiles?"

"Some of the men in this government are absolute bastards," Kojo says.

Amina tries to clear her name. "Hey, I only tried to pass on a hello to someone who would not remember me. It was a joke."

"Do you know there's rumours of a Mr. Bojang who tells doctors what to put on death certificates?"

We all freeze, as in how we used to when small and playing musical chairs.

Amina breaks into the disquiet, "Like I said, I've only met him the once. Don't take me too seriously. It was only a joke."

Kojo has the last word, "Men like that cannot be joked around with."

The early bus is ready to leave. I notice Reuben shuffling near the door, looking around with his hands in his pockets, shoulders hunched. When I think he might notice me looking at him, I turn away and reach for my bottle of beer.

The moon settles into the night. What breeze there is is muddied by the large mango trees standing in its way. We are leaving later with Kojo. Amina is given the chore of explaining our plans to the teachers supervising the tidy up in preparation for the second departure. We help to spill hot coals and scatter them onto sun hardened laterite. Empty bottles clink together as they are put back into the crates and loaded onto the bus. We commandeer a few bottles from the vats of cold water before the dustbins are emptied and the plastic bags of our litter loaded in. When all is done, the last bus starts up. We allow the quiet to hang over the trundle of the engine as it turns out of the gate.

The noises change. The bird sounds are fewer, longer, lower.

"What about snakes?" says Amina, her voice tangled and squeaky.

We burst into delighted laughter. And the laughter and lightness carry the rest of the evening.

Eventually I say, "Should we go now?"

Yuan replies, "Don't want to."

"Should we stay till morning then?"

Amina echoes, "Don't want to."

We knot ourselves into a drift of conversations, starting and ebbing. University crops up again. And what we intend to do with our lives. We talk about the moon, about whether mermaids will come this far up the river, about crocodiles and oysters. The night is stretching itself thin, with no one wanting to break up the easy company until the sky starts to lighten, and we agree that yes, indeed, it is morning after all.

DAYO FORSTER was born and lived in the Gambia. Her first novel, Reading the Ceiling, an excerpt of which was first published in Kwani 1 will be published by Simon and Schuster in April 2007. She is involved in setting up a literary festival in Kenya which has established a linkage with the Hay Festival in Wales. She lives in Nairobi.

Weaving

Alison Ojany Owuor

A weaving begins,
The fingers move through the reeds rapidly,
A repetitive enchantment found with those given a destiny higher than the mundane,
Blood of divinity frolics in the veins of these beings,
An emphasis on the staggering fears of the todays but the unknowings of tommorows,
She questions the beginnings but never the endings,
An introspective thought an allowed leisure by the great divine patterns of pain
that take shape, blunting the sharpness of deformation
Her fingers move in haste a reconciliation of body and earth.

Merchants bargain their wares,
Blind to their trade,
She takes their tears for his blood,
An eternity she shall live her time has come its is here,

The basket is complete so shall her breath on this realm a perseverence
so unacknowledged.
In the past her venom engulfed her within …that was before,
She sang songs not of youth but dirges for the fallen anointed,
Twilight is rendered a dark encasing symphony of crickets
And wind begins.
A merger so meticulous in severity,
Hether stage surpasses the cures of apothecaries,
A wisdom greater than theirs made its choice,
She begins her speech,
Pale wanderers shall come from far.
Tell of paupers who are king and sinners morphed to redeemers,
Breeze to rain to storm so moves this story through our lands.
There shall be many to follow.
The basket is complete so is the prophecy,
The ancestors no longer speak but see her.

ALISON OJANY OWUOR is a student of psychology at The United States University. She has been writing poetry since she was eight. She hopes to become one of the ghosts of Rimbaud. Some of her other work has been published in the UK.

Convention

Steve Partington

Not being Kenyan - and indeed, instead,
my birthplace being England, not the most,
I'm told, propitious place - I am at least
obliged - they tell me - in my writings - if
indeed I *must insist* on putting expat pen to paper - to respect the way
we do things here in literature and write
about a character dictated by
a list that's been prepared for budding bards

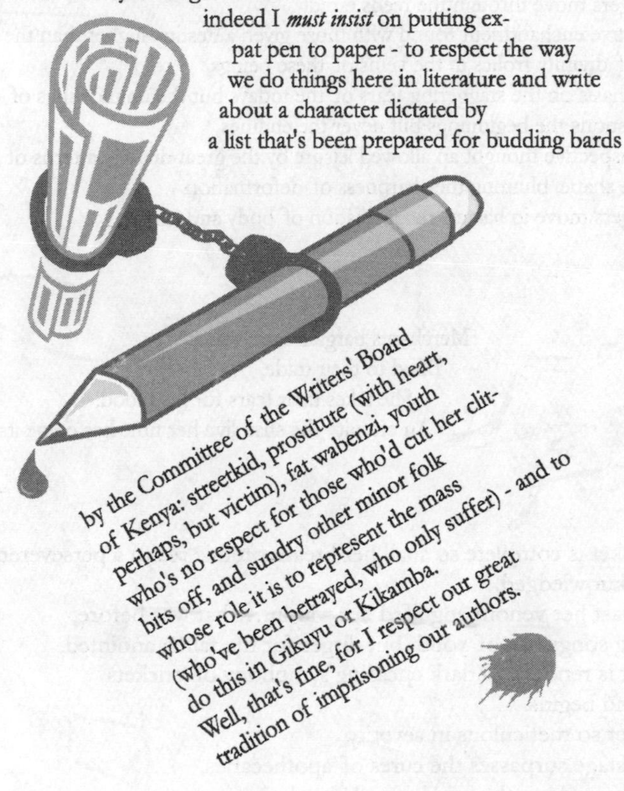

by the Committee of the Writers' Board
of Kenya: streetkid, prostitute (with heart,
perhaps, but victim), fat wabenzi, youth
who's no respect for those who'd cut her clit-
bits off, and sundry other minor folk
whose role it is to represent the mass
(who've been betrayed, who only suffer) - and to
do this in Gikuyu or Kikamba.
Well, that's fine, for I respect our great
tradition of imprisoning our authors.

STEPHEN PARTINGTON is a poet. He has just realised a book of Kenyan poetry titled Sms and Face to Face. He is a schoolteacher and makes bad tasting fruit wines.

The Life Of Brian

BY SHALINI GIDOOMAL

Sunday, Grand Comore. November 1996.

Slivers of white cloud float slowly through the wide blue sky as the afternoon sun beats down on the powder white sand beach of Grand Comore. Turquoise waves lap gently against the shore and an offshore wind cools sunbathers, catching rays before their return to the grimmer winter of the northern hemispshere. An unfamiliar droning sound overhead heralds the first sight of a large metallic bird on the horizon. It quickly comes into focus, moving earthward at speed. Closer and closer it rushes towards the beach, banking steeply to the left, forcing its wings away from the palm trees and the tourists. Now impossibly low, skirting the water, it searches for a spot to rest. There is an audible gasp from the sunbathers as they watch this erratic progress downward towards the sea.

Sunday, Nairobi. November 1996.

It's a lazy weekend lunchtime in the leafy suburb of Lavington. Lobsters fresh from the coast lie immobilized on blocks of ice in a cool box ready for the barbeque. The wine is chilled, the breeze softly plays with the leaves of a large fig tree in the garden. Duncan Willetts, photographic partner at Camerapix, absent mindedly strokes his luxuriant moustache as he chats to his friend, catching up on local Nairobi news. CNN flicks multiple images silently in the background. A red tickertape flash of breaking news stretches across the screen, interrupting the newscast. It informs that an Ethiopian Airways flight making the short hop from Addis to Nairobi has gone off the radar.

While they eat lunch the airplane story moves inexorably up the priority of news items. Glancing at the screen during coffee, Duncan realizes with a sudden start that this could be the early morning flight that his business partners – Mohammed Amin and Brian Tetley boarded to return from yesterday's meeting in Addis.

A flurry of phone calls take place. Duncan calls Salim Amin, also a cameraman, and son of Mohammed Amin to see if his father has called or arrived home. He hasn't. Salim is worried. Sitting with his mother Dolly, they too have seen the news of the disappearing Ethiopian Airways plane. Duncan speed dials Nick Kotch, the Nairobi Reuters bureau chief, to see what he knows. Nick tells him he's been monitoring the story since early morning when the Reuters stringer in Addis first reported the plane heading off course. He's not saying much, but his tone is careful. "You'd better come in." Salim and Duncan speak briefly again before leaping into their respective cars and racing from Lavington through the quiet Sunday streets onto Uhuru Highway, to the Reuters office at Finance House in town to monitor the situation on the newswires.

"We were expecting an emergency landing in Tanzania because of their low fuel situation," says Nick as they rush through the door, "but the plane's turned east and is heading out over the Indian Ocean. We've no idea yet who's hijacked it, or why." More journalists filter into the Reuters office for updates, waiting impatiently for news to come off the wires from stringers based in Ethiopia and South Africa.

Nick gets a call from his Reuters boss in London. "Charter a plane – you need to get there now." The hijack was big news for them—after all Mo Amin, already an international cameraman of repute, was now on the Reuters payroll following their takeover of the smaller news agency Visnews, of which Mo had been bureau chief for years.

By mid afternoon the aircraft is back on the radar moving towards the only speck of land between the east African coast and open sea – a small group of islands known as the Comores. As they monitor the wires churning out reams of news updates, the plane comes down in the turquoise sea near the biggest atoll Grand Comore, destabilized by the wingtip hitting a hidden reef, cartwheeling through the water, breaking into pieces. There's an intake of breath, then a brief stretching silence as the news arrives. "Shit," whispers Duncan, not looking at Salim. Nick picks up the phone to Wilson Airport and begins the process of booking a plane. He draws several blanks from their regular charter companies. No planes suitable for that length of flight are ready to take off immediately. However Air Boskovich, a private charter outfit favoured by journalists, agrees to get a plane ready for the next day. Years of regular use of 'Boskies' means a quick conversation, followed by a fax confirming price, secures an aircraft for a 6am take-off the following morning.

An hour later, still in the Reuters office, they hear that some of the airplane passengers have been picked up out of the sea, or succeeded in swimming ashore. There's a chance that either Mo or Brian could be amongst the survivors. Reuters are sending a crew from South Africa to cover the story. Nick, Duncan and Salim are not going to the Comores in a news capacity at all. Their job is to find out whether Mo and Brian survived the crash.

Monday Morning, 5am, Nairobi.

A tense group of journalists gather in the early morning dawn at Boskies hangar at Wilson Airport. Among them are Nick, Duncan, Salim, together with Reuters photographer Tony Njuguna. They board the small plane for the flight to Moroni, the capital, on the island of Grand Comore. The Boskies pilot, an elderly white Kenyan, swings open the door of the cockpit to get in. "This isn't really legal you know – to fly this sort of distance in a single engine plane," he says. We'll have to fuel up in Mombasa if we're to make the four-hour journey from there to Moroni.

Late Monday afternoon, Moroni.

Nick manages, with the help of a $20 palm greasing and some French-language schmoozing, to get them into the concrete meat storage warehouse serving as a temporary morgue in the Comores Islands. They slip through the plastic flapping curtain strips. Into the interior, slightly cooled by a large rumbling air conditioner that partly converts the humid air outside to a lower temperature to prevent the bodies from decaying too fast. The corpses are laid out in neat rows by colour; black, brown, white. All are zipped into semi translucent body bags.

They identify Mo first – he's easy to recognize. His neck is broken but other than that, the injuries are slight, the facial features clearly distinguishable. Salim leaves the morgue, too upset to continue. Locating Brian proves harder. Eventually in a side row of Europeans they find him. His arm and leg have been ripped off, his face smashed by the impact of the crash. They check below his stomach. Throughout the screaming of the aircraft slicing through the water, the bodies churned and flung together with seats and suitcases, the rudimentary recovery, and the wrapping and laying of bodies in the meat warehouse, his colostomy bag remained firmly in place, and served as confirmation of his identity.

Tuesday morning, Moroni.

Nick and Reuters photographer Tony Njuguna return to the makeshift morgue to collect Brian and Mo, only to find all the bodies in chaos, carelessly thrown around by the Israeli emergency squad who had arrived after them on Monday, and turned everything upside down in their effort to find, tag and preserve their own citizens. With little regard for the other corpses, they'd mangled the neat rows of identified dead– originally facing upwards with handwritten sheets of paper on their chests showing their names through the thin transparent plastic.

Tony and Nick couldn't help walking on the tangle of bodies as they turned them over to relocate Brian and Mo. They were stiffening, but quite slowly because of the heat.

"There were at least 50, perhaps more, but we found our two again quite quickly. I remember shouting at the Israelis in anger," said Nick. "To make amends, they injected our corpses with formaldehyde and allowed us to heave them into the smaller of the two cold rooms—with the Israeli casualties, where the refrigeration was working better."

A day of haggling over paperwork followed before they got the necessary ministerial approvals to take the bodies home. Reuters Comores stringer Mohamed Karadine, pulled in favours from a ream of contacts to arrange the necessary permissions for the bodies to be flown out immediately, instead of waiting for the lengthy outcome of the inquest into the disaster.

And so finally after a gruelling 48 hours, Duncan, Tony and Nick flew back to Nairobi from Grand Comore, freezing, with the airplane aircon up to maximum, to prevent any further decomposition of the bodies. Their colleagues Mo and Brian lay in bodybags, a metre or two from their seats - at the back of the fuselage. They got back to Wilson Airport late in the evening. A crowd had gathered on the tarmac, somberly awaiting their arrival.

Monday morning, Surrey Countryside, November 1996.

I'm staring yet again at a blank screen. Images of my recent visit to the

Mkgadigadi Pans in the Kalahari jumble in my brain– flat, featureless grey salt landscape, red ball sunsets, glowing dust kicked up by the speeding quad bikes racing to get back camp before nightfall. The 'Hong Kong Princess' caking make-up onto her dust covered face. Our demi-god guide sucking petrol out of one bike to siphon it into another. Ostrich shell beads and archeological finds scattered carelessly around the Pans. None of these shifting views make it to the page. My fingers tap the table instead of the keyboard. It's grey outside, overhanging cloud, dribbling rain, leafless trees. This story is late, but sideswiped by illness I'm not having any luck producing the GQ action adventure piece I've been commissioned to write.

Now what would Brian do when he got stuck? I thought. But this didn't happen to him. I remembered one of his suggestions to educate the readers of the unsalubrious tabloid the Daily Sport at which we had both briefly worked. He wanted to run a feature to celebrate the great 17th century French physician and seer Nostradamus' birthday. The idea was absurd for a newspaper renowned only for its combination obsessions of tits, footie and oddball happenings. "Even those who just buy us for the boobs'll like it if we write it right," he argued. "We can make it fun and accessible to them. He persuaded the editor and his story fabulously began: "Nostradamus, or Nozza to his friends."

"Hey isn't this your old boss?" said my housemate, a chubby Cypriot as she waved the *Daily Mail* in front of me while I make a cup of tea. The front page is dominated by the bearded mug shot of Mohammed Amin staring out through his thick-framed glasses.

"Another publicity stunt for maximum self-benefit, no doubt," I muttered, flicking only a brief glance at the photo before parking myself on the sofa sliding my feet underneath a blanket for warmth and taking a large slurp of tea.

"Not so. Don't think he generated this one," she replied tossing the paper onto the sofa beside me. I look again. Pictures of a broken-up plane resting in the water on a postcard pretty beach. Hijack headline. Mo dead. His luck exiting the dodgy African situations that made him famous had finally run out, ignominiously, on a routine business flight I think only of Brian as I race out to the newsagent to pick up the rest of the papers. Was he there? Unlikely, as he hated to fly. The news carried plenty on Mo, and spectacular if blurry pictures of the plane tilting and breaking as it hit the water—images grabbed from a tourist's home video. But nowhere was there any mention of Brian.

We had a block on overseas calls on the landline in the house—too many disputed phone bills. No email either. So it was only on Day Two of the hijack headlines that I finally picked up news of Brian's Tetley's death. Unable to turn to my usual sources in Kenya, the first day's frantic panicked trawling of the UK broadsheets and tabloids had yielded nothing about him, only news of Mo. On the second day, as the larger obits dissecting the achievements of Mo dominated the pages of the UK press, I found Brian, buried as an afterthought almost, in the last paragraph of a *Daily Telegraph* double page feature.

In the rest of the press, despite his Lancashire origins, there was not a mention of this Englishman who had been my mentor. They were more concerned with trumpeting the life and death of Mohammed Amin—referred to as the 'world-renowned cameraman—the man who moved the world" He was lionized— the bringer of the catastrophic 1984 Ethiopian famine images to prominence. The indirect catalyst for Live Aid. Where all colours and creeds collected their coins to Feed The World. At Christmas time. Some listed his awards and decorations for that footage– although not quite all 29 of them— which ranged from the well publicised MBE in 1991 to the more obscure Guinness Stout award (also 1991). Hundreds of column inches worldwide eulogized my contrary former boss now apparently heroically dead, negotiating to the end, his bionic arm—such a salvation in many tricky situations—unable to get him out of this one. A single sentence in those thousands of words was reserved for my friend Brian. "UK-born Brian Tetley, journalist, also died in the Ethiopian Airways plane crash."

Ethiopia had certainly figured prominently in Mo's career. It was the venue for his grandest taste of international recognition, it swallowed his arm and finally this flight back from the capital abroad the national carrier took him and Brian on what was to be their last journey together.

I was livid. As Mo's face popped up regularly on the news bulletins followed by clips of the plane hitting the water, famine footage, Freddy Mecury at Live Aid, and American popstars singing "We are the World," I thought of my return to the UK in spring 1991. I had just finished a six month stint at Camerapix and had left on the BA flight to London at the same time as a posse of my UK based journalist friends worked the phones at the BBC office in Chester House, Nairobi, negotiating for a charter flight to take them into Addis Ababa to report on the fall of the dictatorial president Mengistu. Anxious to keep up with news I switched on the telly at a dull dinner party in Kensington a few days after my arrival in the UK, only to watch in horror as an ammunition dump in Ethiopia exploded in a high drama of pyrotechnic fireworks. Filming too close to the smouldering dump, Mo's arm was blown off when it finally erupted. His colleague, John Maathai, a gentle Kenyan editor more used to twirling dials in an edit suite than chasing stories, was attached to a microphone at the end of Mo's camera. He was killed. Like Brian, Maathai shouldn't have been there. He was under orders to go because the camera's inbuilt sound mike wasn't working, Like Brian, he felt bullied into taking the trip. Like Brian his death also only merited a brief mention as the "Kenyan soundman" before being forgotten in the greater story of Mo's lost arm.

I remember trying to explain my anger to the genial, striped-shirt host of the dinner as I sat crossed legged on the floor, hunched in front of the TV waiting for more detail on the story, while other guests tucked into the Marks and Spencer summer puddings. Spitting out angry, discombobulated sentences about a world that I knew he didn't understand, I let rip in frustration at what I saw as an absolute waste of life. "In my last conversation with John—only last week—before I left Nairobi, he was putting together a promo documentary on tourism, and insisting that this would be the last time he'd let Mo strong arm him into doing the lacky job of soundman. He hated it. It wasn't his game. He wanted to carry on doing what he was hired for – and John was a great editor. It's intolerable that he's now dead."

"Hmmm," muttered my host, lost for words, slowly backing away from me and turning in the direction of the kitchen. "So sorry. I just...m...er...sure I need to see to coffee. Will you have some?"

Fast-forward five years to 1996 and Brian was gone too, just as pointlessly lost in a shambolic hijack venture that was doomed from the start. I picture him, blue eyes goggling with fear, rumpled suit, shambling with his ungainly walk up the corridor of economy class, trying to find Mo in club class, busting for a drink if he hadn't already got one. It was an early morning flight after all. Brian hated flying and hated foreign assignments but his love of beer and his inability to manage finances, or his colourful life, often made him hostage to Mo's will.

Much is already known about Mo. There are two Camerapix published biographies—one glowingly written post-Ethiopian famine by Brian at a time when he needed to curry favour. The other posthumously by their mutual friend, the UK based writer Bob Smith who publicly credits Brian for the wealth of information he had to work with. And more recently his son Salim made a moving documentary of their lives, entitled Mo and Me. Less detail is available about those who worked with Mo, the backgrounders, who made so much of his success possible. Brian Tetley was the most special: the most enduring, and the most colourful of them all.

Tetley—"as in t-bags or beer"—as he liked to introduce himself, was a journalist, a writer, lover of words, women, cricket and beer. A ruddy Lancashire boy, with ruby cheeks and a gravel voice roughened by years of cigarettes, he fittingly made his entrance to Kenya on April Fool's Day in 1968, at the behest of the *Nation* newspaper. At that time it was standard practice for both the *Nation* and *The Standard* to import Fleet Street journalists to work on two-year contracts. He was accompanied by his third wife, Eve, a stout motherly northern lass quite a bit younger than him. Within a week of his arrival he found his job – he had been hired as Features Editor – had quickly been given to another new import, a soft-spoken Scot called Neil Graham.

"I suspect that in those seven days before I reached Kenya, editor George Githii decided that Brian was not really management material. I had never applied for that features job. I was only coming out to work as a sub editor," explained Neil, who is now a professor of journalism in Vancouver, Canada.

In a snit at this sudden change of events, and proclaiming loudly that he'd been shafted, Brian threatened to catch the next boat back to Blighty, but he was stopped, as he loved to recount, by a mosquito.

"It was malaria, luv, it floored me. Couldn't make it back on board the vessel and it gave me time to cool down." Instead he took the alternative position offered to him—a sub-editor on the night news desk at the *Nation.*

In the late 60's The *Nation* certainly wasn't the large conglomerate in its custom built tower that is such a part of Nairobi's skyline today. Back then it was housed in a former bakery on Tom Mboya Street—the brash, upstart newcomer to the Kenyan media scene. Originally conceived in 1959 as a weekly Kiswahili paper, it had quickly morphed into an English daily and, injected with healthy amounts of

Aga Khan funds, had taken a mere nine years to overtake its competitor, the long established settler rag, *The East African Standard,* as the biggest-selling newspaper in Kenya, topping their circulation of around 40,000 with one of 45,000. It helped the *Nation* greatly that the Ismaili readership defected en masse to it due to the Aga Khan's connection – and that *The Standard* had lost a large chunk of its traditional readership of whites when they left the country at Independence in 1963.

But perhaps more poignantly *The Standard* fell victim to the success of its own campaign. Prior to independence, it was something of a voice in the wilderness, calling for a greater role in the media for African reporters. Despite the fact it had a white editor (Kenneth Bolton), it often editorialized about the need for the Brits to move out. That, of course, didn't endear it to many of its traditional readers, who looked and found a replacement read in the *Nation,* which simultaneously embarked on an aggressive readership campaign.

Unlike the *Standard*, the *Nation* largely paid lip service to the Africanisation policy touted by the government and focused on "Kenyanisation" instead. It retained a white news editor and a couple of white expatriate reporters, several Goans and at least one very good Hindu fellow. They also had some Ugandans, including, Barbara Kimenye who was British trained and who had formerly handled media matters for the Kabaka in Kampala, George Mbuguss who edited Taifa Leo. Unlike the Standard, the sub editors at the Nation were almost entirely white or Indian as was production and layout although they were careful to point out that a number of their staff had taken Kenyan citizenship (as indeed did Brian Tetley). *The Nation* also hired an ex-policeman who was sent to England for a year to learn about running a circulation department. Although he was white he was fluent in Swahili, Kikuyu, and Luo, which allowed him to deal very successfully one-on-one with the vendors for each area of the Nation, pushing them to tout the paper to prospective readers..

Meanwhile, Bolton at the *Standard* followed through with his promises to hire young black Kenyans and, by 1970, within two years of the government africanisation call, had an entirely black reporting team. While the Standard's motives were pure, the speed of change didn't allow enough time for training the new recruits to sufficient editorial standards, and in the competitive business of newspapers, this helped ultimately lead to the paper's demise.

First to go was the *Standard's* lucrative Syndication department, which ran a news bureau providing coverage for a range of papers around the world— Japan's *Asahi Shimbuni;* Sweden's *Dagens Nuyter;* British papers including the *Times; Telegraph* etc. They even covered for the *National Enquirer.* When the Kenyan government pushed for Africanisation of the Syndication Department, these contracts quickly disappeared— the writing was not up to the standard expected by the international press. They simply stopped using the department, which very quickly shut down.

Steadily the *Nation* pushed the *Standard* out, and by its 10th year it turned a profit and went public with shares selling at around 10/=. At about the same time Ken Bolton at the *Standard* died, and Lonrho sold the paper. A disastrous editor was appointed who moved on to do PR for the Mazola factory in Nakuru, but not before wreaking further damage to the *Standard's* focus and direction. It never recovered and the *Nation* cemented its lead as Kenya's foremost English daily.

The *Nation* team in the former bakery continued to grow. The rooms were halved and quartered into rabbit warren proportions to accommodate new staff. "Life in the newsroom was tough," said Neil. "It was deafeningly noisy from the sounds of many manual typewriters, which were mostly chained to the desks to prevent theft. Reporters clacked away in competition with the roar of the printing presses. The rooms were cloaked in a fog of smoke as newshounds sucked cigarette after cigarette while they turned out stories, dropping their butts onto the floor until they formed a spongy Sportsman carpet by the time the paper was put to bed in the early evening.

"Everyone worked a lot of unpaid overtime," added Neil. I thought nothing of coming in at the weekend to check pages. I recall plenty of 5:00 a.m. starts to complete work on a Sunday. We took it as seriously as all our previous Fleet Street jobs. Most of us drank a little more than was good for us in those days, both in and out of the newsroom. Journalism was a hard-drinking profession.

But even in that atmosphere of alcoholic excess Brian stood out. "It didn't take me long to work out why the job switch happened," said Neil. "Brian himself was quick to tell me he had worked for 28 papers and been fired from 27 of them. By that time I knew why. Beer after he finished work; beer when he got home; beer in the morning for the hangover; beer at lunchtime; beer during his dinner break at the paper."

As with most journalists in Nairobi, the dingy Sans Chique bar on Government Road (renamed Moi Avenue post-independence) behind the *Nation* was his favoured haunt. It was the sort of place where warm Tusker was served in chipped glasses, and your elbows stuck to the years of history layered on the tables. Brian enthusiastically befriended the coterie of African journalists being brought on board to work for the paper, buying beers all round as he got to know his new mates.

"Owner Pierali Jaffer thought he had died and gone to heaven when Brian appeared," added Neil. "He'd never had a better customer. Until Brian's cheque bounced.

"But he eventually paid up— Brian never left any bills unpaid that I was aware of. He was honourable that way."

While this gave him many friends in the Sans Chique, his predilection for Tusker made him quite a handful at the *Nation* for the chief sub, Jack Regan. He was moved to the more leisurely pace at the *Sunday Nation* under a tougher boss, editor John Eames. Brian wound up writing a weekly column tackling current political events, which later morphed into the very popular Mambo and was moved back to the daily. It was brilliant (most days), and earned him the permanent moniker of Mambo with the local journalist community.

"He was an amazing thinker—so at one with language. He was a journalist—in every bone and sinew...old school...an archetypal Fleet Street hack...plus," said Gavin Bennett, the Nation's current motoring correspondent and a former colleague.

While Neil is doubtful that Brian worked on the nationals back in England it is well known that he made his way unsteadily up through the big regional newspapers. He began his career in the traditional fashion as a copy boy– a glorified messenger, before graduating to reporter and then section editor. In those days hack-dom and alcohol mixed frequently and acceptably– as long as it didn't get in the way of a good story.

"Best training you can get," Brian said to me often. "Don't like this studying journalism nonsense that you see these days. How much can you learn in a classroom? You have to be there, smell the ink, tramp the pavements, weave the story, watch it get spiked, do it again, fight with the subs, and chew it over in the bar later over a pint. That's the learning ground for a real journalist."

It was part of the enigma of this new Kenya recruit that, other than his writing credentials, most of his English background was obscure. It is known that he attended Repton in Yorkshire, a tough all-male boarding school. "Perhaps he acquired many of the characteristics of what the English would call a 'gent' from his time there?" ventured Gavin. "But he also had tremendous blue-collar appeal rarely associated with boarding school types. The signals are that he was working class and had some sort of finishing school type of experience at Repton," explained Gavin. He had a great ability to mix with all classes, all types—an invaluable skill for a good hack.

In those early days at the *Nation* both Neil and Brian had regular contact with Mo and a couple of other ambitious photographers, including Mohinder Dhillon and Azhar Choudry, who were all bringing in photos for publication at that time. Brian and Neil helped writing stories and cutlines for the images they submitted to the paper. As Neil was sub-editing Kenya Farmer on the side and working as a stringer for the South African Argus group, the task fell more and more to Brian, who was always willing to spin words for those who asked, leaning forward over his manual typewriter, tapping them out at high-speed in his characteristic single finger style. He began to get more involved in some of Mo's projects, occasionally disappearing from the *Nation* to sort out a story for him, lured by the promise of instant payment on delivery of this text, or a couple of Tuskers as thanks.

As he settled into Nairobi life, Brian also discovered the Starlight Club a sort of combo brothel and drinking den, and was soon the best buddy of another Scot, Robbie Armstrong, who owned and ran it. Ever tempestuous, Brian had one work tantrum too many after a long lunchtime session with Robbie and threw his typewriter out of the window onto the lane that ran behind Nation House. His days were numbered after that. He had already been hired and fired several times from both papers in his short sojourn there. In 1970, two years after arriving in Kenya he was permanently removed by the *Nation* payroll, and began working more regularly at Camerapix.

"I think Mo especially liked the Tom Mboya thing I did when he was assassinated in 1969—a dazzling piece," said Brian. The *Nation* had stuck Brian, and the then cub reporter Philip Ochieng, in a room with a crate of beer and a typewriter and locked the door, letting them out only when they had completed the definitive obituary. It was a seminal moment for Mo too—his footage of the happenings won him his first award—1969 British Television Cameraman of the Year in the silent film category—and earned him his first contract with the international news agency Visnews.

And so a legendary if fractious union began. Ever the businessman Mo, knew a bargain writer when he saw one, flaws and all. He was not only impressed by Brian's speedy talent, but also by the cheapness of the liquor required to make it flow. Previous writers had stalked off the set of Camerapix at the tough terms Mo imposed, and future ones would continue to do so, myself included. The usual gambit involved working for free for as long as was sustainable, and then for as nominal a fee as he could negotiate.

"I've seen big men come out of Mo's office weeping," said a Peter Moll, another former Nation recruit who worked sporadically with Mo in the 1970's."Some very talented people were broken down by his ruthlessness. There was Mr Qureshi, a wildlife photographer who's images were rarely attributed to him, Afsal Awan and the brilliant Azhar Choudry. He drove people too hard, letting them down often at the last minute with technical small print, stealing their glory. He had peculiar boundaries between business and personal– one minute he would shaft you on pictures or text, and the next would invite you to come eat chinese as a friend."

Brian, with his precarious hold on his finances, needed Mo's trader instinct and drive to sort through the troublesome task of commercial enterprise. He preferred to write to order and leave the marketing of stories to someone else.

"Brian was certainly good enough in talent, spirit, generosity, empathy, caring and courage when it came to work and life," enthuses Gavin, who also credits him as a mentor. "But he wasn't bad enough in those areas of drive and discipline that turn ambition into achievement." Mo was able to provide that element. He would nail the financials before the job. He could organize the logistics. He knew how to put it together.

In some ways they made a good foil for each other— largely as they were equally talented in their fields. Both were full of ideas and enthusiastically passionate about their work. Both were mavericks; running on self-will, definite in their opinions, able to fall quickly into the vision of a story, complementing each other. Mo was able to do stills and video, Brian could whip out crisp precise copy for newspapers, and evocative rich text for manuscripts. In their time together they worked on some 45 books and many of the big African news stories of the time. Brian, however, was far less keen on the operating in the field; with his chaotic personal life he saw little attraction in hiring planes, cars, bicycles and donkeys to put himself in the middle of other people's troubles.

"I remember this trip we did to Uganda once luv—when Idi Amin was newly in power and still the darling of the West," Brian once told me over a beer at the now defunct Westview Hotel on Waiyaki Way.

"We'd actually gone to film images of the Nile for a tourist documentary, when Mo decided to take a little side trip to check out some information he had received. Our little car was quickly stopped and hussled by soliders on a dirt track near Jinja.

One of them pulled me out of the driver's seat and gave me a right crack across the head with his rifle, then began laying into me before putting the gun to my neck.

"He was just about to squeeze the trigger when Mo popped out from the passenger seat, so they bashed him instead until he managed to diffuse the situation with some Swahili sweet talk. They let us on our way then, after declaring us 'worthless Kenyan pigs.' Too dangerous for me, this sort of stuff, and I always told Mo. I mean our Pakistan trips, the gallivanting over Africa. That wasn't my game. I prefer to write it up in an office– you know, close to a bar and my missus of the time.

"Mind you, we got a huge exclusive from that Uganda piece. The barman at Chobe Lodge near Murchison Falls where we stayed a few days later told us of the hundreds of Acholi and Langi people being machine-gunned and dumped in a Nile tributary. He took us to see the bloated bodies floating past that night—horrible. And the stickiness of the bridge over the river—I thought it had been recently covered with tar, but in daylight we saw that it was actually half-dry blood."

The front page exclusive in *The Observer*, bylined only with Tetley's name caused a furore in Whitehall, who insisted that the reported massacres weren't actually happening. The *Observer* refused to stand by Brian, leaving him to clear his own journalistic name. Mo refused to help, since he didn't want his access to Uganda to be jeopardized by linking him to the photos in the *Observer*.

"Took me ages to get vindicated on that story – Idi had to start doing a lot more crazy things before England would accept he was a madman," grumbled Brian. "But it did mean I couldn't go back to Uganda, which I was pleased about. I'm not into hoofing through danger like that. Mo's a complete bastard to have taken me there."

It was a reference they used often against each other. Their bust-ups were frequent and fierce. Brian continued his habits of temper tantrums, typewriter-throwing and disappearing. Mo regularly fired him, only to hire him back the next day. During one of their longer separations in the mid 70's, Brian made an ill-conceived move into the business world—trading his favourite substance.

"I'd opened a bar, luv," he explained. "The Bombax up at Dagoretti Corner —you know, make a profit because, lord knows, I've spent in bars before. Thought I'd try a new venture. Great fun—we had music and so many people. Nairobi was such a buzzing place then.

"Problem was, clients never settled their chits. I had to go to their homes the next day to negotiate prices on the slips they signed. You know what I'm like— they'd bargain me down to a quarter of their spending, and turn up at the bar the next night to do it all over again."

"And then I found out that while I was serving bargain beer, my new missus, Charity, was screwing the customers in the back of their 504's. Only knew when she gave me a black baby. That's when I left her, too."

To get the bar's finances in order he decided on a cash only policy, took his remaining funds and bought a chunky National Cash Register, solid, reliable, a repository for the money he would take from customers.

"It set me back 10,000/- a small fortune when you think that beer cost 5 bob. I had it delivered but it was stolen that night. I never got to use it. It took the club down with it. It was years before I paid those debts back luv. And I never found out which one of those buggers did my wife."

Broke, he went to back to work on a full time basis on publications in 1977, joining Peter Moll Africa, working on a stable of nine trade titles including *Swara*, *Farmer's Voice* and the tourist mag *Karibu*.

"Unfortunately our office was next door to Camerapix in Findlay House," said owner Peter Moll, a former sports editor for the *Nation*. "Even though Brian was on my payroll he would often slip next door to moonlight for a bit of ready cash. Mo couldn't string a literate sentence together so he would offer Brian 1000/- if he could produce finished copy by that evening—he never gave him a penny up front in those days. Since Brian could really canter out the words—he was a splendid editor and rewrite man—he would disappear when he was in need of quick injection of shillings—which was often given the way he ran his life. Really, he was the best in the field, which is why I hired him. The only person I can think of with his talent for purple prose is Wilbur Smith. He could have risen to those heights if he had been able to keep things together for long enough."

Bob Smith—a sub-editor on the *Express* newspaper in London, and long time friend of Brian, agrees. He first met Brian in April 1978, when, with Barbara, his wife of two weeks, he arrived in Nairobi to join the Peter Moll Organisation as production editor. Brian was his boss.

"The plan was to check into a hotel and spend a week acclimatizing," said Bob. "Instead, Brian met us at the airport, bundled all our luggage into his new but very textured Mazda 323 and pointed the car towards Mombasa."

"Change of plan, mate," said Brian, resplendent in garish beach shirt and Panama hat. "We're off to the Coast for a spot of cricket." Less than an hour after touching down in Africa, Barbara and Bob were esconsed in a shebeen somewhere off the Mombasa Road down by the Athi River, drinking warm Tusker.

Brian returned to work and left the couple to a wonderful week's honeymoon in Mombasa, before Bob returned to the dubious delights of magazine production at M'fangano Street, just round the corner from the bus depot.

"That's where I received an education in journalism," said Bob. "I had worked on weekly, evening and daily papers in the UK, reporting and subbing news. Now, under the expert tutelage of Brian, I learned much more, from design, picture and story selection to page composition and writing. Brian excelled at them all, preparing business plans for new magazines, creating dummies for them, providing the words and commissioning features.

"We would write a leader in each magazine to add gravitas. This was new territory for me and I sweated blood over the chore until Brian showed me the way. He had compiled a series of intros and outros which, when applied to virtually any subject, would add the requisite flavour of authority. This became known as the clichograph and we embraced it wholeheartedly. Some stories began with "Much has been said..." or the variation, "someone once said"—The someone being Brian or me. A good rounding off phrase might be "and as the sun's shadows lengthen over the..."

The definitive intro was, of course, penned by Brian. Writing a leader on desertification for *Farmers' Voice,* the official organ of the Kenya National Farmers' Union, he began: "Not since a desert zephyr first blew sand into the eyes of the sphinx..."

"How do you follow that?" laughed Bob. "And there were many more. Brian could churn them out endlessly and effortlessly."

But it wasn't easy working in a shoe box of an office with Brian. Good days were fun. Black dog days were bloody difficult. You never knew what mood he would be in. Sometimes he came straight from a bar, unshaven and unsteady. Then Charles Onyango, the long-suffering production manager, would be dispatched to the Kilimambogo Bar next door for a warm Tusker while Brian sat on his trembling hands in anticipation. With a beer on board and the "twitch" sorted, life would resume as normal. Some days women would appear at the door broke and asking for money. Often there would be an ex-wife, others were former girlfriends. If Brian had money he would never turn them away. Sometimes Brian didn't appear at all.

It's three days before deadline and Tetley hasn't been seen at the offices of Peter Moll. A series of stories need editing and the final layout has to be done. Peter paces through the office, along the corridor and pokes his head into Camerapix to see if Brian is in there. He isn't. He gets into the car and drives slowly around Pangani eyes peeled for Brian. He visits the Starlight and chats to Robbie Armstrong. No sign. He's worried – not just about the magazine, but also about whether Brian has survived intact. He knew that same level of brilliance that could shake and improve the world despite, and even because of, Brian's dizzy heights of madness, fared less well when launched from the platform of blur associated with his evenings.

He paused back at the office to chat to Gavin Bennett. They knew Brian had acquired a new mistress, Mary, who matched his former wife Charity's propensity for aggression. There is no still no sign of him.

On his tour of Pangani the following day, Peter decides he will do a round of the hospitals if he can't find him. Just then, he spies Brian on the street, weaving uncertainly back towards his flat. He stops the car, opens the door.

"Get in Brian—we've been searching for you for days."

"No way mate—bit busy right now, got to sort the missus. Some problem see, a little complicated. I'm a bit broke too, brother. Bless you for looking for me. Sorry Peter."

"Come on Brian—hop in, let's get a beer. I'm sure it isn't as bad as you think. We can sort this out. Jump in."

After four Tuskers, Peter manages to lure Brian back into the office where the atmosphere was divided between frustration and relief at his reappearance.

"Right – what needs to be done," said Brian, oblivious to the tension, shuffling in his safari boots towards his desk, which was laden with papers and photos for the magazine. Tusker by his side, he sets to work, leafing through the copy, laying pictures, swigging his beer, tweaking sentences, rewriting copy. Fully absorbed in putting the final touches to the magazine, he's unaware that he's quoting sections of Shakespeare's Taming of the Shrew under his breath. Word perfectly. He calls for another beer. By the end of the afternoon the magazine is ready to go to press.

It would have taken a lesser editor a week to sort the mess. But even with the gallons of alcohol that went through his system that day, he could still put together a sterling issue in a few hours.

"That was Brian," laughed Gavin. "He was in roughly equal parts a genius—and a shambles. He was almost a great man—his genius survived, and even thrived through his eccentricity. It screamed 'lead, follow or get out of the way!' He performed—though often at horrendous cost to himself. He was this unstoppable, umissable, go-it-alone thunderbolt in our midst."

But for Peter Moll it was the end. In the tradition of most of Brian's employers, he finally got rid of him.

"Peter was reluctant to do it," explained Gavin. "He recognised that Brian's genius did need an external reference point, a patron. A person or organisation perceptive enough to see his talents, wise enough to recognise their values, and strong enough to rescue him from his crisis-to-crisis conduct while waiting for the results to come through. Peter knew his firm just wasn't big enough to support the mishaps.

"For me the great sadness of Brian's life was that no sizeable corporation had the bravery or wisdom to put him on the payroll and let him decide what he should do and when. Engagement of Brian on these terms would definitely have been a loss leader in the short term, but ultimately it would have paid big dividends."

And so Brian returned to Mo, and the Beer for Books deals began at Camerapix A few thousand bob for Tusker money could extract a well-crafted coffee table tome in about three months. The funds were drip fed to him with delicate precision. Enough to ensure sufficient creativity, but not too much for inevitable hangovers to prevent him from working, or going walkabout. Over the years they churned through books— *Journey Through Pakistan* ("such hard work in the mountains and no booze," grumbled Brian), *Magical Kenya,* and then Journey through all sorts of other domains. These were then recycled and rejigged into the Spectrum travel guide series.

While cash poured into the coffers of Camerapix, funds dribbled through and round Brian, as he bumbled along in his career. "Met this poor bugger today who needs school fees—so I gave him my salary," he said, as we met one evening at the New Stanley for a drink. "Poor old Mutua said his wife wanted money for an operation," on another. "My white friends will just have to buy me beer," he chuckled.

On his 50th birthday Duncan Willets, a regular Tusker provider for Brian, and now the only surviving member of the Camerapix trio, wrote him a card forgiving all his debts.

"The response was typical," smiled Duncan. "All Brian said to me when I waived his loans was; 'I owe you nothing in comparison to what I owed Robbie

Armstrong at the Starlight Club.'

"That was Brian—broke, generous, charming. Buy me a beer. Bless you mate. He knew all sorts of people through his knowledge of the bars. He was always so curious and compassionate. Like a little boy really, which got him into terrible scrapes."

"Where's Tetley," glared Mo through his thick black frame glasses. No reply from intimidated staff. One of them had been drinking with Brian the night before, and seen him set off on foot for home, having spent his last cent on beer. His location was now unknown. Mo thumped back to his office, slightly dragging his bad leg, his face scrunched into a scowl. "I'm fed up with Tetley." I'm never going to do a long term project with him."

2am. Only a few regulars left. Most are slumped around their tables, energy for the return to home used in drinking and talking. Bleary-eyed, huffing heavily, Brian counted the coins in his pocket. He would have to walk home from town. When he reached the casino roundabout, by Museum Hill on Uhuru Highway, he was accosted.

"Pass me your money," demanded the fellow, pushing him.

"Brother, look at me. I am a Mzungu. How many Mzungus do you see walking home at three in the morning? Don't you think if I had money I would have taken a taxi rafiki? It's a long way and I am not very fit," reasoned Brian.

"Oh. Then where are you going?" came the reply.

"Uthiru. I am the only white man in the slum."

"But that place is dangerous! You will get killed! I will walk you home."

"Sawa. Bless you."

On the darkened side of the verge the unlikely couple—mugger and muggee walked the four miles back to Brian's house.

"Oooh Bless you mate. Want a Tusker," asked Brian. "I have some beer in the house and my wife's asleep."

"Of course," said the mugger and together they slurped the last six beers in the house. He left four days later.

Brian's escapades pained Mo. They were the antithesis of his own behaviour. He neither drank nor smoked, rose early for prayers, and detested the small talk of social functions. He lived for work, his family sliding into second place if there came a choice. His set face took on a cynical grimace as stories filtered back of Brian's antics, always fuelled by his weakness of Tusker moto.

Not that alcohol was the only thing that Mo felt he had to worry about when it came to protecting his cut-price text wizard. Having been abandoned by his imported wife Eve, who took up with a British corporal early on in their stay in Kenya, Brian collected a succession of African girlfriends and wives, each picked up in moments of half consciousness from the Banana Hill Day and Night Club or the Ngara Pub and Bar. Each one he acquired was younger and larger than her predecessor as he got older, and each one displayed frightening levels of aggression —usually towards Brian.

"It was my dad that fucked me up for women," Brian once told me over a ruminative beer in a pub in Manchester. "He took me all the way to London to see a prostitute when I was 16 to lose my cherry. Made me celibate after that for years. She was terrifying—the prostitute. Very unsympathetic. I didn't want to be there but she said she'd promised my father. I was so ashamed. I couldn't look at a woman for years after that without remembering her and feeling sick."

"Made up for it, I suppose. I'm a bigamist you know," he added as an afterthought. Married Eve—my third wife—without bothering to divest myself of the second. Too much trouble all that paperwork. Couldn't afford maintenance anyway. I prefer it here where you can have many. Made it hard to see the kids from the second wife—I was scared of being arrested when I went back to Britain."

Of the various women he had, I only ever met Mary, the last and most dangerous of his six wives, owing to her tendency to use as a weapon the heavy steel pan they received as a wedding present. Mo seized the advantage to further control Brian's wandering and took to giving her Brian's salary. She then doled out 20 bob a day to him in a bid to take charge of the household.

5am. The phone rings at Mo's house.

"I know you're up early mate, hope I'm not disturbing you or anything."

"I'm awake. What do you want?"

"Well it's just that I need some help see, can you pick me up? It's not far, just a spot of bother last night. Oh, and could you bring trousers and a shirt too, please Mo, bless you."

In the car home from Lavington police station, Brain babbled, "Mary just went into one, you know those rages. I was already in bed when she came after me with a knife so I did what I could—I jumped straight out the window and ran.

"I hoofed it— imagine—a mzungu stumbling bollock naked down the road to the police station. I told them to lock me in for my own protection and they did. Bless them. Gave me a blanket to cover myself up. I had to make sure I was safe from her. Bless you brother for helping me out."

Some six months later though, he was reprimanded by the heavy steel pan on his return home on payday without a shilling in his pocket. "I had to give it all to the taxi driver, luv," he protested. "I needed to pay him protection." Mary's own response put Brian in hospital with bruises to most of his body, a broken arm and three bashed ribs.

It was an inconvenient time for Mo—they had a well-paid expensive commission up in the barren north of Kenya up near Lake Turkana and Brian was lingering in Nairobi Hospital punning his way through explanations of how he had landed up there. A late-night visit, the threat of no future work, and a promise to fix his false teeth, which had been broken in several places in the Mary altercation, was enough to reluctantly persuade Brian to be placed at midnight in the waiting Land Rover outside. In its haste to make it up the jagged road north the heavily loaded vehicle hit one large pothole too many and flipped over. While the rest of the crew worked to fix the car, Brian vanished. This posed a number of problems. They were now short of a writer; and he had been placed in charge of the provisions, which had haphazardly been put together earlier in the week. The ton of unmarked cardboard boxes containing random purchases from the nearest Pangani supermarket all had to be offloaded and emptied in the search for suitable ingredients each time a meal was prepared. In between the few tins of useful food for the three-week journey was 748 helpings of instant mashed potatoes, which is all the expedition had to eat by the time they reached Ferguson's Gulf. You can buy instant mashed potato in Pangani? YES!

Meanwhile Brian had flagged down a passing car after the accident and managed to grab a lift back to Nairobi, settling into the same hospital bed less than 24 hours after he had left it—but with a fresh series of bruises and glass in his eye.

"The nurses couldn't figure it out—and wouldn't believe how I acquired the new injuries. I like those enigma stories," he winked. "Like the Maltese Falcon, one of my best."

New Year's Eve, 1980.

The terrace of Nairobi's smartest hotel, The Norfolk, is decorated with twinkling candles and full of revellers gathered to bring in the New Year. As wine glasses clink in celebration, an explosion that could be felt three miles away ripped through the building tearing apart one of the wings, scattering bodies and body parts through the carefully decorated restaurant.

Mo, feeling the blast, abandons his dinner in Westlands, calls the *Nation*, hears the news, manages to locate a number for a call box in the hotel and rings. Someone picks up the phone;

"Please help, I've just lost my leg. We're dying here."

He grabs his cameras and drives at speed to the Norfolk to be confronted by the gruesome sight of the dead and wounded amongst the rubble, the restaurant destroyed and a massive blaze eating into the main area of the hotel.

Meanwhile Brian, having over-celebrated, is slumped snoring under a table at the Starlight, less than half a mile from the Norfolk. He didn't feel the blast shaking the club, didn't notice Starlight customers leave in panic at the ensuing commotion. Waking up in the morning he's told of the tragedy by the cleaning staff and flurried into action to catch up on the breaking story.

Speaking to *The Sun* newspaper in the UK later in the day, he flails for an added twist to distinguish his piece from the earlier reports filed by his colleagues and competitors. "I have it from an impeccable source that the terrorist responsible goes by the nom de guerre of—The Maltese Falcon. Exclusive information," Brian insists to the news editor of *The Sun*.

Within minutes of publication of the first editions in England, irate news editors from rival papers call to lambast their Nairobi correspondents for not uncovering this vital angle, and demand they unearth information about this mysterious Maltese Falcon found by Tetley.

Brian remains tight lipped about his 'source', and chalks up another 'scoop'. He retreated quietly to the cricket pitch until the fracas died down.

It was in the pretty little glade in Karura Forest to the north of Nairobi that

Brian spent some of his happiest moments. The Starlight Club, in between drinking, fielded a competent and passionate cricket team. Amongst his fellow enthusiasts was a huge Seychellois mechanic named Bob Bresson, built like a hippo, who was a fantastic left hand bowler. He introduced Brian to the rickety charming multicultural Wanderers Cricket Club behind Muthaiga Golf Club.

For Brian the game was his passion. While at school in the UK he once had a trial for Yorkshire and was still a very useful bat. When fielding he would put a warm Tusker behind a boundary marker at each end of the ground to keep him going.

The Starlight Club played fierce but friendly matches against rival teams, pitting themselves frequently against the awesome batting of Jawa Singh, then Kenya's cricket captain.

"I remember Brian was always asking questions—he was really keen," reminisces Jawa Singh. "He batted left-handed, even though he did everything else right-handed and quizzed me constantly about style, swing, everything cricket. He was already talented but was always thirsty for more knowledge."

"He always turned up for cricket," added Gavin. "He could have a panga fight with his wife or wake up in a ditch and still make it to the game on time in perfect cricket whites. He was an excellent batsman, could have been professional if he chose—he was almost as good as Don Bradman in my opinion.

Both Bresson and Brian were keen to encourage local sportsmen to take up the bat and delighted in talent spotting, passing on the knowledge they had to youngsters who they brought into the Starlight Stragglers. Amongst the young recruits he helped were the Tikolo brothers and Odumbe, then about 12 years old; and now stars of the current Kenya team. What does Tikolo have to say about Brian? Didn't manage to get hold of him before I left.

"You'd never really expect that this beery bunch of expats would be interested in furthering the game with locals but they were instrumental in helping out and encouraging youngsters, who've made a name for themselves in later years." laughed Gavin.

"It was characteristic of Brian to really put heart and soul into helping. He wasn't jealous that way at all. He didn't need to reserve glory all for himself. He liked to see people come on in their work and passion. He gave a lot of mentorship to both cricketers and journalists. It is one of the greatest parts of his legacy."

I should know. I was one of them. He was wearing a neck brace when I first met him, which made it hard for him to hunch in his customary style over the reams of manuscript on the beauty of Maldives that he had recently finished without even visiting the country. I had just begun on Mo's customary terms for novices – as a freebie to be initiated into his joint business of coffee table books and African hard news stories. My task was a new Kenya guidebook, also to be produced without visiting most of the country—and to be on standby for any story that broke which may need an extra pair of hands. I had extracted this position after hours of persistent persuasion, standing outside the office of Camerapix in the Press Centre at Chester House waiting for a gruff five-minute audience.

"I've had too many disappointing people here—look at this stack of half-finished manuscripts. They've all let me down," said Mo, gesturing at neat piles of paper stacked in a corner. I grovellingly reassured him I wouldn't. "No pay until I can see what you are worth," was his parting and grudging agreement.

Brian and I worked in a large wooden house built in the back of Mo's garden in Lavington. It was a Swiss-chalet style building, housing the Camerapix archives and an edit suite. The rest of the gently sloping garden out front was dominated by a 20-foot satellite dish strategically placed to get best reception and in full view of the main house. His wife Dolly's disapproving presence could be felt all over the property and I skulked out of sight of the main house, sliding quietly into the chalet each morning. Her home life was dominated by Mo's work. I often wondered about the hours he kept—6.30, sometimes earlier each morning until around 10 at night, when he wasn't travelling. There was little time for family in Mo's life. It was all about the job.

Mo visited the chalet every day at 7.30am to do a bit of admin and to check on staff timekeeping before heading into the main Camerapix office at the Press Centre in Chester House. Brian rarely managed to be on time and neither did I. Jennifer – an American would-be photographer who wound up as the chalet's administrator, writer and receptionist won the punctuality stakes. Not that it did her much good. In the months I was there I never saw her pick up a camera. The occasional visitor from town would arrive to collect papers or disappear to the edit suite. There was little chatting—the boss didn't like, and didn't do that.

I admired the speed and adeptness with which Brian churned out reams of perfect text, stroking his stomach in satisfaction, chuckling at his own sentences and stopping to read aloud those which were particularly perfectly put together to whoever was listening—or more often not listening. A cigarette always lay in a cracked wooden ashtray, flakes of ash scattered around his desk.

"Listen to his luv," he'd say peering over his glasses. "You know those coco de mer fruits—the ones that look like female parts. How about this for a description;

"Honeymoon couples favouring Seychelles as their post-wedding destination frequently find inspiration from the structure of these singular plants found only on Praslin Island. Any man who forgets his duty to savour the fruit of new union cannot fail to be reminded after a short walk around the island." His enthusiasm was infectious and we traded sentences, often in whispers when Mo was around.

I spent three weeks chasing Mo to get feedback on the first quarter of the desk-produced Kenya guidebook. "Fine," he grunted after finally reading it in the car. "Keep on."

Occasionally we made forays into the Press Centre at Chester House to the main office which was adorned with images of Mo with many dignitaries – President Moi with his little red eyes, BBC newsreader Michael Buerk and the Queen when Mo received his MBE. Copies of Camerapix-produced in-flight mags—*Selamta, Singapore Airlines* and *Africa Life* were scattered on the waiting room table. They inevitably contained solemn stories, beautiful but boring. Their real importance was access to free air cargo. The coffee table and guidebook proofs were flown to

Singapore for printing at considerable savings, and then flown across the world for sales through another of Mo's cunning cost cutting business arrangements.

Mo's office was at the end of a long corridor. He mostly left the door open so he could watch the movements of his staff and pick up on most conversations. Public humiliations were frequent. A visiting Australian cameraman remarked how nobody could get away with shouting at staff the way Mo did. It kept us on our toes, mostly terrified—all except Brian. He shouted back. He very quickly became my guide, editor and shield from Mo, taking interest in my work, and interjecting "but she's got it Mo, she's brilliant," when I came in for criticism.

One day, strolling into Brian's office, bored with the guide book, I spotted a sheaf of mail on his desk, rather than the usual manuscripts. Brian looked up from the letter he was handwriting; "Just polishing off the thank-you to the queen," he said. He was drafting Mo's response to Buckingham Palace for the MBE he'd just received. It was then I realised that Brian dealt with Mo's correspondence, answering letters, correcting his spelling and writing speeches. It was clear he played a much greater part in Mo's life than I had originally known, through this access to his most personal and private paperwork. Mostly Mo was immensely reserved—he had little patience for people unless he could directly extract some benefit for himself—but he had let Brian into his inner sanctum. It was a marriage of convenience between two unusual bedfellows. At some level the years of contact had turned into a genuine love, grown out of mutual respect for each other's talent and eventually strengthened by the rollicking domestics over differences in lifestyle. I watched them flow around each other with new eyes. Their bust-ups were frequent, but often soothed with tea, beer and bhajia's, two pairs of feet on Mo's massive desk, trading gentle insults and discussing work. Brian's chuckle and "bless you mate," would float through the door past Mo's grunting acknowledgements and complaints about the shower of cigarette ash.

It made the row that resulted in Brian leaving the country in a huff all the more dramatic. As usual the issue was funding flow. Mo walked into the chalet one morning, beard set firmer than usual. "We're going to Somalia tomorrow—there's no more book work. Make sure you're ready."

"There's no bloody way I'm going there. I'm too old, Mo. You agreed to books. We've been through this before mate."

"I need to go with a writer. I can give you another book in a couple of months. Either come or get out. It's all I can offer you."

As he turned to leave, Brian banged the table, knocking over a half drunk teacup. "Fuck you, Mo—I barely earn any money already with your tight arse. I need to earn mate. You pay me half or less than you should, and now you're reneging on our deal. How am I supposed to live over the next few months? You know Mary. She'll get me for sure unless we can pay the rent. You're forcing me to go, you bugger."

As Brian was still wanted for bigamy in the UK, it was a measure of his outrage at the sense of betrayal he felt from Mo's change of deal that he really did leave Kenya taking up a post at the *Daily Sport* newspaper in Manchester. He suggested I go at the same time to take on the British press.

The Sport, the UK's newest tabloid, was housed in the old Express building, an art deco extravagance, once a hive of activity, until Maggie Thatcher and media tycoon Rupert Murdoch broke the powerful print unions and changed the face of newspaper publishing. Now small sections of the vast press and a large third floor room, with what seemed to be the oldest computers in the UK, made up the office of this latest tits and bums offering. It purported to be more serious than its sister paper, the *Sunday Sport* which was better known for its front page discoveries of a London double decker bus on the moon, and for reincarnating Che Guevara as a pimple on Idi Amin's bum. The daily preferred to deal with real life oddities instead, dousing everything in saucy sexual innuendo.

Here Brian was in his element—old hardened hacks bumped off the *Mirror* newspapers had all congregated to work for soft porn sex phone line seller David Sullivan. Burly men with ringing northern accents strode around the newsroom in kipper ties, cigarettes dangling from their fingers. It was working men's club fantasy world. Brian was offered the job of ghosting Fiona Wright's "5 times a night" advice column. It appealed to Brian's puckish humour that a balding bespectacled middle-aged man with a paunchy belly and a penchant for beer penned Fiona, who was actually a 36-26-36 blonde stripper who hit the headlines over marathon sex sessions with a portly gap toothed member of the Conservative Party. Moreover, masquerading as Fiona meant he did not have to get on airplanes, which landed in a desert region of Ethiopia, or in the middle of heavy fighting in Mogadishu. Here his skill at creating one-syllable words with one pun per line learned on the S*unday Pictorial* 20 years ago earned him as much as the lengthy Journey Through books he flipped out for Camerapix in Kenya—and the beer was better. "I'm just giving a cricket player a huge wicket," he'd announce, his two fingers hammering away at the old Ferranti keyboard, "so he can bat away at his babe. What a good innings he's going to have!"

Meanwhile I was thrown into this new and strange world of topless skydiving stunnas, botched sex change victims, streakers, witchdoctors and hypnotists, most of whom had size 36DD breasts that they would pull out at a moment's notice. The paper had the highest tit count in the land and blazened the number of breasts available for view in a regular tally on the front page.

I was the youngest person working there and one of only two female journalists at the paper. Nothing in my expensive education had prepared me for this side of Britain. Women wrote in sending topless photos to the paper imploring us to use them as birthday treats for their husbands. Pubic hair straightening kits, boob tattoos, and Hunk of the Month photos of chunky pale-skinned men in bodybuilder poses landed on my desk. Once a huge coffin, customized to also work as a double bed turned up at the door, donated as first prize for a Halloween competition.

Brian led me through this unfamiliar, seedy maze of the tabloid world. He taught me to find the one-liners required to describe a topless Tour de France aspirant ("Whaor what a ride!") and how to load a simple acupuncture session with the innuendo required for our lads in the local to read ("as the prick entered me, I felt a tingle all over my body").

He took me to the local pub, the Land O' Cakes, and showed me how to drink cider – enough to participate, but definitely not enough to get drunk. "Drink is the ruin of all luv," he would say glumly finishing off his fifth Guinness and waving his pint glass at Fran the landlady for a refill. The pub was on direct dial from the office so staff could be pulled out from overlong sessions to conjure up a quick story for the final deadlines. Mary stayed behind in Kenya and for a time Brian was free – he had booze, he had words, cash and no comeback.

Some months into our stint at the *Sport,* as the grey rainy Manchester summer turned into an even greyer rainy Manchester winter, a routine visit to the doctor flagged bottom problems for Brian that turned out to be the beginnings of colon cancer.

"Oooh luv, I'm going to die," he pronounced, waving the test results at me in the office, hands shaking more than their normal quake from booze withdrawal. It was the first time I had seen him so afraid, his usual brio squashed by the gloomy prognosis. The doctor decided that an operation was required immediately, which threw both Brian and I into a quandary. He was due to return to Kenya for Christmas and the paper had decided that it could only spare one of us. I was desperate to leave the concrete scruff off the city for my homeland but Brian was senior and—despite his drunkenness—more tactical in organizing his holiday. "Listen sweetheart, this could be my last time to set foot in the country before they chop me up – I can't let you have this one," he said, shambling off to speak to the editor Peter Grinsted, flashing his cancer diagnosis in his face. But in the end I won when the NHS set his operation date for December. For him Christmas would involve getting fitted with a colostomy bag at Salfords General Hospital.

Brian took the news without much of a grudge. The features editor let him use the phone to call Mary in Kenya to explain why he was not coming home for the holidays. She began a tirade as soon as he said he was sick—Swahili invective pouring down the phone while Brian's belly wobbled and he cried silently, his head cradled in one hand, spectacles squiff on his forehead, cigarette ash dripping onto the desk. It was only then that I realized that in all his 20 years in Kenya and with his three African wives and numerous women friends he had never learned to speak Swahili and didn't have the words to explain to his wife how a part of his colon needed to be chopped off and how afraid he was of hospitals. There was a silence in the room – fifteen hardened hacks of the *Daily Sport* trying not to listen to the soft snuffling from Brian and the strident voice of his wife on the other end of the phone when he moved it away from his ear.

I promised to meet Mary in Nairobi and explain to her what had happened and how she would need to fly over to look after her sick husband, so that he would still be capable of sending money over to her. Over a long session at the Westview Hotel—Brian and Mary shared a fondness of beer—she understood that this was not some ploy to cheat her of cash, and agreed to go look after him – as long as I agreed to look after her. Having never traveled abroad, she, too, was terribly afraid.

Brian loved the drugs of the operation. The nurses didn't as he took to wandering the corridors at night trailing his drip and his colostomy bag. "This is great luv," he exclaimed as I bumped into him in the hospital corridor, his eyes bulging from the combined effort of walking and strong painkillers. "I'm a bit bored of soup though —they won't let me eat anything solid in case I jam up my pipes."

As soon as he was released from the grip of the drip he began to make daily trips out of the hospital to the Land O' Cakes, arriving by taxi at 11am when the pub opened and leaving at 7pm when I collected him at the end of my shift at the *Sport*. By then he would be drunk, roaring, "I'm bummed—my colon has become a full stop." Eventually the hospital took objection to his use of their ward bed as a drunken crash pad and discharged him, despite his objections that neither he nor his imminently arriving wife would know how to change his poo bags.

Six months later Brian returned to Kenya having re-struck a deal with Mo to write a glowing revision to the biography of his frontline life. It was to co-incide with the fitting of Mo's bionic arm in replacement for the one lost in the dump in Ethiopia. The new limb, titanium-tipped, could manipulate a camera, crush steel and win arm wrestling contests by flipping the opponents hand so fast that breakage usually occurred. "A much better crowd-puller than my poo bags," grumbled Brian. He had been told to stop drinking after the operation –"technically impossible for me to keep off the warm Whitecap" – he informed me; and so decided that he would prefer to die of liver failure in Kenya than in a grimy flat in Salfords.

I meanwhile meandered through the UK tabloid world for several years, largely on a list of contacts provided by Brian. "Go speak to Hamish at the *Sunday Mirror*," he told me. "He's a great old mate of mine from the *Sunday Pic* days. Here, we got a stormer of a story that landed on the newsdesk; they won't miss it with all the other pervs writing in – this one's mainstream national material anyway. Its about a racing driver called John Hooker. He's had a sex change and turned into Joanna Hooker. And his address is Dyke's End. Fabulous! It's the perfect intro luv. And if they won't have it, take it to the *News of the World*. I'm sure you can persuade Ms. Hooker into a pair of fishnets after that great job you did on the mother and daughter boob-to-boob photo shoot."

His advice worked and I wound up in the nebulous world of 'investigations' at the *News of the World*, 'making my excuses and leaving' from a string of highly unsalubrious stories. During my time in the vast News International complex that housed all of Rupert Murdoch's newspapers I met Nick Rufford, part of the much admired investigative *Sunday Times Insight* team. He'd just been let down by another Kenya hack on a big story they were doing on exploitation by the tobacco industry in Africa and was looking for someone who could quickly find an 80-year-old cancer patient who'd been smoking most of his life. I gave him Brian's number. A week later I bumped into Nick in the cuttings library. "Perfect story," he said of Brian's piece. "It was topped and tailed, needed no editing and turned up on time." Nick seemed bemused that such skilled writing was available from an ageing tabloid hack in Nairobi.

On my return trips to Kenya, I'd often see Brian, sometimes with Mo, sometimes independently, always at a bar, where he would complain about how his op had messed up his drinking. "The beer just rips through these bags—have to keep rushing off to change them. Otherwise I just get too smelly," he said. "Hear that?" he said as a loud gurgle emerged from his side, "that's the stuff coming through. Bloody awful I tell you."

Some years later in 1995, I had a motorbike accident while on holiday on a remote tea plantation in Uganda, which resulted in a hip to ankle plaster cast that put a temporary stop to UK work. Brian immediately invited me over for a subbing stint at the *Standard* where, after yet another fight with Mo, he was now writing a new column 'Off the Wall'—which was one of the first attempts to slyly criticize the repressive Moi regime. It didn't last. A few months in, he overindulged in a heavy drinking spree to celebrate Kenya beating the West Indies in the World Cup, missing a deadline. "Fuck you," he bellowed down the corridor to the hunched retreating shoulders of the newly hired British managing editor of the *Standard;* "This is a historic occasion you slimy ignoramus. Kenya's just shown their greatness against one of the best cricketing nations in the world. Our boys have done it! Of course I'm going to see it out with my mates in the bar. You don't like it, then fire me." They did, and Mary left him at this job loss. Once again Brian turned back to Mo for help. This time Mo extracted the promise of overseas flights from Brian who was to accompany him on his trips across the continent.

"It's so sad – after farting about for all those years he seemed to have forged quite a comfortable life," said Duncan of their final year together. "He found this lovely girl—Lilly—very pretty, who cooked for him and cared from him and didn't beat him up. He was doing well on the book side, and both he and Mo seemed to have mellowed. Maybe it's age, although I guess Mo was more occupied with fighting Reuters (in a perverse twist, Mo was experiencing a microcosm of what Brian had felt all his life—Reuters, who had bought Visnews, had imposed their structures, systems and accountability on him, refusing to allow his maverick tendencies, questioning his expenses, relegating him to the role of bureau chief on their terms. This union was further complicated by a joint venture between Camerapix—Mo's company—and Reuters to produce Africa Journal, a documentary style feature programme. Editorial and control differences between the partners had turned this deal into fractious fight for control of the series). Perhaps Brian and Mo could now identify even more strongly with each other because of that brawl, but he and Brian were going through a long good patch."

The trip to Addis was a routine one – a visit to talk about the airline's magazine. It's a supreme irony that this innocuous trip led to the death of a high profile war-zone persona such as Mo. His self-promoting internationalism, forged through the hardnosed pursuit of exclusive foreign news stories, is what singled him out as the most prominent figure to die in the crash. And his work had serviced mankind through his images, but crucially they had to serve himself in the process. Not so with Brian. He experienced his life in a balance of enchantment and exasperation—almost entirely backstage, not infrequently back-street—in an atmosphere of beer, mates and brawls. But his brand of encouragement, his sharing of talent was heartfelt and generous, handed out freely and personally to a wider audience.

"In most conventional terms you could argue that Brian spoiled his own life," reflected Gavin. "But in certain magical moments he inspired so many others to real and lasting achievements. Never let it be said that the 'Life of Brian' was wasted—because of his impact on, and through others, it will never be ended."

Bob Smith concurs: "There was truly no one quite like Brian. His mind was pin sharp, his wit rapid and his trove of stories endless. He was a flawed genius, able to write on just about any subject with authority and originality. I learned more about the art of writing from Brian than from any other person and I will never be half as good as Brian was."

I had gone to join Camerapix, thinking that work with Mo Amin would bring me the necessary know-how to forge my new career. Instead I too had found Brian, the outward shambling mess, this drinking, womanizing, word enthusiast, who became a focal pivot in my career. His influence pervaded and informed my work, just as his presence popped up frequently and entertainingly in my world. Although I moved back to UK from my final working stint with him on the *Standard* in late 1995 and didn't see him again before his death, his influence remained. So much so, that just as I met him at the start of my writing life, his death heralded a pause in my journalistic trajectory that became as permanent a full stop as that forced on his colon. This story, a decade after his death, has finally brought me out of a writing hibernation to pay homage to this eccentric, loveable wordsmith.

It seemed that the hijackers of that fateful flight 10 years ago didn't really know what they wanted. Nick Kotch, who interviewed the pilot in his hospital bed after the crash explained, "they were young, angry, naïve and on the run after being tortured in prison. They were physically violent with the crew and wanted to keep flying across the Indian Ocean to Australia. It was the pilot who tricked them by approaching the Comores as the fuel ran out, ditching the plane as close to the shore as he could in the hope that some passengers might escape." Coincidentally a doctors convention was taking place in the capital Moroni, and bikini clad medical experts administered first aid on the beach, contributing to the relatively high number of survivors—almost third of the passengers. But my friend and his scavenging bionic-armed boss were not among them.

Both funerals were well attended. Mo's family was joined by a razzmatazz of foreign correspondents and dignitaries—their disagreements with the man notwithstanding—who came to watch his body solemnly shrouded and buried according to his custom. Wailing women stood by as the shroud was lifted and taken for burial. It was a sombre formal event. Affairs of the state prevented the then-President Moi from attending, but he sent condolences and deputies—attorney general Amos Wako and foreign affairs minister Kalonzo Musyoka.

The next day was Brian's turn, and it couldn't have been more different. More than 600 people crowded round his grave at Langata cemetery. They were a fascinating cross section of all stratas of Kenya society. MP's mixed with newspaper hacks, businessmen, cricketers, slum dwellers, barflys and many women.

Brian often said he was "born in UK, but made in Kenya," and this gathering was testimony to that. He had little actual family left—only his brother Peter, who flew over from UK with Brian's two daughters, whom he hardly knew. But a cornucopia of friends and associates that stretched back over the nearly 30 years of his sojourn in Kenya came to pay their respects to this character, who had mixed and merged so comprehensively with so many. Two bottles of Tusker were symbolically placed with him in the grave before a large group of friends retired to Dambusters bar after the funeral to begin a piss up in his honour, which fittingly finished in the early hours of the morning in the Terminal Bar in River Road.

"It was a moving, beautiful day," said Duncan Willetts. "Multi-gender, multi-racial and totally representative of Brian's effect on so many people in Kenya." His send off may not have had the gravitas reserved for Mo, but his impact locally was in many ways so much greater.

So in death as in life Brian and Mo messily twisted together departed. An acrimonious yet fruitful 25-year collaboration between alcoholic and teetotaler, wordsmith and image-maker was over.

It saddens me to think that Brian's worst fears—of dying by plane, or by drowning were both realised. I only hope he was drunk when it happened.

SHALINI GIDOOMAL is a freelance journalist, writer, businesswoman and inveterate traveller, born and currently part- living in Nairobi. She has worked extensively on U.K. and international magazines and newspapers, both high and low brow, and is now making forays into fiction.

Mombasa

Murray Shelmerdine

Night in Mombasa
Under stars precise as a planetarium
Palm trees whisper secrets
Over the noise of the reef
Shapes slither beneath bushes
Or flit through soupy air
On membrane wings
Cicadas chatter with frogs
And things rustle among the leaves

Oath-takers and street-boys
Stand at shanty corners
Stooping in shadows
Watching a watchman
The watchman aims his torch
But sees nothing
Swings his stick
Clears his throat

In the police station a machete slashes
Blood seeps through the mosquito net
Mrs Anopheles turns up her nose
The oath-takers pick up guns
Start fires

Burning thoughts lope along jungle paths
Sink steaming into the sea
And slide into caverns
Where mermaids sit on dead men's chests
Stuffed with emeralds
Beside them on the coral

Crabs crawl through the eyeholes
Of pirate skulls
And skitter over pearls
Froth falls upwards from their mouths
To speck the heaving surface of the lagoon
And night is broken on the coral

Over the beach, the sky grows pale
A woman walks the sand
With a basket of sweet bananas on her head
A smiling boy holds a gift
An ebony crocodile paper knife
And there's a barefoot professor
Sitting outside a makuti hut
Who'll carve your name on it
For twenty bob
While you sleep

of sweet bananas
oy holds a gift
codile paper knife
barefoot professor

MURRAY SHELMERDINE is a poet.

Count Your Blessings

Murray Shelmerdine

What a good thing
There are no homosexuals in Kenya
Eh!
Otherwise we would have to kill them
As it says in the Bible:
Leviticus 4, 13.

What a good thing
There is no more corruption
In the Kenya government -
Now they are all working
For the interests of the people.

What a good thing
I always have enough to eat
And feed my children

What a good thing
I haven't got AIDS.
I know I haven't got AIDS
Because I am a good person
And I only ever had sex
With my husband
May he rest in peace.

What a good thing
He didn't die of AIDS

When I am well enough to walk
I'll go to the church
And thank God
For all these good things.

The Pearl Collage

Patrick Chorya

i.

If only we could learn
the patterns of other races humbly,
never imposing our own wills,
or even if we persisted in our own
ways, that we would grasp the need
for acquired kinship,

to lose ourselves in the aspirations
of other people, blending,
thus ending the grief and crimson
of our prideful becomings.

ii.

Yet even amidst the pain
of an oyster nursing a grain of sand
in its bosom, I am flooded
with the grace of God living in this
country. And all around me I see
lives of pearls built from pain and chastisement
as the Lord gathers us from these
disparate strands grown from history, scattered
from a common loin.

From our separate origins we are
jewels of different shades, a pearl collage,
cemented by a common history,
learning fraternity towards one identity.

And in our oneness, yielding
to the Spirit of the Lord,
we shall see God's glory, and so too
our only true homecoming,
seeing finally our sameness in our past,
surging through out lives and now
the very life of Christ in our midst,
inviting our hearts…

PATRICK CHORYA was born in Kitgum, northern Uganda. He attended secondary school at Samuel Baker School in Gulu. He was admitted for a B.A. (Soc. Sc.) in Sociology and Public Administration at the University of Swaziland, Kwaluseni. He has since been employed in development work, first in a refugee camp, and later with an NGO implementing reintegration and development programs for children and communities affected by armed conflict in northern Uganda. Chorya's first publication is A Time for Peace & Other Poems From A Civil War

Illustration: Peter Elungat

Mrs. Shaw

BY MUKOMA NGUGI

"Hey! You there! You know what you need? A white mother."
I must be mistaken. I whirl around to face the voice. "What did you just say?" I ask.

"I said you what you need is a white mother."

It's her. For a year or so now, almost every weekend I find her here. She is British. I am African. From bar-gossip I know that in the 1950's she lived in my country, lost her husband to our war for independence, taught African history at the University of Wisconsin and now that she's retired, spends most of her time in bars. I assume that bar-gossip has offered the same skeletal details about me; where

I'm from, that I am in political exile, work at the local UPS hub loading trucks and like her I have a penchant for drink. In a year we haven't talked—not even a hello—yet I feel that we are always aware of each other.

She is old, probably in her seventies, maybe even eighties. She is white, very thin though not frail. Her makeup does little to hide her deep wrinkles or the brown age spots on her face. Her red hair is cropped short, but even in the bar light I can tell it has been dyed. She is wearing a thick red sweater and blue jeans that she has tucked into flaming red cowboy boots. I expect to find her smoking but with a thickly veined hand she is twirling a little umbrella that came with her vodka tonic. Her tone is not confrontational, insulting or bitter. She is telling me I need a white mother in the same way I would give a stranger direction to the nearest bus-stop or restaurant.

It is a few minutes into the New Year and a new millennium and it has been exceptionally quiet at the Eagle's Bar. Before her interruption I had been staring at the Billie Holiday photograph on the wall. It is not an original and her uneven autograph is too glossy to have been from her own hand. The other photographs that cover the wall are all copies of a photograph of the original, too. Charlie Parker, Louis Armstrong, Duke Ellington, Miles Davis—martyrs, victims and survivors of this country I have called home for the last ten years.

Billie's photograph—side profile—makeup, even in this black and white photograph, barely covering her bad skin, short hair in black curls, a map of veins along her neck stretched taut like guitar strings, glittering brown eyes half-open to close, smooth hard jaws with skin stretched to an open mouth hungry for the microphone a few inches away—she is pulling back as if taking a deep breath...and my narration ends there. I always wonder what it is she is going to sing; without the song she sings the photograph is incomplete, it always leaves me hungry.

I take a long drink, and lugging my remaining beer skip the three or four barstools between us I sit next to the old white woman. Early into New Years Day, we are the only patrons in the bar – everyone else has a home to go to. This is an exceptionally dastardly time to be alone. We do not speak for a while. The bar-tender and owner of Eagle's Bar looks over to see if we need drinks and then turns his attention to the muted TV tuned to some millennium celebration in New York. He is a former college football quarterback who is ageing like the cliché, and he's a jazz aficionado who delights in reciting names of musicians he met (he can't have; he seems to be in his thirties). He doesn't like me because when I get tired of staring at the dead imitations of the dead, I remind him the photographs are photocopies of the original and that the live recordings he pipes through his expensive Bose system have lost some of their original groove in the machinery of mass production. It is a symbiotic dysfunctional relationship—I am the asshole drinker and he is the asshole bartender.

A home away from home.

"What would make you say such a thing?" I finally ask, feigning annoyance because I am supposed to. I cannot bring myself to hurl an insult at her. There is something about her that reminds me of grandmothers. Old people and children radiate infectious warmth in the same strange way, I have found. Is it the vulnerability that cannot be hidden? There are also aspects of one's culture that remain no matter what the journeys taken. We do not insult our elders (though to be quite fair some people shoot them for their land, their money, because they are old, for a host of reasons) and a few choice words that normally would have ended this conversation are of no use. In addition to her British accent authenticating a relationship that neither she nor I have any control over, I have revealed my hand by moving to sit next to her. I become aware that she knows all these things. I cannot leave until I have heard what she has to say.

"I have watched you for a long time watching our old friend Billie. What you really need is a white mother."

I know exactly what she is doing. She is offering her credentials.

"Why do you say that?"

"Only a white mother can you tell you what happened in your white family. The father, your white father, was a colonizer but you see within the family, he was a husband, a son and father. I can help you understand him," she says.

Coming from any other person these would have been fighting words. Even at another time I would not have taken it but it is New Year's, a new millennium at that, I am alone, lonely, homesick, drunk and hungry for the touch of words.

"Interesting." I say, trying to be sarcastic as I take a sip of my beer. "So the mother and the son plot against the father. Only I possibly can't be your son."

I reach for my wallet, flip it open and point to an old photograph of my father and mother. I point the photographs out to her.

"See, these are my parents. I am as black as them. But I'll tell you what, we can make a strategic alliance."

On the other side of the wallet is a photograph of Wambui. My own personal Billie Holiday. Why do I still have her photograph in my wallet? It has been ten years. I order two beers for myself. She doesn't order another drink; she sits poised, waiting for me to ready myself for what she has to say.

"Alliances! That's the trouble with the world today. Alliances don't work. I am offering...only intimate spaces... a family will work. No plots and counter-plots."

She pauses for a moment, reaches out for her drink and then changes her mind.

"You can be the mother and I the son if you like. It really doesn't matter," she adds, with calculated carelessness.

Probably my father could play the role of her son better than me. His wife, my mother, died in car accident a year after I was born. I do not remember her, though I recognize her in this vague feeling of growing up without balance, as if I had a phantom leg that worked. He told me years later he'd been planning to divorce her. But her death turned him into a widower and this came with duties that he could not pass on to anyone else.

I always wondered what went through his mind as he dutifully tended her grave, planting rose after rose until there was no more space left in the graveyard. His betrayal of her weighed on his conscience because she died before their divorce.

Sometimes I feel that he brought me up in the same way he looked after her grave —doing something that was expected of him—doing his duty. How often has he reminded me that he has done his duty by me?

It was from him that I learned of our past. With a school teacher's zeal, maps, historical documents and a magnifying glass on a ping-pong table that he converted into a general's desk, he would point, pontificate, drill, query, and pull my ear until I understood our history. His version of it at least. He has a favorite maxim; "Love is knowledge, knowledge is love."

Yet in spite of it all I don't think he ever quite believed that the colonizers did what they did to us—put us in concentration camps, poisoned water holes, cut off hands, lips and ears and threw the rest of us in their plantations and mines.

Tracing a colonial map along the River Nile he would pause over a poisoned well and ask himself, "But how could they do this to another human being?"

Yet just a few moments before, he had told me how we were not human beings to them. At other times he would tell me how we lost our land. Often he took me there. The way he held the soil that had been his father's and let it course through his fingers told me that he took me there to remind himself that it was all true, that it had all happened. Yes, I very well understood this trail of broken treaties. I had been walking it since I was born. In fact, I had walked it right into exile.

Unlike my father, I never doubted what I knew to be true—that the same hands that embrace one's child will squeeze the life out of a neighbor's child when war comes, that the same colonizer who built a church to save the native, did not hesitate to burn it down when it housed rebels and that my leaders, black like me, speaking my language and praying to the same God had sanctioned my torture by night and driven their children to school in the morning. Perhaps I was better than my father in that I knew all these things to be true, or I was worse off, more jaded and more tragic. If in my realism I had lost faith in my neighbor, how could I have faith in myself?

But I did learn a lot from my father. I can see him now, telling me how right from the beginning of colonization, there had been skirmishes between whites and blacks. "It is not true that we did not fight back," he was quick to remind me. Movements were formed and banned, leaders jailed, killed or exiled, and whole villages of people put in concentration camps.

"Pretty much the same as it is now for your generation, only your leaders are black," he would say.

The ebb and flow of resistance and repression continued until...

"Happy New Year!!" the bartender yells to a passing friend through the large glass windows. She waves back with a gloved hand. My thoughts interrupted, I turn my attention back to the old white woman.

"Listen, I don't think even my father qualifies to be your son." I say to her.

"Oh! But he does. He didn't believe what he saw with his own eyes and even though you think you're different, neither do you."

Damn it! Had I been speaking out aloud? She reaches into her red handbag which I notice for first time dangling down the bar stool. She pulls out a red lipstick, pouts her lips and I catch a flash of her as a young woman, sexy, confident and self-assured, years before history caught up with her.

"Look, I know more than you think I do... I know after your husband finished raping his slave, he rested for a bit and then turned on you. Many white sons and daughters out there are children of rape. In town he was cheap and a drunk, and in the fields he was a murderer. At home he was much worse because he could not kill, so he learnt to torture his wife and children without leaving scars. Whatever little game you are playing here, know that I see you," I say.

"And I am also judging you," I add more for effect, because it sounds good.

I notice I am clutching my glass tightly and I take a deep breath. Or maybe she is the one losing it because she turns her back and beckons the bar-tender for another drink. The bar-tender returns with a vodka gin and tonic too soon. We both could have used a break from the conversation. She beckons me to continue talking. Instead I walk over to Juke Box and play Kool and the Gang's Celebration; what the hell—its New Year's after all, and the song reminds me of home. The bartender annoyed by the sudden intrusion of sound turns the music down. I knew he would do that, music other than jazz is only OK for young college kids. I ask for another drink. Perhaps she can tell I'm stalling because she is watching my transactions with a look of amusement. Finally I sit down and continue from where I had left off.

"It must have been much worse for you. Our mothers had us when they returned from your homes where they worked as maids, nurses, cooks and gardeners. But you, whom did you have? You had no place to return, no sanctuary. Everyone you would have known would have..." For the first time, she interrupts me. I am doing well; I have hit something so I let her continue. But oddly enough she does not jump right into the conversation. She hesitates, reaches into her bag once again and removes some Wrigley's gum. She offers me one and carefully unwraps one for herself. I can tell she used to smoke by the way her little movements fill nervous space.

"Perhaps it was worse for me. But I wonder if your father let your mother back into the house knowing what my husband had just done to her. He is a man after all. Men speak the same language," she said, emphasizing each word in the last two sentences.

"Had it been my father, I think he would have understood that he had no choice. We are talking about metaphorical fathers and mothers, aren't we?" I ask but do not wait for her to answer. "He would have beaten her up, and the kids too, and kicked the cat and the dog but he would have had no choice but to take it, until he was tired of it and decided to fight back—he had no choice. Nor did our mothers, nor any of us...well, some of us."

We must look quite odd. The whole world is celebrating and here we are, a young black man sitting next to an old white woman in a bar called Eagle's. I wonder if the bartender can distinguish our accents, mine weighed down my Gikuyu yet trained to sound like hers; and hers proper English infected with a Midwestern drawl. Or to him, a typical American, we are both foreigners to be watched.

"You are right but also wrong. I had your mother. Yes, I passed your mother on my stairs as she climbed into my bedroom... She saw the beatings and the rapes on the lily white sheets. She might have thought that I did not see her, that I left the bloody sheets and underwear there because I thought a human machine was washing my clothes. Maybe that is what she would have told you. I don't know. I don't think so. It was my SOS written in blood. There is no way she could have mistaken it... as a woman."

Celebration has come to an end. The bartender walks over to the jukebox, puts in some coins and starts flipping through the albums. "Why are we speaking in metaphors? I tell you about my life and you tell me about mothers and fathers. We've shared this space for a year without speaking. Let's catch up," she says in irritation. She has a good point there I concede to myself.

"I can't speak for my mother. She died when I was very small." I wait for her to say how sorry she is that she dragged my mother into this, or for her death, but she says nothing. "But you want to know what I think? I think she would have hated you. She had her own problems you know...without yours. And you, you would have held on to your white skin. It still would have shielded you from some things...like you never went hungry. But I can only speak for the living; at least they stand a chance to defend themselves." The conversation feels out of hand and uncomfortable. But given where I'd been a few minutes before—in front of Billie Holiday—I'm happy talking with her. The bartender's first selection has kicked in. I can't tell which of Miles' songs it is but I know his voice, a trumpet sound that reminds me of bouncing smooth pebbles off the surface of a pond.

"Listen, why don't you tell me your story, surely, surely we won't get anywhere like this," I say, going for broke as Wambui would say. It feels good to use her words. Ten years and her stock phrases still spill out of me.

"Take me home young man, and I will teach you a thing or two," she says in mock flirtation. She jumps off the bar-stool and offers me her hand. I accept, and pretend to climb down my bar stool. We both laugh for the first time and I feel her warm but vodka laden breath on my face. I ask the bartender if I can buy something to take home. He refuses. I promise him a book on Charlie Parker, a biography. He agrees and we haggle over the price. Eventually the old woman and I stagger out of Eagles Bar. It's just as well we left. It was almost time to close anyway.

Outside the bar everything is covered in snow. It's beautiful. The snow makes everything brighter. It's cold enough to announce winter on uncovered skin, but not oppressively so. A mild wind is riling the snow off the lamp-posts, roof-tops and magazine stands to make a second showing of the snow-fall—an encore. A police office driving up the street slowly comes to a crawl when he spots us. The old lady slips her hand under my arm and laughs. The officer nods his head from side to side, steps on the gas and the car swerves dangerously before it finds a foothold and drives off.

We walk in silence, occasionally slipping into each other on the ice that has formed beneath the snow. Sometimes she slips away from me and I feel an urgent tug of her arm on my elbow. By the time we get to her home, we are no longer familiar strangers. Once the veneer of mutual suspicion had been removed, we find we already knew a lot about each other. From the outside, her house doesn't look like much but it's cozy inside. Not at all what I would have expected had I had more time to think about it. It doesn't have that stale smell that is peculiar to old people's houses. I notice that the lamps have shades made out of stained glass, the kind one would find on church windows. Her wall has all sorts of art on it—all original, she says, with figures contorting in pain or pleasure.

It's hard to tell.

As I'm about to sit on a couch in the dining room, I notice she has a photograph of a Maasai Warrior. I think about Kiliko Town, and remembering how I had escaped into exile disguised as one, I want to check if it was me. Some tourists who gave me a ride couldn't get over having met what they took to be a real live Maasai and they took a lot of photographs of me—a Kikuyu disguised as a Maasai. The absurd, comical, tragic, revolutionary all rolled up in one. I have always felt that I will come across one of those photos in the United States but I'm too tired to get up and check. On the drunkenness count, I'm relieved to find I'm more tired than drunk.

She puts on some Masekela and his voice booms "There is a train..." before she turns the volume down. Now that's strange. The only people I know who listen to Masekela are the African exile types. I open the bottle of Jack and place it between us. She takes a swig and passes it to me. I do the same and we settle in for a long silence. It feels like we are speaking even in the silence. Or maybe we're just making space for room to speak, because she suddenly makes a sweeping impatient gesture and begins telling me about her husband.

"About the violence, you're right. He couldn't leave his work at the office. He delighted in bringing it home." I know what he did even before she says it.

"I loved him at first," she says. I feel like she is trying to convince herself. "But what you need to know is that he was a Colonial District Officer. I have often wondered why I really followed him. Perhaps you can tell me later. Even after all these years I still do not know. For what I went through, love couldn't have been enough." I wonder along with her. She doesn't strike me as the type to fall in love and follow her husband around the world nor, for that matter, does she seem the Florence Nightingale type. It should have been the other way round—her husband following her—but years pass and people change for the better or worse, some become weaker and others stronger; into what had I mutated? Afraid of what's coming, I walk over to her stereo and turn the music up slightly, just so I can have a cushion, something to soften the harshness of whatever is coming. I sit back down, take a swig of the whisky, and pass the bottle to her. Our hands brush and she smiles politely. Placing the bottle back between us, she leans back. She moves forward again only when she starts speaking.

"As a Colonial District Officer he was also in charge of security in his area. So when what we called the little troubles and what you called the uprisings began, he was in charge of collecting information. But his love for what was to become his life's work started even before he came to your country." She said life's work with a twist of her mouth. "He was a large man, about your height but very large, very blue eyes too. It was his eyes... When we were dating, he once told me that he liked to hunt and kill deer because he enjoyed seeing the color of their eyes change from brightness to a dull stare. Nothing should have come as a surprise after that. He was trained to collect information by an expert on African Affairs—Dr. Joseph Howard. You might have heard of him, or read some of his history books. Dr. Howard spoke six or seven different African languages and was an expert of the African mind. In his books, he never revealed how he got his information, but he taught my husband everything."

She pauses, taking another swig from the bottle. I know the types she is talking about, they are still walking around as if they own the continent. Only in Africa, it is written on trucks and buses. How does it feel to be studied, poked with needles and theories and talked about as if invisible?

"Then the little troubles began; the blacks started slapping back and everything changed," she says. I am struck by the way we come to share language. The little troubles—outside how we met, our tragedies, our histories, our stories, those words would have had no meaning. I understand her so well. I understand the words underneath those words. I too am here because of present day little troubles, related to her little troubles. It was the increasing frequency of my little troubles that brought me here. And there are so many all over the world whose lives ebb and flow with little troubles.

"He enjoyed, no wait...he loved his work. He couldn't get enough of it. I was always the chaser after the main course. Work slowed down, I became the main course. We had a garden boy, an old man really...his name was David." I am about to take offense at an old man being called a boy, then I remember we use the same terms, boy, girl or sometimes just an anonymous rude you.

"I can't remember his African name. I was sitting outside with my husband and I was looking at David—nothing sexual, he was just there so I was looking at him. I didn't hear him leap from his chair. "Why are you looking at him? You want to fuck him? You want to fuck him." I woke up later in bed, swollen all over. It excited him to think of me and David. He couldn't even wait for me regain consciousness. Poor David lost his job. Had it been a few months later, my husband would have killed him." I needed a break. I asked her where her bathroom was, went in and washed my face in the sink. My heart was pounding violently. It was quite simple, I was afraid of what this old woman was going to tell me. But even as I thought that, I knew I was going to listen so I walked back to the table. She continued as if there had been no interruption.

"I had to wear dark sunglasses most of the time. Once we had a picnic party where all the women showed up in white dresses, white pearls around their necks, white tennis shows and hats and sunglasses. And we laughed and sipped our wine." She lifts her pinkie finger up gingerly, pretending she's delicately holding the stem of a wine glass. "We talked about our husbands and the little troubles that our maids and servants were giving us. We were a sea of whiteness but underneath...

only tears. I do not know what the men were talking about but as they got louder our laughter grew louder too. It became a madhouse. We were all mad. We needed a whole lot of shrinks." She lets out a laugh that in exile I have come to hear. It ends abruptly, a sudden burst of gas escaping a pressure cooker.

"One morning I woke up knowing I was going to kill my husband when he came home. I was tired. It was getting worse. An epidemic had broken out among our men and the cure was our bodies...My neighbor stopped visiting me, I knew why. Underneath the glasses and white dresses..." I felt her voice waver, as if it was going to break. "And who knew what the black men would do to us when..." she was adding softly.

I can't let her finish. I've been nice enough and played along. But this is too much. It was they who came to our country and they, woman and man, alike got what they deserved. I have no empathy. I need it all for myself. I have to do something, before I lose it. I've come too far. I'm almost healed. I'm going home in a year. Wounds have been slowly closing to form scars. What I and others had sacrificed for had finally come to pass. In the next year elections will take place. The dictator will be elected out of office and my exile will be over because the party I had joined at its inception is going to win the elections. But now, more than opening her wounds for me to see, this old woman is also opening mine, and she doesn't seem to care. I just need to survive another year and I can return and these things will be behind me. People like her are always taking. She is still taking, always taking...

"Jesus Christ!!! Can't you see you are still taking? You are a taker and have always been a taker," I shout, interrupting my own thoughts with speech. "Can't you see you what you are doing?"

"What I am doing?" She asks this very calmly. "Didn't I tell you that you don't know everything?"

"Stories are what my grandmother told me at bed time. This is torture. You deserved your husband!!" I realize too late what I have shouted. She says nothing, letting the silence gnaw me into guilt. I reach for the bottle, take a swig and wait.

"Please, sit down." It is half plea, half command.

I sit.

"Look, things are not as simple as you are making them out to be. It was not just you and your husband. Can't you see that it was not all about you?" I am feeling calmer now.

"Explain yourself". She leans back into her chair and folds her arms across her chest. I go on anyway.

"For starters we had our own lives too... my grandparents worried about their children; they talked about their history, prayed to their God, they kept developing their own philosophies and sense of justice. They did not stop living because you came—that is what you hated most about them. Also, let's face it; you guys were not as scientific as you try to make it sound; colonialism did not move in a straight line—lots of massacres, accidents and lies. Did you know that your Henry Morton was a liar and a cheat?" I pause to catch my breath.

"There is something I want to show you," she says, as if whatever she wants to show me will rest all my doubts.

She walks into another room. I hear a drawer open and close. Whatever it is, she's not fumbling for it.

It could be a gun.

I think of leaving, even though deep down I know I won't. She walks back into the dining room carrying something that round like a soccer ball, covered in expensive-looking rainbow colored batik cloth. She places it on the table. Like a magician, she ceremoniously unfurls it. Something clatters onto the dining table, its jarring sound mixing in with her chuckles. When it finally settles and I lock my shaking eyes on it, I realize it is a human skull. I let out a quick sharp scream.

"What is this? What the fuck is this?" I stand up, abruptly knocking against the table and the skull and bottle dance crazy hula-hoops. "What the fuck?" I notice my right hand, instinctively stretched to save the dancing bottle, is trembling. I have broken into a thin light sweat and with my knees feeling foreign I find my seat but then stand up again.

"This is the price of freedom!" She says lightly, now laughing in pure delight. I can't reconcile her with the old woman at the bar. She looks young.

I can't help it, I start laughing too. I reach for the bottle and take such a long swig that she reaches across the table and gently takes it away from me. She takes an equally long swig. She picks the skull up, gives it a kiss, cradles it in the crook of her elbow, and sashays around the dining room,"well son, this here is my husband," she says in an American Southern drawl.

In this madness, my father's history lesson: The ebb and flow and resistance and repression had gone on for years. Then the Africans made one bold move that changed everything. They kidnapped the head of British National Security, a former District Commissioner who had proved to be very able in Native Pacification Campaigns. They held him for a few days and when there was no sign that the white government would cease its campaign, they killed and buried him in an unmarked grave. The colonial government went on a rampage and killed hundreds of blacks as it searched for the "black terrorists" (my father would say terrorists, this with a wink). This in turn sparked a nationwide movement that gave birth to the People's Freedom Party, the political wing of the People's Freedom Army that eventually forced the white government into a stalemate. And from the stalemate came a stillborn independence and betrayal of the nation by the People's Freedom Party. My father's version was much longer than I cared to remember at this point, but the general point was that the kidnapping and killing of the national security head was the watershed for the first independence. But here he is right before me—the Head of National Security.

"Is this Oliver Shaw? The one and only Oliver Shaw?" I ask as if meeting him for the first time and also announcing his entrance into a boxing ring.

"Yes, this is him." She runs her hand over the smooth skull. "The one and only," she adds.

"What happened to him?"

"He was drunk when he came home. I tied him to his arm chair and sat up all night waiting for him to wake up." She says this like she had been waiting for a loved one to wake up from an illness. "Then I killed him."

"How?"

"He woke up at about 7:00 in the morning. I opened up the curtain and told him to look at the rising sun. It was red and beautiful. I told him to look at it well because I was going to kill him. He didn't ask why. He was a soldier only doing what was the best for his family and country. He was only doing his duty. 'Do you love what you do?' I asked him. He said yes. 'Can I have a glass of water and a cigarette?' His blue eyes darting from side to side like that... 'Isn't that more than you do for the Africans?' He said that wasn't true, 'I always offer a glass of water and cigarette.' 'And the ones who do not smoke?' He grunted nothing. I didn't give him any water. I took a cigarette from his shirt-pocket, lit it for him and put it in his mouth. For the first time since we were married, he said thank you. I took his gun off his belt, placed it on his forehead and shot him." The she adds, "I've always hated cigarettes since then."

I sit down. As I reach over for the bottle I see for the first time the neat hole that went through the forehead, so neat that it looks like it's been filed. I imagine she was dressed in white.

"How did you get away with it?"

"I fed him to the lions and hyenas he loved to kill."

"What about his skull?"

"British soldiers used to cut off heads belonging to Chiefs who resisted. They would boil them until the flesh came off. I have since read elsewhere that it was to keep the victory alive, that to cradle the skull of your enemy is to savor the victory forever."

"You were never suspected? How did you get away with it?" I ask again.

"I waited for a few days, put on my pearl necklace, white dress and shoes, and went to the police station to report my husband missing."

"You did not choke?" I'm leaning into the dinner table. With her leaning forward as well, I imagine we make an arc across the table. I want to know more. I nod impatiently for her to continue.

"No I did not... Remember our white dresses and hats? I stayed on. I was there when the Union Jack was lowered. Did you know that it was done in the dark so as not to shame the Prince?" she asked. My father never tired of telling me this.

"I left when your new president, Samuel Johnston Mburu—that was his full name before he became African again—called to say that I would still get my widow's pension. I could continue farming. Even though he couldn't say this in public, he felt my husband, while cruel, still embodied greatness. I asked him why he would say such a thing. I think he was shocked but I didn't care. His answer? He disagreed with my husband's racism but they had in common a belief in protection of property, law and order. When he vowed to find my husband's killers, I knew it was time to leave. Not because I would be caught... that was Africa for me. You want to know who bought my husband's farm? The President's oldest son, Daniel Muigai Mburu. Was that his name?" I think he changed his English name to an African name that means freedom or liberty. But I am not sure so I let her continue.

"Do you judge my act as revolutionary? But what does it matter? I am part of history even though history doesn't know it."

"And the skull?" I continue with my questions ignoring hers. I want to know the rest of her story.

"No one stopped me at the airport. Once again I was dressed in white."

"Which version of that history did you teach?"

"Your people's version, the only known version. Who would believe me anyway?" She says as though considering the option. "I told you I'm a martyr in more ways than one," She adds dismissively.

"There's DNA testing," I offer.

"What makes you think I want people to know? My history... this is a private party for a single gal. Let the dead remain buried." Underneath the light-hearted tone, I can tell she is serious.

"I disagree. No matter what, people deserve to know how their history was made," I counter, even though I know it is pointless. A secret this big would never be let out, it would remain buried. There was a lot that was buried, all the secret deals that were made, that had made a mess out of things, the assassinations, illegal arms, grab lands, bank accounts in Switzerland and power sharing deals. This would be just one of them. "But where do I fit in all this?" I ask.

"I told you. You are my son," She says seriously.

"No. That cannot be. I have a father and mother. I am not an orphan, not even of history."

"You can only reject me. I mid-wifed your history and died for it."

"Independence would have happened anyway. No. I cannot accept your offer."

"It's not yours to accept..."

I stare at the bottle. "Look," I say, "we make good drinking friends...the rest... in the course of time we shall figure it out," I offer. At the end of it all, she's just another lonely old lady and I... I'm not sure what I am, except that in a year I will wear the punishing moniker of returnee.

There is silence for a while. "...And we already have a skull and a bottle of Jack between us. We are pirates," I say. We laugh so hard my belly aches.

"Now, it's you turn to tell me your story. My grandmother told me bedtime stories too. I don't want that kind," she says as our laughter dies. Our eyes meet, hold for a few seconds and then, past exhaustion, I look at the time; it's 7:00a.m. I take a swig from the bottle and pass it to her.

"If you are leaving there is no point," she says, waving the bottle away. "Come and visit me again—but only if you come bearing gifts," she says, sending a wink toward the bottle which I am still holding out to her. She writes down her number and house address on a piece of paper, one arm resting on her skull.

"You kept it?" I'm surprised when I see the name on the piece of paper.

"Like the skull, it's a reminder. Being called my name is like rubbing a genie bottle—the thing that pops out reminds me of my victory. These independences are elusive. Do you think we are going to lose again?"

"No, Mrs. Shaw." At the sound of her name she smiles a deep gratified smile. It's like a retired general being called by his war name one last time. "I don't think we will lose again." I stand and put on my winter jacket. "Mine is Kamau Wa Mwangi," I say as I tuck the bottle into my pocket. Hearing no answer, I look to find her passed out. Not the most comfortable position to sleep in. I lift her up and stagger with her to the couch, surprised at how heavy she is. I leave her there; makeup, red boots and everything still on—a feisty grandmother sleeping off too much booze. I walk back to the kitchen and turn off the stereo which has been playing dead air for a while and leave.

Outside it had started snowing again. It's January 1st and people are going to work. I feel happy and light. I stagger home and go to sleep.

MUKOMA NGUGI is a Kenyan poet currently working on an MA in African Languages and Literature at the University of Wisconsin. He holds an MA in Creative Writing from Boston University and a BA in Political Science and English from Albright College. His writing has appeared in Brick Magazine, Smartish Pace, Student Under Ground, *and* Teeth in the Wind *amongst others. His poetry has been featured in the following anthologies:* One Hundred Days, Barque Press *and* New Black Writing; *John Wiley and Sons. A political manuscript on Africa,* Conversing with Africa, *was published by Kimaathi Publishing House. He has completed a novel which he is looking to publish soon.*

Homosexuality and the Bible

A gay Kenyan man was talking about how people use the Bible to condemn homosexuality. Well I always felt that anyone can use the Bible to say anything.

Anyway, I decided to do a quick recap of verses in the Bible that mention homosexuality. I couldn't help throwing in my own editorial comments.

The vengeful Yahweh destroyed Sodom for its lechery. The last straw was when the men of Sodom attempted to rape two angels. The punishment against Sodom was not against homosexuality per se but the immorality of its residents. The story about Sodom does not mention God's anger, or otherwise, in relation to consensual acts of homosexuality.

What I find interesting about the Lot story, which to me illustrates the double standard people apply to interpretation of the Bible, is the moment towards the end where Lot and his daughters are living in a cave. The daughters conspire to get their father drunk and have carnal knowledge of him and *huko* he is blacked out.

Now that would make Njoki Ndungu gag but Yahweh is easy. The offspring of that liaison (Ammonites and Moabites) are about the only people Yahweh doesn't end up instigating a war against. In fact they are considered cousins to Israel. (Compare that with the purported crime and its subsequent curse in Genesis 9:20-27, that would be used later as Christendom's biblical justification for slavery and apartheid.)

In the bible, then, incestuous sexual abuse is tolerated, but if your father gets drunk and you happen on him sleeping naked, your ancestors will forever be slaves.

Another time homosexuality is mentioned is in the incidence of the Levite and his concubine. (Judges Ch: 19). This again as verse 22 indicates is a case of homosexual rape;

> "[Now] as they were making their hearts merry, behold, the men of the city, certain sons of Belial, beset the house round about, [and] beat at the door, and spake to the master of the house, the old man, saying, Bring forth the man that came into thine house, that we may know him."

If you care to read how that story is resolved in the next two chapters, you will think God writes Hollywood movies and men wrote the Bible (that is one of the worst stories of sex, gore and objectification of women you will ever read). But as I always say, what do you expect when God is a bloodthirsty Patriarch!

The act of sodomy is mentioned in 1 Kings 14:24:

"And there were also sodomites in the land: [and] they did according to all the abominations of the nations which the LORD cast out before the children of Israel."

(The internet version I am using here uses the word sodomite instead of pervert.

In the hard copy I am reading from—which happens to be my mum's New King James version—in relation to the word 'perverts' it gives a footnote to this effect: "That is those practicing sodomy and prostitution in religious rituals."

In my view then it is not clear whether the crime is in the action or the situation—is it the, *What* that is wrong or the *Where?*)

The book of Leviticus provides the only outright condemnation of homosexuality in the Old Testament:

Ch. 18:22: "Thou shalt not lie with mankind, as with womankind: it [is]an abomination."

Ch. 20:13: "If a man also lie with mankind, as he lieth with a woman, both of them have committed an abomination: they shall surely be put to death; their blood [shall be] upon them."

Now according to the *New Concise Bible Dictionary* (ed. Derek Williams), the warnings in Leviticus "are also primarily aimed at idolatry using the word 'abomination', which is a religious term often used for idolatrous practices." (I am taking that dictionary on its own authority since I cannot speak Greek, and, as I have once mentioned to the Pink Blogger, linguistics is not my forte. That word 'abomination', though, is what his Kikuyu Bible translates into: *thahu.*)

Then came the one of whom much had been written about: Jesus Christ. He that came to die that we may live. The Lamb of Pentecost. The Blood of the New Covenant. Moses' pension plan or is it Nemesis? He was God—Incarnate—walking amongst men, teaching about the way to the father. He taught about this and that but he never mentioned homosexuality. Yet he spoke of sin—and the forgiveness of sin—and his word was God.

The only outright condemnation of homosexuality in the New Testament comes from the reformed Pharisee, Paul of Tarsus.

1 Cor. 6:9: "Know ye not that the unrighteous shall not inherit the kingdom of God? Be not deceived: neither fornicators, nor idolaters, nor adulterers, nor effeminate, nor abusers of themselves with mankind."

1 Tim. 1:9: "For whoremongers, for them that defile themselves with mankind, for men-stealers, for liars, for perjured persons, and if there be any other thing that is contrary to sound doctrine."

(Incidentally, Paul/Saul never met Jesus and had spent his early years persecuting the so called Christians, yet he became the most influential protagonist (in Acts) and author (the

Epistles) of the Christian Canon. He is even considered more Orthodox than Peter, who was the Rock upon which Christ was to build his church, to a point where he won a doctrinal tiff between them: Gal. 2:14 and Acts Ch. 15).

This is just my reading from the Bible, I have used quotations from the Blue Letter Bible. Maybe now that I am at it, I should attempt what I call: 'Sermons of the Anglican'....later!

posted by POTASH at 15:08

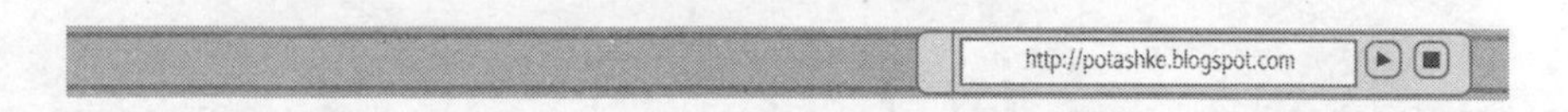

POTASH is a regular mid-twenties Kenyan guy trying to afford his next drop of alcohol. He has been in his mid-twenties for too long. His educational background remaining unknown, he continues to describe himself as a pseudo-intellectual. He detests yuppies, development cowboys and preachers who go bang in the night. On a regular Tuesday morning when you are working, he is sitting on a stone, in the mtaa, drinking, waiting for a half-life and writing about it. He confesses to having a longstanding grudge with Matathia.

Photograph: JNK / The Mindbender

High Stepping

BY

J. MBURU KABAA

In 1976, our family moved from the home in Kikuyu town to our New Canaan-Ondiri Farm. The farm was not far from Kikuyu town, only a twenty minute walk or so, up and down some hills and ridges, and around the waters known as Ondiri Swamp. A 200 acre farm which bordered the swamp. The swamp seemed sprawling. Our nearest neighbours seemed miles away in each direction. As a result, we never developed very close relationships with our neighbours. In fact, it seemed we were constantly mired in disputes over boundaries, and easements, and access to the swamp waters, and irrigation and other adult-like things.

We reared steers, cows for milk, sheep and goats for sale, as well as, chicken and pigs for slaughter. The farm also produced maize, sunflower, and Napier grass to feed the cattle. At its height, the farm probably employed upwards of thirty permanent staff and perhaps forty or fifty day workers – including many primary school-aged children, who supported their family's incomes or were simply unable to continue school for their meagre family earnings.

The rage at Hospital Hill during my middle years was building rival homesteads in the school's sprawling grounds. We called them camps. The camps were like attempts by middle class African children to build social groups, probably imbedded in our customs and traditions, akin to the clan and age group systems of our forefathers.

> The third principal factor in unifying the Gikuyu society is the system of age-grading *(riika)*. Almost every year, thousands of Gikuyu boys and girls go through the initiation or circumcision ceremony, and automatically become members of one age-grade *(riika rimwe)*, irrespective of *mbari* (family), *moherega* (clan), or district to which the individuals belongs They act as one body in all tribal matters and have a very strong bond of brotherhood and sisterhood among themselves! (*Facing Mount Kenya;* Jomo Kenyatta)

Each camp was built 10 feet in length and varying width, depending on the number in the camp. The walls were of grass and leaves, which were in plentiful supply thanks to the abundant grass throughout the school, at some places standing about two feet off the ground. During the morning and lunch breaks, we'd scrabble to get our home-packed lunches or race to buy hot dogs, samosas and mandazis at the "tuck shop," and then race back to our respective camps. The camps forged very close friendships—by eating, playing and sharing stories together in our make-believe homes away from home. Amongst my closest friends were Waititu, Patrick, Maureen, Steven and Edna, who formed the base of our camp. We played games together like soccer and marbles; raced cars; shared lunch and homework, and grew up almost as a family.

One game I enjoyed much in primary school was the game of three sticks. The game was quite simple. All it required was three sticks of about equal size, some flat ground, and a number of competitors. Three sticks could be played by as many people as were available. In the beginning, the three sticks were placed on the ground very close together—perhaps a foot apart. Each participant would have a go jumping over the sticks—one step only between each stick. First the participants would jump over the sticks from one side. Then when all the participants were done jumping in one direction, they would begin jumping in the other direction. The sticks would be spread in either direction according to the point at which the participant who jumped the farthest reached. As the game progressed, the sticks became further and further apart. Participants would then begin to fall out of the game as the distance required to jump widened. Soon only the best at the game survived.

Some students were known for their prowess. Alan was probably the most skilled. Allan was lean, very smart, but also very cocky. He ran incredibly fast. He started off by scaring the competition at the onset with his natural skills—really fast running and really huge jumps. This set the standard and he kept it. His running style was much like a cheetah's—he approached very low to the ground and jumped long, very long. Steven had a somewhat similar style, perhaps, less deftly executed but almost as good.

I too excelled at the sport. But I was not well equipped—being shorter than most of my competition. I did not have much of the personality to the game, either. I didn't take any noticeably different tact from the rest of the participants. And there wasn't much theatrics. But I was also much lighter as well. But as the bar was raised, I compensated with the only hidden advantage I had which was my size. I had an unusual style. Long-jumping technique usually calls for long and wide jumps.

Because I was much lighter I, well, literally flew over the sticks. I jumped high —very high—then propelled by the force and being lighter than the others, I simply went further. Finally, there were only one or two participants left remaining, a few sore with scrapes from the ground, and a lot of eager spectators. Of course, the game had to have a winner—unless the bell rang to return to class. At the end of the game, everybody feted and cheered the winner but camaraderie always carried the day.

By now the family was enjoying the relative comfort of my dad's well-paying job in the government. My mother's career, however, suffered given the attention she had to pay to her growing children and the anachronistic attitude my father had towards having a second breadwinner in the house.

I was still in primary school when my father bought a prize bull from Nairobi International Show. He brought it home and the bull seemed to grow even twice as large as it had been before we acquired it. It became so large it could no longer mount the cows without doing damage – or at least that was what my dad told me. One morning without notice, he told me that the bull was going to be taken to slaughter.

It stood a full meter or two above any of the other bulls and it had a rich dark almost pitch black color.

The bull was trekked about four miles to the slaughterhouse in Kikuyu. A crowd of twenty or so drew near to witness the sacrifice. The bull was penned in and its feet bound. A man with a large axe then mounted it, balancing his legs against the wooden stall. Then, he stood up straight and raised the axe high above his head. He studied and measured his prey.

It was the largest he had ever encountered. He aimed for the area right above its eyes. He drove the axe down into the head of the bull, holding the axe with both arms. The axe landed with a dull thud. The bull stood – almost unperturbed by the instrument. The man raised the axe again. Again, he drove it down into the bull's eye. Again, nothing happened.

I was overcome with grief.

Finally, however, the bull moaned. Then, its muscles began to twitch. The bull began to sway. Its legs buckled. Finally, the great big bull fell under its own dead weight. It would take hours before the head was finally torn from the neck. The head was at least two feet in height and must have weighed 50 kilos.

I stayed around for sometime to watch the carnage. Then, I departed, my heart torn out of me.

It was at about this time I began to become aware of an interest in boys. I don't know when this started or what brought it on. I just know that I began to yearn for the love and tenderness of boys and men. Jomo Kenyatta himself wrote about the practice amongst boys. However, Kenyatta couched it as a sort of competitive spirit or sport. Was Kenyatta winking at sexual practices amongst his people that he knew acknowledging would reveal even deeper, darker taboo subjects?

Whatever the cause I knew the moral high handedness of many Africans.

I began to turn my interest to boys and the things that normal boys liked. Normal boys my age were into riding bikes, boasting about their television sets and accumulating a dizzying array of electronic games.

Around Standard Four, my brothers and I joined Hodari Boys Club, a bicycle racing group which was run by Strathmore College, a Jesuit Catholic School where my brothers attended high school. In Standard Five, I entered into the bicycle race with one of my *commando* bicycles that father had purchased on one of his trips abroad.

The race was divided into three legs and into two or three age groups. I was in the middle league, competing against some boys three or four years older than me. By the end of the second leg, I was coming into the lead. I was about a mile or so from the finish line.

This last stretch, however, required navigating a steep descent down towards Strathmore College. Never fully comfortable at high speeds, I tried to maintain my balance on the bicycle. But as my momentum increased, going down the hill, I lost control of the handlebars. Before long, they were shaking uncontrollably.

Next thing I knew, I was scraping the tarmac road with my thigh, elbow and forehead, and gushing with blood at all three contact points. When I finally managed to get back on my bike and ride it, gingerly down towards the finish line, I was covered in blood. Undaunted, however, I completed the final leg of the race, in fifth place, earning accolades from my friends and family. The scars remained like a badge of honour and a physical reminder to maintain balance, watch my speed coming down, and to always stay the race.

I completed my primary school exit examinations, KCPE exams, in December 1976. I went to St. Mary's school. St. Mary's School was run by Irish Catholics, but this was hardly a perceptible difference for an African Presbyterian, little aware of the numerous sects and denominations within the body of Christ.

St. Mary's School could count amongst its students—the sons of all three presidents, of numerous vice-presidents, countless ministers, and other high-ranking government officials, not to mention executives of the largest multinationals in East Africa.

It also had a large smattering of the children of the well-heeled white expatriate community as well as Sikhs, Hindus, Pakistanis and Arabs and others. One could hardly be blamed if they completely overlooked the school's Irish/Roman Catholic roots or the school's motto being *Bonas Disciplinas Scentia* and simply thought St. Mary's was so named for the most pretentious, petulant, materialistic boys this side of The West.

I was now a teenager, puberty delayed, and experiencing confusing sexual thoughts. I immediately drew the attention of fellow classmates and not always favourably. In my first year, I was often the victim of harassment and beatings by many students in my class and others. Not the truly scary bullying my classmates from Hospital Hill endured at the likes of Lenana School. But the harassment I experienced was a clear example of the excesses of boys when they disliked or denied those aspects in themselves which in others they found aberrant and abhorrent.

I retreated from my African peers and instead sought the friendship of non-Africans. In my first year, my closest friends were mostly Kenyan Indians. From them I would learn many Gujarati and Hindi words – almost all expletives, almost always used first on me.

Second year, we took a trip together to Mombasa, stayed together at Diani Beach Hotel in the south coast. I was the only *Gandu* in the group. The trip was quite memorable. Mostly for the many ways my friends taunted me. I was eager to fit in; and made me perform various humiliating antics. Soon the taunting became unbearable. I began to resent their presence.

Finally, while sitting in the hotel veranda, enjoying the setting sun over drinks and little banter, Chirag targeted me for some blistering insults. I shot back with a tart retort—commenting about his academic aptitude.

Without any hesitation, he shot up from where he sat and slapped me across the face. I was stunned and burned with anger. I thought I could tear off his flesh with my teeth—like *Kali.* But the sound had drawn the attention of the rest of the hotel guests most of whom were white. I dared not to start a fight. I was already feeling uncomfortably out of place, surrounded by Indians, likely to protect their own, and would now have to face the judgment and disdain of the white guests for spoiling the quiet and serenity.

During my first year at St. Mary's, a craze developed amongst my classmates. It was part mischief, part pre-adolescent hormones kicking. While the instructor was teaching, two students sitting next to each other would engage in a bet.

It was quite brazen. The two would begin a competition, fondling each other, in class to see how long it would take before one of the two got a hard-on. Hands would fall under the desk, locate the other boy's shorts and begin to arouse the little snake.

Here was an unwritten rule that you couldn't actually touch beneath the shorts and underwear—but nobody was telling. Students often exchanged places before class began to avoid monotony. I became rather adept at this game.

But I never really stood much of a chance when it came to holding out. This was one game I often lost but was much rewarded in. I developed a crush for a handsome and athletic but shy student in my class called Andrew. Nothing happened between Andrew and me, however, besides exchanging uneasy and fleeting moments of physical intimacy by the swimming pool changing room or after school. That year, I received the General Excellence Award for my class.

I wondered whether the award was not also the result of the camaraderie and closeness I had actively nurtured with many of my classmates.

It was about this time that my father called me to witness the operation of his new projection camera at Kikuyu Country Club. When the screen lit up it flashed the haunting rape scene from the movie *Deliverance.* I was caught shamefaced and turned away immediately. But it was also undeniable – this yearning I felt deep within me.

The scene kindled my nascent feelings of homosexuality. But the violence and the words "scream like a pig" etched in a more sinister message in my mind.

My dad witnessed my reaction with a growing sense of disquiet but said nothing. He simply stared at me.

As many of my classmates started chasing Loreto Msongari girls, I took up other interests. I joined the annual production of the Saint Mary's School Opera. The well-known operas were really renditions of famous American musicals by Rogers and Hammerstein, Bernstein and such. Nevertheless, the production standards were quite high and the leading actors and actresses displayed unusual talent and looks.

The weeklong production took place during the first term and in the evenings. This meant that for weeks, I stayed late singing in the choir lines or choreographing dance steps. The evening rehearsals and productions were a rare opportunity to be out late in school. They also provided the first opportunity to release the pent-up sexual feelings stirring within me but suppressed during class and daytime.

When the auditions took place, I went to try out for the choir. I was shy and embarrassed. Behind me stood all the other boys also eager to vie for a part in the choir. The music instructor tapped on the piano indicating the keys I should sing. I shut my eyes and sang the lines. Then, he tapped some other keys as he tried to figure out my range. I sang.

He repeated the process, this time an octave higher. Again, I sang. He stared at me quizzically. Then, he shifted his fingures again and tapped the keys. I pierced through the quiet like a swan in the night.

"Njoroge," he said, calling me by my family name. "Do you know you're a few keys short of singing like an opera queen?"

I blushed and said nothing. He repeated the process once more, for clarity. Then he shouted loud.

"First soprano!" And I joined a handful of boys and the girls in Form Five and Six singing soprano.

This year's performance was *The King and I.* I had just been on stage with the choir. The play was now coming to an end and I wanted to catch the climax. I took a seat in the back row, near the rear entrance. Just as I sat down, I noticed Andrew, sitting right next to me. My heart began to race. I had no sooner sat down and exchanged greetings before he was eagerly reaching into my pants.

I offered weak protest. I was concerned about it with him in public. But this was such a rare opportunity. He mumbled something and before I could even respond, he was bending forward towards my privates. I starred at the row of heads in front me. To my right was wall that jutted some few feet in front of me which provided some cover. But there were other faces on our row although they seemed to be riveted to the action on the theatre stage.

Even still, I could not imagine such unabashed lewdness in public. I pulled away hastily. Andrew felt spurned. I tried to explain but it was impossible unless I wanted to let everybody in on what was going on.

He angrily left the building. I followed him out. I met him by the school quadrangle. He was still angry. I tried to talk to him suggestively, but he was now embarrassed and angry with me. He turned away and left.

The following year we performed *South Pacific.* But besides starring at each other longing, nothing happened below the equator. Inside me, now burned this unquenched desire to be in the arms of another man.

During the following year's production, *Oklahoma,* we finally consummated two years of tense longing and sexual frustration.

We had just been performing a dance on stage. The dance choreography was an Africanized version of the classic American country western musical. Andrew and I both took part. The dance itself was a hybrid -- half South African gum boot dance, half Country Western dancing. We were dressed head to toe in western country boots and studded belts.

After the dance, Andrew and I agreed to meet behind the school's squash courts. Our blood raced and we were bubbling over with nervous energy. He made quick haste undoing the buttons to my pants. I told him I loved him. He ordered me to go down on my knees and fellate him.

"A blow job?" I had not heard the word before. I surmised his intent by the way he kept pushing my shoulders down to his crotch.

"I can't, Andrew; I just can't."

Then, he stared into my eyes, stooped down to me, and put his lips on mine. Then he placed his arms around my waist. Then he returned to his earlier demands.

"John, ohh, please ... please just do it!"

I promised; if he reciprocated.

I took him in my mouth. Not long after, he groaned, jerked and spurted into the ground.

When he was done, he hastily drew up his pants and made ready to retreat.

I was angry, and showed it. But now he was preaching, and condemning sex with other men as a sin. He was not gay, he said. He seemed sickened by my presence.

Finally he relented. He offered a hasty hand job. When it was over, he left briskly. Although we were in the same class, we hardly spoke again. Andrew developed into a star athlete—playing soccer and rugby. He had also developed quite a reputation, as well, with the girls. His self-esteem seemed unperturbed by the events of that night. His reputation as an athlete, ace student and lady-killer was soaring.

The incident left me bitter and afraid.

I was leprous and could never be cured. I feared it was now readily apparent to everybody. If I became obsessed with thoughts of sex with men, I compensated for it by trying to date women. I devised a balance upon which I endeavoured to balance my iniquity—my feelings for boys against my virtue—scoring with girls.

Dating girls failed. Most seemed little attracted to me. Many saw through my weakly veiled attempt at heterosexuality. With others, I felt worse still, for my vanity, in trying to pawn off myself as something I could never be.

Our old home in Kikuyu town had become the thriving night spot, the Kikuyu Country Club. The Club had a storied past. In its early days, the late seventies and early eighties, KCC, as it was more commonly known, was a meeting place for many of Kenya's African elite. It aspired to be the likes of Karen's Country Club then a haven for Kenya's expatriate British community. Over the years, however, the business and political elite migrated to more ambitious clubs.

KCC's clientele changed and it became a nightclub catering to a moderate-income and younger clientele from Nairobi and its environs.

In December, I made my first foray as a member of Kenya's workforce. I worked weekend's taking gate collections for the disco featuring resident DJ Paddy Moore. Other nights, I played bouncer—quite laughably since I was still pint-sized.

The weekend intrigue, which often included a bar brawl—bottles, fists and all—was a welcome respite from evenings at home. Many guests would opt to spend the night in the club's guest houses. KCC was the place to take your mistress, or somebody you picked up in the wrong side of town.

My mother had been rearing chickens for a while, and received a steady income from selling the chicken to restaurants and other businesses in the city. Realizing I needed only a minimum investment, I purchased my own day-old chicks and began rearing chicken. Although, I had despised farm work, I took to the business quite seriously, which surprised my father.

It was during this holiday that I came to befriend Kamau. Kamau, one of the farm workers, oversaw the milk production, recording the daily output, in the mornings and evenings, before it was transported on the farm pickup truck to be sold. He would also ration the milk for the farm workers, for us at home, as well as the daily portion for the calves.

I would often accompany him in the evenings after feeding my chicken when he measured the milk from the evening's production and fed the calves. Kamau was three or four years older than I was, but was boyish, almost childlike. He was fair-skinned, handsome and had a great smile and a solid physique. He had attended high school and as a result we made easy conversation—switching back and forth from my halting Kikuyu to his broken English.

During this time together we would tease each other about girls or drinking.

"Kamau, you like making me laugh a lot." I said to him in Kikuyu.

"Yes, it is because you are nice and I like you." He replied, the words catching me off guard.

"And why is it you sound like you have a lisp." I responded guardedly.

"Ohh, it is because of my homo!" He said tongue in cheek, simultaneously bursting out in laughter.

My ears pricked up. I was stunned. I said nothing but our eyes joined briefly in a moment of bliss. Had he just dropped an awkward comment intimating he was homosexual?

A few weeks later, he invited me to his house. His house—really a shack—was one of a number of small brick and sheet metal roofed rooms a small distance from the farm house, just by the entrance to the farm. I told my mum I would be with Kamau for the evening.

She appeared unconcerned that I was fraternizing with a farm worker but had been watching our budding friendship with a mixture of caution and curiosity. When I arrived it was still early evening, perhaps, five-thirty or six o'clock. We spent the rest of the evening chatting and laughing. Then my eyes chanced on a piece of newspaper with an article mentioning homosexuality. I asked him to read it, lying that I wanted to gauge his English skills.

He invited me to stay for dinner. His company alone whetted my appetite. We ate a simple meal of *Ugali* and *Sukumawiki.* Then, he asked whether I would spend the night. The prospect of sharing the same bed with him made me tremble with excitement.

I answered yes eagerly, despite not having not my mum I would be staying the night.

Before long, we had shed our clothing down to our underwear and crawled into bed. We lay side by side in his bed, talking, barely touching. Our conversation continued for a little time before it became increasingly punctuated by heavy breathing and awkward pauses. Before long, the conversation stalled. It was replaced by first tentative and then increasingly sensual exploration with our hands.

This was the first time I had experienced such normal, casual intimacy with another person. The bedroom setting gave it an almost familial aura—as if it had just been our normal routine to have dinner and then go to sleep together. In bed, side by side, it seemed the most natural expression of our mutual affection and longing.

Next to him, I felt like a star. My insides burned. Soon we were locked in a tight embrace, squeezing the distance between us like two stars caught in parallel orbit.

Within seconds, I succumbed, begging for sexual intimacy.

Kamau demanded more attention but he too finally climaxed, his muscles pulsating throughout his body. When we were done, we lay side by side, breathing heavily, both enchanted. I felt like a heavenly body, crossing the night. I was light, and free of my past.

But no. In a few moments, we heard a loud hooting noise in the night. It was soon followed by an equally loud knock at his door. I heard my sister's voice,

"John, John, are you there?"

"Yes, yes, I answered." I answered, still sluggish and happy.

It took a moment for me to realize the threat. I dressed quickly and opened the door.

"John, you are in so much trouble!"

And with that, she turned and walked back to the pickup truck, parked a hundred yards or so from Kamau's house. I remained silent and followed her dutifully; Kamau followed a few paces behind.

Within minutes, I was back at home. I found a large group of people had gathered—farm workers, the farm manager, my father, and two police officers.

"Where have you been?" he asked in a high pitched baritone that clanged in my eardrums. His fists descended upon my face, crashing against my jaw.

I fell to my knees. I collected myself and got up.

I ran towards the gate but they locked before I could make it.

"If you leave, don't ever come back!" My dad blared in Kikuyu.

Before I reached the fence of the compound, three men closed in on me. In the background, I could hear my sister and mother screaming. Kamau had sensed trouble and ran away before I did. The police caught up with him the next day and he was beaten and interrogated for hours at Kikuyu Police Station before being released. The day he was released, he was fired from work.

I was taken into the dining room, escorted by the two police officers. I was interrogated for three hours. He noticed some red stains on my light blue three-quarter Capri pants. I had gotten them earlier in the day from eating raspberries.

"What is THAT on your pants?" he again demanded.

"Did he drug you or poison you?"

Apparently, my mother had suggested that her innocent son might have been caught in the clutches of another man; in her mind this was the only reason her son would be caught in bed with another man.

"So what did you do there together?"

"Did you sleep in the same bed?"

"John, are you a—homosexual!"

Was I a heretic, a blasphemer, or an unrepentant sinner? Who were my judges? Surely, not the same employees who seemed quick to lie, cheat and steal to make ends meet? How many times had they relied on my intercession on their behalf? Were they themselves blotless? Surely, not the managers nor the police officers who acted as if they were steeped in corruption? Not my dad? Didn't I know and see with my own eyes what happened every Friday and Saturday night at his club?

"No!" I answered finally, staring him directly in his face, my own fury and anger beginning to stir within me. It was a terse response. It was final.

And it was a lie. It was almost daylight when I finally got to sleep. But even as the sun came up I knew the events of the earlier night had changed my life and my relationship with my family forever.

Perhaps, boarding school could be my salvation. I joined Lenana School, named after the last laibon (leader) of the Maasai who was broken by the British, and who oversaw the conquest and humiliation of his people.

Lenana School whose motto was *Nihil Praeter Optimum*—Nothing but the Best—and had the country's number one reputation for bullying.

In fact, the school's nickname Changez memorialized this reputation—for there, it was said, boys turned to men.

J. MBURU KABAA lives in California.

Blogguy™ GET YOUR OWN BLOG FLAG? NEXT BLOG>>

AUTOEROTIC ASPHYXIATION

Wednesday, May 24, 2006

Personally I blame Dr. Hannibal Lecter for introducing me not only to pulp fiction but also to Auto-Erotic-Asphyxiation (AEA). I can say, on the basis of empiricist data, that AEA works. But it is technically illegal, considering that your local magistrate, not being famous for sexual inventiveness, can only view it as attempted suicide. Though the presence of a partner could be useful in case things go wrong, things could still go wrong—blame that on Sod's Law! If you were to die, your partner could end up spending a lifetime as a Jail House pussy or worse, still, get Auto Erotically Asphyxiated by the Government executioner.

As a matter of record, I would insist that you do not try it at home. But the pervert's Regimental Motto is: a hard on has no conscience, so I know you just might try it. Therefore, as your shrink takes his Corporate Social Responsibility seriously, I recommend that you use a rope with low breaking strain. That could make all the difference between your living to see your next orgasm or not.

Considering that AEA is dependent on an adrenaline high, there are other activities, besides manual strangulation, that could be used to achieve a similar effect and that can actually be seen to achieve greater utility in the punishment-reward equation. Robbing a bank, for instance, is a multiple orgasm experience, not only because of the thrill of the heist but also the subsequent sight of an enormous amount of money. (Incidentally, money can buy you a session of vaginal masturbation—a hooker that is—or a colostomy bag in case a stray bullet connects with your nether viscera.)

In the sex and drugs era, which our juvenile delinquent set referred to as Westland's Summer of '99, I knew a dude named Gogo. Gogo wasn't twisted—heck, everyone was twisted in those days and life was one big hallucination—he was fucked up. He was so fucked up that had he been a white boy, he would have slit his wrists. This dude used to drive out to the open stretch of garbage that demarcates Woodley from Kibera with his 'pussy of the day'. He would leave her in the car, walk over to the railway line, light a spliff and wait for the train.

As the train thundered past him missing him by an ass-hair, Gogo would run back into the car flashing the kind of boner that would make Sebastian, the huge ape at the Nairobi Orphanage, cover himself in shame. Once in the car, the medically provable aphrodisiac effect of Delta-9-Tetrahydrocannabinol, adrenaline after burn and the pheromone studded animal smell of mortal fear conspired to make Gogo the much sought after fuck-buddy that he was.

All that until Nana, the infamous Westie Succubus discovered that in the absence of train games, Gogo was doomed to earn Frequent Flyer Miles on Air Viagra. It wasn't our business to know, but the heck we now did. What a coupe de grace; now Gogo couldn't even have sex with his right hand without the left one sniggering at him. Certainly that *Dawg's* penis had gone to the dogs... it's (Morning) Glory days were over. Anyway come September Gogo left for *Uni* in England—and so did about everyone else.

Psychoanalysts say that it is all in the mind. That in the absence of a deeper physiological problem, a man finding himself unable to rise to the occasion need only believe in himself that he can and he will. The traditional healer at the exorbitant fee of a heifer of one body will give you your own pee to drink and tell you to imagine yourself a simba... *Raauuu... Rauuuu!* Gogo was a lion, in a new concrete jungle. The cock of Nairobi could crow in Northumberland. But first he had to be rid of the Kenyan crowd. His past. So he ignored them.

In his thinking, who needed a past when the future was a rainbow nation of orgasms? ...his name screamed in varied accents... picturesque colour chromatography as ebony dips into sepia, olive, tan or *onlygodfuckingknowswhat* shade of melanin privilege. Gogo was soon spotted by the railway line with a string of eager freshmen. Waiting. Naked. Spliffing. Hey even some of them—those with numerous freckles, braces and, no price for guessing, slit wrists—would walk with him all the way to the line and play the train game. Foreplay!

In those Westie years still, there was a dude named Binji. Binji was a hustler. Okay, his occupation was unknown (who cared about occupations, we were professional bums- Young Urban Posers!) Binji was more blinged out than a hip hop video but most importantly, he had strange merchandise. Stuff like this hundred-dollar bill that was issued by the US Confederate States during the civil war. One day, he showed me something I found infinitely more interesting-a postcard. A postcard made in the Dirty South, circa 1918.

The picture on the postcard is of a lynch party. A dirty nigger hangs from a maple tree. He has shat himself but I do not think he has ejaculated. It is too soon after... you know he was caught...! Huh, but it takes two to tango? I do not know about that but I do know that a Black Widow ain't necessarily black... boy!

At the foot of the tree, a pre-coital mood freeze framed. Men hold up sjamboks and riffles-Phalluses of the Sadists! On the other hand each holds a token, a woman. The men below seem to be wishing that the women will equate what they hold in their hands with what is in their pants. Power! And the women look up. They seem to be asphyxiated by the Auto Erotically Engorged Mandingo.

The Savage is up on the tree—not cutting much of a Christ figure—and the Neurotics down below. Is it a Freudian Point of Agreement between the Mental Lives of Savages and Neurotics? Who knows, but I am a theorist—I can put sex on a pedestal... or up a Maple tree!

Everyone at the foot of the tree looks sex ready. Everyone wants to have sex with someone. But not everyone will have sex with whoever they are most attracted to (sometimes even the plausible Darwinian Theory of the dominant male decides to go wank. In those instances, people will settle for the monkey with the dubious cranial structures and shrug: The heck, I am horny!)

It is a scene loaded with sexual meaning. A scene that proves that both the asphxiator and the asphyxiatee can share a single, fleeting moment of erotic stimulation...

On the upper left hand side of the picture, a mockingbird takes to flight!

posted by POTASH at 11:30 | 19 comments»

POTASH is a regular mid-twenties Kenyan guy trying to afford his next drop of alcohol. He has been in his mid-twenties for too long. His educational background remaining unknown, he continues to describe himself as a pseudo-intellectual. He detests yuppies, development cowboys and preachers who go hang in the night. On a regular Tuesday morning when you are working, he is sitting on a stone, in the mtaa, drinking, waiting for a half-life and writing about it. He confesses to having a longstanding grudge with Matathia.

ph / Illustration: JNK

Phtotgraph: JNK

Lowlife

BY ANDIA KISIA

*T*his isn't my life. This life belongs to some git that not very long ago, I wouldn't have given so much as the time of day, that I'd have walked right past if I'd met him in the street, assuming I'd even noticed him in the first place. If I'd have had the occasion to speak to him, I'd have given him a piece of my mind, told him a few home truths about himself, to get up out of the gutter and clean the muck off himself and think about acquiring the semblance of a life.

This git spends most of his life in the kitchen at Houlihan's, elbow deep in scummy water, pulverising the accretions of the continental menu from an assembly line of plates, side plates, soup bowls and a variety of glassware. Three nights a week, he takes the train to Jersey and spends it house-sitting for three adult nutcases. He is, in a word, a loser.

I am not a loser. No one who knows me would say that I was. In fact, I have a famous intolerance for losers as for all lower forms of life, an intolerance that has cost me more than a few friends.

This git has, however, managed to insinuate his miserable life into mine, so completely in fact that he has taken it over. When he's not at the kitchen sink or babysitting nutters, that git spends large chunks of his life in my living room drinking Bud and pondering the mysteries of the universe which have brought him so low.

I should evict him of course, just pack up his shit and all the evidence of his third-rate life and leave it out on the street. I haven't been able to do it yet. Maybe I'm a nicer guy than I think. Maybe I'm not the asshole that everyone seems to think I am. Maybe I have some as yet undiscovered reservoir of the milk of human kindness.

He's gotten awfully familiar with me. I suppose he must think that deep down, we're really the same kind of guy, that we have lots in common, that we might get to be the best of friends. Of course he knows nothing of my former life, of Haverford College and the full scholarship and my summers interning at Smith Barney and the evenings living it up in all the best spots in Manhattan. I haven't told him any of that yet. Not much anyway. I started to talk one day about something or other but I stopped when I caught him looking at me kind of funny, as if I was a bit touched in the head, as if he was a little sorry for my delusions. He didn't say anything though, just nodded as if he understood perfectly what I was saying. I haven't tried again. That stuff, I keep to myself, it's what keeps me going, what sweetens the bile of this git's life that I'm living now; Houlihan's, South Jersey and a cramped studio in West Philly with filthy wall to wall and gits to the left of me, gits to the right of me, all of whom think I'm one of them. One of the hundreds of Africans who come to America with stars in their eyes which get progressively dimmer in the years and years of scrubbing toilets and washing dishes. The only thing I was sure of when I got to Philadelphia six years ago was that I was never going to be one of them.

I've never had to do stuff like this before. My mother would have a fit if she could see me now. When I was younger, she would throw a fit if I so much as looked in the direction of the kitchen at home and make the maid get me whatever it was I wanted in there. She brought me up to believe that people have their place and that mine was not elbow deep in greasy water at the kitchen sink. And of course there was always someone to do the dishes and the cooking and pick up after me and my brother. A succession of house maids and Joseph the miraculous cook who used to work for some British expat family and had an extensive repertoire of English food that he would whip up and present ever so proudly every night. For all I know, Joseph is still slicing and dicing and whipping up all sorts of amazing food, though for a much depleted household since my brother and I came to Philadelphia and there's just my mother and my little sister at home now.

But of course there's no chance of my mother seeing me. I haven't seen her in years. The last time I talked to her, and even that was six months ago, she asked me how I looked.

"The same, pretty much," I said.

"But you can't possibly look the same, after all this time."

I'm not much given over to thinking about how I look, so I had to think about it for a while. And even then, "Older," was the best I could do.

I have John to thank for this job. John is one of the more prominent members of the Kenyan invasion, Philadelphia chapter. He is the hooker-upper for a certain type of Kenyan who arrives in America every month sans papers. He knows every restaurant kitchen and gas station and care home for miles around. He's one of those guys who came here with their eyes on a prize and are working their four jobs to get there. And going to school. Hats off to them boys. I wasn't interested: I had no need to be. Until now.

We hadn't exchanged more than a few words in all the years we'd known each other, so he was ecstatic to help me find a job, to look pensive and unsure and tell me that he didn't know if it was possible, and that there were dozens of guys looking for a place – he called it a "situation" – and that if my papers weren't on the up and up – Were they on the up and up? No? He thought as much—he'd likely get in trouble, and he couldn't risk that, and a whole bunch of other shit. He was getting off putting the stuck up rich kid in his place, just pissing his pants at the opportunity to give me a hard time.

This has been a recurring theme of my life after Haverford. There's no shortage of people lining up to give me a hard time. For miles and miles behind me there are dozens of still smouldering bridges, bridges I find myself having to cross again.

I waited until he was done getting off—and that took a while—before I told him to cut the crap and just get me a damned job. The way I saw it, I was doing him a favour even asking him for a favour. He laughed at that and said he'd call me in a couple of days. I told him to make it the next day and he laughed again and said he'd see what he could do. Of course he let me sweat for a week before calling to tell me about a situation as a dishwasher at Houlihan's and could I come down the next day for an interview. I told him I thought it was stupid to be interviewing for a dishwashing job. "I've got two hands," I said, "I'm qualified." He told me to quit bitching and just do the interview, that they interviewed everyone, no matter what the "situation" was they were interested in and anyway it was just a formality. So I went in next day and did what I could to hide my utter lack of enthusiasm and had to stop myself from sneering when Ed, the manager asked me with a deadly earnest look on his face why he should hire me and what I would be bringing to the "Houlihan's family," as if I was interviewing for CEO of some *Fortune* five hundred joint. Unfortunately for me, I did get the job, beating out what John assured me was a strong field who must have been pretty pathetic to be turned down for a job like that.

I arrived an hour late for my first day at work. Even though I'd never really been in a kitchen before, I felt right at home in this one. Pretty much everyone else in there was Kenyan too, and they were about as happy to see me as I was to see them. The malice was palpable. It made for a touching homecoming.

They sulked and slouched. No one said a word to me, though they watched me more than a little suspiciously. I knew they were unhappy with newcomers muscling in on their floor scrubbing, adult diaper changing niches. Especially newcomers like me.

Some though, were only too happy to watch me squirm, to see me get into the grimy uniform and grimace at the clammy feel of the gloves on my hands. One hulking guy, looking particularly stupid in his apron asks me what the matter is, "You never washed dishes before?" The others snicker.

A guy like me, a good middle-class boy like me has certain natural enemies, people exactly like the cast of characters around me now—working-class boys with aspirations, with an inflated sense of their place in the scheme of things, who thought that just because you were living the same nightmare, you *was* all brothers and shit. That just being in America was going to be enough to remove the stain of questionable antecedents, to scrub clean the dirty laundry of a childhood in Dandora and high school at Ofafa Jericho. We have nothing in common but our passports and that isn't basis enough for any interaction. At this point, I'm way beyond expedient alliances. Who resented the fact that I refused to be smeared in their camaraderie.

I did what I always do when presented with a cohort of my countrymen, I pretended they weren't there. Still, every day in the restaurant rubbed me raw.

John finds me two other jobs, one looking after three mildly retarded adults and another as a parking lot attendant on the night shift. The git was here to stay.

In the months after that I settled into a relatively simple schedule, pared to the bare minimum, going through the motions and plotting how I was going to get my life back, get the hell out of here and away from these poisonous people. Then I'd walk across the Schuylkill to the Houlihan's on Rittenhouse Square where I was a productive member of the American labour force. My day consisted of steaming hot water, a hose and pulverising the accretions of our continental menu from an assembly line of plates. Two evenings a week, I took the train to South Jersey to the care home and the warming embrace of my three nutcases. Three evenings a week, I dozed in the guard's booth at a parking lot off South Street. Most of the money I made went to rent, the rest I saved. This was meant to be the beginning of what I hoped would be the relatively brief business of reconstructing my life. I should have known it wouldn't be as easy as all that.

One day, after a particularly rancorous day at the office, when I wanted nothing more than to get home and fall asleep with a bottle of Bud in my hand in the company of *Dr. Quinn Medicine Woman,* I get home to find Charlie sitting on my doorstep. I spot him from a long way off. He smiles when he sees me, eyes shadowed behind dark glasses, gives me the treatment, smiles out loud, like floodlights coming on.

"Mato!" He grins and seems genuinely pleased to see me.

That smile is the nicest thing about him, the sudden, unexpected softness in a handsome but hard face. It has a quality in it of childish glee, unfettered and vital, conferring on him a vulnerability which is quite out of keeping with the man I know. That man has nothing left in him of innocence or of softness.

Charlie and I have one of those friendships that arise out of crisis and are strengthened by a continued production of the same, so that when I found him sitting outside my door step that July morning, I knew there was trouble brewing, though knowing Charlie it had probably percolated and was ready to serve. We've had nothing but bad times together Charlie and I, and it's as good a foundation for a lasting friendship as any I know. Better than most in fact because trust is at its very essence. You can get real close to the guy who hides you from the cops and gives you the fare to get out of town. And when you start off like that, you can't go back to small talk and niceties and bullshit. So it was with Charlie and I: conducted in the space between mild disturbance and catastrophe, it was the only real friendship I had.

It might be accurate to say that it is the only friendship I have left, the only one I haven't shed along with my innocence, the only one that has survived the accretions of cynicism and the knowledge that no longer allowed us to excuse the divergences between what we wanted in our lives and how far short the people we knew were falling from that or straight up fucking it up. Then it became impossible to make excuses for them, for their inadequacies and the little cruelties we'd inflicted on each other over the years and which piled up and poisoned everything between us. Perhaps my only friend since I realised the nest I had gotten so cosy in was full of vipers and other unsavoury things.

I met him first three years ago; a good looking man lying shirtless on the couch in a mutual friend's house, smoking weed and playing video games to while away a particularly oppressive Philadelphia summer. He was between deals again and homeless and crashing on a succession of couches in a succession of houses. Charlie has probably seen more couches than most furniture salesmen ever will. Between deals and homeless is his usual state of affairs. When he isn't working, he plays video games and smokes spliff. What Charlie calls work is of great interest to law enforcement officers in several states. They've been trying to catch him for years. Charlie thinks he's too smart to get caught. He maintains a healthy contempt for the police.

After a few months, Charlie found the welcome worn quite thin. Our friend however, hadn't had the courage to broach the subject of his leaving. Charlie's charm mitigates against such unpleasantness. But even he was sensible to the growing hostility and he asked if he could crash on mine.

He has the easy charm that shysters have as a matter of course. Shysters and criminals and gigolos and other likeable rogues. He knew that I had seen what so many other people failed to and he smiled that smile at me, genuinely amused. We hit it off immediately. And then we found out how much we had in common. A deep and abiding contempt for everything. A deep and abiding sense of our own importance even in the face of our vastly reduced circumstances. Well, my circumstances weren't reduced then, all that was still in the future, though not a distant enough future. I still had my scholarship to Haverford and was still a little giddy from a summer interning in New York which had strengthened my sense of all the good things that were just waiting for me when I graduated. We talked for hours, mostly about cricket, Charlie devastatingly funny in his careful, impeccably phrased speech with an accent that swerved wildly between R.P and French. He told me that he'd gone quite young to public school in England from Congo, but the French accent had never quite disappeared. The public school bit rather intimidated me. I had gone to a government boarding school in Kenya, though at a time when government boarding schools were still respectable, even exclusive, when well off families still sent their children there, when we still had bangers and mash for lunch and cake and custard for afters, and called them afters.

Charlie is standing up now, and walking down the steps to meet me. I'm not happy to see him exactly. I love Charlie but he's the last thing I need in my life right now. I slow down, smile back while the wheels turn and turn in my head. He sees my indecision and his lip curls slightly. He doesn't believe I have it in me to send him away and he's right because I bend to pick his bag up off the top step and reach into my pocket for my keys.

"How'd you find me?" I ask him, unlocking my front door.

"Grapevine," he says and smiles again.

I laugh. "No shit."

"Were you hiding?" he asks me.

"What do you think?"

He laughs out loud at that, bending over and slapping his thigh. He knows what I'm hiding from. And he knows as well as I do that it's a waste of time playing peekaboo with yourself. You always know where to look.

"How about you?" I ask him.

"Always," he agrees, still grinning. "Always."

The bag is Louis Vuitton, the relic of an older, more prosperous time. Last winter to be precise. That winter of our content brought also a camel coloured Jones of New York trench coat, two suits made to measure at the Polo store on Walnut Street and five pairs of Allen Edmonds shoes. The guys at the Polo store were a little surprised to see us. They were even more surprised to be paid in cash. They examined it as if it were a souvenir of a far off and rather quaint age. I think Charlie must have looked pretty stupid lugging that bag around on the Greyhound. But then Charlie's things, the good things in life are indispensable as distractions from the squalor he's made for himself. And he never denies himself anything he wants, even if someone else has to pay for it. Inside my apartment, he unpacks his PlayStation and plugs it in. That, too is from last winter.

"What? No couch?" he asks jokingly. He settles down happily enough on the cushions strewn around the floor and begins to play Tomb Raider. "Where were you coming from?" he asks.

"Work," I say, embarrassed. Industry is a deplorable quality in Charlie's eyes. No. Not deplorable, piteous. And then, trying for lightness, "How do you think I pay for all this?"

"What kind of work?"

"The only kind I can get," I say, not feeling very light-hearted at all. "The kind I'd rather not talk about."

He nods and goes back to his game. I join him on the cushions and watch for a while.

"So dude," I ask. "What do you want to do?" when what I really want to ask is "What are you doing here? And more to the point, "What do you want?"

He mimes a smoking motion.

"Nah man," I apologise. "Gave that up."

"That's too bad," he says. "You're not getting all respectable on me?"

"Not a chance," I assure him. Not a chance in hell. Although it's not for a lack of trying.

The thing is, I've been trying for an awfully long time.

Other than the weed and the *Play Station,* Charlie only ever wants to do one thing. When I come back in from the kitchen with a six pack of beer, Charlie makes a sweeping gesture with his hand.

"I approve," he says.

"Fuck. So do I man." Another round of slightly hysterical laughter. There's nothing in my apartment except the cushions on the floor and a few mismatched plates and cups I got at the thrift store. But we've been through worse, Charlie and I. We laugh a long time. Laughter and cruelty, staying the sly thing that was skirting slowly around us.

The thing is, I've been trying for an awfully long time to achieve my former respectability. In the meantime though, I've been in plenty of unpleasant places.

When Charlie had finally run out of friends and acquaintances with apartments and couches he could crash on, he'd asked if he could crash on mine. I had lived in a succession of dives since I'd left Haverford. The house I was living in then was the worst one yet. Even Charlie who had learned to remove himself from the mostly unpleasant circumstances in which he found himself was shocked. It was a mess. Not just untidy, but so dirty that the dirt had become somehow integral to the house itself.

Things got worse every day. On a really bad day, the decline was hourly. Strange stains appeared on the wall. A draught came in through another broken window. The wooden floor outside the bathroom was always wet and began to rot.

I had allowed Abdoul, a Malian friend of mine to move into a three bedroomed house I'd found. Big mistake. There are four official tenants on the lease and between ten and fifteen actual ones. That's how these West Africans are. They take extended family to its logical, disastrous extreme. I had welcomed the company at first after the isolation of my last place, enjoyed the easy chatter, the freestyling and the guitar playing and the endless cups of green tea. By late night, they'd all be gone and I'd have my peace again.

But then the traffic began to get out of hand. The visitors stayed later and later until they'd dispensed with leaving altogether. I'd find someone crashed on a mattress in the living room, then two, then three, and they'd still be there in the morning or in the afternoon when I came in from school. They came in earlier and earlier. They were there in time for breakfast and stayed for dinner. At all hours of the day, the house was alive with the rapid fire chatter of Bambara.

The neighbours are up in arms. When the landlord shows up to do a body count one morning, people disappear into closets with practiced alacrity.

Four people remain in view only two of whom he recognises. He looks around mildly then addresses one at random. "Hello," he says. "It's Abdoul, isn't it?" he asks, reading from the lease. The man nods and smiles. He doesn't speak a word of English. He got off the boat only last week and he hasn't learned to negotiate dry land. Dugan doesn't push it. He counts four people on his lease and four people in the house and makes an exit.

I discover that Bambara culture has no concept of personal property. I find some idiot wearing my dry clean only winter jacket after putting it through the wash. It is barely recognisable. I wonder why he took it in the first place in the middle of summer.

"Who gave you that?" I ask him.

He tells me he found it upstairs. I pull it off him roughly and drag him into the living room.

"Where's Abdoul?" I ask the mob lolling about on the couch and on the floor.

"He went to work," someone volunteers.

"And you are?" I ask.

"Maktar," he says, smiling.

"All right Maktar. Get the fuck out of my house." He doesn't understand. Maktar is used to preamble and dissembling and the practised use of proverb and metaphor and beating eloquently about the bush and approaching the matter at hand from as oblique an angle as possible.

I'm sick of translating my English into Bambara hand signals. I haul him out by the collar along with the clothes thief. A chorus of protest erupts. I come back and haul another guy out. Maktar, smiling bemusedly, is making his way back in. I stretch out a leg and catch him with a vicious kick. He yelps in surprise, but understanding is beginning to dawn. I go back for the others but they're already collecting their things and clearing out. I lock the door behind them and wait for Abdoul.

I tell him that I never want to see any of that mob in here again. He is apologetic, almost obsequious, promising to sort things out. The vermin stays away for a week before the first little critter skitters in again. We settle into a comfortable pattern of forceful eviction and gradual recolonisation. I have to do this alone because Charlie has retreated into a mist of weed and Lara Croft. The neighbours continue to complain and the landlord continues to drop in unexpectedly. But these guys have out-manoeuvred immigration authorities across Europe. They've given the INS the slip. He never catches them.

One summer morning I wake up to find an odd little group ranged along the couch; three young men and an old woman, the Sahelian dust still clinging to them. It is a band just arrived from Mali for a series of concerts in the North East,

Abdoul's latest moneymaking scheme. Needless to say, they will be staying with us. I would object strenuously if I could, but there is no one to object to. Abdoul has had the foresight to disappear.

I give them the finger as I walk by and they smile at me and nod.

I make another discovery. Bambara culture has no concept of rudeness. The visitors smile uncomprehendingly at my most transparent insolences. I try every one I know. I invent a few.

The band practices into the night, singing their plaintive praise songs till the sun comes in at my window and I get up, bleary-eyed and with an edge on my anger that never blunts.

These visitors attract a trail of admirers and hangers-on in larger numbers than before. They cook vile-smelling dishes and eat together from a communal plate, spilling rice and pungent stews all over the floor, talking all the while.

I think that this is what it must have been like at the court of Mansa Musa or Sundiata Keita: boubou'd men with sauces dribbling out of the corners of their mouths, oral histories bellowed around mouthfuls of yassa, audible mastication, slurping and eructation. Where I'd once imagined majestic households peopled by elegant men, men of refinement, haughty men who ruled by divine right and wore privilege easily, like a favourite trinket, now I just saw two dudes with bad table manners and whose hands you probably didn't want to shake.

One afternoon I walk in to find the woman sitting on the couch wearing a bolt of cloth loose around her waist and nothing else. I stare in horror. I am speechless, indignant, aghast. I sign my disapproval to her. She stares placidly back. I demand an explanation.

"She feel very hot," someone tells me. I lose it. I throw everyone out again. The woman's breasts flop about as she runs. The refugees mill about outside the door. The cops come. I'm incoherent with rage. A sergeant placidly records my hysterical statement. I ramble on and on. I think I may have said something about an invasion. I hint darkly that it will not stop at my house. That West Philadelphia is in grave danger, possibly all of Philadelphia as well and perhaps even the whole of the continental USA. I realise that the sergeant has stopped writing and is staring at me, undecided between amusement and a growing suspicion of my sanity. He tells me to calm down. I tell him that I don't know who these people are and that I don't want them near my house. The Malians cover the woman up and cart her away.

Abdoul reappears looking sheepish. He tells me that my mother called last night. I wonder briefly how she got my number, but I have other fish to fry. I complain about the noise, the noxious cuisine. I insist that any half naked women on my couch must look good with their clothes off. Abdoul is genuinely puzzled by my lack of courtesy but he's too polite to get angry. He makes a few placating noises. He assures me that the band will be leaving soon.

A hysterical letter arrives from my mother. I wonder how she found my address. The strange accent on the phone has convinced her that I have fallen in with Nigerians. She warned me about Nigerians before I left home. The implications are ominous. "Are you selling drugs? Are you robbing and plundering?" She calls again and prays for me for half an hour over the phone. The band finally disappears.

At the end of the summer, I tell Charlie that pan-Africanism is an obscenity. The sound of a kora striking up revolts me.

"These people are animals," I tell him. "I have more in common with Jesse Helms."

I've had it with their feudal manners and their chivalry and their decorum except when it really matters. Like what the fuck did they eat that their shit floated like that and required three flushes as a matter of course? And when did eating with a fork ever hurt anyone? And why should I have to convince anybody that I used toilet paper before I came to America?

"You're frothing at the mouth," Charlie laughs. "Have a beer."

My patience has run out and I stare down the possibility of moving in with my brother. But it is already too late. The whole block is up in arms. I find the eviction notice when I get back home. Charlie fucks off to Marietta.

I grit my teeth and submit to my brother's self righteous ministrations, his room and board. I begin to keep a diary. It's full of self-pity and a barely-controlled hysteria. I think that one day, years from now, I might find all this amusing.

But of course nothing has changed. Not only do I not find that summer amusing, but my present circumstances have served to endow it with a certain charm for which I have sometimes grown nostalgic. Nothing but my address, that is. The sordid details of life are now performed on south Forty-Eighth Street as opposed to Forty-Third and Pine. I'm heartily sick of the whole thing. I want out, I was getting out, or at least doing something about getting out. Now Charlie is here and I have a notion that things are about to change, and not for the better.

We drink the beer in companionable silence. When we run out, I suggest that we go out to a bar.

Outside, the heat hits us, heavy and wet, and close on, all the sights and sounds of our growing African ghetto: the Blue Nile restaurant, the White Nile restaurant, rinky dink little stores alive with smells of alien condiments and food. The high pitched guitar of some Congolese band blares from invisible speakers, providing the soundtrack for the groups of idling men and the slow unfolding of lives without purpose.

West Philly was nothing like this when I first saw it. There were only a handful of Africans then. I could weep just thinking about it. There was just me and Charlie and my friend Charlene and Papa who ran two bars that all the Africans went to, and one or two other guys who kept themselves to themselves and didn't bother us too much. Maybe there were others, but they had the courtesy to stay hidden in their holes. Not that I spent much time in West Philly. I was more that happy to stay in the 'burbs and come into town once a month or so. Philly I thought a little down market. West Philly was beyond the pale.

I'm not sure when or how it changed, but one day, walking down Baltimore Avenue, I look around me and do a triple take. It feels like fucking Addis Ababa or Ouagadougou or some shit. I mean, I remembered when we couldn't get a bag of maize meal for any amount of money, but now you could have ogbono and enough *okra* to make you green, and people at the grocery store stayed right with you when you asked for couscous or plantain. At Oscar's deli there was even a "Nigerian Hoagie" on the menu and the owner was Greek. Now they've come out to cavort in broad daylight. I wish they'd go right back where they came from.

I'm still astonished by the disparate realities that can inhabit even such small space as University City, the immiscible universes crammed cheek by jowl, the professor of classics in an apartment above the Aba market woman who had got lucky in the green card lottery. When I first got here, it was classics professors everywhere you cared to look. Now I can count my white neighbours on one hand. The fucking neigbourhood has gone to hell in a hand basket.

Now there was a fucking grapevine stretching from the fucking motherland and spread all around North America and parts of the Caribbean. You couldn't do fuck-all these days without your third cousin six times removed hearing about it in Winnipeg and calling you in a panic.

I look at the street with the old distaste, now softened by intimations of what I'd like to think is imminent escape. I'm out of here, I think. Not too long from now and I'm gone. Beyond the gnarled grip of this poisonous place, beyond its myriad predations and its cloying pettiness. And when I'm gone, I'm never coming within spitting distance of it again. And I'll work any number of shit jobs to do it.

I don't realise how fast I'm walking trying to get away from it all. Charlie has a hard time keeping up. He grimaces, "I can't believe I'm back here. In fucking Philadelphia." He hates the place. "It's hideous."

I tell him that it's just his suburbia withdrawal speaking. "I hate the 'burbs and the block upon block of organised unimagination."

"Like this is any better."

He snarls his dislike through uneven breaths.

"Got a little bigger?"

"Shut up."

"How does a poor guy get so fat?"

He wants to go back home to Marietta. Back home is actually Kinshasa Congo, but after all these years, that's like a foreign country. He can't go back to Marietta because he's broke and he's broke because the last deal didn't work out. When a deal didn't work out, there was always the added possibility that the ink wasn't quite dry on another warrant for his arrest. Then he'd come to pay me one of his increasingly infrequent visits. The logic of our lives, a vicious little circle.

We turn into a side street and the world changes back to the University City I love: the three-storey Victorian houses and the immaculate lawns. It lasts only three blocks. The grit and grime of Walnut Street loom ahead. I wonder how I never noticed how ugly this place can be, and why I'm still here so long after I did.

Took Charlie to do it. Took Charlie to do a whole lot of things.

Tijuana, the bar, is empty when we get there, except for Papa, the owner, taking stock and cleaning up. In the evening it will be a warm and fuzzy caucus of cabbies, dishwashers, toilet cleaners and burger flippers. Africa's huddled masses in the flesh.

Only last year, this was a Mexican restaurant. No one can remember when the last Mexican left. Now the bartender is Rwandese, the cook is Indian and the waiter is Jamaican. The food is inscrutable. It's close enough to Penn that a lot of students still come here. It's an odd mix, the inheritors of the earth and its wretched mingling with little acrimony in spite of the "one day, you'll work for us— if you don't already," subtext.

Papa's not surprised to see me so early in the day. He has served me beer first thing in the morning and last thing at night. If he has any opinions about my drinking, he keeps them to himself. Which means we get along like a house on fire, or as famously as anyone can with Papa. He's the sphinx of West Philly. Says little, laughs less, but obviously has a handle on things. While African businesses are folding all over the place, he's still making money.

"No credit today," Papa says, in an approximation of humour.

Not a problem. I'm flush. In one pocket I have a Visa card with a starter credit line of eight hundred dollars, courtesy of my new working status. In the other I have five hundred dollars worth of cleaning dirty dishes after incontinent arseholes. Until just now, it had assumed and maintained an immutable identity as Mr. Dugan's money. Rent. I absently reconfigure and reallocate my resources. Rent will be late again this month.

Papa remembers Charlie from the last time. Charlie's a hard man to forget, and when he's set his mind to convincing you, a hard man to dislike. Papa is obviously convinced. He gives us our beer "on the house," smiling a half-regretful smile as he says it. I've only once known Papa to give a beer away, and the guy had to lose his mother first. Even then sympathy stretched only as far as two Bud Lights.

"How do you do it?" I ask him, shaking my head.

He smiles. That's how.

A man walks in, pool cue in hand. His name is Berhanu and he's handsome in a pinched, ferret like way. Too much beer and too little food, most of it cadged. He has two upper teeth missing where someone punched them out. I met him two years ago when misery was in active pursuit of company. I must have been pretty damn miserable to put up with him as long as I did. He must have pissed someone off again to have to come in here. The Ethiopians drink in their own bars.

Berhanu has an explanation for all the happenings on Baltimore Avenue and America in general. His theory stretches to include much of sub-Saharan Africa, with the exception of South Africa and Ethiopia. Eritrea is included. One day he shares it with me, leaning conspiratorially close to my ear. "Ze darker zey get," he tells me, "ze dumber zey get." The result of a lengthy introspection.

I tell him to fuck off.

Papa owns 3 bars and a club, the only African club in town. It's a pretty shite place, dark, smoky and with an indestructible smell of fish lurking in the carpets on the floor and on the walls. But it's the only club Africans have to go and listen to African music and to meet other Africans. Pretty much everyone comes there as well as West Indians and more and more African Americans. It's also a place of business. Where African men meet African American women to marry. For a fee sometimes, but often enough from a heartwarming desperation. When 30% of your own men are in jail, it's hard enough to just find a black guy to be with. Africans have the added advantage of a non-felonious culture and an appreciation for hard work. "The Mbira," the club, is Papa's cash cow.

For such a shrewd businessman, Papa is pretty damn naïve where his family is concerned. His nephew Bob runs the bar, although it would be more accurate to say that he runs it into the ground. Bob always manages to be drunker at closing time than the drunkest customer, and that's saying something. Papa just turns a blind eye and keeps him on though the nightly receipts must tell a story of steady incompetence and occasionally of wilful transgression. He doesn't ask the questions he doesn't want the answers to. He just bends over and takes his shafting like a man. For God and for family.

Another nephew just arrived from Malawi last week and is learning American. He's already learned to say "Y'all ain't gotta go home, buy you've got to get the fuck out of here," at closing time.

The two o'clock closing time takes some getting used to. Other than a hand-me-down constitution, a virulent inferiority complex and an enduring awe of London, drinking hard is the only thing the British left us when they checked out in '63. Last call is like a personal affront. Every night a fight breaks out between the bartender and a bunch of Kenyans who don't want to leave. That's where Kevin comes in. No one wants to argue with a 6' 4", 250-pound guy. They drink up and leave, complaining and hurling insults as they stagger out the door vowing never to come back again. But of course they do. Every day.

It's only midday and I figure that I'll be only slightly late for work. I drink too—sweet coke and watch football.

At one I call the restaurant and tell them that I'll be half an hour late. At two I call to say that I'll be at least an hour late. Car trouble doesn't seem to be getting fixed. I think about calling again at four but abandon the idea. I remember my laundry in the washer. I start to drink beer.

I'm still there at five when the first of the wretched begin to trickle in.

Papa, and I'm sure he knows it, is like a coffin maker or an embalmer. He makes his living off the misery of others. There's a whole lot of it thinly camouflaged around these parts. Any night of the week, Tijuana would make the folks at the United Negro College Fund weep. There's a whole slew of degrees going to waste here. There are PhD's working at Wawa and 7 Eleven selling hot dogs and Rough Rider condoms, MBAs driving cabs, good engineering degrees guarding parking lots and pharmacists mopping the aisles at the dollar store. And every evening they came in, sloughed off their miserable realities and stepped into a few brief hours or normalcy and humanity.

Here they could be simply themselves. No need to translate who they were and what they had been into a non-metric quantity, a two-sentence education. Here they were more than the sum of their paltry weekly paychecks. They were what they had been, what they had set out to be, what they still thought they could be. Not just the cab parked outside or the lingering smell of mustard and relish. Everyone had worthy antecedents.

Here we skirted around the lingering bitterness and confusion and talked of better things.

This was perhaps what lay at the bottom of the disproportionately bitter exchanges at closing time. No one wanted to go out into the darkness outside. Into the cold and the anonymity. Just another Zulu.

And every week, every beginning of semester, a new bunch of faces stepped of Sabena at JFK and made their disparate ways to a cousin's in Minneapolis or DFW or Norristown, just until they could get on their feet.

At about nine, Bob walks in with some girl. Experience gives her the once over. It hits me then, how long I've been here, that I felt only weariness at some other bright eyed youngster at the starting blocks. I was exhausted just thinking of what things she had to learn, what battles she'd have to fight, the depths to which she might sink.

No doubt the others saw it too. Eagerness thwarted and then quickly perked up at a fresh bit of pussy. I ordered a triple of bourbon and drank it down.

There were things I had set aside to think about, one day in quietness that I was still so far from. Mysteries that America had revealed to me. There was a theme running through this room. A lack of volition which I had never been able to understand.

As if the surround sound, turn the knob all the way up volume at which the world outside conducted itself froze one into inaction, was too much for those such as us used to sylvan peace. As if an inability or a failure to translate oneself, to augment oneself to the same ear-splitting decibels meant that one became the moral of the story being told along the length of the bar counter and at the wobbly tables in the back. Inagency. Failure.

Distance from reality, the postponement of life which we lived here every day, allowed one to tell oneself the tallest tales, to cultivate and protect all sorts of outrageous half truths and to believe them. And then, when someone pointed out the discordances, to defend it, and that often viciously.

Since that happened often, since men were called upon to defend their life-sustaining fibs and themselves on a daily basis, a fight was bound to break out every day. A fight of such viciousness, all sharp teeth and claws, it was frightening.

Tonight it was Driss who had blundered into an unpleasant reality. His dearly cherished mirage was politics. He talked about it every day. How much he had always loved politics. How he was going to be in government, how well he had prepared himself for this inevitability by taking a first in political science and then an MBA just to be sure. Second in his class. He said it as if the reality of 8 years driving a cab was not a fatal impediment to that eventuality. As if he had a one-way ticket to Togo in his safe at home. As if he hadn't himself caught the disease of involition. As if he wasn't fated to always dream of better things he could never have. When the subject turned to Togolese politics, Driss was in his element. He knew the whys, the wherefores. The minutiae. Someone interrupted him and was shot down. That someone tried again with the same bloody results. Then someone got angry.

"My brother," he said. It doesn't matter how many degrees you have, or whether I never went to school. Your cab doesn't know your degree and mine doesn't know I don't have one."

Don't fuck with a man's illusions.

Driss put his Heineken down on the bar and rolled his sleeves up neatly while the other man watched these preparations with a wry smile on his face. He knew what he had done. And he knew the consequence. He went down heavily under the force of eight years of distilled misery delivered to his jaw. All the venom Driss would have unleashed on life had life had the temerity to dare him to dance.

Kevin ambled over smirking and pulled Driss away easily enough. "Fighting outside." Driss walked out and drove away.

Charlie groans in disappointment at having his entertainment so summarily truncated. The feeling in Driss is too close to something I am consciously trying to suppress for me to derive any pleasure from it. I need to leave. There are more than enough bars in University City to get trashed in.

We get home at three. My phone blinks, pregnant with messages. We sleep the sleep of the damned.

The discourteous explosion of the phone by my ear jars me awake. In the haze of uncertainty, I feel only fear. I do not know what I have done, only that there will be hell to pay. I let it ring until the answering machine kicks in.

It's Ed. He asks me to call him back. I am 20 hours late for work. I begin to count excuses like sheep.

The phone wakes me up again. I am now 24 hours late for Ed. But it's Joanna on the line. She lays it on businesslike and thick as hell.

"Martin?" she says, "This is Joanna calling," as if I wouldn't know that voice from hell anywhere. "I haven't seen you today and I'm wondering what's going on. I must say this is very unprofessional of you and thoroughly irresponsible. I must say I am very, very surprised."

Yeah right.

"As you can imagine, John is very upset and so am I. I took a chance on you giving you this job, and I am very much looking forward to your explanation."

Guilt trip. Very nice. Might have worked on a lesser soul.

"You have my number. Call me."

Fat chance.

I don't doubt that John is pissed. I've been making him look bad at each of the jobs he got me right from jump street. I drift back into sleep.

The afternoon brings back sharp reminders of all the cisterns I have known. I puke and flush, puke and flush for an hour then go back to sleep.

I wake up again at six and just lie there, prostrated by this latest manifestation of my own stupidity. I'm impaled on my mattress by the shaft of a brutal massing of pain between my eyes.

I manage to call Ed and tell him that I'm sick. It's not far from the truth. I tell him that I'll be in next week. No doubt Joanna has fired me by now. Ed I think will keep my job for me. I'm almost sure of it. He'll just give me a tongue lashing and be dramatically disappointed like only a queen can be. He'll ask me to think about whether or not I really want this job. Like, really, really want it, as if I give a shit, then he'll sigh and put me back to work. I'm the best darned grease pulveriser he's ever had. And I was employee of the month just last month. And if he doesn't, there's plenty more dead-end jobs where that one came from.

When I finally get up, I walk to the laundromat and switch my almost dry clothes from washer to dryer then go and get some takeout. We eat in silence. Eight o'clock finds us back on Papa's bar stools.

We come back every day for a week. By the next Sunday I'm broke. I negotiate a credit line with Papa and we drink steadily for another week. Then even Papa begins to make unpleasant noises. With great difficulty, I negotiate another credit line at one of the Ethiopian bars, mostly so we have some place to go in the evenings. Charlie in my apartment all day is starting to get on my nerves.

I see it less and less as my apartment now, and more and more as Mr. Dugan's seriously underperforming investment. My rent is a week late by now. Mr.Dugan's secretary has already left two messages on my phone informing me of her concern about the chronic lateness of my payment. It will take three weeks of my three paychecks to recoup the money I've spent on booze. Trouble is, I only have one job now. I think.

My mortal fear of the mailman returns. I scan his face with trepidation as if he's read my mail and knows what horrors are contained within it—what bad tidings, what summons, what final notices. I have panic attacks at the thought that my mother might have found me again and that I'd find one of the cheap brown envelopes with my name described in her painstaking hand. The pain and the worry incorporated in each laboured capital. Today however, the mailman just waves as he walks by.

I'm surprised by how quickly I have unlearned all my hard earned lessons. Every semblance of the orderly life I had achieved before Charlie got here is gone. It'll take me a while to work my way back to where I started.

We've run out of ideas Charlie and I. Nothing to do, nothing to be done. Charlie is innocent of the unfolding drama. He never mentions it at any rate—not the fact that I haven't been to work in over a week, not the unpleasant messages on my answering machine—and he doesn't lift a finger to help. And he never gets off his arse. When I run out of money, he stops leaving the house altogether. He spends the days on his back with Lara. I think it's a miracle he hasn't got bedsores.

"Hey man," he says to no one in particular. "I'm hungry."

"What the fuck do you want me to do about it?" I ask him. "I'm not your mother."

He's surprised and hurt, but I'm in no mood to be charitable. Between terror of my mother and Mr. Dugan, I think my blood pressure must be about to burst my capillaries and that I'll die in a haemorrhaging mess on the floor. The strain is killing me.

But this is the first verbalisation of the problem I long suspected. Charlie wanting. I know all about his legendary taste, and even though he hasn't asked for anything before this, I feel that I'm somehow falling short, that I'm not giving him all the good things he should have. Unable to fulfill my obligations to myself, I resent these mostly unarticulated obligations to another.

I go to the ATM for my last twenty bucks. After a worrying period of inaction and silence, I am informed in whirring machine speak that the twenty dollars has ceased to exist. I can look forward to a maximum of seven dollars and thirty five cents.

There is only one machine in West Philly that dispenses money in denominations less than ten dollars and it's ten blocks away. The ATM at the Thriftway supermarket, the last machine in this neighbourhood that gave out five dollars, just upped their minimum. Screw this, I think. Screw the credit union and its hidden charges and screw the University of Pennsylvania and its affluent student body and its gentrification of University City.

I begin the unpleasant walk to the Penn Hospital ATM. I am having an angry conversation with the contriver of all things, including irritations like these. If I'm going to walk all this way, I tell him, I'd better be able to get that five dollars out of my account or I'm going to be very angry, and who knows what I'll do then? I insert my card with trembling hands. The old whirring and I'm in luck. Five dollars comes sliding out. It's already budgeted for.

I need cigarettes. I promise myself I'll quit as soon as this is over. My suspicions that I am terminally ill are healthy enough without the additive of proven carcinogens. With the rest of the money, I buy a week's supply of Ramen noodles for Charlie. I don't doubt that he'll be vocally ungrateful. Charlie dreams of medium rare rib eye steaks at Shula's. In his book, Ramen noodles do not qualify as food.

Charlie eats them all, complaining all the while, in one fell swoop. The steaming, watery, unappetising mess disappears down his throat and we're back to square one.

We're about to get thrown out onto the street and I'm spending my time like some cavewoman, foraging for an adult male. "Dude," I tell Charlie, "if I get thrown out, so do you. What do you plan to do about it?"

"I'm working on it," he tells me, sinking slowly into somnolence. "Give me time."

I work my way through my phone book. No one can help me out. There's only one other person on my money hit list. It is important that I maintain an element of surprise. I decide to catch him at home as soon as possible.

When I come out of my room, my coat is gone and so is Charlie. His camel coloured coat is hanging from the hook on the door. Nothing in my wardrobe goes with camel and I know I'll look like an impostor in that coat. But there's nothing to be done. The ambush is only mildly successful. Half an hour of abject begging yields forty dollars. I walk back home with the rank taste of humiliation in my mouth. I think that begging doesn't become me. It pisses me off that the cracks are beginning to show. I never had to share my misery with anyone before. Before I could always find my ingenious way around it. Alone.

I hear footsteps behind me and start to turn, but it's too late. It's the guy I passed five blocks away and he's right up to me. He throws an arm around my shoulders and pulls his shirt up a little to show me the butt of what looks like a glock in his waist band. "This is a stick up he tells me," as if I hadn't already guessed. As if maybe I was thinking that he was an itinerant weapons salesman.

I want to tell him that that's a hell of a corny line. What does he think this is? Boys in the Hood? New Jack City?

It's the fucking camel Jones of New York trench coat. A Market Street, Liberty Place, Society Hill coat. Fucking Charlie and his fucking impeccable taste. The man's arm is still around me. We keep walking down the street, so happy together. We look like brothers or best friends or black queers. Him Tarzan. Me Jane. It's the fucking coat man.

I give him my wallet and he takes his arm from my shoulders. He's pissed when he finds only forty dollars in it. He looks at the jacket and back at the wallet.

"This it?"

I nod.

The dynamic of this relationship irks me. Like how he's just reached his grubby hand down into the guts of my privacy.

"No credit cards?" He says it as if I've committed a terrible faux pas.

I shake my head.

"What, fool?"

Like how he can call me stupid and get away with it.

"I ain't got no credit cards," I say in American, saving him the effort of translation.

"Well-why-the-fuck-not?"

Like how he has the temerity to ask why I don't have more shit for him to take off me. I stop walking and so does he. "Cos I got bad credit," I tell him. "Like you no doubt."

He looks up and down the deserted street then reaches for the gun in his waist band. "You'se a smart mother fucker huh? You think you smart don't you? Huh?"

The momentary bravado has already abandoned me. I shake my head dumbly then underline my point. "That's it man. All I've got." I pull my pocket liners out of my pants. "That's it."

He drops his shirt back over the butt of the gun and puts my wallet in his pocket. He nods at me and turns to go. Then he stops and pats my ass.

I think about that for a minute. I've heard that in South Africa robberies are thorough. Man or woman, they take everything you have. Even if you're a guy, they just flip you over and bang the hell out of you. But this ain't S.A. I catch up with him two blocks on. He's running easy, springy, not worried about being followed and no doubt feeling quite pleased with himself. He hears the footsteps coming up behind him but it's too late. When he turns, I'm waiting. The blow catches him in his windpipe and he crashes to the ground.

"What the ...."

"What was that?" I ask him. "What the fuck was that?" He just clutches at his throat and gasps. "You queer?" I ask him. "You a fucking fairy?" He's in too much pain to answer me or to pose any danger at all, but I hit him again to make sure, then frisk him and take my wallet back. I take his wallet too and the gun. He has way more money than I did.

"Fuck you," I tell him before walking away.

By the time Charlie gets back, my anger has surpassed expression by speech. I jump on him as he closes the door and we grapple with each other for a bit. Charlie is strong and it's good of him to merely push me away.

"What?" he asks when I stop struggling. "What's wrong with you?"

I point.

"What?"

"Give me my fucking jacket back."

"You're that pissed over a stupid jacket?"

I make inarticulate gurgles of anger and he takes if off and tosses it to me. Then he tosses a hundred dollars after it. I don't tell him about the mugger until the morning.

"No wonder you were pissed," he laughs. He tells me to be careful walking around. "Better not let him see you again."

I pay Dugan off later that day but the month's already half gone and rent is due again in two weeks. I'm first in at Tijuana again. I'm well and truly plastered by the time my brother walks in. My stomach drops. He doesn't know where I live. This is the third bar he's been in tonight looking for me. He's with a clutch of my countrymen as usual. I think he is terrified of his own company, that he thinks he'll put himself to sleep and crash his Acura into a lamp post.

I'm certain it's not my company he's after. There must be a problem of appreciable dimensions to send him dredging the less fashionable Philadelphia watering holes for me.

His friends hang back nervously and stare at me like I'm a circus act or something. They ask after my health with an inordinate interest. I ignore them. Memories of the fatherland itch like a scab I refuse to scratch.

My brother dispenses with small talk. "Mum called," he tells me. "She wants to talk to you. She's going to call again in the evening tomorrow. My place." He pauses briefly and then very quietly adds, "You'd better be there."

I know it's taken some courage for him to tell me what to do and so I know that this must be important. His mission accomplished, he leaves, his consort stumbling along behind him. My interview with my brother leaves me abraded. Charlie is gone when I get home and so is the PlayStation and the camel coat and the Louis Vuitton bag. There is a depression in the cushions that I think may be permanent, but that's the only sign that he was ever here.

Dugan's secretary has left a message on my phone. She wants me to come in tomorrow. Urgently. Stress on the urgently. "I'll see you then," she says, and hangs up

---

ANDIA KISIA is not fond of giving out her bio. She likes to enter and win BBC radio plays using pseudonyms. She is six foot tall and intimidates everybody who meets her. She wrote a play, The Roosting, *which was performed at Phoenix Players in 2003. She played the Rooster. Andia also won another major prize, but we are not allowed to say that it was the Mnet New Directions award. We shall continue to respect her desire for privacy. She lives in Philadelphia, and will not come home. It seems. Or communicate.*

B Blogguy™ GET YOUR OWN BLOG | FLAG? | NEXT BLOG>>

Rediscovering Elizabeth

September 4th, 2006

The basket has been churning the familiar looking chameleons at some alarming rates, the past two months headline news simply boasts of these creatures. Changing colours with ease ,never once thinking that their metamorphosis might be a cause of the rising number of people visiting ophthalmologists with sight problems.

Ear plugs are fast becoming a near necessity too for in their transformation losing colour also occasions some loud noises. Justification for their change, perhaps.

Two bonfires and the gibbous moon.

Tales of vanity are not far away.

Her hands gently propped themselves to support her chin, up close the visible pimple was the only blemish on the well served face, hair cropped to lawn grass levels.Years never touched anything as far as these eyes could recall.

There were tales of punched up lines, near misses and some of cows that wandered off their supposed pen into new feeding grounds only for the owner to leave them for an exchange.

"It has been treating you well," she started.

"And so has it been for you," in between a cough.

Patches to get us off on a new footing as the night progresses gently, we settle for sinking ships and sunken straws as our eyes are fixed on the anchored dhow. In the near future it is hoped that something similar to a phoenix tale would steal these encounters.

None the less for what it was worth, the brine filled oxygen and the two stars that were counted an evening well spent. Brief shadows lingered on moments of undefined brilliance before the cake was cut.

"So what has been up since then," it was enquired.

"A proposal that still hangs on air," she said.

"Reasons?"

" Kilos," she answered.

Hidden beneath the apology was the seasoned sheepish smile. A sigh of relief follows as human nature takes stage in the consolation processes.Two weeks' answers will flow and fate as we know it might shine.

Two bonfires and a cloudy night.

Fuck vanity.

Posted in under the table dreaming | 4 Comments »

B **Blogguy™** GET YOUR OWN BLOG | FLAG? | NEXT BLOG>>

Protocol

June 2nd, 2006

Walking down the street, the pauper glances, parting with a grunt in which his hopes that I will nod and do the needful are banked on, instinct drives me to scrap deep into my left pocket, spending a while trying to separate a coin from my bunch of keys, I struggle for eight seconds before I grace my fingers with the touch that is Kenyatta's face. 28 years past the legacy of this man still irks the living daylights out of me; why do we have to follow these traditions while as a country we claim that we are never in short supply of heritage, why not have the image of the highest point on our land instead of this?

I leave these thoughts as I drop the coin into the bowl; I walk away.

Watching the National Geographic Channel one night I saw images of a vehicle called Mars Rover navigating the surface of Mars, for a while I had to fidget my eyes for what the screen had was similar if not exact to the road that leads to my home. The road translates to a painful 40 minute ordeal daily, the bus driver says it's pointless to install new shock absorbers as the craters will only be too happy to gobble them up.

I say hello to him as I walk in, my early morning has paid off, I am greeted by the unfamiliar sight of an empty seat and hurriedly I confine my rear, buckle up prepping myself ready for the ride.The bus gets into life before being suddenly stopped by the lovely sight of a six-month-heavy, polka-dot dressed lady. As she gets on the bus, my reluctance to release the buckle waved from, it's a good thing to the unfamiliar spits of various deodorant types mixed with varied human musks that would meet me if I opted to stand. The road to and from Mars is more traumatising without the seats, eventually resting on the ignore her, I ignore her.

That when you enter a place, you must extend your hand in greeting, at least get them to say something. Millicent tells me that's what we have been taught to do. Habits that we have picked as we get older, mannerisms that mother taught us, fine tuned by society to make us better men. Here is my greeting to you. Behind this obvious pseudonym with these too many anything goes tales of life and sometimes misconceptions of love. We might seem to be strangers yet I know you all so well.

Dropping random numbers that might become my guiding light:

43, 22, 6.

Late night news to sum up my day:

Pictures of the pauper unwrapping the nylon sheets off his leg, after all, it was all in a day's work. My area legislator just won the rather inconsequential by elections.

The polka-dotted lady never lined herself well, however fate and the need to make good would see me play pivotal roles 3 months later leaving me with this forever thirsty edge; need!

Stories for another day ... yes indeed .

Posted in the learning curve | 3 Comments »

Dreams Of Our Fathers

June 5th, 2006

Long before the streets of Calif claimed responsibility for vulgarity on FM radios they played neighbour to a blossoming estate. This middle class estate would eight years later become the capital city of the khat chewing, everywhere spitting, canjeelo eating Africans from the north.

A second generation of middle aged Kenyans had made this part of Nairobi their home, burdened with the difficult task by their colonial masters who opted to affix a *leigh* to the geographical location of the place, the inhabitants largely unaware of the reasoning behind all this were quick to absorb the name into their daily vocab albeit with the e, g and h dropped leaving only the li to go by. Like all the city estates at the time Eastleigh was a decent neighbourhood with adequate amenities to cater for this growing generation. Mosques, Churches, Schools, Health Centres and Pubs completed what was needed to service these inhabitants.

I take off with the pub reference now, not that I was a regular paying patron then though I had my moments, there was nothing like sipping of froth off the old man's beer mug when he was emptying off his white cap. I do though because it was in this pub that I first overheard my dad's grand ambitions for his budding 5 year old son.

On a regular Sunday afternoon he would pack us up and off we would go to his blazing joint, the talk of the town then. MBC as they used to call it, I would later learn that it was the source of anguish for many mothers and the primary cause of the shouting and cutlery throwing that we had to endure from our neighbours across the road. At night the abbreviations displayed the full brunt of the misery it compounded onto society, the initials would show in their true colours of green and red, *Mateso Bila Chuki.*

He used to meet with his regular buddy, a structural engineer who I knew as Uncle Mikey and who also doubled up as Millicent's dad, and they would engage in peeling of white and blue stickers off brown bottles while their voices drowned in music. They would talk about anything under the sun, from the fears that greeted them on the coup day to what they thought were grand plans for their children.

Age has never been a hindrance to some things and you would be surprised what the human brain can store, even at the age which made us to believe that babies were bought and that the balloons we used to see in front of the bar were used to store water. The most vivid recollection of what Uncle Mikey was discussing with his brother still haunts me at selected times when I choose to play back those years. "They would settle down well and what's more our families are close like this together," Uncle Mikey never seemed to get tired of those words, my old man would simply sing along and echo back the same.Twenty four years later, our paths never took that turn; Millicent still amazes me with her daring escape from the convent and I am here still undecided on which shoes to buy.

Posted in 8th Street | No Comments »

http://dobvious.wordpress.com

I'LL BE ON MY WAY

July 28th, 2006

Echoes *of the Beatles* reborn in the nasal outings of Ali Campbell have been characteristic of my past month, sudden silences forced upon by broken ties. An apology for the departure?

Winter has since invaded parts of this land while Alpine inhabitants are slowly being cooked by searing temperatures, they have I am told traded it with near nudity as the battle to contain nature's wrath takes a different gear. Extremes if you may, meanwhile we are seemingly content with the obvious business boom that will be evident after certain gestation periods are truly over. Gloves and blankets find their way onto our washing lines as we make good of the discards from the east.

Back to the landscapes, soundscapes and destiny. June continues to hold significant changes in this life; it is the cleaning house month when everything that never held value in the bigger picture of things slowly detaches itself just like mite having to let go of the abdominal walls when you decide to heed up mother's advice and de-worm.

Never once had I hoped for exceptions; my only surprise lay in the choice June decided to rid me off. A wrong investment decision would be welcome, a sudden fire in the corner of my library that housed aged novels also a good bit; or perhaps thugs snatching this worn out and always empty wallet. The swift nature that it took to extinguish the flame is still a sight to behold.

Was it in grace or pure elegance, the jigsaw pieces fell into place as the shadows that lulled over the misunderstood dozes of silence stopped short of a complete haunting; empty spaces, gaping holes exposing the timid mollusc that was me as a being.

Landing in this place where silence no longer haunts, winds no longer blow and the horizon greets me with golden rivers.

The June light did indeed turn to moonlight.

Posted in under the table dreaming | 1 Comment »

http://dobvious.wordpress.com

Photograph: coutesy of Rasna Warah

What My Dying Mother Taught Me About Living

BY RASNA WARAH

This is not a story about death, or about my mother, but about how the dying teach us how to live. It is about redemption, forgiveness, love, compassion, resentment, anger, all rolled into one. It is about how watching someone die can teach us the meaning of life, and reveal to us the immense resilience of the human spirit. It is about how a woman who never quite forgave me for marrying an African man learned how to accept him by living with us in our home in her dying years.

Death is the ultimate equaliser. When you are dying, when your body and your bodily functions are controlled by others—doctors, nurses, caretakers, machines, catheters—there is no room for false pride or arrogance. When you can no longer do the simplest things—pick up a glass of water, comb your hair, dress yourself, talk or walk—whoever happens to be near you, whoever helps you do these things, becomes your god.

It is difficult for those who have never taken care of someone who is paralysed or incapacitated to understand what it means for the caregiver. What does it mean for a daughter to change her mother's wet diaper, to feed her through a tube, or wash her hair because she can't herself? Many a time, both when my mother was in a semi-coma and afterwards, friends would ring me up and ask me to come over. "Surely, all you need to do is put her to bed, and leave." No, it is not as simple as that, I would try to explain (unsuccessfully), not when the person you are leaving behind cannot walk, or fetch themselves a glass of water, or call for help in case of an emergency. No-one, except my sisters, who took some of the responsibility of taking care of her part of the year, quite understood this, because they were not going through it. How could they?

On 9 July 2003, when my mother, Manjeet Kaur Warah, aged 68, suffered a massive haemorrhage on the left side of her brain, she could not do anything on her own. The stroke paralysed the right side of her body, and for several months left her speechless and motionless. For the first month or so, she ate, drank, urinated and defecated in bed. She couldn't talk, so her eyes became her tongue, blinking when she meant yes, turning away when she meant no. Several weeks of physiotherapy eventually got her speech back and, with some help, she could feed herself, but barely.

Two weeks after the stroke, when my mother was still in a comatose state in the intensive care unit of M.P. Shah Hospital in Nairobi, this is what I wrote via e-mail to my friends abroad:

"Here we are at the end of July and I can honestly say that life has never been fuller. On 9th July, I was forced to sit back and reflect on what is important and what isn't. My mother suffered a stroke, which has left her paralysed on the right side and taken away her speech. Although she is slowly recovering, the first few days really brought home to me the fact that life is so temporary and the little pleasures, like reading and writing (which we take for granted) can be taken away in just a moment, when you least expect it. That's how the doctor described the stroke – "a bolt out of the blue", with no warning signs, no symptoms. I suppose for us, the hardest part was seeing this strong, independent woman lying in a hospital bed completely helpless, unable to talk or communicate. But life is a marvellous thing. My mother now uses her left hand to "talk" to us. Sometimes I think she is smiling, although it is hard to tell with the tubes in her nose."

Two weeks later, my mother had moved in with me. There was no choice. She couldn't live alone as she had been doing before the stroke. With a day nurse, the task of feeding and cleaning her, plus administering the cocktail of medications and a catheter, was manageable, but just barely. Her favourite nurse, Maggie, was a godsend. For 12 hours a day, she never left my mother's side, sometimes reading the newspaper to her after her morning bath, often offering words of encouragement, some straight from the Bible, which she carried with her everyday. Thanks to Maggie and her replacement nurses, it was possible to have some moments on my own.

A few weeks after she moved in, Mummy her said first words, often mixing up Punjabi, Kiswahili and English, like saying "Haan" (yes, in Punjabi) to my husband Gray and "Ndio" (yes in Kiswahili) to me without realising that he didn't understand Punjabi. The brain is truly a complex and fascinating thing. Sometimes, when I would make a joke, she would even laugh, the laughter throatier than I remembered it, more authentic than her laugher during her healthy days. The fact that she could laugh despite her condition was a miracle in itself. Once, she even stroked my face, gently, like a mother does to her new-born child, something I do not remember her doing even when I was little. When I'd put her to bed, after emptying her catheter and giving her a glass of water, she'd sometimes whisper a "thank you". My mother was becoming more human, more intuitive and more compassionate than I had ever known her to be.

Meanwhile, I myself underwent a transformation. I learned to be completely responsible for another human being. Having never had children, this was a new experience for me. The only difference was that while the dependence of a new-born baby brings about a sense of joy and accomplishment, the dependence of a grown adult is painful to watch. Moreover, babies eventually grow out of their dependence and watching them take their first step, pass an exam or get a driving licence, are an attestation of your success as a parent. With an adult dependant with a fatal illness, particularly a victim of a stroke, the process is often reversed. What you are watching is the slow demise and deterioration of another human being, each day survived, each word spoken, each step taken, a miracle. Watching your parent disintegrate right before your eyes is probably the most painful experience a child can experience, especially watching someone who once represented beauty, strength and independence.

But I was also getting increasingly exhausted and disillusioned, at times even resentful. A month after she moved in, and after a week of unforeseen mishaps, I wrote the following to a friend in New York:

"Things this end have not been too good. The day the UN in Baghdad was bombed, my house help had an accident and broke his leg and Gray's car was stolen from our compound. Oh, and I got a Blaster worm on my computer, and then our Vice President died. And all this while I am trying to cope with a paralysed mother. Needless to say, I haven't written a word. No time to think, let alone create. I sometimes wonder if a nursing home was the answer. This is just too tough. I am completely housebound and my computer is my only contact with the outside world. Please keep writing to me."

Gray, still reeling from the fact that the woman who did not speak to him for nearly nine years since we got married, now had to live with him in his own home, took my mother's arrival in our home in his stride. In his typical, forgiving and mature style, he saw it as an opportunity to bond with a mother; his own mother died when he was ten—having Mummy with us gave him another chance to be a son. But since he worked seven days a week on most weeks, his moments with her were restricted to small conversations at dinner, or during the news at nine (which my mother watched diligently in the first year, when she started regaining more of her senses) or on weekends. Our relationship oscillated from very close to resentful. I was told many relationships die in the face of an illness in the family. Sometimes I wondered if the strain of my mother's condition on both of us would eventually lead us to divorce.

But more disturbing was the realisation that I had lost nearly all of my friends, even those I considered to be very close. Never in a million years had I imagined that they would abandon me in my hour of need. Apart from a handful, few picked up the phone to see how I was doing. Fewer still offered to help. One of my closest friends, (whom I have since dropped from my list of buddies), came to see me a whole three months after the stroke. Her first words to Gray were, "How can you bear to take care of a woman who didn't speak to you all those years? Rasna's not working, does that mean you have to take care of all the bills?" Over the months, I got used to such provocative and cruel statements, many from my mother's own friends, who dumped her as soon as she no longer fit the pretentious little Asian women's circuit that she had belonged to until her illness, and which had been one of the chief reasons why she refused to accept Gray in the first years of our marriage. Even today, when I think of all the lunches she took them out to, and all the pretentious little get-togethers and gossip sessions she attended simply because she was bored, my blood boils.

Barely three months after the stoke, a member of her kitty party circuit informed me that the kitty club that my mother belonged to were demanding her share of the kitty, which amounted to Shs. 30,000 and could I please pay up immediately. Although I was disgusted at their total lack of sensitivity, I promptly paid the money, even though at that stage, we were struggling with medical bills and other expenses that were much more important. The funny thing is, none of her kitty party friends came to visit her when she was ill, not once. Yet they happily took the money. If only my mother had known how shallow her friends were, she might have spent more time nurturing other relationships, like those with her children.

In the two years that she was ill, I learned more about human nature than I did in my entire life. In many ways, for me at least, taking care of her was a blessing, a real gift, a learning experience that taught me the true meaning of what is important in this world – love, respect, kindness, the things that cannot be measured or bought.

And in many ways, I think it was for her too. They say one lives long enough to learn one's lessons. My mother learned how to forgive; she died when she knew we had forgiven her too.

My mother had always been a beauty, dainty, with hazel eyes and a perfect complexion. She was not just run-of-the-mill beautiful, but according to several of her age-mates (including the hospital administrator, who told me this) she was stunning, the toast of the ball, the one every man at my father's cricket club secretly desired. Her biggest regret was that her daughters had not taken after her. She was constantly scolding me about my weight or my sisters about their complexion. "You will never find a husband", she once told me. "Just as well you have brains."

Fortunately, perhaps in rebellion to her constant chidings, I decided that if I could not be beautiful, I could be smart. Unfortunately, the more I studied, the more disturbed she became. "Surely all those books will not find you a husband." How different that world was to the one we have now, where parents compete with each other to see whose kids perform better at school. "Oh, your kid is in America, that's easy, mine's in England, at Oxford, and you know how hard it is to get into that university," I have heard many an Asian parent say. I was spared all this, because I went to university not because my parents wanted me to, but because I applied, was accepted, and they basically didn't have a choice but to send me.

Papaji was different, of course. Surrounded by women – a headstrong wife and four doting daughters – he had no choice but to succumb to his fate. He was the nurturer, the one you ran to when you fell and hurt your knee or when your boyfriend dumped you. It wasn't that Mummy didn't care. "She finds it hard to show her emotions," he once said, while rubbing my head with Vicks when I had a fever. "But she loves you." I found it hard to believe then, because even though minutes later I heard him tell her to come to put Vicks (the Robb of those days) on my chest "because I can't, she's a growing girl", she never came to me.

There have been times when I wondered if maybe she herself was neglected as a child and therefore did not know how to relate to her own children. Or was it because we were all girls? Was it a case of "oppression-of-the-self"? In my 20s, I came across a book by Nawal el Saadawi that provided some answers. In *The Hidden Face of Eve,* the author and medical doctor describes the sense of betrayal she felt at her own circumcision at the age of six:

"I did not know what they had cut off my body, and I did not try to find out. I just wept, and I called out to my mother for help. But the worst shock of all was when I looked around and found her standing by my side. Yes, it was her, I could not be mistaken, in flesh and blood, right in the midst of these strangers, talking to them and smiling at them, as though they had not participated in slaughtering her daughter just a few moments ago."

Saadawi concluded that her mother, like most Egyptian women of her time, was not in a position to make any decisions, let alone whether or not her daughter should be circumcised, hence was not responsible for what happened to her.

Was my mother, like Saadawi's, just acting out the patriarchal wishes of her community? My mother tried several times to have a son, largely, I believe, because my father's family expected her to have one. (Sons are the gods in Asian families, the ones that rule the roost, in many cases, "controlling" their own mothers.) In all cases, the foetuses miscarried. Only the female foetuses (me and my sisters) survived till birth and beyond, a confirmation of the biological fact that, unlike the XX chromosome, the XY chromosome easily succumbs to its own demise when confronted with adversity. Her last attempt, in 1974, was successful, but just barely. The boy died within 24 hours of birth.

Ironically, despite her yearning for a male child and her somewhat sexist attitudes towards her own daughters, my mother did not conform to many of the female norms and traditions expected of her generation. Unlike many other Asian women of her age-group in Nairobi, my mother did not hesitate to do things on her own, to be the maverick in the stifling world of Sikh and other cloistered Asian societies in the city. It may not seem like a bold step now, but she was driving her own car long before many of her peers were even allowed by their husbands to sit at the steering wheel. (My own sister was not allowed to go out on her own in the first years of her marriage.) She defiantly wore make-up and saris at a time when it was considered too "modern" for Sikh women to show their bellies or wear lipstick, and worked a full day when women her age were sitting at home learning recipes and doing the gossip circuit. She never gossiped, not once. She said she didn't have the time, and besides, who cares what others do. But she prayed every single day. It was her deep faith, I believe, that kept her alive when most others would have given up. (During her illness, I played *shabads* (Sikh hymns) for her every single morning and evening. It was during this time that I also learned that Sikhism is probably the most musical religion in the world; no prayer is complete without a *shabad*, and apart from being highly knowledgeable about the philosophy contained in the Sikh holy book, the *Gurbani*, Sikh priests also have to learn to be musicians.)

When our father died in 1989, my sisters and I thought that our mother would step in and take over the nurturing role. But it didn't happen. Her sense of disappointment in us was clearly stronger than her maternal instinct. We all married the wrong men, especially me. "What will people say? What kind of daughters did I raise?" We were a constant disappointment at least that's what I thought. All my sisters had married young, to men of their choice. They were beautiful, not in the same way as my mother, but sufficiently enough to attract men who wanted to marry them; at least that's what I believed until Gray asked me to marry him. (Did I say yes to affirm to myself and to my mother that I was indeed beautiful, I often wonder – even when I knew that she would disapprove of the man I was marrying?)

In the end, I think all I wanted was her approval, even when she lay incapacitated in her bed, frail, weak, confused. How else can I explain the fact that even when I knew that she was in no position to scold me or show her disapproval, I constantly found myself doing things to please her, like finally learning to cook her favourite Indian dishes, or censoring myself from doing things that I knew she disliked. Maybe I thought that after years of disapproval, Mummy would finally approve of me, that she would know – at last – that I was a good child, someone who deserved to be loved and cherished. This need for her approval was so overwhelming that even when I knew she was fast asleep, I would find myself telling Gray not to smoke in the living room, knowing how much she hated cigarette smoke, or hiding the bottle of red wine from her view, hoping she would think that the beverage in my glass was Coca Cola.

On the other hand, I also suspect that if my mother had been doting, protective and smothering, I might never have taken risks, or branched out on my own. I may never have been a writer. If there was one trait that she did pass on to me, it was her independence, and, in some ways, her rebelliousness.

She was also fearless in many ways. Once, when her car stopped in the middle of Uhuru Highway, she walked home alone, almost a mile, without calling for help. She lived alone, at a time when crime in Nairobi was at its peak. Once, when thieves broke in and stole her TV while she was asleep in the next room, she shrugged her shoulders and said, "I never liked that TV anyway, now I can buy a new one." Only once have I seen real fear in her face – when she told me that she knew she was going to die. *"Main nai bachna"* (I will not survive), she said in Punjabi, crying like a baby. I cried too, but in the other room. I wanted to hold her and to say, "Yes, I know. But let us value the time we have left." But I couldn't. How do you tell someone you know is dying that they are dying? How?

A few months later, she suffered her second stroke, this time, more serious than the first one. It was 31st March 2005, ten days after my younger sister's husband Tushar, her favourite son-in-law, died suddenly at the age of 47 and two-and-a-half months after my older sister Rupa had a near-fatal car accident that fractured her skull. In an entry dated 16thMarch 2005, this is how Maggie, her nurse, described my mother's morning:

8.00 a.m.	Main routine done.
9.30 a.m.	Patient relaxed as per her instructions
11.00 a.m.	Bath and massage
12.30 p.m.	Physiotherapy done. Spasms. Tense. Looks so down, confused, no good speech. Admitted being fed up with life. Feels useless.

Mummy never came out of the coma. It was almost as if she had willed herself to die, two years after doctors had first diagnosed that she would not survive a week. The hospital doctor, like the one who attended to her the first time she slipped into a coma two years before, informed us that the likelihood of her descending into what he called "a vegetative state" were high, and advised us to look at the option of "not to resuscitate" – in medical jargon, this means not taking any extraordinary medical measures to keep a patient alive, in other words, letting nature take its course.

Around the same time, there was a legal struggle in the United States, where a husband was trying to keep his wife Terri Schiavo, who had been in a vegetative state and on life-support since 1990, alive. He lost the battle, but according to public opinion, letting Teri go was in her best interest. As columnist Anna Quindlen wrote in an April 2005 issue of Newsweek, *"Once the feeding tube was removed, polls showed that the majority of Americans believed Terri should die. That's probably because they've been there. They are the true judges and lawmakers and priests. They have been at the bedside, watching someone they love in agony as cancer nipped in the spine, as the chest rose and fell with the cruel mimicry of the respirator, and the music of personality dwindled to a single note and then fell silent. They know life when they see it, and they know when it is gone."*

Reading the article convinced me that letting her go was the only option we had because being alive and living are two completely different things. "Mum's gone, whether we like it or not," I wrote to a friend on 5th April 2005. Three months later, Mummy died.

Photograph: courtesy of Rasna Warah

RASNA WARAH is a freelance journalist based in Nairobi. She is the author of Triple Heritage: A Journey to Self-discovery *(1998); a book that explores the social, economic and political history of Asians in Kenya. From 1994-2002, she worked at the United Nations Human Settlements Programme (UN-Habitat) as editor of* Habitat Debate, *a quarterly periodical focusing on shelter and urban issues. She is also a keen photographer and has held exhibitions in Nairobi, Fukuoka and Amsterdam.*

B **Blogguy™** GET YOUR OWN BLOG | FLAG? | NEXT BLOG>>

October holiday galore

Sunday, October 22, 2006

At the rate at which we are going, you'd probably be forgiven if you thought it is January 2007. After all, we have had quite a number of holidays so far this October, and there are more on the way.

Hope you had a happy Kenyatta Day, and are now enjoying the fruits of independence, dear readers. What a glorious day of remembrance it was, perched on my favourite seat in the pub, debating the virtues and vices of a NARC administration gone wrong; of a country's hopes and dreams bungled over the years. Sometimes, I sit here and wonder where those 43 years have gone, watching this fledgling nation's fortunes wane over the years and we are now international beggars of repute. Who would have thought, all those years ago, that a promising band of new leaders would have started this sorry state of affairs and misrule? How much more ironic could it be, that a batch of mau mau "rebels" who fought for independence, could have probably charted a better path for Kenya had they not been pushed aside by the educated politicians we call the 'founding fathers'? Oops, I almost forgot, Kenyatta day is a holiday for patriots who appreciate their independence heroes, and as we all know, patriots never question the motives nor the decisions of those in charge.

So with a bottle of Tusker on my fist, fresh from Ruaraka, the home of the top taxpayers in Kenya: Exactly from whom are we celebrating this independence? I mean, as a Kenyan in this dark day and age, I've found myself anything but independent. Sure, I sit in the safe boundaries of this country, getting paid real Kenyan money to offer my services to an employer who appreciates my input, but Kenyan politicians have recently demonstrated to all and sundry that they are out of touch with the reality in the country. Fuck, I drove an imported (and used) Japanese vehicle to the bar, fuelled by Saudi Arabian oil, and I'm wearing a used American shirt sewn together by young Third World Asian hands. My used shoes were stitched together in the Philippines, the glass I'm drinking from was wrought in France, and the musicians prancing across the television screen have American names. Believe it or not, the very streets you walk on in Nairobi have been designed abroad for colossal amounts of money. Could it be possible, in all this vanity and self-worship, that a day dedicated to an event that took place many years ago is just a sham? Perhaps in the same manner that a King depends upon the taxes of his rulers to live his life of luxury, that we sit on this throne funded not by our own taxes but by the efforts of seemingly trivial loans from several foreign coffers? Consider this tonight; when you sit in front of your TV and watch the news (without Swaleh Mdoe to tickle your funny bone) to find out what Kibaki was up to. We depend upon:

- The World Bank and the Interfering Mother Fuckers (IMF) for loans to fund our spending;
- The Western world for our used clothing;

- The Internet for cracked computer software;
- Europe for our cell phones;
- Japan and Germany for automotive engineering;
- South Africa for eggs;
- Pakistan for rice;
- Tanzania for electricity poles;
- The USA and the UK for approvals;
- The Middle East for our petroleum (and those masochistic oil company cartels to boot);
- Scandinavia for premium liquors; and
- Uganda and Tanzania for bullshit political support and general jack-assery.

Once upon a time, a mob of pissed-off patriots had had enough shit from their oppressors and packed up for the bush to fight for a better way. A new way. And a New Kenya. On this Kenyatta Day weekend, you should remember exactly what that New Kenya has become: a charade of political clowns and executive pimps, whoring your patriotic asses out for the fat shilling in the offshore bank account. The government tells you the lies, the media relays the lies, and you, the gullible Kenyan, live the lies. The Narc dream, the vision, the role of our leaders to spur exponential economic growth and the elimination of poverty and tribalism is a vast illusion. No, Central province, the motorcade finally crossed River Chania, there was no Mumbi nor Gikuyu, and your President is a lying bastard. No, Western Kenya, there will probably never be a Luhya president. No Kalenjinland, William Ruto does not think about you even once, he just needs power to enrich himself, and he'll never be president anyway. No, Maasailand, 'your' land will never be returned, so stop bitching and move on with life.

So I beg you, on this weekend commemorating the imprisonment and deaths of our independence heroes, to look up from your feet and the newspapers, and pay attention to what is actually happening. You're not celebrating independence from anything, not your past of letting Kenyans die of Malaria as drugs rotted away in Nairobi godowns and Ministers drove multimillion limousines, your legacy of igniting and ignoring tribal genocides as we approach elections, the reputation of your leaders for exploiting the voters. You're not celebrating your right to sniff pussy in K-Street, your ability to masturbate in the sovereign abodes of your household and to own your own land. You're not celebrating your freedom from international oil pricing, the effect the Central Bank's controls have had on the fate of our agricultural exports, or what the KRA is going to do to your economy. And you're certainly not celebrating what those mau mau fighters had in mind when they armed themselves and went into the bush to push out the mbeberu.

You're celebrating their ignorance.

Ignorance of what Kenya would become, ignorance of all those dead Kenyans across the Rift Valley, ignorance of where your tax money is going or what those MPs are doing or who's raping who as the police watched. Ignorance of exactly what that flag you squirm to attention when it is hoisted and lowered signifies.

And your own ignorance that right now, that in your own country, a Kenyan is dying from a curable disease, another child goes without an education and a homestead is burning.

An elected official probably lit the match. A highly paid appointed spokesperson briefed the gathered press. A police officer held you back from the side of the road. A cameraman was robbed of his film. An editor, a total stranger, warped the words you read. An unfamiliar face on the TV read them to you in that assuring voice, with Swaleh Mdoe chained and en route to a probable deportation. And you believed them.

You believed every word they told you.

So why don't you believe me?

Ponder this: The Asian community controls about 70% of the Kenyan economy, their vote does not count in elections (except in some wards in Westlands and Kisumu!) and yet yesterday they were celebrating Diwali, their new year and yet this was not a Public Holiday. Our Muslim brethren on the other hand, control a smaller portion of the economy, mainly at the coast and the vast nothingness that is the North Eastern Province, and when they break their fast, it is a Public Holiday (as shall be on Tuesday 24 October). Christians on the other hand, make up the masses, their politicians double up as their tribal chieftains and the richest people on the land (coincidence? Nah), their vote counts, they control the smallest portion of the economy, mainly through the chieftains and yet you and me engage in a lot of chest thumping over freeing the land from the colonialists, while the benefits are clearly ending up elsewhere!

The only entity of which you're operating independently is the truth.

Celebrate that, fellow brainwashed Kenyans.

This blogger—Stackofstiffys—describes himself as an easygoing kind of guy who cares less about the majority of things, situations and people around him. The only thing he cares about is his family, friends and making a few guys laugh occasionally.

POTASH is a regular mid-twenties Kenyan guy trying to afford his next drop of alcohol. He has been in his mid-twenties for too long. His educational background remaining unknown, he continues to describe himself as a pseudo-intellectual. He detests yuppies, development cowboys and preachers who go bang in the night. On a regular Tuesday morning when you are working, he is sitting on a stone, in the mtaa, drinking, waiting for a half-life and writing about it. He confesses to having a longstanding grudge with Matathia.

Illustration: The Mindbender

Selling World Power

BY BILLY KAHORA

Jemima Kariuki is becoming Chinese.

'Charity begins at work,' she says breathlessly at every desk she stops at, licking her lips. A nervous habit from childhood. A few join: Mama Kitu the Domestic Revenue Manager's soon-to-retire secretary who had a sausage and 'Buru Buru free range' eggs business.

Bob Onyango "just call me Barbie," who offered green card opportunities for a price at the office, started asking her whether she could 'hook him up' with 'Red Cards' to go to China. He said he needed a new product and he saw potential in working together.

"I'll tell you the new Kenya is Dholuo and Gikuyu; working together. Kama

Kenyatta *na* O.O. Okuyu meets Kisum City," he said. Many at the office who had bought 'Green Card' promises from Onyango were yet to go to America.

Soon the office's informal marketplace couldn't stop whispering about Jemimah's new Chinese thing. Wires and Cables who were content with the money they made from stolen copper cables started deriding it. Accounts started looking for small things to deduct from her salary. All the messengers wanted to join but were unable to raise the Ksh. 500.

She stands in the queue with other junior clerks from Domestic Revenue, ExtelComms Inspectorate, Nairobi Lower Hill, at Mama Jacinta's. The kiosk has a smoky stillness and midday sunbeams bullet through the recycled wood walls. Once in awhile there is large crack as the iron-sheet roof suddenly expands and contracts from the lunchtime sun and a cloud of hot *githeri* gas washes the interior. It is the smell of boarding school dining halls and nostalgic village life.

Bessie, Jemimah's 'best friend from work,' is closest to her in the queue. Her back is to the counter so she does not notice she's holding the queue. Assumpta, a tall and beautiful engineer, stands in front of her. Three cheap suits from Accounts breeze past her and get their lunch, the corners of their eyes stretch, like tongues to lick at Assumpta.

One turns to her and says, "Sasa Beejing?"

And they start to giggle.

Beejing was conceived in Domestic Revenues, spreading to Wires and Cables and Accounts and finally legitimized in Field Division.

Jemima does not notice them. She is speaking to Assumpta, who is nodding graciously, her eyes roaming, panicked. Her eyes are hypnotized by Assumpta's mouth – large, large and soft and painted carefully, and never grimacing or stretching awkwardly. Bessie calls it a "Private sector mouth. She will never last here."

"Not America, Chaina is the next world powa—everyone knows. You need to buy new Made in China. Thas why I'm selling Made in China," Jemimah says. "Na-Sell World Power," Feeling confident.

"Yes, yes," says Assumpta seriously, "I went shopping in Cheng Du last year. Their kitchen tiles are very good."

"Korea, Iddian, Firipino watever," says Bessie with a glare. "I forgot my purse in the office. Can you pay for me?"

Jemima has become used to forgotten purses and lost handbags since Bessie lost her Nigerian boyfriend two years ago and stopped living what she used to call her *la vida loca.* Obi was thrown out of the country, leaving Bessie momentarily rich and propertied.

Jemimah still remembers the time Obi started sending his associates back for it all: the dark platinum 5-series Beemer, the Hutchings Biemer furniture, the Yaya 'executive' apartment. Bessie was left with some Dubai 24-carat gold trinkets, a pair of Dubai Donna Karan outfits, a Queen-size gold bed with a smaller mattress (concentric squares), her stocky puppy, Boss, who looked a bit too much like Obi, and an almost life-size poster of a Dubai Tiger, all yellow and gleaming and photo-shopped and crouching in a jungle of cartoon-like jungle-ness.

Bessie lived with her for awhile and they became friends. Jemima knows she is Bessie's only company at the office. But the days of doing Chinese, Japanese or seafood for lunch are long gone.

During friendlier moments like month-ends Bessie commiserates on their present vertical immobility in life with a standard sigh:

"My sista mon, Jemmie," She says this in her slow, stalking and deliberate way, in a passably bad Nigerian accent that with time has acquired old Jamaican reggae lyrics.

Bessie is long rather than tall—like a gawky giraffe calf.

'Jemmie' suggests to just about everyone that Bessie is unlikeable because she has a high center of gravity. She hates it when Bessie calls her 'Jemmie' though her short quirkiness has learnt to shrug this off - like many things about Bessie. Part of her understands that her plump round-shouldered lightness is complemented by Bessie's dark long looks.

"Kwisha. Kaput!" says the young man behind the counter, with a smile, and a flourish of the *sufuria* lid. He bangs two lids together, *"Chakula kwisha!"*

Accounts are already seated, enjoying what was supposed to be Domestic Revenue's *Chapati Madondo.* Beans and chapatis.

"'hhh bana...Camon Kitchen Toto, not again!" Bessie says skewing her eyes, elbows aflutter.

Kitchen Toto laughs, "And where is last month's money, by the way? Mama Jacinta *anakutafuta."*

He bangs his lids again, and a cheer rises from Accounts.

Domestic Revenue has to do *Chapatis* and Stoney Tangawizi. They aren't happy and all leave the queue except Jemimah. Bessie glares at Jemimah who is left talking Chinese products to Jacinta, who made her way to the till when she saw Jemima.

"Kianshi is Chinese. They do multi-level marketing. Selling Chinese products. Wait a minute ... here it is," she says to Jacinta, as she riffles through her bag.

"As it says here... I will photocopy this for you. No you don't have to pay for photocopies. I'll do them at the office."

Jacinta holds up her hand. *"Ngoja,"* she says. Wait. She quickly scribbles on her receipt book. Photocopy—J to Pay.

"Kianshi is a large-scale global enterprise group. Advanced biotechnologies. Advanced... you understand. Kianshi boasts a rapid average annual growth rate. 270%..." Jemimah suddenly remembers the video presentation, and juts out her chest to project her voice.

The kiosk is quiet with chewing. Light beams shooting through the holes in the *mabati* walls slant as the sun moves across the sky.

"Three years minimum I plan to be Kianshi head marketer. You have the 500 shillings to join for me."

"Dengu Chapati," shouts a late customer, pushing Jemima aside. Jemimah sits down, ignoring Bessie's glower.

As she eats, she counts, in her head, everyone in the building they work in; Mlima House. All the Ministries, Labour, National Planning and the defunct

Heritage; 5 askaris at the gate, the women selling felt pens near the chain fence around the compound, the two police and four Receptionists. Eighteen storeys in the building, fifty people per storey.

She turns to Bessie.

"Like the wheel of a bike, every ka-spoke is No 1. With ten percent of *kila mwananchi* in our building has ninety people," she says to no one in particular, removes a pen from her bag, and starts making notes.

"I need to invest in a scientific calculator," she says.

Everyone sitting at the Domestic Revenue table laughs.

'Shock on you," Bessie says to Jemmie, "Somebody told that me the Aloe Vera products are better," she leans in to whisper, "the cream tightens it down there."

That Friday afternoon there is no one in the Domestic Revenues' cardboard and urine smell office, 4th floor Mlima House. Everyone is running around, collecting money for the coming weekend from their various office enterprises. *Saa nane na forty.*

It is quiet. Jemimah is relieved and exhausted after 2 hours of detailed calculations in Mama Jacinta's small hot office. Mama J is a member of: GLD, AMWAY, ALOE VERA, HERBATRONICS, and five merry-go-rounds.

But, But, when Jemima hears this, "Kianshi is special. All members are a FAMILY. Chaina is the next World Powa."

Friday traffic and street shouts and smells rise from the street, like *Githeri*-gas, the burning blue saucer of sky outside the curtainless windows, grit in her eyes and the perpetual smell of urine and chemical lemon: the things she is trying to get out of life.

VISUALISE, said the video: driving up 'Community' the hill that leads to her office. Passing by and drifting towards leafy Nairobi suburbs, going West into Hurlingham, Adams or Karen,- a non-working and free woman unencumbered at 3p.m on a weekday afternoon. Following the setting sun in the opposite direction to her 5 p.m. reality; Downtown-Eastlands.

She has calculated. With hard work it could take up to two years. She finishes drawing the generational multi-level mind map structure for Mama Chanua and quickly writes up lunchtime projections for her sponsor—Mr. Han So. He is the head of Kianshi Multi-marketing in Kenya.

Mr. Han So has asked her to come up with a more identifiable Kenyan name for Kianshi. She was his choice for that select assignment among many other Kianshi hopefuls and when she looks around the tired office, she knows she will be leaving soon. Jemimah underlines beneath the projections she has placed on paper—NOT TOO SHABBY!—then starts working on the new name.

"Chenya, Kinya," she mutters rolling her tongue. Trying to enunciate the vowels. She does not see the slouching figure before her for a moment. When she opens her eyes the intern she is assigned to train that afternoon is standing at her desk. She ignores his hands both placed on her desk

"... Er Sammy." Her head is still on the Kianshi figures and names.

"In-this-department-we-deal-with-telecommunication-revenue. We-get-photos

–from-all-over-the-country-that-show-pipeline-meter-readings. Edit-and-forward-to-IT," she says in staccato.

"Eh."

After going through the meter counter photos for half an hour with the intern she looks around and, making sure there is no one within earshot, pulls back her shoulders and says in her best 'multi-marketing voice', smiling:

"Ever heard of multi-level marketing? While everyone is doing silly *tu*-small businesses in this office there is money to be made."

The intern jerks back, startled, 'Is this part of my internship?'

Jemimah ignores the Friday lunch alcohol under his breath, noting with surprise the expensive patterned yellow shirt he is wearing. Han So has taught her to look for potential signs.

"Nice shirt. I can always tell a dyed in the wool multi-level marketer," she smiles.

"What you doing after work?" he asks. They are alone in the office- 3.30 p.m, 'By the way....my name is Walter.'

"I could have sworn you were Silas? Ha!"

He grins.

Even better, she thinks. A thick skin. Not easily offended.

"*Skiza,"* he says smoothly, "I can't join you. Marketing training seminar. Four-thirty, Westlands."

The intern walks away and picks up the phone at the next desk and starts dialing, all the while looking at her with a new insolence.

She ignores him and fishes a small mirror from her bag, admiring the new red suit with padded shoulders that she chose in the morning. It is one of a batch she bought in Ngara market after joining Kianshi.

She still remembers, now with disbelief, the chiffon dresses with erratic hemlines and balloon shoulders that she wore when she just moved to Nairobi from Karatina.

She then graduated to buying softer skirts with shorter hemlines and white blouses from Wangari Posta. Even if they weren't half bad Bessie always made fun of her saying they made her blend in like a good Made in China weave. After Obi left, and her own dreams of a Nigerian on a white horse, she started attending motivational classes and wearing suits.

Feeling the intern's eyes still on her she purses her lips like she's about to whistle at her compact mirror. She notices a growing cold sore on her lip but applies lip gloss anyway.

Some men from Wires and Cables have joined the intern in looking at her from over the far corner of the partitioned office. One imitates her with a clipboard. She ignores them: she is meeting Han So.

Jemima did not ask Bessie to join the multi-level marketing venture. She suspected her *'sista'* would be highly successful. Lately she has thought of introducing Bessie to Han So's brother-in-law, Jin-Shu. But decided he's too short for Bessie.

After the mandatory one month's training she now judges everyone around her as either a 'multi-level marketer' or a 'non-marketer.' Or even worse, the bottom of the marketing heap—the 'traditional marketer.' This is something Han So has trained her to be wary of. Traditional marketers like the father of her eight-year-old son Kim. And her parents back in Karatina.

Even with Han So's training the criteria she uses to judge 'marketers', 'non-marketers' and 'traditional marketers' is vague and instinctive.

'Many people are like that in Kenya. They prefer luck to hard work.'

This is something she never tires of telling her focus group during the seminars Kianshi has arranged. She gives her own personal testimony whenever she gets a chance. Talking of her first years in Nairobi when she attended Christian Sunday morning seminars in the city where everyone seemed too happy and clappy for her. Hoping that the Lord would make them rich.

"When I first arrived in Nairobi two years ago, I lived with my relatives... *Mbari ya Mundia*. They hated me but I loved them. You will meet many people like that when you go out there selling," she says. In reality the Mundias were vaguely hostile and pleasantly indifferent to Jemimah.

"I thank Mundia *wa* Steven for getting me my job but not for making me take Word Processing 3 and Sales Certificate 4. So I quit and moved to a high-rise bed-sitter in Kayole. In Nairobi you start with a small inch so I started saving. And I am here now."

She never tires of playing testimony with the five other telemarketers in her Kianshi group. All have undergone the one-month training period together. Jemimah can't always remember their names.

They are such a sight—an exercise in Han So's faith. An old recovering alcoholic who lost his senior marketing position at one of Kenya's largest HMO's, some bright kid just out of International School of Kenya, Han So's ever grinning brother-in-law Jin Shu. The rest hover on the edges of Jemimah's memory.

The nervous oddity of the group doesn't matter in the face of Han So's motivational speeches, "Magnifying glass catch sun, bring power, focus energy. Then fire! Catch potential!"

They all cheer and become one.

Since she joined Kianshi she finds that she also categorizes aloud: national politicians, newscasters and people starring in TV ads as they come on into either 'traditional marketers or 'telemarketers. Her 'come we stay' husband, Miano, curses and mutes the TV: "Okay, Let's listen to YOU, *nye nye nye ... nye nye nye,*" he says. "All the time. *Nye nye nye ...* Go on and on. *Endelea ...*" he urges with vicious relish.

Once during these regular TV battles, Jemimah switched the TV off in a huff during one of his favourites: *Nderemo ya Mabingwa.* Win-A-House Contest. She then watched him mentally calculating whether her action warranted some form of physical action. He gave her a look saying: "I guess if I win the house you won't be coming." She ignored him as he walked out of the door and made him sleep on the floor after he came back after three days, drunk, meek and dishevelled.

"Being multimarketer, very challenge," Han So has told her.

MADE IN CHINA

Jemimah recognizes the uneasy 'détente' that becoming Chinese has provided between her and Miano. She finds him useless now that she has more money but likes the new sense of power over a man. She wonders what he'll say when she tells him about her son. She is too busy for now to engage in retaliatory agression.

A few months after they met, she kept waking Miano up with screams from a recurring bad dream. Her son Kim would appear in a field of maize. Kim would be wearing his grey, black and white boarding academy uniform. Starting at the foot of the field he would wander into the long stalks and she would helplessly watch as the lilting green leaves started to whir like blades as he walked in harsh sunlight.

Miano would wake up to her thrashing and, still semi-drunk from the previous night, find this arousing. His gropings, which came to nought, would calm her down. He stopped asking what was wrong when he decided Jemimah was not epileptic. Though he found a payslip lying around, full of scribbles and evidence that there was another budgetary presence in her life, he said nothing.

And so Kim went undiscovered.

On Monday, happy and high after three weekend meetings with Mr. So, Jemimah comes to work dressed in a dress from China.

"It is 'Qipao," Han has told her. It is a long, flowing, deep blue garment—with aquamarine herons on the breast flowing over the shoulder to the small of her back. She ignores the snickers from Wires and Cables.

"Also called Cheongsam. Not only for Chinese woman but beautiful all woman," Han So says.

"Come in many style. You can sell here in Kinya???"

Her boss PK Maina calls her into his office. *"Kama unataka kuvaa hiyo stupid* national dress you do it in your home."

"This is Chinese silk! It is called Kipao." She storms out of his office People stare and laugh through the glass partition of PK Maina's office.

"Mambo ya wanawake," he mutters shaking his head.

Jemimah notices Bessie is as usual irritated about Kianshi.

"I can't see myself coming with a Nigerian *Agbada* to work. If and when I could. And Jemmie you know what I mean—I had the money and the man."

She places her fingers on the sides of Jemimah's eyes and tugs upwards: "Chinese."

Sideways: "Japanese."

And downwards: "Portuguese."

Bessie then puts her hand flutteringly to her chest, leans back and says: "Nigerian."

This starts both women laughing hard.

During the next two weeks Jemimah notices that Han So is getting more and more interested in her work. He keeps on asking about ExtelComms products —and even asks her to get copies of shipment invoices, credit notes and LPO's.

Then one day he says: "You know ... er how you say it ... where government company you work for buys..."

He makes as if to pick up something. She can tell he means a telephone receiver and handset.

"Your boss is good man?"

"He's a traditional marketer," she says dismissively, thinking of her affair with PK Maina two years ago. Then PK Maina was not the present brusque, top-heavy man given to picking his teeth to distraction in the afternoons at the office. She was still in the white blouse, tight skirt phase. Jemimah stopped sleeping with him when he started telling everyone he was "eating Beejing."

Soon after Jemimah met Miano and moved in with him.

At Jemimah's dismissal of PK Maina as a 'traditional marketer', Han So turns furious, his eyes glazing over from behind his thick glasses and he curses in Chinese. "No time for joke. Time for serious. You introduce me?" he says with a furious smile, tapping his chest and almost pushing his hand into her face.

She decides not to tell Han So about Maina's recent scorn at the Chinese dress he gave her and invites him to work and introduces him to her boss. Han So and Maina talk for two hours. They are intent and huddled, through the transparent government glass. Then they laugh and shake hands. When Han So comes out of PK's office she walks him out.

"Beejing, Beejing," she can hear loud stadium whispers. Bessie laughs out loud. "Jemimah is furious."

"Now you know how I used to feel when you'd call Emenkua, 'Obi."

"Your boss he good man."

They are outside in the hot sun. She realizes for the first time, that he is shorter than her. She can put her hands all around his upper frame. Until now, she has never contemplated physical contact with him. He has small tight thrusting hips, and a charcoal coloured mouth—smoke and beer and certain knowledge. She wonders what their children would look like.

Pink to medium brown depending on the time of day, she decides.

"He agree to buy Chinese phone phone. We soon talk about computer."

"I have come up with a name that sounds Kenyan for Kianshi-Kenshi," she eagerly tells him. He nods absently.

"When are our products arriving?"

"Factory in Shanghai burn down. Six months."

Later that afternoon, PK Maina passes by her desk and whispers: "I like your *kajamaa. Anaelewa* Kenya. He taught me some Chinese words—you know what *kuma* in Chinese is?"

The moment Jemimah has been dreading comes.

Han So is to visit her two-room Highrise bedsitter in Kayole. She wonders whether they know each other well enough.

She has postponed visiting her son Kim at his Academy in the Athi Plains that weekend. This she can tell will be another trigger on the escalating hostility from her mother – like Miano, her mother is another looming front.

Jemimah makes sure the maid removes all the wet clothes hanging in the small corridor leading to her room. She removes the *vitambaas* from the red velvet jumbo sofa set, looks at them and puts them back. She opens all the windows trying to make the room larger and removes a cracked mirror that hangs on top of the TV.

She stares at the small pile of books from her days at Maseno University.

Looking at a household list on the wall—an account from one of the local shops where she has scribbled the little Chinese she has learnt, Jemimah suddenly feels small and hopeless. She crosses out the Chinese words. They are from a book Han So has lent her. She takes her monthly shopping list down from the kitchen wall.

Mwangi Shop List – July

Mafuta Boy 1kg
Milk (30 pkt) Milk =
Bread (8) Bread
Ugari Maizemeal
Ketepa
Tomatoes
Waru
Boga
Degu
Beans
Bebe
Hey-Ho
Mchere...

With nothing to do but wait until Han So calls her on her cell-phone, she walks out of the door and, while looking down from the abrupt balcony her phone suddenly rings.

"*Haai,*"

"*Mathee,*" she hears. It's her son Kim.

As she looks down she is surprised to see Han So emerge from a small Canter parked outside the block of bed-sitters. She had hoped he would call first.

"Mathee..."

"Kimani."

"I couldn't make it ...this weekend. Sorry."

"Mathee. Una homa? You sound funny."

"Kimani. English. English. Argh..leave that Sheng daddy....how are you?"

Kids have gathered around Han So, "Jackie Chan, Jackie Chan."

Chopping their hands and kicking in the air. Han So laughs and shouts and with a flourish takes a Kung Fu stance: "Ha."

He looks up, sees her and waves her down. Relieved, thinking he might not come up after all, she clacks down the five flights of stairs in heels, still on the phone. Looking at the huge white quarry at a distance she feels a sudden heat on her face.

"Mathee. Mi si mlami."

"Kimani!"

"Okay. When are you coming. Will you bring *Kenchic?"*

People are lighting *jikos* everywhere. Saturday maize and beans, *githeri* gas everywhere, the smells of her mother's life. There is a burst water pipe. Water overflows from the third floor to the second in a stink.

"Soon. Soon. Your school is so nice. Green, big. Like where I grew up." Jemimah sighs.

"Mum, *imejaa wa Cambodia.*"

"Kambas are not as bad as some people in Kenya. Are there any Chinese?"
"Hakuna ma Jackie Chang."

She paces herself, tiptoeing through the last flight of stairs—she wants to finish with her son before she meets Han So, who is cut off from view by a wall. On the ground floor she sees some of the bigger kids playing with Han So. He can't see her. The kids are looking intently at her phone.

"Bye Dadee... I will call tomorrow."

"Like leettle monkeys," Han So smiles, looking at the crowd of kids gathered around when she finally appears.

Jemimah is thankful that Miano is not home.

Soon Han So's men start stacking boxes everywhere in the small house. When one box falls down the stairs Han So curses furiously. "Carefle. Carefle." Small containers and packets of seasoning Royco fall out. Han So hands out an armful to Jemimah.

"For you. Good friend of Han So. Loyco."

She laughs. How long did it take for her to stop saying: "Loyco."

As the men go up and down she notices an oil stain on one of the boxes. "For cooking. Fat for cooking. Some for you. Good friend of Han So."

She is happy when he doesn't ask to go up to her house. He seems more interested in the shops metres away from where they stand.

"Come let us dleenk soda dleenk," he says his hands busily fishing into his pockets. He also waves the kids over and ends up buying over 50 sodas and 30 *mandazis.*

"Ha ha ha. For good fliend of Han So."

Once inside Han So leaves her and goes to talk to Mwangi, the owner of the mini-market shop. Han So then goes outside. His men bring in five cartons. Jemimah sitting at the table sees Mwangi shaking his head.

"Angalia hii label. These Omo packets are torn."

"Half plice. For good friend of Han So," Han So says. Mwangi laughs and shakes his hand.

"Money half yours," Han So whispers to Jemima as they walk out. She likes his lips, his hair tickles her ear, and his breath is strange and exciting.

"Electical....silk... Some to sell. Toothpick, clockradio. Big and small. Yes? Till Kianshi product come from Shanghai."

Han So never comes back to Kayole after his one and only visit. The Canter comes every Monday at 11 a.m to Jemimah's house to pick up boxes. Miano says nothing when he notices the full shelves in their kitchen, their small bathroom laden with Vim and Jemimah's dressing table full of Lady Gay and Limara.

Han So now frequently comes to the office to see P.K Maina, many a time just waving from a distance at Jemimah. He comes over to her desk when she has money for him from the Royco seasoning, Vim toilet detergent, Kiwi shoe polish and Eveready batteries that she has sold in Kayole. After about six months Jemimah and her focus group are still waiting for Kianshi products.

One Friday, PK Maina comes wearing a deep blue silk shirt and a glossy tie with herons that shimmer in the office dust.

"People are saying that your Beejing boyfriend bought him a car," Bessie tells her.

After almost a year since Jemimah started her Kianshi adventure she is the biggest supplier of consumer products in Phases 3,4 and 5.

She knows it-she has come far since the '97 'floods' when she moved there. Getting home at midnight after wading through half of Nairobi and pushing matatus. Now Kayole is no longer nights spent staring and listening to the rushed pounding of rain on her ceiling at three in the morning waiting to start the next day.

One Tuesday morning she climbs into her usual five a.m *matatu*. As the *matatu* pulls into the City Center a dirty brownish light fills the sky. It is August again and the cold months are behind Nairobi. By the time the *matatu* gets to Lower Hill, ExtelComms offices, she is warm from FM 101.8's Breakfast Show offering cash prizes and a climbing sun.

Later that morning three men in brown and grey suits and grim bland and smiling faces wordlessly show up at ExtelComms. They directly walk into PK Maina's office. Everyone can see something is wrong. Two of the men sit in PK'S visitor's chairs and the third, a fattish individual with folds of skin for hair sits behind PK Maina's desk. PK Maina remains standing, alert like a schoolboy with his hands behind his back. He never sits down even as the others stand and pace;

leaving empty chairs to sit on.

Very little work is done in the office that day. Wires and Cables is hushed—the department could be under investigation, being the most lucrative in Extelcomms. Jemimah doesn't even pretend to work after she notices P.K Maina pointing her out to the men. The fat guy in the brown jacket fingers the folds of fat on his scalp, rubs the top of his head hard, all the time smiling through the glass partition.

Later she sees him feeling P.K Maina's mauve silk shirt between his fingers. The other men laugh silently behind the glass.

Bessie is full of information, *"Msichana,* they are coming for you! It is for you. I know that bald guy. I recognize him from when I was with Emenkua..."

Jemimah looks angrily at her: "Do not compare China to Nigeria. Nothing will happen. I tell you. Nigeria and China. How can you compare a world power with a *foo foo* drug culture."

Lunch time comes and goes and the men are still in PK Maina's office when everyone comes back from *madondo* and *chapati*. It's that time of the month. No one can afford *nyama* and this makes the atmosphere at the office more oppressive. Finally the men leave at around four pm; carrying a phone handset.

"Nothing. Nothing," PK Maina tells her when she rushes in.

"Han So is in China. His mother is sick. Can I leave early?" she says, somewhat aimlessly. PK Maina wearily waves her away. She picks up the heavy bag of Gukki designer clothes and Pansonic electronic samples she brought for some people at the office on the way out.

The next day the three men come back. This time they carry a large paperbag and walk straight into PK Maina's office. After a few minutes PK Maina comes and calls her, "These men are from the State Research Bureau. Nyakundi, Kaboga and Rutto."

In the office the men look at her without a word and spill cans, bottles and packets on PK Maina's desk; Royco, Vaseline Petroleum Jelly, Cooking oil, Omo, Tea, Kiwi, Homecup Chai, Lady Gay.

"Tese tings are costing the Kenya Refenue Othority 1 pillion a year," Fattish says. He is Nyakundi. Today he wears a green suit.

They hand her a *Nation* newspaper, opening it up in the middle: "FAKE OR REAL: THE CHOICE IS YOURS," it reads. There are photos of all the items on the desk. "Don't worry Matam. This can go away, as we told your boss and our friend here, Mr Maina. The Trade Descriptions Act just needs you to prove that you did not know these are fake. And I'm sure you did not know this was a crime. That is the law for you. Ignorance is your defence." PK Maina shakes his head in agreement. Droplets of sweat fly.

Nyakundi beckons to her to come to the corner. He whispers into her ear: "Nyakundi and Co understand. But te magistrade..... Even your boyfriend Mr Han-Chu. Good friend of everyone ... We need to find him. Dondi worry. He is our friend."

Jemimah tells them everything.

The verdict:

Café *TwendiOne*. Kenyatta Avenue. four pm. *Alafu tumalizane*. Bring forty thousand.

A week later there is a knock at the door in the early evening. It is Mwangi, the mini-market owner. Jemimah has never seen him like that. Dishevelled and unkempt. It's time she brought up moving out of Kayole with Miano she decides. They can afford it. Everybody either looks drunk or criminal.

"I thought we've already paid for our monthly milk account," she says as she turns to get her handbag.

"Wait ... you know the police had put me inside for one week selling curry powder mixed with flour as Royco," he shouts. "Your Royco. Your Omo. Asking me why it is doesn't wash. Kiwi *yako* hardens my customers shoes. I've closed shop. Njuguna and Kimemia also bought from your boyfriend and are still inside—Buru Buru police. Wait till they get out and you'll see."

"Fake or real the choice is yours," Jemimah shouts at his back, as he thuds downstairs. She can see the city's tiny lights in the distance; they are almost touchable.

"That's why they were half price! *Shenzi!*" she shouts into the night.

Miano comes to the door and drags her in. He explains it's just a matter of time till the police pick her up even if they have already given Nyakundi and Co. forty thousand shillings.

That night they hurriedly pack and move out in the dead of the night. They also carry Han So's remaining boxes and bags full of clothes and electronics. All they leave in the small apartment are the Kianshi brochures.

Jemima got to know about Kianshi for the first time when a vendor handed a small promotional leaflet in a *matatu*.

'Make Money. Sell Chinese products. Call no. 0740444888 and attend seminar at K.I.C.C. February 5th' the leaflet said. That's when she met Han So. A small man wearing a flashy tracksuit and dark glasses with an even smaller identical half standing by his side. Jinshu, his brother-in-law, wearing exactly the same clothes. There were about two hundred people. Han So's helpers sent away all those without employment I.D's—leaving about twenty-five people in the small hall.

She met Han over the next few weeks for 'interviews' before she signed up with Kianshi. Once, during these meetings she asked him what China was like and for the first time since she had met him he grinned.

"There is story of famous Chinese government official with heart of general. Name is Lin Tse-hs. My father named me after him but don't use that name here. In 1830...1840, I not remember exact. He refuse British product but greedy Chinese government official agree. British then bring opium and people become weak. British first say they sell to China world power. British say British products are world power. And that Chinese will become strong. But come opium. And then opium war or Anglo China war. Me not like that. Want to make China strong and Kenya strong. Bring products that make Kenya and China strong. Bring Kianshi. Bring World Power."

As the *matatu* swerves past Globe cinema, Jemimah pictures Miano and Kim, who have no idea the other exists, sitting in a shop in Karatina town. She already has a name for the shop. She will call it 'World Power.'

Illustration: Peter Ngungui

BILLY KAHORA is the Assistant Editor of Kwani? *and a freelance journalist. He writes fiction and is published in* Kwani 3 *under the penname B Karanja Wa Njama. He is currently an M.SC student in creative writing at Edinburgh University, where he is working on a novel based on his short story* 'The Applications' *and a collection of short stories.*

How Did I Get Here

Sunday, July 23, 2006

No one has ever accused me of being sane. And they're not going to start now.

A Kenyan's Guide to Kenya- Vol. I

I've often been terribly disappointed by the tourist guidebooks written about Kenya. Most of the time they tell you stuff you already know, like "you can go on safari and see some lions." That's probably why you wanted to come here in the first place, so that's not helpful. Other times they give you all manner of useless information. For example: what's the point of telling you how to ask for directions in Kiswahili if you're not going to understand the answer? (Sometimes they seem to be written by a malicious Kenyan who hates tourists. One time I was lying on the beach and was accosted by an earnest American who said, *"Jambo. Nyinyi muna kula viazi?"* First of all, no Kenyan says "Jambo." Secondly, I was lying on the beach, I was alone and I definitely wasn't eating potatoes.)

These books never tell you about all the amazing people you can meet in Kenya, or how to understand what they're saying. Determined to correct this horrible wrong, I'm issuing the first of many useful, practical tips for our many visitors. Behold Volume I of *"A Kenyan's guide to Kenya."* (Disclaimer: this is written from a Nairobi perspective. Other parts of the country are a whole other story and will cost you extra.)

Here's what you should know:

When we want you to pass us something—the salt, say—we'll point with our mouths. Example: We'll catch your eye then say, *"Nani."* Then we'll use our mouths to point at the desired object. This is achieved by a slight upward nod followed by an abrupt thrusting out of the lower lip, which is pointed in the object's general direction. There's no explanation for this. (*"Nani"* can be roughly translated as, oh I don't know, "Whats-your-face," "You," or "Thingie." We're unfailingly polite.)

Frequently, and for no reason whatsoever, we'll refer to a person as "another guy." However, this MUST be pronounced/ slurred thus: *An-aa* guy. This also applies to "the other day," which is when some momentous event in our lives always took place. We do the same thing with Kiswahili words like *'bwana'*, which is pronounced *'bana.'*

Example: "I was driving in town the aa day and this guy comes from nowhere and cuts me off, bana. Man I abused him!" 'Abused' in this sentence must be drawn out and emphasised for maximum effect: a-BUSE-d.

We claim to speak English and Kiswahili, which technically means that we should be able to communicate with the English-speaking world and Tanzania. What we really mean is that if you're not Kenyan you won't understand a damn word we say or why we say it.

Example: *"Sasa"* in Kiswahili means "now." We use it as a greeting.

Correct usage: *"Sasa?"* "Ah, *fit.*" It confuses us that Tanzanians don't understand this.

We also, just as randomly, might greet you by saying, "Otherwise?" Common response: "Uh-uh." There is no explanation for this.

Kenyans are multi-lingual, but all that means is that we believe that if we translate something word for word from one language to another it will make sense. A Kenyan might say, for example, "You mean you're not brothers? But you look each other!" Be kind, they just think that *muna fanana* can slip into English unfiltered. Speaking of filters, that's why some people (tribe/ethnicity withheld to protect my uncles) will claim to 'drink' cigarettes. If you're not Kenyan you won't understand this. Let it go.

We can buy beers at police stations. Grilled meat too. Heck, in some cop shops you can even play darts. I am NOT making this up.

Example: "Man the aaa day I *pitiad* (passed through) the Spring Valley cop station after work. I was leaving there at midnight, *bana*. I was so wasted! I told those cops to just let me go home."

Oh, that's another thing: when we're leaving a place (your house, a wedding, the cop shop bar...) we tend to say, "Ok, me let me go..." We're not implying that you're holding us against our will; we're just saying that we'd like to go. (The plural is, of course, "Us let us go.")

When Kenyans say that you're mad, it's a profound compliment. "Man this guy is mad. You know what he did..." then they'll go on to recount some of your admirable exploits. It's high praise. Smile modestly and accept it. By modest I mean look down, draw a circle in the dust with the toe of your shoe (or just your toe) and then smile, draw your mouth down into a brief frown, and smile again. Alternate quickly a few times. This is known by English-speaking Kikuyus as The *Nyira* Smile, or The Sneering Smile. Then say "aah, me?" in a high, sing-songy voice. However, only do this if you're female.

On the other hand, if Kenyans ask, "are you normal? (Sometimes pronounced *"nomo"*), then they're getting a bit concerned about your state of mental health. Reassure them by buying another round.

Which brings me to Alcohol- our national pastime. You know that myth about Eskimos having thousands of words for 'snow?' Well, our beloved drinks are known by a thousand names and phrases too. Kenyans will 'catch pints (or just 'catch'),' 'go for a swallow,' have a 'jweeze,' *'keroro,' 'kanywaji,' 'jawawa...'* really, no list can be exhaustive. Be aware, though, that the words you use will immediately tip off your audience about your age. (For the Kenyans reading this, no I was NOT born during the Emergency, you swine.)

Our other pastime is religion (what a contradiction?). If you're broke on a Sunday—and your hangover is not too bad—stroll over to one of our parks and catch some open-air preaching. Jeevanjee Gardens in town is a prime location. There you will see us in our full multi-lingual, spiritual splendour. There is always, and I mean always, a freelance preacher thundering in English while his loyal and enthusiastic sidekick translates into Kiswahili.

Sample:

Preacher: And then Jesus said...

Sidekick: Alafu Yesu akasema...

Preacher: Heal!

Sidekick: Pona!

Preacher: HEAL!

Sidekick: PONA!

It's hypnotic. We suggest you go with a Kenyan who understands both languages because sometimes the sidekick nurses higher ambitions and, instead of translating, tries to sneak in his own parallel sermon.

If you're bored in Kenya it's because you're dead.

As you've probably figured out, we like abbreviating things. (Why would the word 'another' have to be any shorter than it is? Why would the Kenyans reading this find it odd that I keep talking about 'Kiswahili'?) This can lead to unnecessary confusion. But by now you should have figured out that when you're catching and someone says, *'Si you throw an-aa ra-o?'* they of course want you to buy another round of drinks. Don't worry about the *'si;'* like so many words in Swa it's impossible to translate. Embrace it, sprinkle it liberally in your speech and move on. There are several such words, which will be tackled in Volume II.

Coming up in Volume II: why you shouldn't try to understand sheng (and please dear God don't try to speak it), why your strange ideas about forming queues won't work here, and why Nairobians love pornographic chicken. Contains a glossary of untranslatable but essential Swa words (like *'ebu,' 'ati,' 'kumbe'* and *'kwani'*).

posted by Kenyanchick at 10:51 AM | 22 August, 2006 03:14

Photography: Jackie Lebo Illustration: The Mindbender

Running

BY JACKIE LEBO

A diner has skipped out on his bill and indicated to the waitress we will pay. We talk amongst ourselves and it emerges that no one can recall seeing the man, who, apparently, was seated a few tables away. We lean out of the veranda and scour Iten's main thoroughfare. The waitress dutifully follows. It is early morning and traffic, human and otherwise, is still sparse. He cannot have gone far but we don't see the diner among the few people walking, huddled into sweaters and jackets, bracing against the chill. Attempts to get a description are futile. "Was he a runner?" someone asks. The waitress shrugs. The only thing he said before he left was that he was from up the road. We cannot ascertain if he meant his workplace. One last look and still no one; he seems to have vanished into thin air leaving only a white receipt for two cups of tea in the waitress's hand.

When she hands the bill specifically to Alex Kipkosgei, we attribute it to his 'counsellor' status. Alex is the Head of Maintenance at Iten District Hospital. He has also been professional athlete for ten years, runs an organization named Aldai Sports Development Association and is the liaison for a Holland-based agent. His multiple roles connect him to all sides of the community – the runners, civil servants, businessmen and farmers. Walking through the town is a slow progress. An unkempt man with wild hair from the Ministry of Works, who looks like he has been drinking all night and not made it home, pulls him aside for a few minutes to talk about a project at the hospital. A group of eager young runners, their leader in a Nike t-shirt with a *swoosh* and 'Run' emblazoned on it, stop to ask about management, key to breaking into the lucrative European Circuit. In another town, Alex could easily pass unnoticed. He is small, quiet and looks younger than his thirty-three years because of the constant athletic training. But in Iten, where there are 400 to 700 runners during peak training season, he is sought out for his connections in the running world.

Iten is a town with no centre. It has formed around a T-junction, the shops on the main street of the town lining the tarmac road that comes from Eldoret and goes to Kabarnet; the other shops line the road to Kapsowar. From Eldoret, thirty kilometres west, the town is hemmed in by farms, from thousand acre tracts to small subsistence plots. The land is flat, with fertile red soils suitable for grain, mainly maize and wheat. The even expanse of the Uasin Ngishu plateau drops spectacularly into the Kerio valley at the edge of the town. Sitet Complex, a hotel built near the cliff, offers tea with great panoramas, but its curtains are often drawn against the view. It is testament to the fact until now land value was weighted a lot more on productivity than vistas. Cliff land, which used to be given to unmarried women in Keiyo society, has gone up tremendously in value as hotels that cater to elite runners and foreign managers are built.

The valley is dry, with thorny acacias, and people eking out a living from the thin soils, in contrast to their better-off neighbors in the plateaus above. A deep narrow gorge at the bottom of the valley holds the Kerio River. Crocodiles sun themselves on a sand bank and the small boys with fishing rods a little way down the river seem unconcerned, clambering up the rocks to sell their catch on the side of the road—delicious whiskered catfish. It is said the crocodiles, which knew the taste of vanquished warriors from old feuds, had come to taste the blood of modern feuds, too. Most of the day the Tugen hills on the far side of the Kerio are blue, but the late afternoon light shows the hills to be green as the sun changes position and they seem to move closer; Kabarnet, on the spine of the hills, can be seen beginning at twilight as a cluster of lights. On a clear day you can see beyond the Tugen hills, which separate the Kerio Valley from the Rift Valley, to the Laikipia plateau. The formation of the valleys pushed up the adjoining areas into high tables of land with altitude conditions that ideal for training, thus the profusion of athlete training camps on both sides, in Nyahururu and Iten.

While waiting for Alex to finish speaking to some acquaintances, I see a bench on the side of the road. There is a man with cut earlobes sitting on one side of the bench selling his wares: shaved tree barks, multivitamins in plastic containers, and a thin brown liquid in a Keringet bottle that reminds me of a foul-tasting concoction my grandfather boiled from barks and prescribed as a cure all. He places a sack for me to sit on the damp bench and we watch the comings and goings of town. *"Daktari,"* his clients call him as he wraps a mixture of barks and vitamins in newspapers for them and places it in a plastic bag. Matatus to Eldoret and Kabarnet crowd in front of the brightly painted post office. Those to Kapsowar and Marakwet line up on the opposite side. Tractors and pick-up trucks carrying milk tankards fuel at the petrol station owned by Christopher Cheboiboi, a former steeplechase runner turned marathoner.The gates to KCB, the only bank in town, open and people begin to trickle inside. Daktari's commercial instincts kick in and he starts to ask deeply personal questions about my reproductive health. I escape to take pictures of the post office when a local council official starts to question my presence in a wary manner, with a view to perhaps levy some small amount of money. "It is because you are not from here," Daktari says. It speaks of a close-knit community, where a stranger is instantly recognized and easily categorised. "We read the newspapers and know what is going on. Just because we sit here quietly..." he continues, summarizing people's views on Nairobi inhabitants' preoccupation with themselves as the center of gravity for the country.

The camp is a few hundred meters down the Kapsowar road at mwisho wa lami, the end of the tarmac. It is a two bedroom rented house across the road from the hospital housing where Alex lives. There a lot of camps like this, set up by individuals, mostly experienced or retired runners. I am told a farmer in the area is running a camp on his land, to support something that has become a regional industry, and also hoping the runners will offer him some part of their winnings when they get to the international circuit. He will have no way of enforcing the remittance of the earnings, as by this time, they will have signed contracts with foreign management that will cater to their needs, and will no longer be dependent on him.

There are four athletes staying at the camp. Two, Evans Ogaro and Onesmus

Nyerere, are experienced runners who have raced in the European circuit for some years. The other two, Felix Keny and Christopher Korir, are young, still in initial training, and have not yet left the country. Rent is paid by their manager in Holland, who visits two or three times a year on recruitment trips and to check in with the athletes; in between, he relies on dispatches from Alex. The furnishing is spare, the conditions martial, like soldiers in barracks, with not much regard for privacy, just the common training objectives. A jiko in the kitchen, various utensils scattered about and the ubiquitous thermos for tea. There is one bed and a couple of thin mattresses with blankets crumpled on top on the red cement floor. Gauzy curtains covering the window look tacked on, like it was done hurriedly. The walls are painted blue; most of the houses I visit in the town have the same aqua blue interior. It appears it was either a fashion or a contractor with the local monopoly ordered an excess of blue paint. Outside running shoes stained by the distinctive red mud of the region dry against the wall and varied athletic attire of all brands hang on the wood fence: Adidas socks, Puma warm-up jackets, Nike shirts, Fila tights.

On this particular morning, the athletes lean against the fence and talk about the long-run. Christopher has pulled his mattress outside on the grass and is basking in the sun while offering everyone hot milky tea with lots of sugar. It is some of the best tea I have ever tasted. He cooked it on the jiko and it absorbed the smell of smoke. People in the Rift Valley drink tea with almost religious devotion, at least three times a day, at breakfast, mid-morning and afternoon, more if anyone visits, then the thermos is brought out without question and tea automatically poured. The only question the visitor may be asked is how many spoons of sugar they take, and sometimes they are saved from making this decision as the sugar was already added in the pan. To refuse is to insult your host and will only bring inquiries as to whether they can prepare it differently for you, perhaps leave out the sugar. Visitors to homes often drop in unannounced, laden with tealeaves and sugar to replenish supplies they will undoubtedly use, and prices of these commodities are followed carefully. A study conducted by an American university on the nutrition of Kenyan athletes concluded, almost with amazement, that milk and sugar in tea are among the top sources of protein and carbohydrates respectively for runners. It is one of those continuous attempts to extricate the one thing that separates Kenyan runners from their counterparts elsewhere in the world, without looking wholly at the tea-drinking ritual that is cemented into everyday life, becoming more than basic nutritional sustenance.

Training is all-consuming. The day begins at 5:30am and by 6:00 am the athletes are gathered at the starting point of their morning run, which lasts forty-five minutes to an hour. They return, have breakfast, rest, and then prepare for the main training later in the morning. At 9:30 or 10:00 they have day-specific training for six days of the week. Mondays, Wednesdays and Fridays, an easy to moderate run. Tuesdays, speed-work at Kamariny track, Thursdays are alternated between hill-work and Fartlek training and Saturday, a long-run of 30 to 40 kilometres, where they reach as far as Moiben. Sunday is the only day of rest, with most of them going to church and the family men leaving, perhaps once a month, to visit wives and children in other towns.

Alex has told us a big group of athletes meet every Thursday at nine am for *Fartlek* training, a funny-sounding Swedish word for an exercise that simultaneously builds speed and endurance. It is about 9:15 and there are only five runners in front of us. One of them comes to the car to talk to Alex. His name is Amos Mayo. He is twenty-three, tall with long strides, and has never been to Europe. He is slated to go in September and appears to be in excellent condition. He will lead the group of runners today. Within a few minutes other runners arrive, bringing the number to thirteen, and start warming up with rapid kicks, legs bent at the knee.

The group seems large enough but we are waiting for Jason Mbote, who came in second at the Seoul Marathon a few weeks before. Jason is a strong runner, easily the strongest of the group that will be running today and his presence will be a big advantage as he will push the group to perform harder. Among the runners are a 10,000 meter Commonwealth champion and a pacesetter at the Seoul Marathon. The larger the number of strong runners in the group the better – they will maintain the high pace that the group will adhere to, making the training that much more beneficial. It is the same reason there are two women training with the overwhelmingly male group.

At 9:30 Amos tells us that the group will move to the starting point. It seems they will train without Jason. It is supposed to be his first Fartlek since he returned from Seoul. It is cool, almost cold. It will still be cool at midday – another reason Iten offers ideal training conditions. It is never too hot, so athletes can train all day. The group takes off at an easy pace, running in a tight pack. They cut across a field to avoid the matatu stage and join the road to Kapsowar, past the venerable St. Patrick's Iten High School, which has produced more world-class runners than any other institution, past the district hospital and long narrow rental houses, which house a number of the athletes training today. Nobody on the road pays much attention to the runners: they are a common sight. We are almost at the starting point when Jason passes with a small group including his wife, sister, brother and two friends. Running has become a family enterprise for them.

There are about thirty runners now gathered at the junction of the access road in conversation. They look relaxed; the five-kilometre run from the main road has barely exerted them. The core group, including Amos Mayo, Jason Mbote and Alex Kipkosgei, are affiliated with the same management. They train together, support each other and scout new athletes for their management based on their local knowledge of upcoming talent. The rest of the athletes are friends and acquaintances, who join them for the benefits of group training; many athletes live and train in Iten for this reason – you can constantly pit yourself against the best. Amos Mayo comes to the car. "One minute slow, one minute fast," he says. Alex sets his combination wristwatch-stopwatch. The group of runners starts off at the slow pace they used to get here. We follow at a distance.

In a minute Alex's watch beeps and the runners take off at a furious speed. Feet pound the road, soles of shoes flashing in rapid succession and arms move piston-like at their sides. They keep it up for one minute, which seems like an eternity, then slow down to a one minute recovery jog. They will repeat this alternation twenty-five times for a total of fifty gruelling minutes. After four or five intervals, one of the women in the group drops back. We pass and hear her laboured breathing over the sound of the engine. Her sweat-soaked shirt is plastered to her back and her strained face is set determined lines as she measures the rapidly widening distance between herself and the group.

At thirty minutes, the group is still almost intact. The leaders keep up the relentless pace on the fast sections of the interval. Each subsequent interval is harder, the recovery jog losing its restorative power. The group mentality kicks in, the individual pegging performance on the group, transferring individual tiredness onto the pattern that can be followed automatically beyond each runner's endurance. I struggle to reconcile the loose, relaxed stances of the runners a short while before to the collective will at work here, determined to press forward at all costs, and fall convert to a trite phrase I have heard uttered by many runners: 'Train hard, win easy.' Still, a few more people fall back, their bodies failing beyond the point they can get reserves from the group's progress. We pass them and they are now going at a steady jog. "Well, those ones are just doing a long-run now," says Alex, noting they do not do the speed alternation. We leave them behind. They will try to catch up during the slow sections.

The course takes us through long stretches of access roads that pass between farmland, ploughed red soils preparing for planting, or newly planted with maize. It is dotted with things running winnings have built: we pass Michael Kite's farm with a stone house, and a large tractor parked outside. He is not shy about the cost of these things, 1.2 million shillings for the house and 800,000 for the tractor. Passing cars tilt to one side of the narrow road to let the runners by. At one place with a deep puddle of muddy water, the athletes form a single file and run on a thin sliver of dry land the edge. If it were the fast part of the interval, they would have had to splash through. Of the people we pass, only the children show excitement and wave, even running behind the athletes for a little while. It is easy to see them as future athletes, easy to see continuity: the children following the runners, mostly young and not yet in their prime earning years, training on roads that take them past symbols of running success. Their time will come and the ranks will keep rejuvenating themselves.

"There are two really bad hills coming up," Alex says. Until now the course has been rather flat. They are not as fortunate as with the puddle, the climb up both hills comes at the fast-paced part of the interval. The human body straining at maximum output is a thing of marvel, pounding up the hill and round a curve only to encounter the second hill. Jason is toward the front of the group, which, surprisingly, stays together. He is a gauge for the younger runners. With his experience and high placement in races, they know that their training is going well and will have confidence of measuring up in international meets. There is a flat section and we are back to where we started, having covered a distance of about 17 kilometres. A few runners are bent over, lungs bellowing, sweat evaporating from their foreheads. But they recover quickly, and apart from their soaking shirts, you can barely tell they have just completed an arduous physical task. Various groups leave till the core five runners, who were there first in the morning, remain talking, resting their feet against a stump. They will eat, rest and go for an easy run in the evening. When one of the runners passes me in town an hour later in his civilian clothes—a slightly oversized blazer and pressed trousers—he looks like any other farmer on the streets of Iten and I almost don't recognise him.

Alex never intended to be a runner. He played football while studying at Kenya Medical Training College, KMTC, eventually signing up with Mafuko Bombers in Meru. He attended college during the week and practiced on school grounds, before travelling during the weekend from to play for the Bombers. With the state of Kenyan football being what it is, he decided to switch to running. As he points out, "All you need are two pairs of running shoes and some sports clothes." He began training seriously after college, living with athlete friends in different parts of the country including Njoro and Nairobi. After entering some local races, he came to the notice of a German manager and was soon racing in South Africa. But it is not until he went to Germany and began racing in the European Circuit that he started making good money. Utilizing his KMTC training, he found a job at the hospital in Iten and started training before and after work. The job is flexible, allowing him to race several weeks during race season in Europe and come home with ten or fifteen thousand dollars a year.

For every Boston, New York, London, and Vienna marathon there are many smaller races—the Würzburg 10K, Sevenaer Run, The Great Scottish Run, Zwitserlootdakrun—10K, 15K, half-marathon events modelled after their more prestigious counterparts. The events are part of the towns' social calendars, with media coverage that attracts sponsors. The races also raise money by charging entry fees to the general public, who in turn enter for the challenge, to raise money for charity, or for just plain fun. Race organizers work with agents and managers to secure places for the Kenyan runners, who set credible race times, and whose formidable reputation brings a certain prestige. This leads to a whole class of middle-tier of athletes who run, not to represent the country in Olympic or world championships, but to make a living. They are journeymen with no illusions; in other words, true professionals.

These middle tier runners live and train in Kenya, and go to Europe for up to three months a year. They stay in small apartments with other runners under the same management, driving from town to town to races every week. The perception of running centres on elite runners who dominate the news. It is far from reality, where a talented, but not necessarily outstanding athlete with training, the right connections to get into the right races, can make enough money to live on, or in some cases to supplement their incomes. This in itself is not an amazing discovery. There exists a whole system to support this industry, from the governing athletic body that oversees the relations between agents and runners, to athletic visa guidelines in the Nairobi embassies of host countries. This is a widely known practice among officials and other sports professionals, but not in the general public consciousness, where running is still a thoroughly nationalistic sport.

On Saturday night we go back to Amani Café, site of the bill incident, to have the evening meal. The waitress still doesn't know who exactly left the bill, nor has she seen him since. The town is slightly raucous and there are still a lot of people walking around. Saturday represents a kind of loosening for the runners, as they will not train the following day. Strict diets slacken as we order the only thing left on the menu, chips and fried chicken of a texture that is generously described as flinty. Any other night and we would have insisted on rice or ugali with vegetables. Accompanying us is Elias Kiptum Maindi, Alex's team-mate and friend. They both come from Nandi and went to the same primary school. Their professional lives converged three years before, when Elias came in third at the Aldai half-marathon held every August by Alex's organization.

Elias is young, confident and believes he will be running a 2:06 marathon within a year; his half-marathon best is 1:03:06. The world-class time is repeated often, with a mixture of seriousness and jest. He describes an incredible negative split he saw, where the last half of the marathon was completed in three minutes less than the first. He has been competing professionally for two years and this year made good time in various road races, and paced champions including Felix Limo and Martin Lel in the London, Rotterdam and Bonn marathons. The optimism is clear in his open, ready smile. Women like him – from the waitress to the pregnant neighbor who comes often to visit the house he shares with Alex. He tells me she is very happy, believes the baby is good luck, and she will run faster after she delivers. Alex, ever rational, says it must be something to do with the stability attained when they have families that enables them to focus. The whole weekend, Elias is on the phone with someone named Sos. Sos is a friend who works in a bank. The 4,000 dollars (288,000 shillings) he earned pacing the London marathon was wire-transferred by his agent to Sos's account and he needs to pick up 100,000 shillings to pay for a piece of land, an eighth of an acre, he wants to buy in Iten.

The athletes sleep early on weeknights but today they are among the people walking around. I am curious to see how far this Saturday slackening of their rigorous routine goes. Big races are televised on Sundays at a hall behind the main line of shops. On other days, the community comes to watch European League football. This particular hall belongs to Arsenal fans, and at the bar attached to the hall we find a couple of runners drinking. The walls are the hard-to-escape aqua blue and there are Arsenal posters, banners, ornaments everywhere. The sign above the door reads *'Highbury.'* Alex, for one, is a strong proponent of the analgesic and sedative powers of alcohol after the Saturday morning long-run. But I have never seen him drink. Elias asks for a soda. At less than sixty kilograms, and coupled with the infrequency of their drinking, the table is really cheerful after only two drinks. There is dancehall music playing and the proprietor takes a turn on the floor. When they find out I am a writer, they ask adamantly not to be identified and the mood dampens. It seems an altercation is imminent when I make assurances of their anonymity and Alex intervenes to back me up. They do not want to be known to race organizers as drinkers and carousers. One of them yells over the music, "And nowadays on the Internet, these things can be seen all over the place. You think anyone will want to book you!"

The place is cramped, with a wooden table and two benches on one side and a small cleared space for dancing. A young woman with blonde braids and skin the same color as her hair comes and sits on one of the runner's lap. They talk for a few moments then she looks as us and leaves. When she stands I notice her expensive trainers. Even the prostitutes in Iten wear running shoes. I am told there is a small but growing number of prostitutes in the town, drawn by the runners' money. But the training exhausts them and they rarely came out except on Saturdays: they make for slim business. They continue to come as long as there is money. The runner's life does not lend itself well to vice. Excessive slackening – rich food, a little too much beer – is immediately felt in one's performance. Disappointingly, everyone goes home by ten-thirty. The bar will close at eleven.

The following day, we are in a Toyota Townace matatu, a seven passenger model that fills up quickly, racing towards to Eldoret. The day is clear, skies a deep blue. Farmland stretches on each side for miles, broken by small shopping centers every couple of kilometers. Elias accompanies us both to pick up his winnings from Sos and to see Felix Limo, whom we intend to visit to try and gain some insight into what distinguishes a champion from the journeymen. "There is the plot," Elias says, excited. It is a few kilometers from Iten, just off the main road. I can barely distinguish it from the surrounding farms till he points to a fence as a marker. He hopes to begin building by the end of the year so he can have a permanent residence close to where he trains, and entertains thoughts of starting a family.

Since Felix Limo has asked that we take no pictures of his home, I am not sure what to expect from the athlete ranked at the top or near the top of Road Race Management winnings list for the last two years. The listings for 125,000 to 150,000 dollars do not tally with what I hear on the ground, which estimate his yearly earnings, including a contract with Adidas, at 200,000 to 300,000 dollars. Thunder rumbles above. I ask which way the rains usually go and Alex points to the direction of Mt. Elgon, now obscured by deep gray clouds. "It won't rain here," he says. The house is simple, neatly constructed with thin wood boards and an iron sheet roof. The windmill that generates electricity is turning on a rudder to catch the strongest gusts of wind. When you notice Felix, it is for his stillness and unnervingly direct gaze. He has just returned from a win at the London marathon. Casually dressed, the only outward clue of his athleticism is the Adidas cap on his head. Felix is from a village in Nandi not far from where Alex and Elias come from. He gestures for us to sit outside on two wooden benches. A small white Toyota is parked in the middle of the compound. There are a few chickens scratching about and four sheep so puffy with wool they look like overstuffed pillows that have split. He says he is looking for someone to shear them.

We launch immediately into a discussion on his career trajectory. "I realized that I can do something when I almost beat Tergat in the Brussels 10,000. I ran 27:04. I realized also I can beat also all these other big guys," he pauses for a moment and I look to the side. The merinos have moved close behind us, and are just standing there, trembling. "In 2001 I realized my potential also was on the road not on the track when I broke the world record of 15 Kilometers, beating Haile Gabresellasie." He left track for road racing, posting a 2:06 time in 2003 in Amsterdam, his first marathon. He has been running 2:06 since then, and boasts one of the top ten fastest times ever posted in marathon running.

Before that, his primary goal was to complete his education. After finishing high school in 1995, he was called to Maseno to study Information Technology. A fruitless search for a sponsor to pay his fees closed the education avenue and led him to running. His early years were a struggle; training in starts and stops when the shoes he bought in mitumba wore out. A manager made promises of races in Europe that never materialized. "I consolidated some money from my uncles and bought some shoes," he says, and resumed training till November 1998 brought his first race in Europe. He wants to go back to school when he retires from running, but will not divulge his specific plans.

Felix trains in Kaptagat, a lushly forested area about 30 kilometers south of Iten. He is at home 100 days in the year, races about four weeks abroad, and spends the rest of the time in camp. "You should be at the camp to focus... very important to focus." He looks around, "You can't be thinking about rain is coming... The cows need pasture... You have to be away. So that they can be independent. So that they can think for themselves." The they he refers to are his family, his wife and two children, and other inhabitants in the compound.

An agent I speak to attributes a big part of Felix's success to the strategy of limiting his events. He races sparingly, attending only four events a year—two half-marathons, and two marathons. "I normally call this half-marathon tune-up race. I have to go see... test. I go there one month before the race [marathon], when I come back I have to evaluate. Where was my weak part? Was it endurance? Was it speed? So I have to work on my weak part so that during the race I know that I am comfortable." Commentators at the half-marathons have mistakenly written off his performances, not understanding their purpose in his overall strategy. He returns to 'prepare for the real war now.' His keen tactical sense is only matched by a fiercely competitive spirit. "You should be thinking about how am I going to win it, and you know winning is money. I am not saying I am not after money. I am after money, but I don't put money on my mind because it will destroy me during the race. I put it... what I put in my mind is winning."

Felix is more guarded than any of the other runners I have met so far, balancing the necessity of interacting with journalists while controlling accessibility. His environment is far more telling, the simplicity of his home deceptive. He owns two well-sized rental houses down the road and points to fifteen acres of maize. When Elias asks the price of an acre, Felix holds up eight fingers, one for each hundred thousand. I am also told of houses in Nairobi and possible shares abroad. He preempts what he expects to be my question on the lifestyle he has chosen, which is very deliberately not ostentatious, when he speaks about runners buying big cars and properties they cannot maintain when the earnings slow to a trickle. He seems to be acutely conscious that this is something that could end abruptly, because of injury, and also because high-level competitive sport by its very nature is a temporal pursuit.

After the interview, he loosens up considerably and invites us inside the house for tea. His wife brings out a Jeroboam of a flask and we drink one cup after another. Her waist is swollen with their third child, and the others play outside. She has a warmth and radiance, and as she pours the tea he talks about IT courses she is taking, perhaps moving the family to Nairobi so she can have better job opportunities. As with most runners I meet, a family was always in the calculations, with none of the cynicism toward family structures exhibited by my peers. There are other visitors in an adjoining sitting room and the flask moves back and forth between our table and theirs. A visitors' book is passed around. There are a lot of recent entries, from Kapsabet, Eldoret and elsewhere, congratulating Felix on his London victory; there is one from a pastor that wishes blessings on the house.

At some point he turns to me and asks why I haven't started a family. I feint and dodge with murmurs of this and that. I get a view of his 'It isn't over till it's over' competitive streak when he points to Elias as a candidate, not alarmed at the prospect that Elias is seeing someone; he cites margins I can exploit in order to ensure the results turn in my favour. The message is clear: this is still an open field. I look to Elias for help but he just grins accommodatingly. As Felix walks us to the matatu stage at the end of the road, he is more expansive, gesturing to his maize farm, the shoots about knee-high. Neighbouring children gathered to play follow our progress along the fence saying, shy at first, but growing more insistent, *"Habari mkimbiaji! Habari mkimbiaji!"* He is a little amazed at the attention he gets from his little neighbours. Until London, he could walk around in relative anonymity.

The profusion of runners in this region makes jogging as a layman a thing of bravery. Encountering a man on an evening jog in Eldoret's affluent Elgon Veiw neighbourhood, shirt stretched so tight over a tumid belly you could see the indentation of his navel, a friend remarked archly, "Definitely not one of ours." So when the runners at the camp offer to don their trainers, on a Sunday no less, and take me for an easy five or seven kilometres, I point to the sandals on my feet and say perhaps another day. We have tea and mandazi near the camp at Victory Café. Again I marvel at the blue walls. We ask for the bill but Elias has paid already and stepped outside. Evans smiles, *"Wacha alipe. Si bado ana Euro."* Let him pay, he still has Euros. After breakfast we go to the Keiyo forest a little way off the Kapsowar road and walk the forest courses. Some parts have indigenous and some plantation forest planted by an area sawmill. Sing'ore Girls, another high school athletic powerhouse, is nearby. On a clearing at the edge of the forest, a few cows graze lazily and the children herding them have fashioned hurdles out of sticks. We watch their game as they race and jump over the obstacles. *"Angalia vile wanafanya tizi,"* Evans says at their play. He points to one of the children. *"Huyo atakuwa mkali* sana... Unaona vile ako mweusi na mserious hivyo." He laughs, *"Sikuwa nimeona watu weusi namna hiyo mpaka hapa."*

Evans and Onesmus are from Kisii. They tell me of the decline of the running tradition back in Kisii. When Evans was in primary school, if you were on the track team, your school fees was reduced and if you excelled, your schooling was free. The schools used to nurture runners but have now stopped. So the athletes are getting older and there is a gap between them and the next generation, who are not picking up running shoes, but looking for other pursuits.

"People are allowed in the forest with animals?" Onesmus asks. Alex turns to him. "There is a forest ranger station in there... You try to come even with a knife." Onesmus has used his part of his winnings in Europe to establish a timber business with his father back in Kisii. Elias points to him, "Huyu alijaribu kubeba power saw kwa hand luggage." This one tried to carry a power saw in his hand luggage. Howls of laughter follow as incidents of airport scrutiny are remembered, removing shoes, the paranoia carrying even a nail cutter on board can cause. There are speculations about the forests Onesmus must have cleared with his power saws in Kisii while we examine a fallen tree. But from the rough scar, it appears have fallen from other causes.

The runners are well-traveled, more than most Kenyans. Among them, they have been to Asia, South America and the Caribbean and most countries in Western Europe. Yet, they travel very specifically to race, staying in hotel rooms or apartments. It is like a businessman who stays in conference hotel for the duration of a seminar abroad and sees little else. The 'been to' airs, that supposed cachet that comes with international travel, are little in evidence. There is consciousness of a deficiency, being from a small town; one of them expresses anxiety about navigating Nairobi despite having been to various European capitals. When traveling, the runners usually depend on their managers. Visas are arranged by sending a letter to the Nairobi embassies of host countries and the Kenyan athletic federation. Managers also handle air tickets, housing and local travel. The famous 'breakdown' is given to the athlete at the end of the competitive season, sometimes on the way to the airport. Onesmus shakes his head, *"Hata hiyo chai mlikunywa itakuwa hapo... Na wewe umekimbia race ya 20 Euro."* Even that tea you both drank will be on the list... And yet you have run a race of 20 Euro. He tells the story of when he was still new in the circuit and kept accepting his agent's generous offers of tea throughout the season, not knowing he was the one paying for them. It is at this time the agent calculates your net earnings, which are your winnings minus air ticket, food, accommodation, transport, incidentals, and, because it is business, his own 15% cut. Usually, the breakdown will include the mileage of the trip he has taken driving you to the airport, and the parking fee he will pay leaving the airport after you are long gone, flying over some ocean on your way back to Kenya.

Just before the line of trees there is a hill with a deceptively gentle gradient. We climb halfway, turn to look at the bottom, then walk the rest of the way with a new respect. It is the hill-work training site, where athletes will run, ten to twelve abreast, up and down the hill fifteen times. I ask if they jog back home after the exercise, "You run?" Christopher says incredulously. "You walk without a word... Then you lie down for a while before you even organize some water to bathe." The plantation forest is dark and quiet. The limited, slanted light hits the barks on one side to tenebrous effect. Damp, dead, brown needles underfoot muffle footsteps as we walk in the evenly spaced trees. The silence is broken when a wild bray rents the air. It sounds like something otherworldly and the effect is enhanced by the atmospheric shadows and silence of the forest. There were squatters here, evicted when the shamba system did not work out. They abandoned their donkeys, which are content to frolic around, no longer beasts of burden.

Any given morning driving the 30 kilometres from Iten to Eldoret, one will encounter groups of runners training; and from Eldoret another 45 kilometres southwest to Kapsabet. For the first part of the trip Alex sits in the back row of the Toyota Townace with agent Gerard van der Veen, owner of Volare Sports of Wezep, Netherlands. The Townace matatu has been rented for the day and has a 'Private' sign on the dashboard where the destination sign ordinarily sits – we are on our way to the Nandi North track and field district competition at Kapsabet's Kipchoge Keino stadium. Alex and Gerard map out the schedule for the day – a visit to Martin Lel's camp before the stadium to meet athletes, meet athletes at the Kapsabet competition, on the way back, stop in Eldoret and meet some athletes, and return to Iten and meet a few more athletes before the end of the day. "Every week I get four, five, six emails from athletes asking for management. But I want to screen them. Because, of course, I am looking for the strongest athletes. Alex does the research for me and when he says ok that is a strong guy or strong lady, I try to invite them for five or six races where they earn back their ticket and make some money." After these initial small races, Gerard will evaluate their performances and decide whether to invite them back the next season. But the athletes also have various managers to pick from. Amos Maiyo, who led the *Fartlek* training a few weeks before, has decided to sign up with another agent and is now racing in Brazil. For Amos the chance to race immediately, as opposed to waiting out the months till September, was the decisive factor. "He couldn't wait," Gerard says, shrugging his shoulders. "But there are many athletes."

Gerard is in Kenya for a week and a half to visit the runners he represents as well as recruit new athletes. He is animated and has a loud expansive laugh and his face tanned and red. He is dressed in track pants, a red sports shirt and has brought some Adidas goodies for everyone, because the Volare athletes are sponsored by Adidas. Dark running shades cover his eyes and inside a pair of prescription lenses are attached onto the frame, so that when indoors and he needing to see something he will squint then put on his shades. He started out as a footballer playing semi-pro in The Netherlands. At 32 his career was cut short by injury that left him unable to play. He had hoped to play until at least 35. In 2004, two months before the Athens Olympics, Pieter Langerhorst, a fellow Dutchman and husband to Lorna Kiplagat, asked if he was interested in taking over Pieter's management practice, he jumped at the chance to get back into sports. At 50 he had remained around sports, helping organize an annual race in his home town, but he now worked for property management company, overseeing the rental of 10,000 homes in the northern part of the country. He still expresses a little anxiety at leaving the stability of a good steady pay for something far less certain.

"But this year I get this guy into London on my own," Gerard says, pointing to Elias. The race will promote Elias's name among organizers and soon they will invite him as one of the elite athletes—the natural and upward progression from pacemaker. I ask if it is truly a competition if the pacemakers can't finish the race and he tells me that along with the 'Pace' back tags they wear, they are usually given chest numbers so they can complete the race, but that is not in the strategy. "He will be ready for marathon next year... maybe year after," Gerard says. Pacemakers are chosen from road racers with good 10K, 15K and half-marathon times. They have to be fast and lead the elite athletes up to contractually agreed-upon distances then they drop out, leaving one of the elite athletes to break the tape at the finish line. The elite runners are not always content to follow the 'Pace' jerseys and are known to put on the pressure. At Bonn, Peter Chemei would come dangerously close to overtaking the pacemakers while exclaiming, *"Chunga Unga! Chunga Unga!"* Guard your flour, or take care of your bread, which you will lose if I pass you. Tegla Lorupe had male pacemakers when she set the women's marathon world record. Some race organizers protested, but when their complaints were not heard, they started to use male pacemakers in their own races. The first year London used male runners to pace the female athletes, Paula Radcliffe broke the record by three whole minutes. "I don't care if they brought in fresh pacesetters at 15 kilometers. As long as they did not pull her or carry her, then that is her record," says Alex, ending that discussion for now.

We get to Martin Lel's camp and there about twenty athletes around in that uniform I have learnt to recognize as what they wear during rest: sports shirt, jeans and clean running shoes, a different pair from the ones used in training.

Elias points Martin's car and Gerard responds, laughing, "Yes, you can buy good car when you run good marathon." Elias trained at this camp before moving to Iten. He is eager to repay the favour by introducing Martin Lel's runners to his agent. "Arsenal, Oxygen!" says Gerard, shaking Martin's hand vigorously and pointing to his shirt. "I am sorry I couldn't come to London. We already had four races that day and I promised Wilfred Kigen I would go to the Hamburg Marathon." Gerard's daughter accompanied Elias to London, where Martin came in second to Felix Limo. Along with his daughter, Gerard's son-in-law has scaled back his work week to three days to help build the agency and accompany the athletes when there are simultaneous races in different cities. They go to the house and talk prospects for various runners while the young athletes from the camp sit outside.

By the number of athletes in the 5,000 meter heats at the Nandi North district competition, an onlooker can be forgiven for thinking it is the provincial championships. According to the MC somewhere in the depths of the red-roofed podium on the far side of the field, 25% of the athletes who will go on to represent Rift Valley in the nationals will be from this district. The disembodied, amplified voice acknowledges Gerard's entrance into the stadium with, "Sasa hata ndio huyo mzungu ameingia," drawing attention to Gerard, who, since it was said in Swahili, continues to move obliviously to the centre of the field. His purpose here immediately recognized and a few coaches and runners approach. Gerard and Alex are particularly interested in the 5,000 meter and 10,000 meter runners as they have the most potential to turn into road racers. The coach talking to Gerard has four athletes in the front. He shouts to them as they pass, "Stride! Stride! Arms! Those are my boys," he says pointing to them. "I tell them don't overtake on the straight... only on the curve."

The flag blows in stiff intermittent breezes above the podium, which has structural columns painted in horizontal bands of black, red, white and green. The tamped earth track is marked with even white lanes, and the middle grassy part has an official yelling at people crossing, unaware they might be in range of missile shot put balls and discuses. There is a 200 meters heat with an electric finish that has spectators standing and shouting. The races are interrupted by a brief intense rainstorm with big raindrops that pockmark the soil on the track. Spectators take cover in the few shelters then return to their places around the field to cheer the 800 meters heats. The races are also interrupted by official speeches punctuated by 1-2-3 *funga fungua* claps that barely register with the spectators across the field and seem to be restricted to the podium and the seating area immediately behind it. The MC issues an effusive invitation to the new District Commisioner, who has popped in to watch the competition for a few minutes. The DC looks across the field and wonders at gaps in the spectators lining the field. He asks the local council to support the athletes, as they will return home to invest their winnings. "Even though they invest in Eldoret... It still helps." There is applause as more officials jockey for position and a chance at the microphone.

The district competition is one of a series organized by Athletics Kenya (AK), formerly Kenya Amateur Athletics Association (KAAA), the body that administers athletics in Kenya and is responsible for, among other things, scheduling the athletics calendar, ensuring meets are carried out according to the International Association of Athletics Federations (IAAF) standards, protecting Kenyan athletes by vetting foreign managers and agents, and selecting and training the teams that represent the country in international events. Their headquarters is Riadha House near Nyayo Stadium, where the executive committee sits. The Executive Committee is replicated in each of the fifteen provincial offices made of the eight administrative provinces, the large ones broken up and entities that have historically produced talented runners in sizable numbers. They are: South Rift, North Rift, Southern (South part of Eastern province), Eastern, South Nyanza, North Nyanza, Central, Western, Nairobi, Coast, North-Eastern, Public Universities, Armed Forces, Police and Prisons. There is a concerted effort to discover talent from all over the country, and in organizations with a culture of recruiting runners and nurturing them.

There are two seasons: cross country from January to April, and track and field from early November to January. The process for organizing each season is the same. AK schedules five weekend meets during the track and field season and invites the fifteen provinces to bid for them. The provinces bid and five provinces win. These events will be held at least a week apart, sometimes as much as two weeks apart to give athletes a chance to recover. The events provide the stage for runners to show themselves and meet agents and managers. It also enables teams from different parts of the country to compete against each other and gauge their strengths and weaknesses. AK then opens the calendar for the provinces, organizations and sponsors to co-ordinate events and submit them to complete the calendar. The AK curtain raiser race is open to everyone who can afford to go. Participants have to pay their own transportation and accommodation costs. Individual runners, groups from camps, organizations and universities will all attend bringing together athletes from the breadth of the spectrum. The same applies to the other four AK events held in different provinces during the season. In between the five AK meets are events organized by corporate sponsors such as banks and telecommunications companies, usually open to all, and events restricted to geographical location and organization, that is races within the province or within the armed forces. The geographical races move from districts to provinces in a bracket that gets smaller as the best runners qualify. The armed forces and all districts will compete on the same day one week. Prisons, police and all administrative provinces will compete on one day the next week. The races are scheduled on the same day so that the same person is not running for Prisons and North Rift, giving the maximum number of people a chance to qualify. This culminates in the national championship, where the team to represent the country in international competition is selected.

AK does not run a permanent national training camp. The selected team goes on to train at a teachers college or other facility near Nairobi for two months, before they proceed to the international championships. Considering the success that Kenyan runners have had and continue to have in the world, the gap is evident and surprising. This is a frustration expressed across the board in the running world. AK in turn points to the Ministry of Culture and Sports, and the lack of policies related to athletics. Asked about the policies in place, a former AK official laughs ruefully and looks at me, "What policies? In my day when you went to ask the Ministry for money, they say they have finished the budget... Taking choirs to sing in State House." The appointment of officials on a political basis regardless of qualification, or more importantly interest in the field, has been cited as a problem in policy making. A former head of the Committee of Stadiums was once heard to ask, *"Hiyo 800, wanapiga kiwanja mara ngapi?"* That 800 [meters], how many times do they circle the track? Of AK's nearly 90 million shilling income in 2005, 49 million was a grant from Nike, 13.6 million from the IAAF and 1.5 million in agent fees. Local grants are up with Standard Chartered Bank at 19.1 million. The Ministry of Sports contributed 3.4 million. The bulk of the money was spent on administration (19.7 million) and athletic meets (60 million). Only 6.6 million was spent on developing talent.

At the same time people complain about the lack of development resources and the athletic federation's entrenched bureaucracy being resistant to change, they take matters into their own hands. Two places in particular, Kip Keino's Training Center and Lorna Kiplagat's High Altitude Training Center, are setting new standards with high-level facilities. The Kip Keino Training Centre is listed by the IAAF as one of seven High Performance Training Centres in the world. It represents an investment in the third and fourth generations of Kenya running. The centre is located on a section of several hundred acres of farmland that Kipchoge Keino owns just outside Eldoret. There is also a children's home and a primary school on the farm. Once the home of EATEC, which used to grow wattle trees to tan leather, but has since gone out of business. The growing middle class and newly affluent, including a few runners, has bought land here. There are still 'For Sale' signs along the road, and tilled deep red soils and muddy roads, like elsewhere in the Uasin Ngishu plateau. Lines of wattle trees have been left on the borders of the farms to act as windbreakers. There is the vague smell of wattles in the air, not as overpowering smell as when it was a plantation. In the distance is the old factory and small houses where plantation workers used to live.

There is a marked contrast with the athletes' quarters in Iten, but still far from luxurious, more neat, ordered, and comfortable. The stone house with two wings feels like part of a well-run national school. The door opens into a huge lounge with a high ceiling, various books and posters on running, including a poster of Kipchoge during his competing heyday, and a long dining room with seating for thirty. "My work here is development," says Ian Choge, director of the centre, as he looks at the gym facility. The centre favours long-term training plans and is training athletes for the 2008 Beijing Olympics, focusing on middle distances. They only train athletes who are young and do not have management yet.

The IOC sponsors athletes they pick at various meets. They pay $1200/month per person. Sometimes countries without training facilities also sponsor their athletes to train at the centre. There are athletes here from different countries from the recently completed commonwealth games, from Mauritius, Guyana and Malawi mixed in with Kenyan runners. The runners stay two to three in a room with private bathrooms in each. There is a room attendant, a cateress who is also a matron, two coaches and a physiotherapist. Progress is measured in numbers, more specifically in qualifying times. Though the centre's specialty is middle-distance, there are also two sprinters training for 400 meters. "It takes many years to build a sprinter," Ian says stressing something I hear when I talk to people in the athletics world. As a country, Kenya has capitalized on traditional strengths in middle and long distance running, extending to cross country and marathon, without developing new events. But there is a history of sprinting, evidenced by the gold medal win in the men's 4 x 400 meter relay at the 1972 Olympics in Munich.

Nearby Eldoret shows in its changing skyline new ways that runners are investing: commercial real-estate. Moses Kiptanui, acknowledged locally to be one of the most successful investors, owns the large five-storey Komora Plaza that leases two floors to Tusker Mattress and the other floors to offices. There is a new hotel belonging to Moses Tanui at the edge of the town. And the two adjoining buildings of Sakong plaza in the middle of town belong to Sammy Korir. There is also the continued farming culture. Athletes can be seen at Will's Pub on Uganda Road before buying feed for their cattle, fertilizer at the agricultural supply shop next door. People acknowledge them with a wave, but they are part of the town and not usually regarded any special attention. Eldoret was for many years a farming town and many enterprises are farming related; the feed and fertilizer shop, the seed shop, the tractor shop are common sights as you walk the streets. With the coming of Moi University, the town has seen an influx of people. In addition to the runners, the university lecturers, staff and students have brought new wealth into the town. I count five campuses: Main Campus, one just outside town for the MBA program, Chepkoilel on the road to Iten, Eldoret West near Kenya Pipeline, and the huge medical school complex in town complete with classrooms, teaching hospital and dormitories that has converted the town into the leading regional medical center.

About a year ago I was walking down a corridor of an international financial organization in Washington DC—the kind that makes headlines withholding aid to poor countries—when I got lost. At the assistants pool in the middle of the open-plan floor I stopped to ask for directions and a girl looked at me in the way Kenyans recognize each other at 500 paces when abroad then studiously ignore each other or burst into conversation. One of her co-workers was near and witnessed our conversation then remarked on my height and asked if I ran. I grudgingly admitted to erratic jogging. The Kenyan girl's name was Njambi, so it was obvious she was from the central part of the country. She could not tell from my Christian name, so asked where I was from; and from name and place of origin we could tell each other's tribes without having to ask explicitly. It was also the region where a large percentage of runners come from. Njambi laughed and said to her friend, "They run, but we run the economy."

Kenyan running is still perceived very much as Kalenjin running, yet the time we feel most Kenyan is when we see the athletes standing on the podium, sometimes on all top three places, draped in the national flag. Since the Kenya team first came out in 1954 in the Commonwealth Games in Canada in 1954 and the Olympics in Melbourne two years later, the country has rallied around sporting events. By the 1968 and 1972 Olympics, Kenya athletes had come of age, winning gold medals and cementing the reputation of Kenyan running in the world, continuing athletic dominance in the successive decades, until present day.

With all that has been made of the base advantage of Kenyan runners: high altitude, the lack of modern amenities that have them running long distances to school or to fetch water or to raid cattle, great amounts of milk drank and unprocessed foods eaten, the observable is far more awe inspiring than the mythical. Large reserves of mental strength are required to face the Iten morning chill, along with laser-like focus to overcome the tedium of daily repetitions training sessions and the endurance to take the punishing physicality of the sport. The question of why people excel at anything is more and more convincingly answered with the perfection of a skill through vigorous training. And not just consistent training, but training geared to specific goals. Of course some people are more athletic, but without the years spent training they would never have become the champions they are today.

On my last Sunday in Iten I go to church with Elias and Gerard. The road to the church has women with headscarves and embellished cardigans, men in jackets and little girls in frilly white dresses. Nike caps placed on the bench trainers indicate the athletes. Elias stops outside to greet the priest, who is waiting at the back of a procession that spans the length of the church. We enter through the side doors, while the procession sings and dances and leads the priest into the church. The church roof is high, with high narrow windows and the fourteen stages of the way of the cross depicted on the walls. The service is in a mixture of Swahili and Kalenjin, with the priest given to bursting into popular songs and swaying. His sermon is about identifying oneself as a Christian in the world and mixes the religious, secular and political. He defines Christianity as a party just like a political party and soon has soon the congregation frantically making the sign of the cross, waving one figure, two fingers, three, and then a fist. Just outside stands St. Patrick's Iten, the center of an athletic movement that spilled outside the school boundaries and became and integral part of the community. And young people will continue to be drawn to Iten and surrounding training centers as long as running is the most lucrative opportunity open to them, and the infrastructure to make their dreams a reality exists, and also because the champions winning medals, marathons and making money are not remote figures, but people they know from their villages and towns.

JACKIE LEBO *is from the Rift Valley and grew up among professional runners. She is a great writer and hates long bios. So Binyavanga is adding: ....this extract is part of an ambitious non-fiction project to document, in compelling prose, the lives and careers of Kenyan runners.*

C.C.T.V

Kitu Sewer

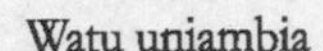

Watu uniambia
Kitu sewer shampoo
Lyrics zako na-gospel kama bamboo
Utadhani rap ni nywele na studio ni bafu
Ni kuchafu Mpaka siafu zinabuy viatu
Pwaguzi na pwagu wargue kuhusu lyrics zangu
C.C.T.V camera zinazoom katikati ya town
Nikawanyama kuwa zoo
Kwa bush watu wanakufa darfur na njaa
Ye naG-8 wametumwa shuttle kwa moon
Wametoka tour ya kuokota diamonds
Sierra leonne ndio ndio akicompose wimbo
Mapya akue nab ling za kufloss
Iyo song inaituwa world war four
Iko sure kukuweka on toes super powers wana try kufight fyucha
Gavaa inahide huduma
Shahidi wakoshy kutua ushuhuda
Juu fine wawalitoleana judge unasikia
Kujinyoga ka judas
Mind inachukua muda kuelewa
Shetani ka hawakimbizi
Amewamark masura

Illustration: Celeste Wamiru

All Things Remaining Equal

BY BINYAVANGA WAINAINA

Milka sits in the boot of the Toyota Land cruiser next to the coolers, spread out on cushions, mouth sticky with dried watermelon; sweat, thick and salty dripping into her eyes, her book lies face down next to her. Her body, suddenly jagged and long, has not yet figured out new ways to arrange itself, two new bumps under her pink t-shirt have become a perpetual reminder that everything has changed.

It is too bumpy to read her book. She will play *cominatcha*, her favourite thing to do on her new computer: she always puts on some *Kleptomaniacs* on Windows Media Player. They rap, loud, in her earphones, and she watches the *cominatcha* visualisation on her screen.

She has learnt over the past few roadtrip months, to play *cominatcha* with landscapes, rather than with digital galaxies on her computer. She faces the back window, and blurs her eyes, and dust and road and trees rush to hit her, and whiz past her.

They are driving through Pokot district: brown loose dry earth, stones, rocks, and skeletons of trees that Gordon had told her will spring to lush and useless life when it rains.

Prosopis juliflora.

They were introduced, he said to the occupants of the car, as a donor-funded NGO project—by Food Aid Organisation. Some life-saving plant, he said, a plant that could grow anywhere, and provide fuel for when the world's oil reserves started to run dry.

It spread, thorny and impassable, and turned out to be poisonous for cattle —no international market seemed interested in it for their fuel tanks.

"Fucking dictators, aid organisations. They say they care. Bullshit. Doing anything they want is all the fuckers care about. This plant is why the Pokot are starving. We are going to sue."

She had a nightmare last night: soft squealing shapes of fear, a dripping tap, lips of a fridge slap open solemnly, and a solid slippery sound rises. It ripples under her feet, and she slips and slides on it, now it is a gelatinous mouth-organ of laughter. Soft corkscrews of fear and pleasure coil in her stomach, and hard rural faces nudge at her ankles, with cold noses and warm welcoming breaths. They are laughing, like phlegm and donkeys.

Like the village: a traditional Gikuyu accordion, and squirming, squealing, dying night-insects in her ancestral home in Nyeri.

Like poverty and the smell of boiling sweet potatoes. She wants to stop leaping up in fear, wants to let go. And she does, and slides into the sound, which strums and rolls over her body, then the ripples of laughter and Gikuyu accordion whorl thickly into her breathing, and she jerks awake, choking.

Mum is pregnant. With Gordon's baby.

Mum sits at the front, with Gordon. Her face is moist, dripping, but she looks soft these days, smug, her stomach stretched taut and hard. Three months to go.

A girl. This is what Milka wants. With long curly doll hair and skin like milky coffee, pink full lips, green eyes.

Gordon is teaching her physics, now that she is in a British system school, in an advanced class, her physics and maths honed, but naked of context, coming as she did, from a strict Kenyan boarding school, X-ellents Academy, where failure was unacceptable, and frills frowned upon, and physics was numbers, never anything else: numbers and exams.

She has always easily topped her class, and is anxious to do the same in this strange new school, where learning is friendly, and classes chaotic. For the first few weeks she sat in class, watching people laugh rudely at their teachers and waiting for something to fall, or explode.

All other things remaining equal, he said: *Ceteris Paribus.*

She struggled to understand this, but now she has made it a swing. If the poles of the swing are not there, the swing will flop to the ground. Something has to stay still. Control things.

Since Gordon married mum a year ago, things seem consistent somehow: routines, possibilities, money, school fees.

The flowers outside the car are making her nauseous. At first the bright pink and white flowers of the desert rose, a plant shaped like a tiny baobab tree, were fun to watch, but now she is tired of them, they go on and on, saying hey hey we have flowers in this dry place too, and she is tired of listening. In this dusty, stony place, they seem clean, as if people washed them in the morning, in anticipation of visitors.

The desert rose has the false cheer of the plastic flowers and the framed print photograph of 'Dubai! Shopping City in the Sun' on their former living room wall. Dubai at night seemed a wondrous place—strings and swishes and eyes of light.

Dubai at Night was like Mum in perfume and makeup, going for a date in the far-off, so-near, shiny city, Nairobi, which, from far enough, could be like Dubai at night.

Milka and her mother have lived in almost every part of Nairobi: for a year, they lived in an aspirational semi-detached house in South B when mum had a perm and business suit job at Barclays bank; then they moved to a strange giant concrete house in Githurai, which they shared with a fat woman, who had a carefully even-toned face with shiny eyebrows shaped like sulking slivers of quartered moon, and a fondness for *Cinzano Bianco.*

The woman kicked them out one day, left all their things outside the metal gate, screaming: *Malaya, Malaya,* prostitute, prostitute, at her mother, her eyebrows unmoved by her anger.

They have lived in a servants quarter in one of the gated rich houses of Lavington, where mum worked as a maid for some expatriate people from Sweden who worked training people in HIV awareness. They smiled a lot.

They have lived in a slum, Kibera, just after mum lost her job at Joska (Josphat Kamau) Investments, where she was a receptionist.

Before Gordon arrived, they lived in a one-room house near Second Avenue, Eastleigh, only a few metres away from the open markets, and book exchange stalls. Milka loved Eastleigh.

Now they are back in Lavington, in the main house.

Gordon walked into their one-room home late one night, a year ago, with mum.

Milka had spent the day in some anxiety. Mum wasn't home in the morning, or when she had come back from school. As the sun set, lights and shadows fidgeted, and she retreated into her 'room'—a bed, with a cloth screen closing it off, and she lost herself in her happiest book: The *Darling Buds of May.* (A Love Gift from the People of Liberty, Mississipi).

Then there was a scratchy squiggle of a key in the lock. Rain and wind and laughter burst into the room like a loudspeaker. Gordon's voice was deep, and nasal, and it slid off the walls with static, as sure as television. Mum sounded drunk and erratic, her voice mewing and laughing, and Milka knew to be cautious. The light came on, and brought with it giant shards of shadow. Glasses clunked on the coffee table, and liquid gurgled loudly. She felt naked—knew that she was a moving, shadowed lump in their eyes. All her movements were too loud, her bed a stage, facing the sofa.

"Milka?" Mums voice was soft and toned to comfort, scary. Milka wrapped a '*khanga'* around her nightie, from the chest, for the first time in her life, not from the waist. She slipped out of her room.

He sat on the sofa, leaning back, hands behind his head, leather-shod foot over knee, his skin angry and red, and she wondered for a moment if it hurt. He smiled and called her Young Lady, which she liked, and she took her finger out of her mouth quickly, and clasped both hands in front of her, which seemed grown-up. Mum's eyes were bright, and she kept trying to pat her weave back to life. It hung limply, wet from the rain, shining from hair spray.

The car jumps over a rocky bump. It is too hot to read; too hot to think; too hot. There is a song her granny used to sing to her...*maua mazuri zapendeza*...and it would climb into the chorus, then slide downhill so sweetly, zoom zoom zoom *nyukilia we..*

Milka fought with mum this morning, for the first time since she was a child. Over the sheer, torso-shaping, frilled-at-waist pink t-shirt, bought for her by Auntie Linda. She had planned, for weeks, to wear it somewhere: her birthday, Parent's Day at school, their weekend shopping trips to Sarit Centre. She was always losing nerve at the last minute, always somewhat despondent after failing to put it on.

So this morning, the t-shirt stood between them: her mother pulling it one way, Milka pulling it towards her. And before her fear of her mother could overwhelm her, Milka let out an urgent breath of words, from her stomach, in Gikuyu: I'll tell Gordon. Her mother gasped, let go, and turned away. They have not spoken since this morning.

Gordon is driving the car, and mum is sitting next to him. The two TV people, and Linda, a friend of Gordon's, sit behind them.

Earlier, she could hear them whispering, the CNN woman saying, "Look at his head... shaped just like gravitas isn't it?" And they both laughed, and Milka could see the top of Gordon's large and square head bobbing in front of the car seat, waves of grey and black running down his head. CNN has over the years, called Gordon a 'Maverick American Missionary', A hero to 'The Forgotten Peoples of Africa'.

There is a race. Milka is now aware

of something she has felt under her skin for weeks now: that mum's will crack before the baby is born, and Gordon will leave her. Them.

Mum has said it already.

"We will move to a bigger house after the baby is born."

"Don't worry baby, *Cucu* will come to visit us when the baby is born."

The baby will allow mum to snap at Gordon, make him take off his shoes in the house, allow her to ban smelly people from the house; allow her to remove the eyeless Nigerian masks from the living room wall, the beaded Masai leather tunic on the wall that smelled of old age and smoke and fear.

Milka has often wanted to touch his hair. Those waves are the same every day; each wave precisely in the same place, yet the hair is blowing in the wind! How does it fall back in place so reliably? Does his barber know the shape of each wave to keep it this way? That hair is too flimsy to be so reliable.

Gordon has two types of friends: those she often hears laughing and drinking whiskey on the veranda, dressed in Bush jackets, or t-shirts distended by overuse, and dirty jeans, talking about places like Rwanda and Congo and Propaganda and Iraq, and choppy verbs: grabbed, shot, burst, hit, gripped.

Guerrillas, *Milishia* – which she thought would make a nice name, Milishia. Aisha. Maybe a Somali name. They sit by the swimming pool for hours, and she sinks into sleep upstairs, her head dizzy with the overheard detail. The stories rush always from location to location: "—left window, across the street, swung his cameras over—Bunia, Kigali, Club Tropicana, RPF, SWAPO Janjaweed ...and then we got on a lorry and dropped off in Kisangani."

She cannot understand yet the connection between these people and those places, has not yet grasped the idea that people make the worlds they occupy, and cannot see anything clearly outside of what they have made. All worlds belong utterly to whoever is talking about them. What were they doing in Bunia? Why didn't they go to Zanzibar, or Ruwenzori or to the Serengeti, where beautiful things were?

Sometimes she sat around them, answering only when directly asked a question. She hoped one day to test out the jumble of language and thought and books that she kept simmering inside her.

One day, over dinner, one of them mentioned Kibera, where she and her mother had lived for one year –and it seemed not like a place she knew, mundane, and full of small neighbourly entanglements, smelly, cosier than Lavington. It became a place they had built themselves, in that wondrous, Swishy-Light-in-Dubai way that white people built things. This Kibera had choppy verbs: Flying Toilets, Death by Machete, AIDS, a whirlpool. Slumlords. A thriller.

What a possibility! That Kibera was all those things!

"Didn't you live in Kibera for a while?" Gordon asked.

"Yes." She said, and sentences rose and fell and crashed into each other in her head, "Near the sub-chief."

There was brief awkward silence as she retreated.

Solemn: a word she associates with the way lips that are sealed by silence, part flesh visibly when quiet people speak.

Francois the Canal France guy broke into the thick air:

"Catherine Peale was fucking the SPLA commander. She always knew what they were up to before anybody?"

"Didn't they send her to Iraq?"

"David Clarke married his Mombasa prostitute."

"Noooo!"

"Yep. Some American marines came with their women and started a fight. Wigs flying. Dave and his wife spent their wedding night in Mombasa police station."

There is Linda, another friend of Gordon's, another type, who sits with the two CNN people in the car, and who always says things like, He didn't understand that I needed some Me-time... People are dying...You'd think they care...or...It's such an empowering book.

'Empowering': a word Milka associates with the rising steam, and bitter smell of njahi beans, which mum cooks with coconut when Linda comes to visit. Linda is a vegetarian, the only friend of Gordon's that mum likes. Linda hates the System– a word that is swirling around Milka, a slow tornado collecting samples everywhere, which will turn in on itself and solidify to one idea, in one startling moment.

Linda works with AIDS orphans, for an NGO called *It Takes a Village.* She used to work for the UN. She has introduced new words to Milka's vocabulary: DIFFID, DANIDA, MSF, USAID, SUSTAINABILITY, and EDUCATING THE GIRL CHILD.

Sometimes she comes to write funding proposals for Gordon in his study. Gordon always sounds irritated when talking to her, and Milka does not understand why they are so close.

He hates 'DevelopmentSpeak'.

Gordon's other friends are all black Kenyans, Indigenous Peoples Linda calls them: Masais, Pokots, Turkanas, all men. They come home with him from his dusty field trips, all of them are bewildered and shy, none of them speak English, and Milka's mother loathes them all.

They all smell the same: like blankets left too long in the sun; like smoke, and paraffin and sweat and sometimes there is, steaming around them, the sweet, intolerable, seductive, fermenting smell of *busaa.*

They never spend the night. Mum cooks a large pot of ugali, fries up sukuma wiki with onions and tomatoes and crushed peanuts, cursing all the time: these people, these people in her home. Gordon unloads a crate of warm beer and they drink from the bottles for hours. Mum bangs things in the kitchen. Gordon barks in his nasal, slippery Kiswahili, struggling to harden his consonants, and presenting this hardening as clipped instructions – a ubiquitous way the language is presented when spoken by white people and Gikuyu tycoons: not full of gentle negotiations, it becomes a way for a man to issue directives, 'in an African way'.

One day, Gordon issued an especially crisp instruction, in English, but sounding deliberately African: vowels rounded, standing straight, not slanting, consonants hit hard against the walls of his mouth, when mum had been sharp with Ole Tomanga, over the toilet:

"Stop it! Do Not Make Him Lose Face!"

Ole Tomanga, one of the regular Masais, always speaks slowly, an old man, taking soft chesty paths to his point. He has an accordion laugh, it wheezes in and saws out in one gentle windy movement, and she always waits for it.

Lose Face. Lose Your Face. Three days ago, in her new school, Milka pushed a pencil deep into Lisa Macharia (of the Funeral Parlour Macharias) – just to see her smug face break. Why couldn't she make them stop laughing at her?

She knows Ole Tomanga's fragility – the wrong words will quickly cut him to violence or departure. There is no way for his behaviour to adjust to insult. He has nothing to negotiate in this leafy suburb.

Face. Face. Face. Television: woman laughs, pulling on tights, saying: 'WAIT! I haven't put on my face yet!'

Faces have spun in her mind for weeks. *Face Off!* Drums blare, trumpets promise drama on FM Radio Current Affairs, and government ministers compete to insult each other, the whole country riveted. Lets Face it, says a woman on TV, bouncing energetically in tights, with a KISS FM accent, with lips cut clean and symmetrical and ruby coloured, never wobbling, Pads are boring.

Matte, gloss, lined lips, new eyebrows, so many possible faces! You look like a prostitute, said her mother, when she was caught playing with lipstick.

Gordon is telling them all about his conversion to this place.

"The church did not understand, sending fucking lurve gifts, talking about bringing people to the heart of Jesus! Jesus! Do you know what Jesus means to the Pokot? During the colonial era, there was a great wave of conversion here. A Kalenjin woman, I forget her name, told people that Jesus was coming. She was going to lead people to the Promised Land. They were all carried by the ecstasy; and the Pokot converted en masse, and a huge mass of people set off to gather and meet Jesus. Coming over a hill, they were seen by a British District Officer, who shot at the crowd, and some died. The Pokot struck back – the British brought reinforcements to crush them, and the Pokot went home and never stepped into a church again."

Linda, "Aren't they just beautiful? So sleek and lean and sexy?"

Gordon's voice is grave, "Man has lived here, maybe longer than anywhere else. The Turkana who live not far from here, have been found to be the oldest society of humans so far to be traced by DNA tests. It is here that man evolved, we know these landscapes in our bones."

Milka sees a group of young Pokot stand by the road, staring at the car without guile, as startlingly improbable as the desert rose. The men are more spectacularly dressed than the women, one has cut his hair into a small disk at the top of his skull; blue beads decorate this circle. His torso is taut and ridged, and around his neck is a little clue and red choker. Milka avoids the naked breasts of the young woman, who is smiling shyly at the car.

Gordon has opened up his library to her, a whole wall of books in his study. It took a while before she let herself in—it seemed impertinent to spend time in his room. She has managed to restrain herself from being too familiar in the house. She no longer has a source of books. She used to exchange books with street traders for thirty shillings on the street wherever they lived. Mum was free with money for this, never minding how many books Milka found. She is still trying to steel herself to broach the school library which sits behind a jagged bottle-neck of American accented girls, stopping to chatter where four corridors meet.

She does not understand Gordon's taste in books; she was sure, is still now convinced, that he must have, somewhere, solid, reliable books (Like *Oliver Twist,* or Mark Twain or Wilbur Smith or Robert Ludlum or *Black Beauty* or *To Kill a Mockingbird,* her favourite book). Steady books, like him—not books so slippery and difficult to escape to. *The Electric Kool Aid Acid Test* had jumpy sentences that she could not train her eyes to.

Slippery. Like her mother. The thought stood up suddenly in her mind, and turned. There is a certain elegant upside-downness about this idea: mum, slippery and unreliable, life see-sawing, reading Reliable American Romance Novels; and Gordon so steady, so finicky about the smallest things (packing the car!), so strange in his tastes for books.

One day she carried one of Gordon's Africa books to her room. After rubbing her toes against the duvet to make it warm, she opened the Africa book, and saw the pictures: dead bodies, some skeletons with clothes on: Rwanda. She dropped the book, and said her prayers fiercely, frowning and trying to close off her mind,as her mother's voice rose up the stairs, drunk: laughing, music playing. Gordon's voice spooled in the background, almost inaudible; all she could hear was regular, comforting waves of bass, which touched her. And that night, she wished with all her heart, promised God that she would be good, would make Gordon like her; would read his books, and talk to him about places like Propaganda and Bunia. Would be good to Ole Tomanga. Would not be shy and stiff, would be bendable and laughing, comfortably rude even, like the children of his white friends.

Late late that night, unable to sleep after the Rwanda pictures, she heard mum squealing, like the wet wheels of a fast car, and Gordon growled in regular wheezing breaths, as if he was the grainy road that kept the car from slipping out of control, and the desperate regularity of his gasps seemed to suggest that one day mum would slip off the kerb, beyond him.

The car rolls past flat lands covered in small rocks; the road is bumpy now, and fine dust has squeezed through the seams of the doors and windows, everybody's hair takes on brown highlights.

Mum sits at the front passenger seat, reading a Zebra Historical Romance, and sipping a cold light beer. She hasn't spoken to Milka since they left, and Milka misses her already. She uses less foundation these days, it barely covers the skin-lightener scars and patches. No perm anymore. Gordon does not like it—now mum always has braids, with African beads (made in Taiwan) woven in.

"You okay sweetheart?" Gordon's eyes crinkled in the rear-view mirror.

"Yes.....yeah. Yeah am fine?"

"What do you think of Pokot?"

The faces in the back seat in front of her turned to face her, all smiling, and she could not release the solemn. Her pink t-shirt seemed wrong now, the wrong thing to wear here.

"I like it. It's nice."

"They're so real, aren't they?" Linda winked at her.

"Yes."

Mum used to have a thick transforming night mask: new eyebrows, mouth smiling carefully, top lip tapping bottom lip gently and regularly expelling a soft whispered pout, face expressionless, and blemish-free. Or no makeup when she was at home: dressed in a khanga, ruthlessly cleaning. Scrubbing that one room. Perm under a headscarf. Rollers on. Scrubbing. Often moody from the night before, sometimes singing from the night before, soft and happy.

Milka brought another Africa Book for this trip. She had browsed through it, and the prose read like Gordon sounds. There is, in this collection, something by a writer called, Kapu...Kapu-scin-ky...

She sort of hoped that Gordon would see her reading it, and say something warming. He loves Kapuscinsky. He hadn't yet. After the city's starts and stops, and the startling fogs, the climb, so high they could see clouds below them, and it was cold. Then they spiralled down the Rift Valley Escarpment, a giant view spread out before them: Mt. Longonot and two lakes. When they got to the dry flats past Naivasha, she opened the book, and read, and was caught by a shocking paragraph. She gasps.

"Good book?" Gordon had said, smiling at the mirror for her.

"Yes, he sounds like you." And everybody in the car except mum had laughed, and the CNN camera guy had taken the book to look at it.

" Ah! Kapuscinsky. Fucking amazing. Did you read *The Emperor?*"

She tries to speak, but her mouth is stuck in solemn again and Gordon feeds the car with anecdotes about people he knows who know Kapuscinsky. And the Kapuscinsky paragraph rings in her head, like a choice.

> "The European mind is willing to acknowledge its limitations, accept its limitations. It is a sceptical mind.
>
> The spirit of criticism does not exist in other cultures. They are proud, believing that what they have is perfect."

Mum has hardly spoken since they left Nairobi. This is not her scene. As is usual when Gordon is with his people, they only spoke to negotiate tasks—Is there enough water? Did you switch off the geyser? Pass the watermelon, baby.

"Here it is!" Gordon booms, "The museum."

He stops the car, and they open the doors, which shrug off brown earth. They unpack themselves. All groaning and stretching, and Milka makes her ears pop, her back crack, and makes one lip two lips, breaking the solemn, and then grimacing wide as if to test run the limits of jollity.

Spread out all around them is a flat, stony plain, soft dry earth under her shoes.

Museum?

Gordon looks happy, blocky, and bronze, wrinkles in him are not a loosening of skin, they are cuts and crevices.

"You good?" he asks Milka, and she smiles shyly. He winks and whispers, "I like the t-shirt."

The CNN man fiddles with the camera, and then hoists it over his shoulder. The woman looks around her, irritated for a moment. "What museum?"

"The Pokot museum. See these stones over there?"

They all turned, and on the ground was an enormous circle of small rocks.

"Imagine this," Gordon is magisterial, and the cameraman scrambles to get a shot, "Stones piled on each other in a perfect circle, a wall, an immaculate and simple camp. Thorn bushes surround this wall to keep wild animals away from thousands of cattle."

"That's great," says the cameraman, "Could you move a little forward? Yeah yeah..that's it..."

"Can I go on?"

"Yeah."

"Imagine—a young moran sits that night on that tree to the left as the lookout. Imagine the Masai defeated. This great empire of warriors has had to retreat – they have been pushed out by the Pokot. Years of drought, and Rinderpest and civil war had brought them to this. This is their last camp before the migration to Laikipia and the Mau hills. Soon, the British will..."

"Hold on, hold on – could you walk around it as you speak, keep your eyes on the camera."

Gordon frowns, and waits for the cameraman to move around him as he turns and circles the stones. Everybody follows behind.

"The British will soon completely remove any threat they offer, then immediately adore them. Imagine the recently circumcised warriors, bellies swollen from stuffing themselves with meat, eyes ready for war, some wounded from the weeks of battle. Sullen that the elders have said they must give in and move on. Young boys and girls restless and excited; cattle bicker in the corral, unfamiliar with being in such a large gathering. Did the elders have any trouble restraining the Moran? Did the Pokot warriors follow them, or line alongside jeering?"

They all stand. Quiet. Moved, but not quite able to assign so much drama to this bleak landscape. And Milka thinks of Ole Tomanga, and turns to look at her mother who is uncapping a bottle of water, disinterested.

The CNN woman breaks the silence, "So what about now? Aren't they getting Food aid?"

Gordon turned to them again, "You see. Now the Masai, the Pokot are cursed by the greatness of their past. Accepting what they need to change in order to thrive makes the past irrelevant. Those that had weak cultures, like the Gikuyu, gave it all up for modernity."

Mum turns to Gordon, mouth turned down to a sneer, and the cameraman swings to her direction, *"Ai! Ngai!* What did you say? When the Masai were crying for help in Narok we were fighting the British in the forests. It is us Gikuyu who are building this country – while these people sit here and beg. And all of you get happy because they suck your breasts and say nothing. Why didn't you marry a fucking Pokot if Gikuyus are weak?"

Milka sees Gordon's jaw swelling and receding. She can't bring herself to move. Gordon does not say anything, and mum turns back into the car and switches on the radio.

The CNN people ask mum to turn the radio down. Mum is sulking on the front seat, and Linda has snapped at Gordon, "Fuck you Gordon! You're such a fucking Patriarch!" Linda goes to the car to comfort mum.

Gordon is rescued from awkwardness by the arrival of a lean, ropey young man in a crisp white shirt and trousers. "This is Simon—the sub-chief of this area!" The TV people pounce on him, and they walk with Simon around the museum. Gordon and Milka follow.

Simon is telling them, "These stones are not touched by anybody...they are our memory of a great time....even children know not to touch anything...Us Pokots do better than most tribes at school, but most of us leave all that to come back here. When I finished at University they sent me to Masailand to be chief there, but I couldn't live there. Then they sent me to Kericho, but eventually I came back home... "

Gordon swells up again, and soon is summoning majesty for the camera, eyes gazing out to the distance, framed by crisp lines, "Is it that we see our way of living as life itself? Is this man's greatest gift? His curse? That we will not relinquish our way, whatever our intelligence tells us?"

He spreads this arms wide, to the landscape, "We will live our way, and walk free across fenced land with our herds of cattle; or build ever-larger buildings, and guns. Not even a wall of fate in front of us will make us give up our way. We will crash into it at full pace, convinced our way will push us through. And often it does, and sometimes it does not."

A few minutes later, Gordon slaps Simon's back, and grabs Milka's neck into a soft hug, while the cameraman takes shots of the landscape. Mum had turned the radio loud, and was asked to switch it off by the TV woman. They board the car and head for the borehole and tanks—Gordon's World Bank funded water project.

Milka knows her sister will speak like television, like International School of Kenya, like We Are the World, We are The Children. Like, Make It a Better Place. This baby will not share mum, like she had – she inside Mum, layers of shared secrets and lies separating them, tying them together; she aloof from Mum, mum open to her – both of them silently agreeing not to acknowledge this situation. And Milka knows herself, already, as mum's assistant in this endeavour: less a daughter, more a partner. For the past year, she and mum have been uncertain around each other. Mum has been afraid of her, has alternated between over-affection and sharp, hot, threatening whispers, far from Gordon's hearing.

One night, some months ago, Gordon and mum went for a party at the UN Headquarters, and came home early, catching her in front of the mirror in the living room, dressed in his drawstring pyjama trousers, and in mum's loose and baggy cardigan, dancing hiphop to some angry South African *kwaito* music, which was blaring out of the music channel on television. She turned to find them standing at the door, and was ashamed. In the moments it took to tune down the television, the living room: the masks, the creaking and crackling rattan furniture, the framed prints of various tribal peoples Gordon had met in his work in Kenya and Papua New Guinea and Malawi; the collection of manly oddities on the mantelpiece: old Congolese beer bottles, black and white photos of naked Nuba men, a little goatskin tobacco-pouch, a grimy old pair of binoculars; the bright and beaded collection of pygmy knives, spread out in a fan—and Gordon, weather-beaten in khakis, diminished in force by the bright television colours, by the rat-a-tat rap, by the wide mouths, and pointing fingers, so close to the screen, they seemed to be addressing each person in the room.

Mum groaned and covered her ears. Gordon muttered, 'Rubbish', and his eyes remained on the screen, until the volume button on the remote control rendered the musician's movements ridiculous.

Cominatcha is not working for Milka on the trip back to Nairobi, there are too many small frictions in the car.

Simon is squashed between Linda and the CNN woman, legs angling sharply, thighs as taut as forearms under his trousers. Linda is speaking animatedly, her voice less prickly than usual, asking Simon about Sustainability of Local Institutions. Linda's hand is on Simon's thigh, and the cameraman keeps glancing at them, and smiling to himself.

Simon turns to Milka, asks her name, and which school she goes to.

"International School" and she is ashamed to say this; can hear how much her accent has changed, as she speaks to him.

Two young women step out of the brush in front of them, in leather tunics, with short mud-coloured mops of dreadlocks on their heads. They stare the car down fiercely and turn back in the bush.

Simon points at them, "Those are initiates. They were circumcised last month. They have to live in the bush now until the next ceremonies. No men can cross the line on that road. They will kill

any man that approaches them."

Linda gasps. "You support this? That's terrible! How can you support mutilation?'

Simon laughs, and Milka squirms. She has found herself, so many times, hearing some comment from some member of a group of girls, that cuts her deeply, and she laughs, and her whole body loses instinct for a moment, everything is heavy and awkward, as she tries to arrange her face not to care.

Milka's voice bursts out, louder and shriller than she would like, "They look like warriors. I want dreads like that!"

Mum laughs, an edge behind it, *"No Mau Maus* in my house girl!"

Gordon is grave, "Some women run away to be circumcised. We try to stop it."

Linda is facing the window, tears running down her cheeks. The CNN people want to stop and film. Simon says no, sharply, his body suddenly concerned with its seating—he closes his knees, and places two hands awkwardly on them, like an uncertain schoolboy. A hard nut swells and thins on his jaw. Linda vows to nobody in particular that she will come here and have a gender mainstreaming workshop, if she can find the funding. The car dips into a suddenly verdant strip, trees above them, and Milka's skin is bombarded by thousands of leaves of cooling shadow. They cross a stream, and are out again on stone and dust, and goose bumps prise her thoughts out of the group, and spread warmly through her body. Her t-shirt is dusty, and she is uncomfortable in it. Pink dirties badly.

Milka leans closer to Simon's back. He smells of sharp clean sweat, a charcoal iron, lifebuoy soap, and sunlight. She wants to touch the bones that run down his white shirt.

"Uncle Gordon?" she asks, "Will Simon come and visit us at home?"

Mum slaps her tongue loudly against the roof of her mouth, and Gordon turns to look at her sharply.

"Simon is a busy man. You must ask him."

A group of young men walk in front of them, and the TV woman sighs, "They are so beautiful. I wish I could take one home."

Gordon growls, "Don't be silly."

Linda peers out of the window, squinting at the afternoon glare, "They don't seem to be malnourished and they don't have ring worms like the people in Ukambani."

Gordon responds, "That's because they haven't yet met enough tourists and the fucking church and modern life. Just you watch and see how they will be when the World Food Programme is done with them. Already people here have adjusted their habits to Food AID. The young men refuse to take the cattle to the mountains to graze when there is no rain. The old men drink *Busaa* all day in Loruk and the women wait for food packages. They are finished."

Simon's face has not changed. Milka sees his back tighten, a train of bones reels down his back, his hands become string instruments, tight cords climb sharply to knob cliffs. She is prickly and hot and soft. Her hand reaches out, and she fists it and curls it back into herself.

He smells of ironing and charcoal and sweat and truth.

"If you drop me off here I will be fine," he says. Gordon drops him off, and says goodbye in Pokot. Simon ignores him, and Milka shouts, "Bye!"

Milka turns to watch him walk away; he swerves off the road and into the bush, his walk springy and alien. His shirt and trousers flap in the wind, suddenly ugly and fragile as brown dust and thorns threaten.

And soon they are on the tarmac—built by Gordon's physics, Linda's donors and Kapuscinky's mind—straight and clean and making equal rock faces, and escarpments and geology and hundreds of unknowable hominid fossils, and ten or twenty tribes and five or ten towns and five lakes and rain and sun and grimy city suburbs and leafy city suburbs and the tensions Milka knows will make the house unbearable this evening. This once Great Rift Valley, which held First Man prisoner for tens of thousands of years, will be comfortably digested by cushions, power-steering, and a two-hour session of mental *cominatcha*.

BINYAVANGA WAINAINA is the Editor of Kwani? *He writes when he can.*

B Blogguy™ GET YOUR OWN BLOG | FLAG? | NEXT BLOG>>

Kenyan National Crisis That Everybody Ignores

Saturday, October 07, 2006

As we approach the general elections, there is one disturbing issue that most Kenyans are aware of but do not want to talk about. Or can I say, dare not talk about.

Over the last few days, readers of this blog and visitors from a neighbouring country have openly discussed this issue of how they relate to each other. The comments have shocked and alarmed many, but they have reflected the true picture of exactly what citizens of the two nations feel about each other. I am confident that from all the hurt feelings and charged emotions, Kenyans and Tanzanians can now begin to find a new way to relate to each other free of any hypocrisy.

While that spirit is still alive in this blog, I think it is only fair that we Kenyans look inwards and start to tackle an equally thorny issue (which our neighbours have mentioned again and again in their comments on Kenyans).

This is the way Luos relate to Kikuyus. It is widely believed that the members of these two tribes hate each other. Is this true? And if so why?

Regular readers of this blog will know that I happen to be (very happily) married to a Kikuyu beauty (tena from the heart of Kiambu, am I a total man or what?) and therefore I have had the privilege of observing the house of Mumbi from very close quarters. I will speak my mind in the coming days.

I also happened to have been born in Kisumu (although I am not from the Dholuo tribe). One of the closest and best friends I ever had was a Luo. We were very close and he happened to have also married from the house of Mumbi, a marriage that cost him his life (more on that later). I will however not spare the Luos either.

I think this background qualifies me to be a good observer and referee in this blog. My fellow Kenyans, what can we do to solve this national crisis that everybody pretends does not exist?

This Luo-Kikuyu thing, if allowed to continue will always impact negatively on the politics of the nation. I firmly believe that it needs to be addressed; let us start by honestly telling the rest of Kenya why it exists.

posted by chris at 3:21 AM
20 Comments:

Anonymous said...

Kumekucha, u going 2 far man! I enjoy hating those uncut, arrogant, lazy, brilliantly intellectual lakeside fellas who will stop at nothing to win the presidency. Remember Jaramogi begged Moi to allow him to seat on the presidency for just one day.

Raila will stop at nothing (even a violent bloody coup) to be Prezo. It is as simple as that.

Why spoil the fun kumekucha? Stick to Tzs.

Benji.

9:22 AM

Luke said...

Hi Chris

Once again, thanks for your most recent posts on this blog. As usual, I will introduce myself (avid reader of this blog, faithfully following kumekucha, have made in the past numerous comments etc.)

Does anyone even remember why and what it is Luos and Kikuyus hate each other so much or they fight each so much for?

I'm a luo and I can't remember (honestly though I don't know and maybe naively I don't want to know)

Keep it up Kumekucha—this is a relevant topic

9:39 AM

chris said...

@ Luke

My dear brother, I know what you are feeling and maybe you have been hurt many times by what Okuyos have said.

However it is important for the nation that both sides understand this thing and that both sides treat each other with respect.

In 1958 when the first eight African leaders were elected to the Legco (legislative Council - parliament in those days) Tom Mboya (a Luo) beat at least one Kikuyu candidate in Nairobi to win those elections. Guess what tribe the majority of voters were in Nairobi were?

They were Kikuyu.

So why did we go backwards at independence instead of forward?

Because some Kikuyu land grabbers in the Kenyatta government were being outsmarted by young Mboya (whom they called Kihii secretly) that means uncircumcised, they decided in the name of security of the state to kill Mboya.

Yet Mboya had done so much for Kenya to get independence, his own ambition not withstanding.

That was the beginning of the Kikuyu/Luo saga. It was quickly followed by the incident in Kisumu where Jaramogi Oginga Odinga confronted Kenyatta. Some emotional Luos in the crowd (I am repeating this story from somebody who was at the scene that day in 1969) threw a chair at Kenyatta. One of his security people caught it in mid air before it hit Kenyatta. Then chaos! The security guys of the president opened fire on the crowd killing a number of innocent Kenyans (that is still a state secret).

It then became in the interests of the Kenyatta administration to fan hatred with Luos.

A good place to start is for the Kikuyu to apologise to the Luos for the sins of their fathers. And then the Luo have to make an effort to stop being so emotional, (you don't throw anything at the President).

10:11 AM

chris said...

I know some Kikuyus reading this, like Benji, will pretend that there is nothing that we are discussing here.

But let me ask our Kikuyu brothers and sisters a simple question. Why is it that in most cases when a Kikuyu reveals to their family that they are getting married to a Luo, there is trouble? WHY?

Sorry I get a little emotional discussing this. You see my best friend was murdered in Nairobi two years ago. A guy walked into his office and shot him twice and then walked away without taking anything (he had nothing anyway). At that time he was having problems with his Kikuyu wife whose friends and relatives had convinced her to abandon him when he was going through a difficult time financially (Kikuyus always do that. So far the only Kikuyu I have met who doesn't do that is my mother-in-law. She is poor but when I had problems she went to her shamba and brought us food regularly).

It was clear that he (my Luo friend) was a hindrance as she enjoyed herself with a guy who had more chums.

To date the murderer has never been arrested.

My dear fellow Kenyans, my biggest ambition is for this Kikuyu/Luo thing to end. I will do anything...

10:20 AM

Vee said...

I don't know where to begin... this always ends up being an emotional discussion for me.

I'm a young, Kikuyu woman (from Kiambu) who consistently & constantly dates Luo men. I mean, I am not entirely sure what the deal is but it's like I am magnetically attracted to them; and I can't begin to explain why I never feel even 50% of that attraction for my own tribe-mates. Yet I've heard some snickering comments from family members over how that won't work...the whole Luo/Kikuyu.

I know a mixed couple that has a son and both grandparents didn't approve of the marriage. What happens now is that when the child is in Kikuyu country they call him Maina* and in Luo country Odhiambo*... the poor child is definitely going to be very confused. Another couple I know got a child out of wedlock. The guy was told by his parents that if he disowned the girl and the child that they would continue to pay for his education and give him land (he is the Kikuyu so you understand the significance of land). The girl on the other hand was told bora she raises that child on her own rather than rely on a Kikuyu man. That was four years ago, they are still keeping strong after they've both been disowned by their respective families...

So I join you on this question Chris... What can be done? If we don't handle the simple issue of how families relate to each other then DON'T EVER expect any sort of political understanding. It's sad that it is the 21st century around the world but in Kenya we are still stuck in a time bubble called the 60s when a Luo threw a chair at a Kikuyu. We can't be serious!!!

11:27 PM

chris said...

Vee, you always inspired me so, now I know why. It's coz you're from Kiambu...

Just kidding (about the Kiambu part, and not about the way you inspire.

After the Luo threw a chair at the Kikuyu, the Kikuyu killed many Luos and after that the Luo has never trusted the Kikuyu again.

And the Luo also sulked (wouldn't you after so many of your buddies were killed in cold blood and buried in one mass grave?)

The other tribes found the Luo sulking and believed the lies and propaganda of the Kikuyu. That is why to this day Luos are said to be unreasonable and too emotional.

And that's why some politicians are claiming that Luos are unelectable as President. What nonsense!!! (I know some kyuks will label this blog a Luo blog, just because of that last comment, so I will add the following rider). Raila may be unelectable mainly because of his confessed activities of August 1982. But there are dozens of other Luos who should shrug off this label of being unelectable and stand for Prezo. I have a dream that one day the Prezo will be from Luo Nyanza.

That is the whole sad Luo-Kikuyu story.

3:12 AM

Anonymous said...

Have a small Q 4 u Kumekucha.

R U Cut? Be honest man!

A cut guy can not write these things. No way!!

3:30 AM

chris said...

I AM CUT. But being cut is not being a man. Wangari Maathai is not cut but she stood where no cut man at the time would dare stand and because of her we still have Uhuru Park today.

Courage has nothing to do with circumcision. Any coward idiot can walk into a hospital an have their foreskin cut off. It's happening to kids all the time.

This must be Benji. The guy who always manages to be irrelevant at that critical moment...

But now that you have brought it up, let's discuss it. How relevant is being circumcised when it comes to finding a good leader for Kenya?

Let's face it head on. Kyuks always bring this up when they want Luos to shut up.

Anybody want to comment?

3:52 AM

Luke said...

Hi Chris

As I said earlier, this is a relevant topic for me. Now I know a little about the genesis of the Luo-Kikuyu tribal issue—I never did before. I also wish to see its end. I never had—and will never have—anything against another Kenyan, but I heard it all the time, and was raised up hearing it, and I see it in our society...

It troubles me to think that someone else, having heard as I did all I heard growing up, won't feel the same way I do and will instead want to hate me, maybe even make life difficult for me e.g. I was away from home at the time of the referendum, and when I came back after it, I was shocked. From the outside looking in, I saw division—that is when I came face to face with all I had ever heard about.

I just want to be able to live peacefully side by side with everyone......

5:12 AM

Anonymous said...

Chris you have a dynamite of a discussion here. It is commendable the way you fearlessly tackle hitherto biting, screaming "dragon" type issues. The reality on the ground is pathetically so. The Luo/Kikuyu 'hatred' percolates and infects our motherland.

Please allow me to point out a few facts you should consider when attempting to dissect this tribal hydra. Remember that the Kikuyu social, political and economic policy was hijacked by the 'home guards' and their kin. These Kikuyu impostors have thereon propagated their immoral methods of operation from the local to the national stage. This genesis is instructive. Note that the Kikuyu masses honestly acknowledged Raila as a njamba during the post '02 elections. Who muddled the waters after uhuru??? Who muddled the waters after the chair was thrown??? Who muddled the waters after we defeated KANU in '02???

Secondly, the dynamics of this 'hatred' should not be perceived from the spectacles of petty bourgeoisie, urban-based, armchair-sitting, remote-control-cradling Kikuyus and Luos. If we are to objectively seek the reasons and forecast its development (or demise) you should obtain the attitudes/prejudices of the rural men and women—in both regions.

Finally I think the opposite cultural positions of both tribes vis-à-vis each other has exacerbated the conflict. What do I mean? How easy has it been for the Kikuyu to shed stifling customs? How hard has it been for the Luo to shed stifling customs? Looking at both tribes you find two dialectically opposite cultural ideologies (if there is such a thing). I would even go as far as saying that in comparison to one another the Luos come out as ultra-conservatives while the Kikuyu can be perceived as ultra-liberals. How then can they co-exist with social and cultural outlooks that are polar?

I look forward to reading your opinion(s), Chris.

5:36 AM

chris said...

I did a quick small research with all the Kikuyus that I could find quickly. I asked all of them two simple questions.

My questions were:

1) Are you aware of the Luo/Kikuyu prejudicial hatred for each other?

2) What do you think the cause is?

Everybody I asked answered "yes" to the first question. To my second question, everybody answered that it is because Luos are not circumcised.

This really surprised me.

I believe that this is more evidence that this hatred has been fanned by politics and propaganda. The same Kyuks who talk about Luos not being circumcised will rush for mzungu men at the drop of a hat. Many Europeans do not circumcise. In fact guess how Hitler used to flash out Jews? Yep. They dropped their pants and the guys who were circumcised were bound to be Jews because most of Europe DID Not circumcise.

Kumekucha.

3:37 AM

Anonymous said...

Indeed Chris, indeed. The 'hatred' is based on a fallacy i.e. circumcision. The simplicity of this prejudice points at instilled propaganda. For a lie to succeed it must be simple, easily understood by capable and limited intellect. Thus the circumcision. If that is the symptom we can see that the malady has a source that is external and deliberately sowed.

3:49 AM

chris said...

Now we are on the right track.

The Kenyatta administration saw Luos as a serious political threat and chose the cowardly path of propaganda and falsehoods.

It started with the whispers within the inner cabinet against Tom Mboya, they always called him Kihii (meaning uncircumcised). Mboya was circumcised and understood Kikuyu very well, so this was always done out of his earshot.

When they had murdered Mboya, the next target was Jaramogi Oginga Odinga. Same simple strategy persisted.

When Moi came to power he attempted to relaunch Jaramogi's political career, but powerful Kikuyu forces (that had supported Moi's ascendancy to the presidency, naively believing that they could take the presidency back at a later date of their choice like AG at the time Charles Njonjo) would not have it.

After '82, Moi needed little convincing that the Luo were a threat to his administration and that "Kenyatta had been right all along."

So the uncircumcised thing continued to be used.

Kenyans need to apologise to the Luo community for national healing to start.

My take is that the Luo may be labeled many things, but they are certainly NOT COWARDS!!

I am not a Luo and I have no links with the Luo, but I weep for these sons of Kenya.

4:10 AM

3N said...

I am not sure issuing apologies on either side will solve anything. What ails the two tribes is misinformed perceptions about each other.

I believe the only way this hatred will be solved is through time. I do not believe that our generations of Kikuyu's and Luos hate each other as their fathers did.

And those citing cultural differences would be advised to note that there are other tribes in Kenya whose cultures contrast yet they do not 'hate' each other.

This hatred is purely a politicized cultivated one and only time will heal it.

2:08 PM

Anonymous said...

Am neither a kyuk nor a jeng. But the Kikuyus are very subtle, and can never be trusted in a deal. Where there is a good deal they always have some thing up their sleeves. Be sure when you deal with one them you are dealing with a whole group of a clan. Theirs is a network strategically positioned. They never care taking advantage of others as long as they benefit. Clearly characterised in the dishonour of MOU in the last elections and in the referendum where they fully rallied in their favour drew sharp divisions that will take a generation to heal. IMO as long as distrust exist so shall the division be.

5:08 AM

Anonymous said...

The hatred between the two is not culture conflicts, but it's all politicized since independence between Kenyatta and Odinga. I bet they are trying to outdo each other over power and it's not about to end until a Luo is in power. Why is the ODM refered as a Raila thing hence the Luos despite having Kalonzo and Ruto who are not Luos?

Ms Cart p

5:19 AM

Vee said...

Well Chris inasmuch as I'm from Kiambu I've recently learnt that I don't look it. Which to me is a great thing; I don't want to be associated to my tribe because I am a Kenyan child.

"What ails the two tribes is misinformed perceptions about each other." I agree with that 100%... therefore, now we've identified the problem, what can we do to contribute to the solution. Do we need a "RECONCILIATION: DHOLUO AND AGIKUYU FORUM 2007" or what cuts?

Speaking of "cut" I can't even believe that is an issue anymore!!! Do people still get cut to fulfil their societal obligations or is it a necessity in terms of hygiene and increased sexual pleasure!? Educate me...

11:57 PM

chris said...

This 'cut' thing is probably hygiene more than anything else, although if somebody remains clean, I don't really see a major issue here. In fact I am informed that uncircumicized gives better sexual pleasure.

This whole Kikuyu/Luo saga is a study at how powerful propaganda and misinformation can be and the extent of damage that it is capable of.

I think your "RECONCILIATION: DHOLUO AND AGIKUYU FORUM 2007" is a great idea that should be looked into more seriously.

P.S. Luos have often come across as arrogant and violent and difficult to deal with, but where this exists, it is reactionary attitude more than anything else. It is defensive after all the years of abuse. I saw it in my late close friend. What he said and how he behaved sometimes did not reflect his true inner feeling. I am yet to meet such a caring human being.

Kikuyus should remember how they behaved during colonial times when they were so opressed and treated unfairly. Wambui Otieno still behaves the same to this day. .

2:37 AM

Luke said...

Hi Chris

Wow! what a debate this has been! As a Luo, I for one would seriously consider RECONCILIATION: DHOLUO AND AGIKUYU FORUM 2007—possibly the first of many more to come? Because I don't assume this will be an easy and simple problem to deal with!

However, my concern, Chris, is taken from a previous post of yours here in this blog. I am concerned that there are those who will view us (on the internet blogger forums) simply as a "noisy and opinionated lot."

Unfortunately, I have experienced this personally before-out in the Diaspora where I am temporarily based. I seem able to think differently and give expression to the same-however, the moment I am back home, "something" (sick) happens......!

I have no desire or wish for future generations to grow up hearing expressed (from me or anybody else) the same tribalist sentiments I heard growing up, about my fellow Kenyan— who is simply just another human being like me!

I'd relish an opportunity to change this aspect of living in my society and country!

8:12 AM

Anonymous said...

As a strong beautiful Kikuyu woman in a relationship with a caring Luo gentleman, it doesn't matter to me whether we have issues in our communities. We do love one another and that is it.

According to Dr. Maathai in her book 'Unbowed,' there were differences on settler farms as workers from all over the country converged there in a bid to join the cash economy and pay their taxes. On those farms, they did not live together, as the settlers decreed. As a result of observing one another, certain biases arose; Luo is like this, Kikuyu is like this, Kipsigis like that and so on. Such biases outlived the time and cemented themselves in the collective mindset of the people.

Tom Mboya was a great Kenyan, so was JM Kariuki and Wambui Otieno, a freedom fighter and landmark case fighter. Dont forget the many who were detained together under torture. Ask them whether they suffered because they were of a particular tribe. Ask their mothers in Release Political Prisoners' Group.

For as long as we shall have this Luo-Kikuyu issue, we shall never advance. Let us refuse to be roped into the yoke left by colonialism.

6:58 AM

EDITOR'S RANT

Flushing Books First Down the Toilet...

Usiless!

Lovers of books must be happy to know that there is a chain of bookshops in every Nakumatt. A couple of years ago, Books First were accused in local media of not stocking or promoting local writing. They gave a vigorous defense, and promised to do more.

In the years we have worked with them what we have found is quite the opposite. For all the pretty words, and even prettier words on their walls, Books First is quite disinterested in working to make Kenyan literature vibrant.

Kwani? has now sold over 12,000 copies countrywide. All the stores of Books First have never sold, in total, more than Prestige Bookshop, a small and very proactive bookshop on Mama Ngina Street. Right through, Books First has sold less *Kwani?* titles than all other bookshops, even though they are well-positioned, with large shelves and situated in places with high-spending human traffic.

Why?

1. Branch Managers are forced to order their books from head office. Head office is chaotic and so branches rarely have stock. We used to get calls every week from customers frustrated that they could not get copies from the bookshops. But head office has always had stocks. We have had meeting after meeting and strategy after strategy, but where there is no will...
2. Books First buys up books overseas that are remainders (books about to be pulped), which cost next to nothing and ships them to Kenya cheap. In our last meeting they decided to ask us to cut our offer price to them to an unacceptable level—and *no* other bookshop in Kenya has made such a request. We pulled out of the store.
3. My impression: the management has an attitude that Kenyans are bourgeois people who want mitumba imported books and find it nearly impossible to believe that something local is worth pushing or marketing.

We bent over backwards, did readings, created expensive publicity material for them and called endless meetings, but talk is talk. Ultimately, they simply did not want to engage us in any meaningful way.

And this is why the largest chain of bookstores in Kenya is now the biggest hindrance to local publishing....and within their business strategy, Kenya remains a mitumba country that cannot sell, distribute or create its own products and ideas.

Good luck with your enterprise Books First. And thanks for sharing.

Some comments about Books First from Muthoni Garland, who was shortlisted for the Caine Prize for African Literature in 2006.

"The nearest bookshop to my house in Westlands, in the heart of Nairobi, Kenya, Africa, hardly stocks books by Black African writers. They do not promote or facilitate the development of local writing. They seem to lack pride in the country and continent that feeds them. This bookshop is a member of the largest chain of bookshops in Kenya."

"Perhaps they perceive that the market does not like to read books by Africans. Or that their clientele is expatriate—what a depressing and short sighted approach to business. Perhaps they do not realize that tea, soap, mobile phones (and and and...) were also foreign commodities, but due to aggressive promotion over the years they are now a ubiquitous part of our culture."

"Since this bookshop claims to be mad about books, I expended my charm persuading them to stock Kiriamiti, Mangua, Gazemba, Meja, Njau, Kibera and Ngugi wa Thiongo books by Kenyan writers. They brought in one carton of books by local writers. I personally bought about half the carton over several visits and encouraged them to promote the works with posters, prominent placement, readings, and author signings. Of course, that did not happen. The books lurked on a bottom shelf and each time I asked for one, the staff asked if I was a teacher."

"Finally, when the carton was sold off, I waited for more local books. ...and waited. Although I've spent thousands in this shop over the years, the sales staff seemed bemused rather than enthused by my badgering. Perhaps they are only mad about foreign books. I will no longer shop there, and encourage the many patriotic writers and readers not to shop in that chain until it becomes part of the solution rather than part of the problem."

Muthoni

Here is a report by Mike Mburu, our sales manager, about our relationship with this company:

BOOKS FIRST REPORT

INTRODUCTION

Books First is a chain of bookshops with book stores in all Nakumatt outlets. It has approximately fifteen retail outlets and also distributes books to other book shops. Consequently, to get placed in all these other bookshops a publisher has to go through Books First and their requirement for hefty discounts that deplete the publisher's profits.

Kwani Trust held a meeting with Books First in February 2006 to discuss placing of the journal *Kwani?* at their stores.

Below are the minutes of the meeting:

Kwani Trust Meeting with Books First Management

Date: Thur 23rd Feb.

Agenda:

1. Central Ordering of Books
2. Placing of Books
3. Promotions

Present:

1. Tom Randiki , Books First
2. Kairo Kiarie, Kwani Trust
3. Mike Mburu, Kwani Trust
4. June Wanjiru, Kwani Trust

1. Promotions

Kwani Trust is invited to utilize the Prestige / Lifestyle / and Nakumatt Mega Books First for a reading or other literary event. It was pointed out that the initial concept behind the Books First stores was to have people buy books and read them as they relax at the restaurants.

It was decided that Kwani Trust was to provide 20 A3 and 50 A2 sales and promotional posters for use in various outlets. These outlets include seven in Nairobi and one in Nyali, Kisumu and Eldoret respectively. It was also noted that Books First also distribute to Tusker Mattresses and Uchumi Supermarkets.

2. Ordering

Depending on the location of the Books First stores, prices may be marked up by significant percentages to absorb expenses. The centralized ordering system is undergoing adjustment difficulties. It is recommended by Books First that Kwani Trust call Tom Randiki directly, on his mobile phone, when an outlet is found to have insufficient stock levels.

3. Placing of Books

Books First was to arrange for placing at Nakumatt points-of-sale as long as Kwani Trust provides up-to-standard display stands. Books First will have the stands painted at their expense. They have recommended a carpenter who is familiar with their specifications.

Inside the store, Kwani Trust is invited to display books strategically, making use of in-store facilities and also providing desk top display stands for the point-of-sale areas.

4. CSR

Books First will collaborate with Kwani Trust in the provision of children's books to various charitable institutions, specifically Twana Twitu Childrens home and MYSA libraries.

It was discussed at length and all parties were content with the agreement that Kwani Trust would give Books First 25% discount on all books. Books First would in return place the books at all its outlets. Some of its outlets are:

1. Nakumatt Ukay
2. Nakumatt Nyayo stadium
3. Nakumatt Prestige
4. Nakumatt Embakasi
5. Nakumatt Nyali
6. Books First Airport
7. Nakumatt Lifestyle

As it would turn out Books First ignored the agreement and continued to ask for a 50% discount which meant that they would be getting our journal at cost price. The import of these was that we would end up selling our journal without the possibility of recouping our expenses.

Naturally, we pulled out of this arrangement. It had become evident to us that Books First wasn't planning to carry our product. As we go to print, none of the above pre- agreed matters have been realized and we do not feel, at the moment, capable of anticipating an amicable solution from these stores in the immediate future.

Kwani? *wishes to congratulate its writers of the year:*

Muthoni Garland

Muthoni Garland for being short listed
for the Caine Prize for African Writing Award in 2006
for her short story,
Tracking the Scent of my Mother,
published in the 2005 Caine Prize Anthology.

Muthoni Garland's enchanting fiction has been published
in two past editions of Kwani?: *01, 03 and in this issue.*

Dayo Forster

Dayo Forster for the publication of her novel
Reading the Ceiling *(Simon and Schuster, 2007).*
Excerpts from which were published
in Kwani? 03 *as "The Deed."*

WAGES OF GARBAGE

WITH PHOTOGRAPHY BY BRENDAN BANNON

STORY BY CHARLES MATATHIA

One of the most inspiring bits of news coming from the Kibaki administration is the statistics on economic growth. The last set of figures set this growth at 5.8 % per annum which is nothing but impressive. Yet some people insist on questioning these figures. They say that they cannot see the evidence of this growth on the ground. These must be the people who haven't seen the Dandora dumpsite.

You can tell the way people live by looking at their garbage, and the Dandora dumpsite, with its accelerated growth and increasingly yummier morsels, tells a story of fine living. The exponential growth of the dumpsite is not something you can blame on the government because it is merely indicative of growing consumption which is, in of itself, a function of the existence of disposable income. Look around you, supermarkets, trendy restaurants and all this nouveaux riche 'Kengen' millionaire types trying to outswipe each other at the credit cards' counter. They are eating and trashing, then they are shitting; and all that ends up in Dandora.

The Dandora dumpsite sits on the spot of land that had been set aside for Dandora phase six. In the end, in a world where people yearn for beachfronts and riverfronts, all the residents of Dandora Phase Two and Phase Four got was a garbage front. Across the murky river that borders the dump is Lucky Summer, to the right and Ngomongo to the left. Within stinking distance is Korogocho. The last time Korogocho was in the news, the First Lady was telling the World Bank Country Director that her Muthaiga was not Korogocho—Indeed!

When the NARC Government came into power, they embarked on extensive programmes to clean up and bring order into the city. Hawkers and street children were cleared off the streets. The government even managed, not for long as it has turned out, to bring rationality and organisational structures into the matatu industry. These ambitious projects have come a cropper because they were the initiative of a distant bureaucracy and textbook economists who continue to take a dim view of Kenya's informal sector; maybe because it does not exhibit or work within the organisational fundamentals of their corporate world.

As the streets were cleared to give way to white collar enterprise, the formal sector grew, a yuppie middle class emerged and conspicuous consumption skyrocketed, the Dandora dumpsite grew bigger. Many informal sector jobs were lost but certainly not all. As the dumpsite grew in tandem with the 5.8% of the national economy, enterprising individuals continued to make a living out of all that garbage. At least they did not have to wait for a roadmap from JICA, a government White Paper or a corporate Blueprint to feed their families. All things considered, that 26 hectare (and counting) sprawl of urban detritus—dead foetuses notwithstanding—at Dandora 'Phase Six' is a veritable goldmine for a particular group of people who have learned how to literally smell out an opportunity.

Certainly the existence of the Dandora dumpsite is shrouded in irony and political intricacies. As a majority of Dandora's residents bemoan the environmental degradation and the health hazards it poses, a minority continues to draw sustenance from it. Understandably, the residents want it moved, but inside the filth and murk of the dumpsite exists a class of 'scavengers' and their recycler benefactors who will have none of that. These are the 'ghetto cowboys' who have discovered the economic value of garbage and who constantly sift and sort trying to turn it all into shillings.

Without a doubt, there are advantages to be gained from the dumpsite if the images coming from Dandora are anything to go by. All those trucks coming in and leaving heavily laden either way. All those box-fresh industrial size bags filled with recyclable and reusable litter. The shiny new weighing scales that tip under the weight of garbage paid for by the kilo. Obviously there are neither cash tills nor Electronic Tax Registers here, but that doesn't mean that cash is not changing hands. This here is the undocumented economy—care to ask the garbage lords for the statistics?

BRENDAN BANNON is a documentary photographer. He works regularly for major NGOs and newspapers in the US and UK. He is based in New York. bb@brendanbannon.com

CHARLES A. MATATHIA attended Starehe Boys' Centre and School and is a graduate of the University of Nairobi with a degree in Sociology and Philosophy. He is an essayist, freelance researcher and writer specialising in Development and NGO speak.

THE MINDBENDER PRESENTS...
GABRIEL'S BIZARRE TALES.
'Killer Necklace'
Sometimes our own words no matter how seemingly inconsequential have a huge bearing on other people's lives.
WHY ARE YOU LOOKING AT ME LIKE THAT, DEE?
YOU KNOW WHY, CEE...
I CAN'T HEAR YOU TOO WELL FROM THIS DISTANCE.
COME CLOSER.
THAT'S A BIT BETTER.
YOU KNOW. I'VE BEEN THINKING...
MMM HMM....
...MAYBE ITS TIME WE SHOULD-
WAIT.
WHAT'S WRONG?
SHHH!
HEARD A NOISE FROM DOWNSTAIRS. MY AUNT. SHE'S PROBABLY BACK FROM THE SHOP BY NOW.
QUICK. YOU NEED TO LEAVE.
WAIT! WAIT! WAIT!
WHAT DO YOU WANT TO DO FOR YOUR BIRTHDAY?
YOU KNOW WHAT I WANT CEE.
O.K. SEE YOU MONDAY!
YES, I KNOW WHAT THAT *%#$# WANTS!

GOLD NECKLACE!
STYLE
GOLD
GOLD NECKLACE!
WHERE THE HELL WILL I GET THAT MONEY FROM?
I HAVE ZERO!

HEY CHRIS! WAIT!
AAGH! JONAH.
SUKUMA 5/=
FROM THE WAY YOUR FACE IS FOLDED I KNOW YOU'VE JUST BEEN WITH THAT RICH GIRL, DAMARIS.
MGANGA

SO, HAS ALL THE ACTING PAID OFF?
THE GIRL WOULD KILL YOU IF SHE KNEW YOU WERE FROM THE SLUM.
NOW, WHAT KIND OF PLAYER WOULD I BE IF SHE DID?

SO, DID YOU?
MAN, YOU SHOULD HAVE BEEN THERE TODAY. I WAS THIS CLOSE...
...AND THEN HER AUNT CAME!

SHE WANTS GOLD FOR HER BIRTHDAY.
NEED AT LEAST 36K.
WHERE THE HELL AM I GOING TO GET THAT KIND OF MONEY FROM?
TELL ME SOMETHING CHRIS.
HOW FAST CAN YOU RUN?
WH- WHAT DOES THAT HAVE TO DO WITH ANYTHING?
I CAN GET YOU THE MONEY FOR YOUR BLING.
GHETTO
I JUST NEED ONE FAVOUR. A DOWNTOWN SNATCH JOB.
I'D DO IT MYSELF BUT THE COPS ARE LOOKING FOR ME.
THEY WON'T BE LOOKING FOR YOU.
HIGHWAY TO HEAVEN
JONAH, I HAVE NO PROBLEM WITH AN ESTATE JOB, BUT TOWN... THATS CRAZY THESE DAYS.
LOOK MAN. 10 MINUTES. 80 THOUSAND SHILLINGS SPLIT IN THE MIDDLE.
BLING.
IS THAT A YES I HEAR?
DOWNTOWN, MONDAY MORNING.
JONAH IS THE DEVIL ON MY SHOULDER.
I CAN BARELY THINK WITH ALL THESE BUTTERFLIES IN MY STOMACH.
CITY BUS
BUS STOP
BUT I NEED TO PULL MYSELF TOGETHER. AT LEAST FOR DEE'S SAKE. YES...
KENPO HOUSE
LODGING
USIKOJOE HAPA
..YES. FOR YOU DEE... I WILL BE SUPERMAN.

THEY ALL CLEAR MY PATH AS I WALK THE STREETS.
THINKING MAYBE SOME SKIN DISEASE OR SMELL WILL STAY WITH THEM.
VERY FAT WOMAN WITH A BLUE HEAD-SCARF LEAVES THE BANK AT 9.05 A.M WITH A RED HAND-BAG.
POT O GOLD
ULTRA GLUE
JUST LIKE JONAH SAID
GLOBE BANK
GLOBE BANK
THE TARGET PROCEEDS TO CROSS THE AVENUE.
SHE'LL NEVER SEE ME COMING.
I CREEP UP FROM BEHIND HER LIKE A LION AND POUNCE.
EASIEST 80 THAO I HAVE EVER MADE.
THEN SHE MAKES THE SILLIEST MISTAKE EVER AND FOLLOWS ME. I'LL NEVER FORGET THE LOOK ON HER FACE JUST BEFORE IT HAPPENED.
P.S.V
813
GET HIM!
I MAKE TRACKS AS FAST AS I CAN. NO ONE COMES CLOSE.
I DISCARD MY DISGUISE IN THE BACK STREET NEAR THE BUS STOP.

THE MINDBENDER was asked for his profile, but couldn't think of anything interesting to say.

write write

WRITE

KWANI ?

WRITE IF YOU THINK YOU CAN WRITE
WRITE IF YOU THINK YOU CAN
WRITE IF YOU THINK
WRITE IF YOU CAN
WRITE
WRITE
WRITE

IF YOU THINK YOU CAN WRITE
IF YOU THINK YOU CAN
IF YOU THINK
IF YOU

IF YOU THINK YOU CAN WRITE
IF YOU THINK YOU CAN
IF YOU THINK
IF YOU

IF YOU CAN WRITE THEN WRITE COZ YOU MIGHT CHANGE

Illustration: J.K.N

About The Illustrators

AMUNGA ESHUCHI has been reincarnated as a scripwriter, filmmaker, chef, graphic designer, musician and computer technician. He is currently dabbling in the arts world and his affinity for images has landed him where he (thinks!) he wants to stay: as a social documentary photographer. He's in love with words and pictures. Email: *amunga@gmail.com*

CELESTE WAMIRU is an experienced illustrator and cartoonist based in Nairobi. She has illustrated children's books and numerous other publications.
Email: *cwamiru@yahoo.com*

JUDY KIBINGE'S (JNK) concepts, illustrations and photographs appear this edition of *Kwani?* When she's not doing creative work for her company Seven, she's out making films.
Email: *judykibinge@hotmail.com*

KWAME NYONG'O is an illustrator and animator based in Nairobi with a passion for bringing Africa's stories to an international audience. Email: *me@kwamenyongo.com*

LENJO MAZA is a visual communicator, poet and dreamer. He is au fait with digital and web graphics and engages in commissioned semi-abstract paintings. His harmonious and inventive layout and illustration skills have brought the poetry in this issue of *Kwani?* alive.
Email: *mazalistik@yahoo.com*

PETER ELUNGAT'S huge oil-paint canvases of dream-like women have become a highly sought after collectors items in the eight years since he began painting. He calls his long-necked women "portraits of my soul." Email: *elungat2005@yahoo.com*

RAY GICHARU is a digital artist with many years experience who hopes to give Dreamworks Studios a run for their money in the not-too-distant future. He likes to get paid his body weight in chocolate. Email: *m_gicharu@yahoo.com*

THE MINDBENDER was asked for his profile, but couldn't think of anything interesting to say. Email: *themindbender2001@yahoo.com*

SEVEN is the multimedia hotshop that put this issue of *Kwani?* together. Email: *info@seven.co.ke*